DATE DUE

JUN 27 2011	
MAR 1 9 2012	
SEP 2 5 2012	
APR 0 3 2014	

BRODART, CO.   Cat. No. 23-221-003

D0845562

Comanche Society

Number Twenty-three:
Elma Dill Russell Spencer
Series in the West
and Southwest

Comanche Society

Before the Reservation

Gerald Betty

TEXAS A&M UNIVERSITY PRESS

College Station

The paper used in this book meets the minimum requirements
of the American National Standard for Permanence
of Paper for Printed Library Materials, Z39.48-1984.
Binding materials have been chosen for durability.

Library of Congress Cataloging-in-Publication Data
Betty, Gerald, 1965–
Comanche society : before the reservation / Gerald Betty. — 1st ed.
p. cm. — (Elma Dill Russell Spencer series in the West and
Southwest ; no. 23)
Includes bibliographical references (p.   ) and index.
ISBN 1-58544-190-2
1. Comanche Indians — Kinship. 2. Comanche Indians — Social life and
customs. Title. II. Series.
E99.C85 B47 2002
305.897'45 — dc21
2001006546

For my parents,

Mary Demetropolis Betty

and

Claude William Betty, M.D.

Contents

List of Illustrations   ix

Acknowledgments   xi

Introduction   3

1. Comanche Kinship and Society   13

2. Comanche Migration and Geographic Mobility   46

3. Comanche Horse Pastoralism   74

4. The Nature of Comanche Economics   96

5. An Explanation of Comanche Violence   121

Conclusion   139

Appendix 1. A Discussion of Theoretical Issues   145

Appendix 2. A Timeline of Comanche History, 1706-1850   151

Appendix 3. Glossary of Spanish Terms   177

Notes   179

Bibliography   215

Index   227

Illustrations

Figures

1. Comanche Kinship   22
2. Tenewa Kinship   39

Maps

1. New Mexico in the Late Eighteenth Century   14
2. Jupe Migration to Texas and Cuchanec Divisions   31
3. Caddoan-speaking Tribes of Texas and Louisiana   37
4. Indians Living within the Boundaries of the Peters' Colony   40
5. Southern Migration of Comanches into New Mexico
    and Texas   52
6. Comanche Raids of Mexico   55
7. Spread of Spanish Pastoralism in New Spain   81
8. Texas Trading Posts along the Brazos River   112

Acknowledgments

I especially wish to thank my parents; my siblings Leigh Anne, David, and Mary Kathryn; and my family for their general and unconditional support. I also thank Cookie Juárez and all of my friends (too many to name individually) living across the State of Texas, the United States, and the world for their incredible friendship and encouragement.

As for my intellectual and scholarly development, I am deeply indebted to two men. I am especially grateful to Lyle Steadman of the Arizona State University's Department of Anthropology for expanding my interest far beyond the discipline of history. His insights into human cultural behavior through the perspective of evolution by natural selection have made a tremendous impression on me, inspiring my development as a professional scholar and historian. I am also grateful for the tremendous support and encouragement provided by Peter Iverson of the Arizona State History Department. As the committee chair of my master's and Ph.D. programs, Peter demonstrated an incredible patience with my development as a scholar. Were it not for his confidence in my abilities, I would not be in any kind of position to realize my dreams.

Finally, I would like to thank those individuals who are responsible for making this publication possible. The persons who read the original manuscript version of this book provided me with great insight and support. Carol Higham of the Department of History at Texas A&M University and copyeditor Kevin Brock have been particularly supportive and helpful in getting this project off the ground. I thank them and the staff of Texas A&M University Press for their efforts and cooperation.

Comanche Society

Introduction

QUANAH PARKER IS PERHAPS THE MOST WIDELY RECOGNIZED and celebrated Comanche Indian to have ever lived. Why is this? We know very little about Quanah's life prior to his settling upon the Comanche and Kiowa Reservation in the southwestern corner of Indian Territory (modern Oklahoma). Despite our lack of details about his early life, the popular image of the man stands out as a great chieftain of his people commanding the expanse of the southern plains. Maybe Quanah's status as being one of the last Comanches to surrender to the U.S. Army in early June, 1875, contributed to the celebrity status he acquired and maintained for the remainder of his life. It is also possible that Quanah's great stature came about as a result of his role as the official leader of the Comanche people in the late nineteenth and early twentieth centuries. As such an official of the Comanche Nation, Quanah played an instrumental role as a mediator between his people and several prominent Texas cattlemen who leased great tracts of reserved Comanche land in order to fatten up their livestock. Also, the chief oftentimes appeared at governmental and recreational events in Indian Territory, Texas, and Washington, D.C., as an official dignitary of the Comanche people.[1] Despite Quanah's achievements as someone who stood fast against the U.S. Army, as an official political leader of his people and as a popular and notable representative of a disappearing way of life, the development of his stature as a celebrity figure and his recognition among Americans as a champion of traditional Indian life is probably due more to who he actually was.

Quanah's past family history is the stuff from which great legends are made.

3

On May 19, 1835, Comanche and Kiowa raiders abducted nine-year-old Cynthia Ann Parker from Parker's Fort, situated along the Navasota River in eastern Texas. It is generally understood that Cynthia Ann eventually married a Comanche chief by the name Peta Nocona, although there is little documentary evidence of the existence of a person by that name. Nevertheless, she did marry a Comanche, and this union begot three children, one of whom was given the name Quanah. As a son of Peta Nocona and Cynthia Ann Parker, Quanah could therefore identify a preceding line of Comanches and one of Anglo-American Texans as his ancestors. This feature of his identity may have contributed to the difficulties he and his brother experienced among the Comanches after their father was killed and their mother and sister, Topsannah, were captured by Texas Rangers on December 18, 1861.[2]

Deprived of the care of their parents, the young boys had to rely upon their relatives. Unfortunately, since their mother was not a Comanche, the boys lacked the number of Indian relatives who might have supported them if both parents had been of that ethnicity. The death of his brother sometime later further contributed to the demise of Quanah's Comanche family. This dearth of identifiable kin may have also contributed to Quanah's association with the breakaway Kwahada band of Comanches that appeared sometime during the 1860s. It was with them that Quanah participated in the June, 1874, attack on American bison hunters stationed at Adobe Walls on the north bank of the Canadian River in the Texas Panhandle. When Quanah finally submitted to the U.S. Army at Fort Sill in the Indian Territory the following year, he was identified as a "Quah-de-re," or Kwahada.[3]

Interestingly, Quanah communicated his desire to make contact with his surviving Texas relatives shortly after becoming settled on the nearby Comanche and Kiowa Reservation. Fort Sill's commander, Col. Ranald Mackenzie, wrote to Isaac Parker in Texas announcing Quanah's wish that his great-uncle acknowledge him as a member of the Parker family. Unfortunately, the Parkers of Texas refused to accept the Kwahada chief as kin, and they never responded to Mackenzie's petitions. Nevertheless, Quanah bucked Comanche tradition and insisted that he be identified by his mother's surname.[4]

Despite the lack of acceptance among his mother's family, Comanches and other Texans and Americans recognized that the chief was both a Comanche and Texan by birth. The acknowledgement of Quanah's multinational parentage among the Indians and citizens of the United States allowed him to establish strong social ties within each community. It is on the basis of this kinship that Texas and American cattlemen sought out Quanah in order to make use of the vast pasturage resource available on the Comanche reservation. As a result of these dealings, Quanah developed strong relationships with the Harrold and Ikard livestock concern out of Illinois and famed Texas cattlemen such as Samuel Burk Burnett, Daniel Waggoner, Col. B. B. Groom, and Charles Goodnight.[5]

Although the nature of Quanah's kinship might have been detrimental to his status among Comanches prior to their settlement near Fort Sill, it served as a great advantage to the chief in the "new world" of reservation residency.

The chief's celebrity status among Americans and Texans emerged out of the social relationships Quanah established with prominent politicians and businessmen. He often made official junkets to Washington, D.C., and public appearances at events such as the Texas State Fair in Dallas and the Fort Worth Stock Show at the invitation of Texan friends like Burk Burnett. Quanah seems to have felt that it was important to interact with a people with whom he publicly recognized a kinship. In 1907 he wrote to Governor Campbell of Texas and declared his affinity with Texans, stating, "I am a Texas man myself." The following year the frozen relationship with his immediate family there began to thaw as Quanah sought out the grave of his mother, Cynthia Ann. Responding to a newspaper advertisement, a cousin offered his assistance in locating the site. Another cousin also responded to Quanah's outreach to his kin by inviting the chief to a family event in Athens, Texas. Quanah poignantly summed up his perception of his relationship to Comanches and Texans in a moving statement he delivered in a eulogy at the reburial of his mother's remains in Oklahoma. He observed that his mother "loved Indians so well no want to go back to folks [in Texas]. . . . All same people anyway." From Quanah's perspective, Comanches and Texans were indeed all the same people, for the chief was the link that made them so.[6]

His genealogical identity as a Comanche, a Texan, and an American probably best helps explain why the chief became a leader among the Indians during the reservation era and later such a celebrated figure in American history. People generally respond in a positive fashion to recognized kinship connections. Although, as the Parker family's detached attitude toward the relationship demonstrates, the simple fact of kinship does not oblige one to behave a certain way toward persons who share an ancestral heritage. Yet people are strongly encouraged to extend sociable behavior to those who share a kinship. This custom begins to suggest why Quanah's family in Texas started to warm to establishing a close kinship relationship to the chief over time. But, even before Quanah's own family accepted him, other Americans in Texas and throughout the United States acknowledged a sort of kinship with him, and this became the basis of their interaction with and respect for the prominent Indian leader.

Quanah Parker's experiences and behavior during the late nineteenth and early twentieth centuries provide some insights into the structure of Comanche society. His strong concern for his genealogical identity hints at the importance of kinship among Comanches. Concerns associated with this issue probably played a fundamental role in the hardships Quanah suffered after the tragic Texas Ranger raid that destroyed his immediate family. At the same time, his kinship ties to Comanches and Texans placed him at a cultural nexus that allowed the chief to exert influence among a diverse population of individuals in the southern plains and throughout the United States.

This book focuses on the framework of kinship that formed the foundation of Comanche society. Although the pages below focus on a time period preceding Quanah Parker's rise as an important man among the Comanches and in American history, it should become apparent that the historical figure of Quanah can be seen as a metaphor for Comanche society in general. His story may not be as atypical as it has been presented in the past. The chief's mixed heritage and the various social and economic relationships that emerged from such a birthright provide a unique glimpse into what it meant to be a Comanche. The following discussion is an attempt to uncover the framework of that society in order to explain not only why Comanches exhibited the behavior that they did but also why the Comanche community evolved as it did.

Many people do not realize that Comanches are originally descended from Shoshone Indians living in the eastern Great Basin and western Rocky Mountain regions of Utah, Wyoming, and Colorado. At some point prior to the early eighteenth century, certain Shoshones became intermarried to their Ute cousins residing to their south. As a result of this union, Comanches found themselves introduced to the Spanish province of New Mexico around 1706. Utes had maintained an occasionally strained relationship with the region since the 1630s, but their ties to the area became strengthened as captive Utes found themselves living in the settlements and pueblos of northern New Mexico. Throughout the early eighteenth century, Comanches went about that province and the Great Plains region to the northeast, harrying Spanish and Pueblo horse herds and waging an incessant war against Plains Apaches and Caddoans. By the 1730s, Comanches broke away from their Ute kinsmen, and by the 1740s, they proceeded to push south into Texas with their new Caddoan Wichita allies fast on the heels of their mutual Apache enemies.

The period between the 1730s and the 1780s was a time of on-again, off-again peace and war in New Mexico, and a period of migration and hostility in Texas. The Indians oftentimes visited New Mexican villages such as Taos and Ojo Caliente for trading purposes. But Comanches just as frequently waylaid those communities with which they engaged in trade. Over the years, frustrated New Mexicans conducted various expeditions against Comanches, with varying levels of success. Stability finally came to Comanche–New Mexican relations when the Indians suffered a grave defeat at the hands of New Mexico governor Anza in 1779. After making several initiatives toward establishing peace during the early 1780s, a large contingent of Comanches met at a site called La Casa de Palo along the Arkansas River in 1785 to choose a supreme leader and to discuss peace with New Mexico. By the end of February, 1786, the Comanches, under the leadership of Chief Ecueracapa, agreed to a treaty of peace with Anza and his people. The treaty ushered in a long-lasting period of social and economic interaction and cooperation between Comanches and New Mexicans that extended well into the nineteenth century.

The situation in Texas paralleled that in New Mexico to some extent, but it later became fairly complicated due to the unique historical developments taking place there during the first half of the nineteenth century. As Comanches accompanied Wichitas and other Plains Caddoans in a push toward the region, they vigorously pursued Apaches and attacked Spanish outposts and settlements that they saw as providing protection to their enemies. One of the most famous events resulting from the Indians' clash with Apaches and Spaniards in Texas occurred at an isolated Franciscan mission along the upper reaches of the San Sabá River. Comanches and their Caddoan allies wiped out the complex in March, 1758, and proceeded to push the Apaches farther to the south. The Spanish erected other missions and presidios along the upper Nueces River, but marauding Comanches eventually forced the abandonment of those locations by Spaniards and Apaches alike. With their Indian enemies all but banished from Texas, Comanches began to target Spanish ranches and villages for plunder in the 1760s and 1770s. As the situation in Texas turned in favor of the Comanches, the Spanish authorities made an effort to establish peace with the Indians. Their efforts were ultimately successful, and the Comanches agreed to a formal peace with the province in 1785. Thanks to the efforts of Spanish moderators there, Comanches even started to establish peaceful relations with Apaches in the early years of the 1800s.

The situation in Texas once again became unstable shortly after the turn of the nineteenth century. Americans appeared on the periphery of the Mexican province in Louisiana and began to cultivate trade relations with various Texas Indian tribes, including Comanches. Instability also seized hold of the Spanish administration in San Antonio as the Mexican struggle for independence spread into Texas during the early 1810s. One way the Spanish sought to deal with the insecure nature of the province was to allow the immigration of individuals from the United States to establish colonies on lands granted by the Spanish government. Although Mexico became independent from Spain in 1821, its government ultimately recognized the validity of the Spanish land-grant contracts and allowed Americans to settle within the boundary of Texas.

Unrest also gripped those Comanches living farther to the north along the Arkansas and Canadian Rivers. Beginning in the 1790s, Pawnees, Osages, Kiowas, Cheyennes, and Arapahos had begun to appear in these northern reaches of Comanche territory. Although Pawnees and Osages occasionally proved a hindrance to Comanches, they became embroiled in conflict with Kiowas. After several years of discord, Comanches and Kiowas agreed in 1806 to what would be a lasting peace. The 1820s and 1830s brought about a conflict with those Cheyennes and Arapahos making inroads into Comanche country from the northern plains. Tensions between these Indians climaxed at a large battle along Wolf Creek, where allied Comanches and Kiowas suffered a serious defeat. Comanches and Kiowas established terms of peace with the interlopers in 1840.

The period between 1821 and 1850 also saw the arrival of the Americans and the displaced Civilized Tribes into the vicinity of the Arkansas and Canadian Rivers. Santa Fe traders encountered Comanches on numerous occasions, and the Indians sometimes attacked the trains heading to and from New Mexico. Comanches also resented the constant encroachment from the east of those Indians removed to the Indian Territory in the early 1830s. They occasionally confronted Cherokee, Choctaw, Chickasaw, Creeks, and Seminoles as the members of these tribes hunted and settled on their lands.[7] The southern plains Indians suffered another annoyance as large streams of Americans passed through Comanche country on their way along the southern routes to the goldfields of California.

One effect of the relative stability of the New Mexico and Texas frontiers in the late eighteenth and early nineteenth centuries was the beginning of Comanche raids into the interior of Mexico. As the nineteenth century proceeded, marauding parties struck farther and farther into the depths of Mexico. During the late 1700s, Comanches began to cross the Rio Grande and penetrate into Coahuila and Tamaulipas as they chased after Apaches and pestered isolated Mexican ranches. By the 1820s, numerous warriors began assailing the haciendas of Chihuahua. By 1850, Comanche raiders became a serious problem for Mexican authorities, soldiers, ranchers, and villagers throughout the northern two-thirds of that country. Amazingly, the Indians made their way deep into Mexico, reaching faraway places such as Durango, Zacatecas, and Sinaloa.

Although enjoying incredible success south of the Rio Grande, serious troubles confronted Comanches in Texas by the 1830s. Unlike the Spanish and Mexican Texans, those of American descent generally refused to interact with the Indians and took a relatively hostile stance toward them. This situation led to a great deal of suspicion between Comanches and Texans, resulting in numerous robberies, abductions, and other hostilities. Tensions between these populations increased after the establishment of the Republic of Texas in 1836. The issues of robberies and captives especially played a central role in the deterioration of Comanche-Texan relations and precipitated the infamous 1840 Council House Fight in San Antonio, where thirty-five Comanches were killed under the pretext of peace negotiations. Needless to say, actions like these left individuals on all sides extremely embittered. Not surprisingly, from that point on, the main issue in Comanche-Texan relations focused on the establishment of a boundary separating the Indians from the white settlements. Unfortunately, this could hardly be resolved as the Texas frontier rapidly advanced to the west. Frustrated Comanches lashed out against settlers in their traditional fashion by stealing livestock and taking captives.

By the end of 1850, Comanches enjoyed the continuation of peaceful relations with the inhabitants of New Mexico. They launched more raids into Chihuahua and to points beyond in search of livestock and captives. Relations with Texas continued to be strained despite the assumption of authority by the United States. Nevertheless, the U.S. government began to initiate measures such as council meetings, treaties, and the distribution of goods in order to stabilize relations with Comanches. The commencement of the decade of the 1850s was the beginning of the end of traditional life as the Indians had known it. Beginning in late 1854, Comanches began streaming into a region along the Clear Fork of the Brazos River that had been designated as a reserve for their nation. Although, the establishment of the Clear Fork Reservation did not bring about the end of Comanche life on the plains, it foreshadowed future developments. Only the ominous events associated with the American Civil War and Reconstruction delayed the finale of the rich pageant of Comanche Indian life on the southern plains in 1875.

The British historian Christopher Hill once stated, "history is not a narrative of events. The historian's difficult task is to explain what happened."[8] This book takes that aim a step further. Not only should one strive to understand what happened, one should endeavor to understand why the past happened the way it did. The following pages attempt to uncover why Comanche Indians exhibited the behavior they did during their existence on the southern plains from 1706 to 1850. One will not find a narrative of events outlining Comanche history. Instead, the focus is on particular characteristic features of Comanche Indian life. Because the aim of this work is to understand behaviors that transcended historical periods, there is a general lack of chronological organization. Also, due to the topical nature of this study, the narrative will sometimes retrace specific historical events. The occasional return to particular events is sometimes necessary in order to understand the full significance of an occurrence with regard to its implications for understanding the various facets of Comanche society. It should be noted that this study aims to advance a comprehensive understanding of the community of men and women who composed the Comanche Nation. Although a considerable amount of evidence for the nature of their society prior to the 1850s focuses primarily on the actions of men, women's contribution to the Comanche community should not be eclipsed by the paucity of information in the documentary sources. Hopefully, the importance of Comanche women's fundamental contribution to the creation and maintenance of their community will be evident in the following discussion.

A detailed chronology of Comanche history is provided, presented from the Indians' point of view. The product of this approach is a chronology that features the historical events and actions of Comanches over those of non-Comanches. The events and actions of the history associated with Euro-Americans are evident only as they related to Comanches. For instance, familiar historical developments such as the Bourbon reforms of the late colonial era in New Spain, the Mexican struggle for independence, and the Texas Revolution are inconspicuous in the timeline. Nevertheless, one should be able to sense from it the shifting sands of historical developments that transpired outside of the Comanche community. The point of the timeline is to provide readers with a reference that can be used to place the numerous examples discussed into a framework of a Comanche-centered history. Readers interested in the relationship between Comanches and Euro-Americans should consult the fine works of Elizabeth A. H. John and Thomas Kavanagh for a thorough chronological treatment of Comanche history within the broader context of Euro-American history.[9]

The first chapter focuses on Comanche kinship and social behavior as the key to understanding the organization of their community during the eighteenth and nineteenth centuries. The realization that human social behavior arises from and is epitomized by a mother's sacrifice for her children implies a direct association between kinship and the organization of the Comanche community. The Indians' ability to identify relatives through the use of kin terms and family names encouraged the extension of such sacrificial or social behavior toward one another. These types of social relationships formed the basis of the Comanche community. This analysis seeks to develop an understanding of the community from the perspective of individuals' familial social relationships as opposed to group-focused and culturally deterministic explanations. This approach helps explain behaviors that are traditionally associated with the historical Comanche community, such as camp residency, clan origins, and rank and hierarchy. The discussion of the foundations of the Comanche community establishes a conceptual foundation for the rest of the book and provides a framework for interpreting the more conspicuous behaviors Comanches demonstrated in the past.

One of the more elementary questions students of Comanche history have pondered over the years pertains to the Indians' migration into the southern-plains region and their subsequent nomadic behavior. Comanches' geographic relocation to New Mexico and Texas and their nomadism within these regions have generally been understood as a response to the availability of regional material resources. Chapter 2 proposes that traditional materialistic explanations for Comanches' geographic mobility are largely insufficient by suggesting that the nature of their movements is best construed within the context of their kinship and social relationships. Material considerations such as the availability of bison, horses, pasturage, water, or wood certainly influenced where Comanches moved, but these concerns should only be understood as motivating factors and not determinants. Familial social relationships, likewise, did not necessarily determine geographical movements, but they had a strong influence on mobility because Comanches actively recognized the advantages kinship relations provided to peoples competing for physical resources. The chapter concludes that the distinctive character of Comanches' migration into and within the southern plains was essentially a consequence of their widespread kinship social relationships.

The third chapter primarily features a discussion on the topic of horse pastoralism among Comanche Indians during the eighteenth and nineteenth centuries and explains the role of culture and tradition in Comanche society. Their inheritance of Old World pastoralist practices resulted as an effect of humans' general ability to learn and copy behavior from other humans. Any behavior acquired in this fashion is cultural behavior. The acquisition of horse pastoralism by Comanches, therefore, emerged as a consequence of their interaction with individuals who maintained kinship and social relationships with persons living in the Spanish province of New Mexico. When cultural behavior is passed down from ancestor to descendant, it is called tradition. That the tradition of pastoralism has existed for several thousands of years and has spread throughout the world implies that it has been greatly beneficial in helping people cope with various environments. At some point in the past, Comanches recognized the benefits of this cultural behavior and passed it down to their progeny as a tribal cultural tradition.

Chapter 4 discusses the nature of Comanche economic behavior and examines their trade from the perspective of their kinship and social behavior. It appears that trade and economics emerged among humans as a result of kinship social behavior and a division of labor. Although people's selfish wants and needs encourage trade, such transactions are fundamentally social acts in which all participants benefit. For the most part, Comanches' commercial relationships in New Mexico, Texas, and within the so-called Comanchería essentially reflected the many lines of kinship they recognized among themselves and traced to others. These social relationships formed the basis of Comanches commercial activities, but trade could also be established to non–related persons through contacts set up by relatives or through other social acts such as gift giving. This chapter departs from the traditional economic models that previously applied to Indians in favor of an alternative explanation that emphasizes the influence of Comanche kinship and social relationships on their commercial endeavors.

The fifth chapter seeks to explain why Comanches often demonstrated hostile, violent, and warlike behavior toward rivals and enemies. Again, the explanation of this behavior is based on an understanding of Comanches' kinship-oriented society. In traditional cultures like that of the Comanches, people favor their kindred over outsiders when competing over resources. The kinship behavior that encouraged this favoritism among Comanches also encouraged high levels of hostility and violence when they felt threatened by people with whom they did not recognize any relational affiliation. Another aspect of Comanche violence stemmed from their competition over women. This rivalry often pitted Comanches against one another and was a source of considerable contention among them. Cases of wife abductions could be settled by a material fine, corporal punishment, or death. Although Comanches tried to discourage kin from stealing wives from one another, they encouraged their young men to abduct women from their enemies. The main point is that the violent and warlike actions exhibited by Comanches in the historical sources are not usually examples of mindless brutality. Although the immediate aim of this type of behavior varied among individuals, its ultimate motivation is best understood through an appreciation of kinship social behavior.

Finally, a concluding chapter summarizes the arguments spelled out in the preceding chapters and hints at the implications for further interpretation of Comanche history. An appendix discussing the methodology employed in this discussion of Comanche society is provided for the benefit of students and scholars who wish to have a clearer understanding of the line of reasoning employed in this study.

CHAPTER 1

Comanche Kinship
and Society

EETING SOMETIME IN NOVEMBER, 1785, AT A PLACE ALONG
the Arkansas River called La Casa de Palo, various Cuchanec (Cuchantica), Jupe, and Yamparica Comanche clans discussed the prospects of
forging a general peace with the inhabitants of Spanish New Mexico.[1] Several
months earlier, on July 12, four hundred of these Indians had journeyed to Taos
in search of reconciliation, particularly for amicable trade opportunities. Comanches had oftentimes visited the pueblo since their ancestors first appeared in
the province around 1706. An uneasy relationship based on intermittent commerce and violence existed throughout the eighteenth century, benefiting and
bedeviling both New Mexicans and their Plains Indian visitors. Trade fairs such
as those held occasionally at Taos, Pecos, Ojo Caliente, and various other sites
could be transformed from an orderly, congenial affair into a violent maelstrom
in a matter of minutes. At one such event held in Taos sometime during the
1740s, the Comanches in attendance, uttering various grudges, capriciously retrieved their weapons and attacked the pueblo in retaliation for some apparent
extortion exacted by the settlers. The eighteenth-century governors of New
Mexico repeatedly issued proclamations imposing strict regulations upon commercial interaction in an attempt to maintain order throughout the province.
Officials often decreed harsh penalties, including confiscation of property, fines,
jail terms, and whippings, for those citizens who violated the edicts. These measures, however, invariably failed to arrest permanently the violence between
Spanish subjects and Comanches.[2]

As officials became frustrated in their efforts to establish tranquility within

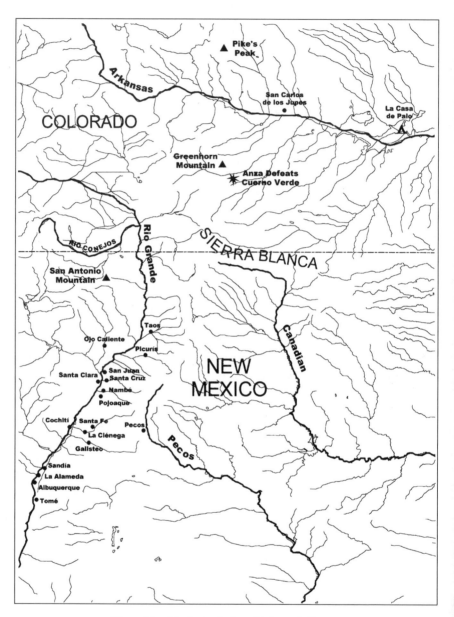

Map 1. New Mexico in the Late Eighteenth Century

the province and amity with the "wild" tribes of the frontier, they periodically conducted military campaigns aimed at punishing those malefactors whom they perceived as threats to the stability of the colony. In October, 1716, a force of 112 soldiers, settlers, and friendly Indians assembled in Taos and set out northwest for San Antonio Mountain, where they punished the Utes and Comanches encamped there. Gov. Thomas Vélez Cachupín, commanding 92 men, chased down and cornered 145 raiders in a canyon cul-de-sac in 1751. One of the most impressive and successful campaigns conducted by New Mexicans against Comanches took place in 1779 under the leadership of Gov. Juan Bautista de Anza. Taking a circuitous route through the mountains of southern Colorado, Anza surprised and overran a *ranchería* and later killed the formidable chief Cuerno Verde. The latter event, in particular, disrupted the continual cycle of trading, raiding, peace, and warfare that had consumed New Mexico and the Comanchería.[3]

Cuerno Verde's demise at the hands of Anza clearly demonstrated the governor's fortitude in dealing with Comanche belligerence toward the province. Nine months later in May, 1780, some tribal leaders communicated their desire to arrange a peaceful relationship with the governor. Peace, however, would not come immediately or easily. The leaders of New Mexico had to consider the opinions of their Ute and Jicarilla Apache allies concerning the establishment of an armistice with these tribes' hated enemies. Nevertheless, the process of reconciliation was earlier established and negotiations recommenced in 1783. Because some individuals resisted the peace process and continued to molest the Spanish settlements, Anza communicated to the Indians that he would offer a treaty to them only if they secured the good will of *all* their people. Leaders of the Cuchanec Comanches particularly desired a general truce and responded to the governor's demands in decisive fashion by the end of 1785. First, they arranged the assassination of the belligerent chief Toro Blanco and mollified most of his followers through persuasive force. Subsequently, tribal representatives meeting at La Casa de Palo that autumn inaugurated the Cuchanec chief Ecueracapa as commissioner general of the Comanches, formally establishing among the Indians a disposition of goodwill toward Spanish New Mexico.[4]

Ecueracapa wasted little time initiating accordance with Anza. By the end of January, 1786, two diplomatic missions under Chiefs Paraginanchi and Cuetaninabeni had visited Santa Fe, where they informed the governor of the prior events and the tribal consensus accomplished by the designation of Ecueracapa as principal leader of the tribe. Pleased by this news, Anza extended the Comanche commissioner general an invitation to meet with him in Santa Fe. The chief arrived in the capital villa on February 25, 1786. Greeted in ceremonious fashion and escorted into the whitewashed *palacio gobierno* by the executive entourage, Ecueracapa stated his terms for peace to the officials present. Anza simply replied that he would agree to the chief's request if he repeated his demands at Pecos pueblo before the contingent of Comanche leaders gathered there.[5]

Once in Pecos, Ecueracapa strode into a large conical-shaped tepee followed closely by eleven fellow Cuchanec captains. Inside, the Indians arranged themselves in a successive order upon skins placed for them on the grassy floor. Ecueracapa sat at the head of the delegation, followed by Tosacondata, then Tosapoy, Hichapat, Paraginanchi, Cuetaninabeni, Quihuaneantime, Sonocat, Canaguaipe, Pisimampat, Toyamancare, and finally Tichinalla.[6] After these individuals settled into their respective positions, thirty-one other followers filled the remaining empty space afforded by the stately hidebound lodge. After a short address given by Tosapoy, the official speaker of the assembled Cuchanecs, the governor announced to the attentive crowd that he had accepted their leader's overture for establishing amity between Comanches and the people of New Mexico. Anza agreed that the Comanches' basic requests were reasonable and even desirable for both constituencies represented that late winter's afternoon. As stated by the esteemed representative of the Spanish Crown, the accords imposed an inviolable peace upon the Indians; provided them royal protection and permission to live within the bounds of His Majesty's realm; allowed for free and unhampered communication and commerce between the two peoples; established a formal military alliance with the goal of waging incessant, open war against the Apaches; and officially commissioned Ecueracapa as the plenipotentiary of all Comanches. With the proclamation of these terms, Anza presented a ceremonial saber and banner to the chief. The Cuchanecs reciprocated by digging a hole in the ground in which they placed "various attendant ceremonies." Upon the conclusion of this ceremony, they covered the ritualistic items with the remainder of the loose dirt. These symbolic deeds effectively buried the longstanding state of intermittent warfare that had consumed the province since the 1710s and heralded a newfound optimism among many Comanches and New Mexicans in a future where cooperation would eclipse violent competition once and for all.[7]

The spirit of cooperation became manifest several months later in the form of a campaign conducted under Ecueracapa's leadership against Apaches living in the Sierra Blanca.[8] The operation, executed sometime during the period from May 19 to July 5, succeeded in seizing sixty-five horses and twenty mules, killing six Apaches, and taking two others prisoner. Out of the 347 Comanches participating in the venture, only 8 received battle wounds, one of whom ultimately succumbed to his injury. Captain Ecueracapa himself single-handedly killed one enemy and suffered two superficial wounds in the apparent melee. According to a tally sheet recording the events of the campaign and submitted to Anza in July, 1786, the Indians mobilized five columns against the Apaches, totaling 347 warriors.[9] That same month, the commissioner general underscored his desire to collaborate with the New Mexicans by sending a contingent of young men to accompany a joint Spanish-Navajo campaign against Gila Apaches living in the mountains along the Rio Grande to the south toward El Paso. Anza had originally requested eight Comanches for the expedition, but Ecueracapa sent twenty-two individuals, including his three sons, Oxamaquea, Tomanaguene, and Ta-huichimpia. The brothers explained to the governor that their father had sent them "so that they might shed their blood with that of the Spaniards in the service of the king."[10] Even though the ensuing campaign only enjoyed moderate success, it further demonstrated the Comanches' commitment to friendship and cooperation with the province of New Mexico.

The establishment of the Comanche peace in New Mexico altered the relationship between the Spanish colony and the numerous Indian tribes who inhabited its bordering regions. This episode has been of general interest to students of the Southwest because of its pivotal influence on the region's historical development.[11] Finally achieving stability along the eastern periphery of the colony, the treaty allowed for the emergence of an equilibrium and secured unanimity and relative prosperity for New Mexicans and Comanches alike.[12] The great desire for this prospect encouraged Spanish officials to carefully document the course for peace. For that reason, the records of this historical process contain careful observations disclosing information on Comanche behavior. From the overview of events taking place in the eighteenth century outlined above, patterns of the Indians' social behavior become somewhat apparent. The mention of clan and personal names, tribal leadership, order of seating at councils, political intrigue, and cooperation in military operations all hint at a subtle context of social conduct.

The basic assumption among social scientists has been that humans are social because they live in groups, that group living is social. This implies that social behavior is simply interaction among humans within groups. Hence the inordinate attention scholars have traditionally paid to the structure of groups in explanations of social behavior. Besides the problems associated with understanding human behavior this way, another problem arises when social behavior is defined as interaction. Interaction is neither necessarily social nor is it a necessary condition for social behavior. The episode surrounding Toro Blanco's assassination implied interaction between the followers of the slain chief and those of Ecueracapa, yet the conflict clearly cannot be classified as social behavior.[13]

Social actions imply at least one individual helping another. Cooperation occurs when two or more individuals help each other. The participation of Chief Ecueracapa's sons, Oxamaquea, Tomanaguene, and Tahuichimpia, alongside Spanish and Navajo troops in a 1786 summer campaign against the Gila Apaches exhibited such cooperation and, consequently, social behavior. Cooperation implies social behavior because the individuals engaged in assistance are accepting, or assenting, to one another's influence. In other words, when individuals make themselves vulnerable to another's interests, they are sacrificing their own interests in favor of the other individual's. Ecueracapa's sons' cooperation with the Spanish troopers against the Apaches can be seen as a social act due to the threat combat posed to the young men's lives. By sending them off to fight alongside

the Spanish, Ecueracapa himself demonstrated social behavior, and their acceptance of their father's and Anza's authority demonstrated theirs. The presence of
Ecueracapa's three sons on the expedition clearly broadcasted the chief's acceptance of the New Mexico government's influence at the expense of his own offspring. The statement made to Governor Anza by the young men upon their arrival at Santa Fe, that their father had sent them "so that they might shed their
blood with that of the Spaniards in the service of the king," vividly communicated the chief's intention to make a personal sacrifice on behalf of establishing amicable social relations (implying future interaction) with the Spanish
province. Interestingly, Ecueracapa had unwittingly imitated Abraham's sacrificial behavior as depicted in Genesis 22.[14]

Identifying Ecueracapa's peace overtures to Governor Anza in 1786, his subsequent personal leadership of a military campaign against Apaches on behalf of
the Spanish, and the offering of his sons to assist troops in another pursuit of
Apaches as "social behavior" does not explain why he acted in such a manner. Indeed, how can we account for the social behavior the chief extended to related
and nonrelated persons alike? Furthermore, how can we account for his extension of social behavior to former New Mexican enemies? Answering these questions requires an understanding of the association between altruism and human
kin relationships, otherwise known as kinship behavior.

Kinship literally implies a genealogical relationship based on the birth of one
individual from another. Kin are those individuals related through one or more
birth links.[15] Whether one is deemed one's ancestor, descendant, or co-descendant
is relative to the birth linkage between two people. The relationship between
Ecueracapa and Oxamaquea, Tomanaguene, and Tahuichimpia helps illustrate
this point. Because the chief's reproduction was necessary for the existence of
his sons, he is considered their ancestor. The brothers are considered descendants
of Ecueracapa and their mother since their existence depended on their parents' reproduction. The siblings are co-descendants of one another since they
share a common ancestor, a parent. Aunts, uncles, and cousins likewise are co-
descendants as long as they are able to trace a linkage to a common ancestor. If
two individuals, living or dead, are acknowledged as being either co-descendants
or one is the ancestor of the other, then they are kin no matter how distant that
relationship may be in terms of birth links separating them.[16] Spanish authorities
in New Mexico only knew that Ecueracapa, Oxamaquea, Tomanaguene, and
Tahuichimpia were closely related to one another because they were told so. But
how did these Comanche men know the true nature of their relationship?

Humans identify kin and kinship distance through birth. Mothers, in particular, play a crucial role in the process of social learning among offspring. Oxamaquea, Tomanaguene, and Tahuichimpia's mother, like all others, identified the
young men as her offspring by the consequence of their birth. During their in-
fancies, the sons then came to identify the woman as their mother and each other

as siblings through her parental behavior toward them. Fathers, however, are identified by different means. Ecueracapa's paternity of his sons was based on his sexual relationship with his wife. His children, consequently, recognized him as their progenitor through their mother and later through the fatherly care he extended to them. As a result of their sibling relationship, the brothers would have been able to identify each of their wives' children who, in turn, would have distinguished each other as cousins. The kin terms associated with these birth relationships — "mother," "father," "brother," "uncle," "aunt," "cousin" — imply a precise genealogical distance. They do not themselves determine an individual's behavior, as several students of kinship have assumed.[17] When "close" terms are used for more distant relatives, as they often are, they are used metaphorically to encourage the same type of behavior enjoyed by close kin among people who recognize a more remote birth link.

Tracing ascending birth links allows people to identify ancestors more distant than their mother and father. A consequence of this is the ability to identify distant co-descendants. Humans use descent (or family, ancestral, or clan) names to facilitate the recognition of distant ancestors and thereby distant co-descendants. By identifying an individual with a line of ancestors through one of the parents, genealogically distant co-descendants may come to be identified. Unlike kin terms, descent names do not indicate exact genealogical distance between relatives. Instead, the inheritance of a descent name allows a person to identify co-descendants too distant to trace birth links. Family or clan names identify all individuals having a particular name as co-descending from an ancestor who may have lived hundreds or even thousands of years ago. Consequently, the Comanche band, or clan, names Cuchanec, Jupe, and Yamparica allowed individuals to identify co-descendants whose actual birth-link connection had been obscured by tradition and time.[18]

Such names also allow the identification of distant co-descendants who do not actually bear the same name. People everywhere recognize individuals with their mother's family name as co-descendant relatives. (Of course, in societies that pass along family names through the mother's lineage, the father's co-descendants are also recognized as relatives.) It has been claimed that Comanche children "belonged" to the band of the father. Both male and female offspring inherited the clan name of the father, but only the males passed along the name to succeeding generations. Thus, it can be safely assumed that Oxamaquea, Tomanaguene, and Tahuichimpia belonged to the Cuchanec family since Ecueracapa had this ancestral name. But it must not be deduced that the three sons acknowledged only fellow Cuchanecs as kin. It should be remembered that they were also the children of Ecueracapa's wife (or wives). Ethnographic studies have suggested that Comanches prohibited marriage between people belonging to the same clan. In that case, Ecueracapa's spouse would have belonged to a clan other than Cuchanec.[19]

Spanish observations in the late 1780s identified Jupe and Yamparica as the only other band names among Comanches. The mother of Oxamaquea, Tomanaguene, and Tahuichimpia presumably bore one of these names. Knowing the clan affiliation of one's mother has great implications for being able to identify a greater number of co-descendant relatives than those known through the clan name actually borne by a person.[20] For the benefit of discussion, let us say that Ecueracapa had only one wife who belonged to the Jupe clan. This detail would suggest that Oxamaquea, Tomanaguene, and Tahuichimpia's maternal grandfather carried the Jupe name. Their uncles (their mother's brothers) would have also inherited the Jupe name from their grandfather, and their sons (the brother's first cousins) would have been identified as Jupe as well. Consequently, Ecueracapa's sons, all Cuchanecs, would have identified all Jupes as their kinsmen too because of their mother's heritage. Indeed, these relatives would be as closely related as any of those identified by their own clan name.

We know that Ecueracapa's father had to be a Cuchanec because Comanches inherited their clan name through the male line. This suggests that Ecueracapa's mother belonged to a clan other than Cuchanec. Now let us assume that his mother had been a Yamparica. Ecueracapa would have been related to those Yamparicas on his mother's side of the family in the same fashion. The clan names Cuchanec, Jupe, and Yamparica gave individuals the ability to identify a large number of co-descendants, the sum of which they referred to as "*nuhmuhnuh*" and to whom the Spanish authorities collectively labeled "*los comanches.*"[21]

The co-descendants an individual Comanche identified through his or her ancestral name did not form the basis of a social group. Descent identification and social groups are two independent features of human behavior, despite the continuing insistence among social scientists that one implies the other.[22] While on a peace-seeking expedition to the Comanches during the summer of 1785, Pedro Vial and Francisco Xavier Chaves noticed that Comanche "*rancherías* are formed according to the *capitanes,* each one trying to have his own." Thirty-nine years later, David Burnet, an American who lived among the Comanches in 1818 and 1819, reported that these Indians identified their "villages" by the name of the most prominent individual of the community. Spanish officials and servicemen copied this practice, often referring to individual camps as "*ranchería de*" Ecueracapa, Canaguaipe, or some other person recognized as a leader.[23]

Burnet's observation alluded to the idea that individual *rancherías* acquired the clan identification of the person it centered around. For example, documents indicate that Spaniards and Comanches referred to Ecueracapa's *ranchería* as a Cuchanec camp. But does this information mean that everyone in the commissioner general's encampment also belonged to the Cuchanecs, as some scholars have suggested? Vial and Chaves commented that Comanche camps did not have "a fixed number of subjects." Individuals, they declared, "adapted to the character [identity?] of each *capitán.*" Interestingly, Burnet made a similar assertion about individual *ranchería* membership, claiming that each member had the "liberty to withdraw from one village and unite with another, as caprice or convenience may dictate." Burnet applied this statement particularly to the high frequency of individual mobility he noticed between residential groups he identified as "Comanchees, Yamparacks, and Tenaways."[24] The information supplied by Vial, Chaves, and Burnet implies that bands or divisions could not have been autonomous social groups since people moved freely and often among camps of different band affiliations. The continuous movement of individuals between *rancherías* also suggests the probability that many of those living in Ecueracapa's encampment did not even have the Cuchanec ancestral name. If members of a residential encampment might not have the same name, then who made up these vacillating residential units?

Among traditional peoples throughout the world, residential communities include an ever-changing set of co-descendants and their spouses. Individual communities are referred to by a family name that identifies a common ancestor that almost all individuals living there had descended from (except for spouses, of course). Knowing the clan names of one's parents, grandparents, and great-grandparents allows a person to identify up to seven different ancestral birth links representing, potentially, eight different family lineages. A person could reside in any residential settlements in which they could trace a connection to a clan name of the ancestor common to that community.[25] Just by tracing his or her genealogy only three birth links up, an individual could identify a number of ancestors among whose descendants he or she would have been welcomed to live with. Of course, most of the ancestors would have a different descent name than the one the individual possessed.

Comanches resembled other traditional peoples in their naming of residential communities and in their changeable settlement practices.[26] They knew Ecueracapa's *ranchería* as a Cuchanec community because Cuchanec was the common ("founding") ancestor of those living there (other than spouses). Likewise, the camp of the Jupe chief Ysarumachi was known as a Jupe one because the defining or common ancestor had that name. Since only three ancestral names have been identified among the Comanches living in the 1780s, individuals probably did not have to trace far back to be able to identify a kinship connection to each clan name. Consequently, individuals and their families could have lived in *rancherías* associated with any clan name as long as they could establish their relationship with the particular ancestor of the settlement. Thus, Ecueracapa's encampment consisted of Cuchanecs and their co-descendants along with their spouses. Even so, most of the individuals living in that particular camp probably had other clan names. The offspring (male and female) of male Cuchanecs and their wives would be the only ones in the *ranchería* to have inherited that descent name. Other co-descendants, those who had Cuchanec mothers, grandmothers, or great-grandmothers married to Jupe or Yamparica men, could have resided

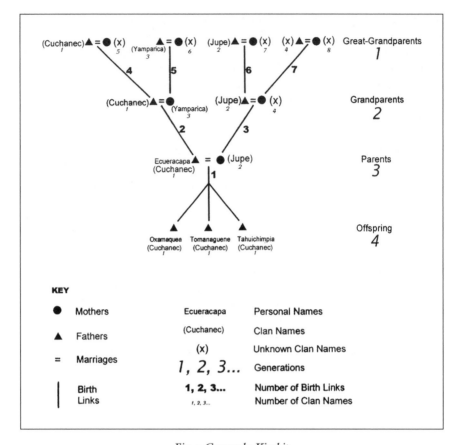

Fig. 1. Comanche Kinship

among Ecueracapa's encampment even though they had descent names identifying them with other ancestors. Naturally, the husbands married to the female Cuchanecs had names other than the one possessed by the residential gathering. The makeup of Comanche residence communities resembled a large modern-day family reunion, where most of the people attending have ancestral names different than the one that the reunion was organized around.[27]

The seemingly confused Spanish accounts identifying the clan affiliations of the chiefs Huanacoruco and Tanquegüe (also known simply as Quegüe) help illustrate that individual Comanches associated and lived with members of both their father's and mother's lineages. Huanacoruco first visited Santa Fe on May 9, 1786, and was identified by Spanish observers there as a Cuchanec. He had accompanied Tosacondata, the Cuchanec chief who sat alongside Ecueracapa at the monumental Pecos peace conference of the previous February, and two Yamparicas named Tosporua and Pasahuoques. At the end of 1803, Huanacoruco made an appearance in Chihuahua, the capital of Provincias Internas. In a letter to New Mexico governor Fernando Chacón, Comandante General Nemesio Salcedo identified Huanacoruco as belonging to and representing the Yamparica branch of Comanches.[28]

The details associated with Quegüe's clan identification resemble that of Huanacoruco's. As with the chief, Spanish observers linked Quegüe to Yamparicas and Cuchanecs. While visiting Salcedo in Chihuahua, Huanacoruco mentioned Quegüe to the *comandante* in reference to a political dispute over the leadership of the Yamparica clan. Several years later, on May 16, 1808, the Spanish trailblazer Francisco Amangual came across three Comanches hunting bison as he trekked across the southern plains en route from San Antonio to Santa Fe. The Indians informed Amangual "that they were the subjects of the big Yamparica chief named Quegue [*sic*]." However, in 1805 three Yamparica chiefs had appeared in Santa Fe and requested that Gov. Real Alencaster recognize Chief Somiquaso as the leader of the Yamparicas "in the same manner as Quegüe for the Cuchanticas."[29] Finally in 1818, reports associated Quegüe with the Cuchanec clan after Spanish authorities received word that the "general of the Cuchanticas named Tanquegüe" had died on the road.[30]

Huanacoruco's and Quegüe's association with the Cuchanec and Yamparica clans stem from each man's ability to identify with the lineages of their fathers and mothers equally. Because the men belonged to each line, they were able to interact with and represent both families at various times. This ability explains why Spanish authorities received reports associating each chief with different clans at different times. However, the question of why Huanacoruco and Quegüe might be identified with a specific clan at a particular point in time is related to the various issues associated with their rank and authority within the family. (These issues will be discussed in greater detail below.)[31]

Students have been confused by the various Comanche band names that have appeared throughout the course of their history. This confusion stems from the failure to realize that family names do not necessarily endure. Clan or ancestral names fluctuate through both time and space. Each male individual of those societies that trace descent and ancestry through the male line has the potential to be himself the source of a new lineage or clan name.[32] Conversely, the lack of reproduction by certain males in such societies also has the potential to be the ultimate source of a lineage's demise. These points have tremendous significance for understanding how clan names may disappear and persist and how they are generated over time.

Ancestral names traced through male lineages will perish when all males bearing a particular name fail to reproduce sons. Some factors that might have a detrimental effect on the reproduction of the sons of a particular Comanche lineage could simply be the random failure of women to successfully give birth to boys, diseases which either killed or sterilized males, or violent competition with its caustic concomitants of murder, massacre, and abduction. At the same time one clan name is reduced, individuals with other names may have large numbers of reproductive sons, increasing the proportion of others already in existence or giving rise to new clan names and traditions.[33]

Something similar to this scenario possibly befell the Jupe ancestral name in the late eighteenth and early nineteenth centuries, for it had practically disappeared in New Mexico by the early nineteenth century. A year after Ecueracapa made peace with the New Mexicans on behalf of all Comanches, the Jupe chief Paruanarimuco approached Governor Anza and requested urgent assistance in building a permanent settlement called San Carlos de los Jupes for his followers along the Arkansas River in what is now southeast Colorado.[34] Students of Comanches have traditionally understood this request as a behavioral anomaly encouraged by Spanish pacification policies, but the attempt to build a Jupe pueblo may have been a desperate response by Paruanarimuco to cope with various historically induced hardships that confronted him and his followers. The weight of these difficulties could have seriously affected the survivability of this particular lineage.

There is very little direct evidence to suggest that Jupes made up a powerful Comanche faction at the time they were first mentioned in the Spanish records of the 1770s. At the very least, it may be presumed that individual Jupes maintained positions of greater influence in the 1760s and 1770s than they did in the 1780s, when the Cuchanec Ecueracapa consolidated his power over the Comanches. The insinuation that the two powerful chiefs (a father who died on September 30, 1768, and his son who died on September 3, 1779) both known to the Spanish by the name Cuerno Verde possibly identified themselves as Jupes also lacks sufficient documentary verification. This conjecture is generally based on the association of these men with the geographical region along the *Río de Napeste* (the upper Arkansas River), identified as Jupe territory on Bernardo Miera y Pacheco's 1778 map of the Domínguez–Velez de Escalante expedition.[35] Indeed, the Cuerno Verdes could have been Jupes, but the possibility equally exists that they may not have been associated with this clan name at all. The same problem surrounds the clan identification of the recalcitrant chief Toro Blanco, who was assassinated by followers of Ecueracapa. Mention in the Spanish sources that the ill-fated chief enjoyed most of his influence among the Jupes and Yamparicas suggests, at least, that he probably did not identify with the Cuchanecs.[36] So far, no documents that positively verify the clan identity of Toro Blanco are known to exist. Nevertheless, for the sake of demonstrating how clan names may go out of existence, let us assume that the two chiefs known by the name Cuerno Verde and the one known as Toro Blanco were all indeed Jupes.

Vacillations between war and peace characterized Spanish-Comanche relations in the 1750s and 1760s. These decades experienced a couple of intervals of amity interrupted by a relapse into mutual hostilities from 1754 to 1762.[37] By the late 1760s, after several years of peace, discord once again epitomized the relationship between Spanish New Mexico and the Comanche people. Gov. Pedro Fermín de Mendinueta's reluctance to place a great deal of faith in the truce former governor Thomas Vélez Cachupín engineered with these Indians led to a series of clashes that could conceivably have prompted a decline of the Jupe ancestral name.

Convinced that Comanches could not be fully trusted, Mendinueta established a garrison of fifty men on San Antonio Mountain, along the Rio Grande northwest of Taos, in order to keep watch over that extremity of the province. In late May and early June of 1767, four hundred Comanches entered Taos with the intention of engaging in commerce. About the same time, one hundred or so other individuals approached the northwestern outpost of Ojo Caliente from the north via San Antonio Mountain. The Spanish troops stationed on the mountain surprised the Comanches as they approached and sent them fleeing for their lives back toward the Rio Grande. Once word of this ambush reached Taos, the traders hastily departed the villa, fearing that they would be accosted in a similar manner. Prior to their departure, however, the Comanches killed five settlers and a Taos Indian who had been trading with them in their camp at the time they received this unsettling news. Despite Mendinueta's argument that the appearance of Comanches at Taos and those on the trail to Ojo Caliente was part of an elaborate scheme devised by the Indians to attack the latter settlement, he cited no firm evidence for this conclusion.[38]

Notwithstanding the lack of proof that Comanches entered the province with the intention of committing hostilities, later that summer Mendinueta pushed northeast toward Jupe territory along the Arkansas River in pursuit of the Indians. After twenty-one days of searching for signs of Comanches, the Spanish force of 546 soldiers, settlers, and friendly Indians happened to come across two young Comanche men tending to a small horse herd. The Ute and Apache auxiliaries accompanying the force rushed out prior to the governor's orders, carelessly alerting the two individuals of the troop's presence. The herders fled posthaste and warned their kinsmen, who quickly disbanded and escaped.[39] These disconcerted actions of the late 1760s initiated a calamitous twenty-year episode of unrest in Comanche history. By 1786, Comanches had suffered not only from fighting against Spanish troopers, militiamen, and Indian auxiliaries but also from violent conflict with one another. These hostilities, possibly in conjunction with a smallpox epidemic and other uncontrollable factors, may have taken a disproportionate toll upon the population of those bearing the Jupe ancestral name.

In late September and October, 1768, parties of Comanche warriors retaliated by attacking Ojo Caliente and Picurís. A raid on September 26 upon Ojo Caliente was particularly disastrous for the Indians, resulting in the deaths of twenty-one out of twenty-four Comanches. The elder Cuerno Verde returned to the villa a month later with a force of five hundred seeking to avenge the death of his kinsmen and a devoted comrade killed in the previous attack. However, tragedy once again transpired at this frontier outpost on October 30, when the settlers discharged a volley of musket fire, knocking the chief and his horse to the ground. Unsettled by this turn of events, the Comanches recklessly retrieved the body of their fallen chief and retreated southward down the Ojo Caliente River.[40] The demise of Cuerno Verde at the hands of Spanish settlers impelled his followers to swear eternal vengeance upon the province of New Mexico, thrusting Jupes into a violent cycle of retaliation and death. The defunct chief's son, also known as Cuerno Verde to Spanish authorities, took up his father's crusade in the following decade.

The 1770s were a particularly tumultuous time in New Mexico and the adjacent territories. In 1772, parties of Comanches, up to five hundred strong, beleaguered the pueblos of Pecos, Picurís, and Galisteo. Cochití suffered at the hands of another five hundred warriors in 1773. Governor Mendinueta pursued these raiders northward to the Rio Conejos but failed to succeed at punishing them. Attacks on Picurís, Nambé, Santa Cruz de la Cañada, San Juan, Pecos, and Albuquerque in the summer of 1774 resulted in the death and capture of many settlers and livestock. These aggressions precipitated a retaliatory campaign that eventually tracked down a Comanche *ranchería* of more than eighty tepees. Most of the inhabitants of the camp, more than four hundred individuals, either died in battle or were taken prisoner by the Spanish force.[41]

The following year, New Mexicans across the province witnessed almost total warfare as Comanches accosted one settlement after another. Residents of Pecos, Santa Fe, Taos, Nambé, Sandía, La Alameda, and Galisteo all endured some form of destruction that year, including robberies, abductions, and murders. The devastation wrought upon the province by the numerous small-scale raids and larger offensives conducted by Comanches and other Indians seriously reduced the colony's horse herds and hence their ability to successfully defend themselves against the Indians. Comanche incursions upon the settlements of New Mexico continued through the following two years. At La Ciénega, Comanches killed 10 persons on June 20, 1776. An attack on Tomé on May 26, 1777, resulted in 21 deaths. Albuquerque also suffered from Comanche aggression in 1777 when, on August 27, 11 persons lost their lives. Spanish forces responded to these assaults later that fall by destroying two Comanche *rancherías* discovered in the Sierra Blanca Mountains. The 1778 raiding season resembled those of the previous years. Marauders revisited Tomé on June 3, slaying 30 more individuals. In all, Comanche war parties captured and killed 127 persons that year from villages throughout the province.[42]

The Comanches' prolonged and far-reaching offensive against the various settlements and pueblos of New Mexico reached a turning point in 1779. In that year the specter of misfortune returned to haunt the Jupe leadership and their followers. Determined to shore up the defenses of the northern territories, the Spanish command began implementing a revised frontier policy that included the consolidation of small and widespread settlements for defensive purposes, a reorganization of the defensive line of military settlements, and steps toward establishing peace with the hostile Indians. The newly commissioned governor of New Mexico, Juan Bautista de Anza, attempted to force the issue of peace upon the Comanches by leading six hundred men on a campaign against the Indians in August and September. After seventeen days on the trail, Anza's forward scouts espied a Comanche encampment on the plains along Colorado's Front Range southeast of Pike's Peak. The moment the Indians discovered the Spanish troopers advancing upon their *ranchería,* they suddenly took flight upon their mounts. After a chase of about three leagues (eight to ten miles), the soldiers finally overran the Comanches, killing eighteen men and wounding many others. Additionally, the regiment captured thirty-four women and children and more than five hundred horses. An interrogation of two Comanche prisoners revealed that the younger Cuerno Verde had gone to campaign in New Mexico with four of his principal captains and many other warriors, and they expected him to be returning soon. A couple of days later, the governor stumbled upon Cuerno Verde's column south of the Arkansas River. The two-day battle that ensued resulted in the deaths of the chief, his first-born son, the captain Aguila Bolteada, three other leaders, a medicine man (*pujacante*), and eighteen others.[43]

The fall of the younger Cuerno Verde, his son, and the others contributed to the devitalization of the Jupe ancestral line. Indeed, the death of the elder Cuerno Verde's son and grandson may have dealt the Jupe name a grievous blow. At most, that particular branch of Jupes that the Cuerno Verdes belonged to could have perished as a result of the battle with Anza, especially if there were no other male offspring produced by the descendants to pass along their ancestral name. In all, hundreds of Comanches lost their lives or were captured as a result of fights and skirmishes with Spanish troops, militias, and Indian auxiliaries from the late 1760s through the late 1770s.[44] Certainly, a great number of individuals who affiliated with the Cuchanec and Yamparica ancestral names also lost their lives in the continuous fighting during that violent decade. However, the vulnerability of the Jupe lineage may have been affected either by a disproportionate amount of Jupe deaths or the possibility that there were fewer individuals identifying with that name to begin with. Nevertheless, Spanish sources dated after 1786 identify fewer individual Comanches as Jupes than either of the other clan names then existing.

An apparently violent conflict among Comanches possibly contributed to the demise of the Jupe name. The continuous warfare within Spanish New Mexico during the 1770s may have been the source of this antagonism within the Comanche ranks. Governor Anza noted in his campaign diary that many Comanches harbored a seething resentment against Cuerno Verde and his followers for "forcing them to take up arms and volunteer against the Spaniards, a hatred of whom has dominated him [the younger Cuerno Verde] because his father . . . met death at our hands." Apparently, many Comanches, especially Cuchanecs, had become weary of fighting by 1779. Indeed, with the cantankerous Cuerno Verde out of the way, some individuals solicited Anza for the establishment of peace sometime before May, 1780. The process of reconciliation initially got off to a slow start. Serious negotiations between the Indians and the Spanish authorities began in 1783.[45] An obstacle to an armistice remained, however. A Jupe named Toro Blanco along with his followers continued the longstanding war upon the settlements of New Mexico. The exact relation between Toro Blanco and Cuerno Verde cannot be established, but if they both identified themselves as Jupes, then they were probably identifiable co-descendants. Regardless, Toro Blanco's raiding activities became a source of contention among Comanches, splitting the nation into two factions: those desiring peace under Cuchanec leadership and those Jupes and Yamparicas who did not. The Cuchanecs gained the upper hand in the debate over the issue of an armistice when, sometime in 1785, they arranged for Toro Blanco's assassination and the subjugation of most of his followers. A small ragtag band of fugitives continued the recalcitrant chief's crusade against the New Mexicans by attacking Pecos in January, 1786. Peace-faction Comanches apprehended the perpetrators of this assault almost immediately. In unforgiving retribution for this misdeed, the Cuchanec Ecueracapa personally took the life of the rebel band's leader, finally ending years of Comanche hostility toward New Mexico. It is obvious, however, that the Jupe name did not disappear in the mid-1780s. Several individuals that identified with this clan name appeared in New Mexico in 1786 and in the early 1790s. These persons were identified as El Chama, Queremilla, Ysaquebera, Tuchubarua, Encantime, Paruanarimuco, and Ysarumachi.[46] Probably more individuals possessed this particular ancestral name, but just how many more is impossible to know.

The biogeographical concepts of minimum viable populations and population viability may have some implications for understanding why the Jupe lineage dwindled around the beginning of the nineteenth century. Research on animal extinctions suggests that once a particular species, or lineage, reaches a lower population level, the likelihood of its demise increases proportionately. Different factors, some human caused and others the results of disturbances beyond the pale of human prediction and control, can increase the uncertainty surrounding the survival of particular lineages.[47] In the case of the Jupes, the human-caused and controllable factor of warfare and internal violence with New Mexicans and other Comanches seems to have weighed heavily upon their potential to survive. But uncontrollable factors may have also played a role in their decrease. Drought, spotty bison resources, and disease probably affected every Comanche family negatively, but the Jupe descent line would have been more susceptible to an aggregate decline given that their numbers, presumably, had been seriously diminished by the incessant fighting of the 1770s and 1780s.

Dry conditions are known to have occurred in and around New Mexico during these decades too. Fray Francisco Atanasio Domínguez observed in his 1776 description of the Pecos mission that scarcity of rain had reduced that pueblo's agricultural output to the point that "what few crops there usually are do not last to the beginning of a new year [January] from the previous October." It seems that the dry conditions also had a negative effect on the distribution and availability of the bison herds roaming the plains to the east. Anza took note of the scarcity of bison in the Arkansas River region while campaigning against Cuerno Verde in 1779. Since the majority of the Comanche diet consisted of food products procured from plants, bison, and other game, any decrease in those resources would have had a detrimental effect upon the potential survivability of each individual. Indeed, a drought lasting from approximately 1787 to 1790 severely reduced southern plains bison resources, forcing Comanches to rely on shipments of almost three hundred bushels of corn from New Mexico in order to avoid widespread starvation. Concha reported to Ugarte y Loyola that several individuals living among the Cuchanecs died as a result of this crisis. Presumably, persons associated with each clan suffered from the consequences of the drought conditions of the late 1780s.[48]

Disease also placed a great deal of stress upon the Comanche population in the late eighteenth and early nineteenth centuries. In early September, 1785, Pedro Vial and Francisco Xavier Chaves learned from the two chiefs Camisa de Hierro (an agnomen for Ecueracapa) and Cabeza Rapada that in years previous, two-thirds of their people had succumbed to a smallpox epidemic brought to them by French traders from Arkansas.[49] It is impossible to know whether the figure stated by the chiefs referred to the total Comanche population or simply the sum of those individuals that lived in the camps of the two leaders at the time the Indians acquired the sickness. Nevertheless, this figure suggests that a good number of Comanches succumbed to the calamity.

Diseases that afflicted horse herds not only threatened the well being of those animals but also indirectly affected that of their owners. One of Ecueracapa's sons arrived in Santa Fe on April 30, 1786, and reported to Anza that his father had been unable to make it to the capital for his planned monthly meeting with the governor "because of the high mortality among his mounts as a result of an epidemic."[50] Diseased horse herds affected the well being of individuals because the animals would not have been available for hunting and transportation, and they also would have impaired the ability of a camp to defend itself against an attack by enemies. The grave possibilities a sick horse herd represented to its owners and the other individuals who relied upon them suggest why Ecueracapa found it more important to focus his energy on tending to his herds than on delivering his monthly report in the presence of Governor Anza. Like diseases that directly afflict humans, those among domestic herd animals also have a negative effect on the survivability of humans. It might be assumed that Jupes also suffered from the diseases that Ecueracapa described to Vial, Chaves, and Anza because of the interrelated nature of Comanche relationships (as explained above). Networks of relatives across groups would have facilitated the spread of illness among people and horses. It would have taken only the slightest contact for these diseases to disseminate throughout the Comanchería.

Variables generated by human and nonhuman elements probably produced certain deleterious effects upon the Jupe clan, seriously reducing the number of people identifying with that lineage. Even though the existence of Jupe individuals can be verified by the Spanish sources of the 1780s and 1790s, the nature of the Indians' reproduction and offspring cannot be fully known. Apparently warfare, starvation, and disease occurred among Jupes to the degree that it severely diminished the numbers of individuals who might have bestowed that clan name to male progeny through which it would be propagated. Since the name practically fades from the documentary sources of the early nineteenth century, it must be surmised that the number of surviving Jupe males had decreased. Paruanarimuco's attempt to establish a fixed settlement along the Arkansas River may represent the trepidation of individuals who envisaged the possible demise of their family unless exceptional steps were taken to ensure the survival of the clan.

The story surrounding the demise of this Comanche settlement exemplifies the peril looming over the Jupe lineage. San Carlos de los Jupes foundered only a few months after the Indians had taken up residence in their new homes in October, 1787. The death of one of Paruanarimuco's favorite wives the following January induced a sudden exodus from the village. Following tradition, the Comanches abandoned the site of the death and returned to a nomadic mode of life on the plains.[51] The loss of Paruanarimuco's wife not only discouraged the successful settlement of Jupes in a fixed village but also further reduced the ability of Paruanarimuco to leave more descendants who might carry on his family name through that particular wife.

Interestingly, even though the Jupe lineage experienced a severe decline in New Mexico, it did not completely die out or disappear. The passing of the word *Jupe* from the documentary sources by 1830 seems to suggest that this lineage became extinct by then. However, it appears that the disappearance of this name in the form familiar to New Mexicans resulted from historical developments associated with the migration of clan members toward Texas and the arrival of a large number of English speakers to that province. A close analysis of David G. Burnet's 1824 description of the geographical location of the Comanche "Tenaway" band suggests that he may have actually been describing southward-migrating Jupes. He claimed that this family "range[d] through a mountainous district that separates the waters of the Rio del Norte, from the rivers of Texas, and they ex-

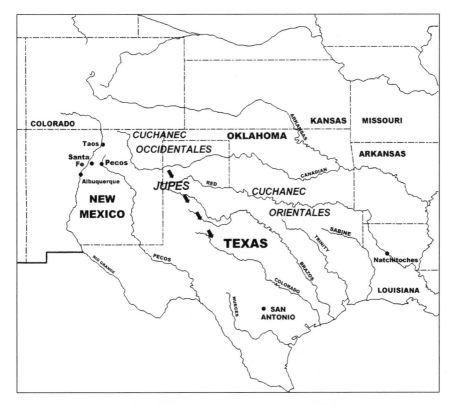

Map 2. Jupe Migration to Texas and Cuchanec Divisions

tend their perambulations to the head waters of the Red River of Natchitoches." Obviously, the area Burnet described is the region of the southern high plains that includes the Pecos River valley and the Llano Estacado. His mention of the headwaters of the Red River suggests that members of this clan frequented the broken canyon country lining the eastern escarpment of the Staked Plains. This area is far to the west of the middle Brazos River region, where Tenewa family members generally lived. Instead, the high plains region of eastern New Mexico and northwestern Texas would have most likely been a territory Jupes migrated to as incoming Kiowas, Cheyennes, and Arapahos pushed them south out of the Arkansas River valley. Burnet's observation that the Teneways "often mingle with the Yamparacks [*sic*] when traversing the southern extreme of their [Yamparicas'] range," strongly suggests that he was confusing Jupes for Tenewas. Anza had previously noted the close relationship between Jupes and Yamparicas in his 1786 report on the events leading to the Comanche peace in New Mexico.[52]

By the 1830s and 1840s, a new Comanche clan name appeared in the vicinity of Texas. Various spellings of this name appeared in regional documents, including "Júez," "Hoish," and "Ho'is." These forms closely resembled the Spanish pronunciation of the words *Jupes* and *Jupis* (pronounced "HOO-pays" and "HOO-pees" respectively) commonly found in New Mexican documents prior to 1830.[53] The realization that names such as Jupe represented familial lineages, as opposed to geographical groups or bands, strongly suggests that the Hois, living in Texas in the 1840s, were the direct descendants of the Jupe family formerly living in the vicinity of the Arkansas River northeast of New Mexico in the 1790s. Consequently, it must be assumed that male Jupe births occurred at a level sufficient for the succession of the lineage. Despite a long period of warfare, disease, starvation, and decline in the eighteenth and early nineteenth centuries, Jupe individuals ultimately endured the historical difficulties associated with life in the Comanchería.

Despite the continuing persistence of the Jupe family name in Texas, there is no doubt that some Comanche lineages succumbed to extinction. The Pibian name, identified as a Comanche band by New Mexico governor Francisco Marín del Valle in the late 1750s, may have been such a dead-end lineage since this name had disappeared from the documentary record by the 1780s. Nevertheless, the number of Comanche clan names appears to have increased from 1780 to 1850. In the early 1890s James Mooney identified thirteen Comanche clan names.[54] It can be surmised from his observation that the ten names that did not exist earlier in the century must have initially branched off from the older Cuchanec, Jupe, or Yamparica lineages.

In order to understand fully the evolutionary process of family names and the identities associated with them, one needs to determine how these names come into existence. Though each male in a society that inherits clan names through the paternal line can be the source of a new lineage, the process in which new clan names appear is fundamentally different than that involved with their demise. When an ancestral name disappears, it can no longer serve to identify co-descendants — that lineage is a dead end. The appearance of new lineages is not reliant on the disappearance of former ones. New ones are necessarily generated from those already in existence. The split of the Cuchanec lineage around the turn of the nineteenth century demonstrates the dynamics of clan segmentation. While it has been argued that the eastern and western Cuchanecs eventually became two separate divisions due to political and material differences, a close look at the evidence suggests that this clan eventually divided into two separate lineages, due in part to the isolation of a large number of co-descendants across a vast territory as well as intrafamily disputes that revolved around issues of authority.

By the mid-1780s, Spanish authorities recognized the widely distributed nature of Cuchanec Comanches. Those Cuchanecs living in the territory lying between the Wichita villages along the Red River and the territorial capital of San Antonio de Béxar became known as "Orientales" (easterners). The Spaniards applied the label "Occidentales" (westerners) to those Cuchanecs living in the vicinity of New Mexico. Though Pedro Vial and Francisco Xavier Chaves mistakenly claimed that the Occidentales "are known as the Yambericas," they informed Gov. Domingo Cabello of Texas in 1785 that approximately 150 leagues (approximately 380–400 miles) separated them from those Comanches they knew as Orientales. Spanish officials in New Mexico also reported the distinction between the eastern and western branches of the Cuchanecs in 1786. Apparently, they learned this information from various interviews with Comanche chiefs visiting Santa Fe around the time of the establishment of the peace between the province and the Indians. Specifically commenting on the Cuchanecs, Governor Anza reported that they "extend from the cited river [Arkansas] south as far as the Colorado [Canadian?] which is distant a few days travel from New Mexico . . . , separated on the east . . . from another group of their *kinsmen* living in the direction of the Jumanos or Taguayaces [Wichitas]" (emphasis added).[55]

Despite the geographical separation between the eastern and western Cuchanecs, the various individuals identifying with each of these branches would have been further dispersed owing to the nomadic nature of Comanches. This behavior further distributed Cuchanecs across a vast territory covering southeastern Colorado, southwestern Kansas, eastern New Mexico, western Oklahoma, and much of Texas. Interrogated by Thomas Vélez Cachupín in March, 1750, the French *voyageur* Pierre Satren informed the New Mexico governor that Comanches "were dispersed, with their large droves of horses, for which reason they could not live together." Athanase de Mézières, the lieutenant governor of Natchitoches and who later served Spain as a diplomat to the northern tribes in the 1770s, described the relationship between Comanche mobility and the dispersal of people across the landscape to Texas governor Juan María, Barón de Ripperdá. He noted that the Indians "divide themselves into an infinite number of little bands for the purpose of seeking better pastures for their horses, and cattle [bison] for their own food." He stated further that "this explains why they separate from their chiefs, following out their individual whims." About sixty years later, Jean Louis Berlandier made a similar observation on the distribution of Comanches in Texas, stating that "they are scattered in little tribes around the headwaters of every river in this country [Texas]" and leading what he called "a wandering life." Dispersion of co-descendants across space is necessary but is not itself sufficient for the segmentation of an ancestral lineage. Indeed, vast geographical scattering seems to have been at least one compelling impetus in the development of this process among the Cuchanecs. However, the area of distribution need not have been great.[56]

Even though the Cuchanec lineage branched into two geographical areas and dispersed themselves over an enormous territory, they seemed to have identified as a single descent group, or clan, until sometime in the early nineteenth century. Spanish sources regularly recorded a close association between individuals who were known to have affiliated with each branch. Vial and Chaves encountered the Cuchanec chiefs Camisa de Hierro (Ecueracapa) and Cabeza Rapada between the first and eighth of September, 1785, at a Comanche encampment along the "Río del Mermellón," in what is now North Texas.[57] The Spanish envoys described the chiefs as commanding "much respect and attention because they are considered as the bravest of all among them." Texas authorities reported that the chiefs also possessed the highest prestige among the Comanches residing near that province. Governor Cabello reported to the *comandante inspector* of the Provincias Internas in April, 1786, that Cota de Malla or Camisa de Yerro (also known as Ecueracapa) commanded preeminent authority among the eastern Cuchanecs. Cabeza Rapada enjoyed the status of second in command. His authority, Cabello suggested, followed closely behind that of Ecueracapa. After Cabeza Rapada, the governor named in successive order eight other eastern chiefs: El Lobito, El Sorrillo, Quinacaraco, El Guaquangas, La Boca Partida, El Español, El Surdo, and El Manco. Three or four other lesser chiefs followed these, but Cabello did not provide the *comandante* with their names.[58]

Spanish observers witnessed other known eastern Cuchanecs besides Cabeza Rapada associating closely with New Mexico Cuchanecs in the late eighteenth century. En route from Santa Fe to San Antonio de Béxar, José Mares encountered the Comanche chief Quenaracaro in eastern Cuchanec territory along the upper Brazos River in March, 1788. New Mexico sources later recorded that an individual named Quenarucaro accompanied by Ecueracapa and Hachacas arrived in Santa Fe on September 16, 1792, and reported the successful results of a campaign they led against Apaches earlier that summer in June. Quenarucaro and Hachacas again appeared in Santa Fe along with nineteen others on October 1, 1792, as they stopped over in the villa upon their return from yet another campaign against Apaches.[59] All the above spellings of this name are very close, and it is almost certain that they represented the eastern Cuchanec whom Texas governor Cabello identified as Quinacaraco in 1786. If so, then it is apparent that this "eastern" chief often interacted closely with western Cuchanecs.

In all, several individuals associating with the eastern Cuchanecs visited Santa Fe in 1792. On June 8 the eastern Comanche chiefs Pisimampi and Pujibuipuja appeared in the capital with fifteen other persons. Pisimampi most likely was the Cuchanec identified as Pisimampat at the peace ceremonies held at Pecos on February 25, 1786, and may have been the person identified as El Sorrillo ("skunk") by Cabello that same year.[60] Indeed, this individual's participation in the 1786 meeting and his conclusive identification as an eastern Cuchanec in 1792 suggest that the Orientales and Occidentales cooperated very closely with each other in the late eighteenth century.

Asserting that the Cuchanecs living in New Mexico and Texas may have recognized themselves as a single ancestral lineage in the late 1800s is not meant to imply that the "east" and "west" labels affixed to the different geographical parts of this lineage were simply a consequence of the inherent autonomy enjoyed by the frontier administrations in Santa Fe and San Antonio de Béxar. Colonial officials based their observations regarding the Cuchanecs on information supplied by the Comanches themselves. The mention of the Cuchanecs' geographical division in the documentary sources merely reflects the beginnings of a segmentation process between the co-descendants of this lineage.

Partisan rivalry among Cuchanecs in the 1790s and the early nineteenth century implies the ever-widening split between the eastern and western factions. Ecueracapa's authority over the whole Cuchanec clan had apparently been firmly established prior to the acceptance of his influence among Jupe and Yamparica clan leaders in 1785. Unfortunately, the chief succumbed to "grave wounds" he received during a campaign against the Pawnees sometime during the first half of 1793.[61] Ecueracapa's death probably dealt the critical blow to the preservation of the Cuchanec family hierarchy that had united the eastern and western branches.

Cabeza Rapada, the eastern Cuchanec cited by Vial and Cabello as second in command under Ecueracapa, had died earlier in 1786 at the hands of Mescalero and Lipan Apaches along the lower Pecos River, weakening Ecueracapa's authority over those clan members living in Texas. Ecueracapa's vengeful pursuit of Cabeza Rapada's murderers in July of that year suggests that the two chiefs must have been close co-descendants. Cabeza Rapada's death thrust the leadership of the eastern Cuchanecs into collective confusion as they attempted to sort out who was to succeed the fallen chieftain.[62] The inability of the easterners to agree upon an immediate successor hints at budding distinctions between the various sublineages within the Cuchanec family at this time.

The demise of Ecueracapa seven years later probably greatly exacerbated the general confusion over the issue of who possessed authority over those Cuchanec family members living in the east, for his death may have severed an important link between the clan's two branches, furthering the genealogical distance between them and stoking the flames of intrafamily rivalries. This rivalry reached tragic proportions in 1797 when an eastern leader named Soxas murdered one of Ecueracapa's sons and fled to the village of the "Taguayases" (Taovayas and Wichitas) along the Red River in search of protection against the enraged kinsmen of the influential victim.[63] The homicide of one of Ecueracapa's sons clearly demonstrated the disintegration of the family authority structure that previously unified the eastern and western Cuchanecs as one clan.

The evidence further suggests that the Cuchanec clan splintered into more than just eastern and western factions. There appears to have been a consanguineous relationship, from past marriage, between some eastern Cuchanecs and Caddoan families living within the Comanchería along the Red, Trinity, and Brazos Rivers. The Caddoan speakers along the Red River and in north-central Texas were some of the Comanches' first allies in the southern plains region, and this relationship may have been the basis for the settlement of a branch of

Cuchanecs in the east. The two peoples first formalized their friendship along the Arkansas River in 1747 after previous years of conflict. The only serious break in the alliance came in 1770 when Comanches reportedly objected to the desire of the Caddoans to meet in council with Spanish diplomat Athanase de Mézières in order to discuss the prospect of establishing peace in Texas. The relationship between the Indians began to stabilize by the last years of that decade, though. The alliance strengthened in the 1780s with the onset of peace in Texas and New Mexico. Vial and Chaves took note of the good relations, mentioning in 1785 that the "Cumanches [*sic*] Orientales have as friends the Tavoayaces and Guachitas [Wichitas]." In the 1790s, Spanish authorities in New Mexico witnessed the amicable relations between these peoples when on July 29, 1792, four Comanches "orientales" accompanied by two "Jumanes," or Wichitas, arrived in Santa Fe, where Governor Concha regaled them with gifts totaling 46.6 pesos in value. This minor incident hints that Comanches and Wichitas may have intermarried on a limited scale by the early 1790s if not before (perhaps 1747).[64] Soxas's refuge among the Caddoan settlements also suggests the prospect that some Comanches may have been closely related to those peoples living along the Red River.

The example of the Cuchanec chief Sariarioco, who was also known as El Sordo, further illustrates the interrelated association that existed between these two peoples in the late eighteenth and early nineteenth centuries. In October, 1810, Spanish authorities in Texas held a council in which they discussed the possibility of waging war upon the Indians of the province. The records of this meeting mentioned that El Sordo, reportedly upset with Gov. Manuel María de Salcedo's prohibition against commerce with American traders, took refuge among the Tahuacanos (Tawakonis, a Caddoan clan) after committing several retaliatory robberies in the province. The council further disclosed that El Sordo had disavowed his former Comanche wives and married Tahuacano women instead. The residential relocation of the "restless and obstinate" chief was not a solitary act. Several other Comanches accompanied him to live among the Caddoans.[65]

El Sordo's close association with the Tahuacanos probably came about more as a result of intense rivalries within the eastern Cuchanec clan than with any disagreement over the Spanish policy concerning trade with Americans. The events surrounding the chief's imprisonment in San Antonio in 1811 suggest that a good deal of discord existed among the Comanche rank and file at this time. In response to El Sordo's arrest by the Spanish, the Yamparica leader Oso Ballo organized a council of war with the Tahuacanos and Tahuayases (Taovayas) on the Red River in early 1812. At this meeting the Indians demanded El Sordo's release and discussed a plan to enter San Antonio under the pretext of peace, liberate the chief, and kill the governor. The hostile meeting did not sit well with those Comanches who opposed the followers of El Sordo, Oso Ballo, and the associated Caddoans. In April a chief named Joyoso communicated to the governor of Coahuila that he and five other captains were not interested in Oso Ballo's de-

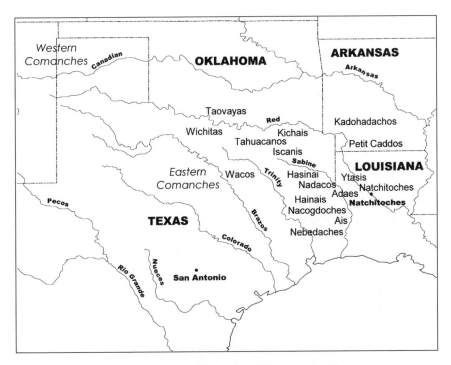

Map 3. Caddoan-speaking Tribes of Texas and Louisiana

signs and that they would take up arms against their compatriots on behalf of the Spanish should hostilities erupt.[66] The antipathy ingrained in Joyoso's siding with the Spanish in this "El Sordo affair" alludes to the existence of serious divisions between individual Comanches over issues surrounding the hierarchy of individuals with regard to clan authority.

The search for refuge among Caddoan clans by El Sordo and his affiliates mirrored Soxas's flight to the Wichita villages on the Red River after he murdered one of Ecueracapa's sons. Both of these incidents suggest an intrafamilial conflict and the existence of a physical kin connection (i.e., intermarriage) between Comanche and Caddoan families because Soxas and El Sordo would have been able to seek the most effective asylum among relatives or in-laws. Most importantly, the incidents surrounding El Sordo suggest one way new clans emerge from those already in existence and how Indians, through marriages, eventually established kinship ties between families of different cultures.

The geographical separation necessary for development of a new clan was inherent in the chief's move to the Tahuacanos. However, this move would not have been sufficient for the recognition of a new lineage. Even though there is no evidence of this chief's reproduction, let us assume that he had children with at least one Comanche and one Tahuacano wife. These children would have considered one another as co-descendants (half-siblings), even though they would not have shared all the same ancestors. From that point on, some Comanches would have had some Tahuacanos as relatives and vice-versa since they would have also been able to trace their ancestry back through their mothers. As long as El Sordo's Comanche and Tahuacano descendants actively recognized the chief as the link to their relationship, then they and others could acknowledge them as potentially a separate clan on the basis of their consanguinity. This situation probably led to some contention, for detached loyalties of certain individuals to particular families would have antagonized those who professed an exclusive allegiance to the various Comanche and Caddoan clans. It is conceivable that the differences among Comanches that surfaced during the El Sordo incident were related to preexisting issues revolving around kinship and individuals' recognition of family authority.

The Comanche clan known as the Tenewas appears to have been comprised of individuals who recognized eastern Cuchanecs and Caddoans living along the Red, Trinity, and Brazos Rivers as co-descendants. The 1838 report of George W. Bonnell, Republic of Texas commissioner of Indian affairs, to the secretary of war in Houston hints at the close connection between El Sordo's Comanches and Tahuacanos in the formation of the Tenewa clan. Speaking on the nature of Comanche councils, Bonnell describes the proceedings as cacophonous, "not unfrequently terminat[ing] with a battle between the different tribes [or clans]." He further states, "this sometimes produces permanent enmities, and the chief of the disaffected tribe, as in the instance of Towacany, separates from the nation, and sets up for himself." The chief Bonnell referred to as "Towacany" closely resembles El Sordo. Later in his report Bonnell describes the Indians known as "Towacanies" as "tak[ing] their name from Towacana, a disaffected Comanche chief, who flourished about 30 years back." The year 1808 implied in Bonnell's report corresponds very closely to the time when El Sordo and his followers made their break from the eastern Cuchanecs. Also, it is evident that the word *Towacanies* was an English adaptation of the same word the Spanish spelled "Tahuacanos." Despite Bonnell's confusion over the exact identity of these Indians, his information concerning the individual he identified as "Towacana" more than suggests that the descendants of El Sordo became those Indians known as the Tenewas. A decade later, Robert S. Neighbors, U.S. special Indian agent to Texas, also noted the close connection between the Tenewa Comanches and the various Caddoans living in the northern part of that state. Expressing his concern over the proposed Peters' Colony in North Texas to officials in Washington, D.C., Neighbors observed that the boundaries surveyed for the settlement "pass[ed] directly through the country . . . occupied by the Keechies, Wachitas, Wacoes, Tah-wac-caros, Caddoes, Ionies, and Ten-a-wish [Tenewa] Indians."[67] Neighbors's observation placing the Tenewas clearly within the geographical re-

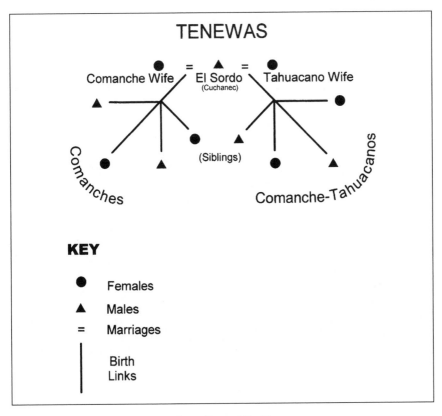

Fig. 2. Tenewa Kinship

gion commonly considered as the territory of various Caddoan clans in 1848 lends further credence to the idea that the Tenewa clan emerged from various individuals' recognition of their Comanche *and* Caddoan ancestry and their co-descendants.

The circumstances surrounding the decline of the Jupes in New Mexico and the splintering of the Cuchanec family into independent but related lineages allude to fundamental questions pertaining to the relationship between kinship and hierarchy. These events suggest the presumption that the cooperative and factious behavior demonstrated by individuals such as Ecueracapa, the two Cuerno Verdes, Cabeza Rapada, Soxas, El Sordo, and others was set within a context of an authority structure or hierarchy based on kinship. Ecueracapa's assumption of command over the Comanches in the 1780s demonstrates the existence of such a "political" system. It has generally been presumed that a person's prominence stemmed from their control of various material and immaterial resources.[68] But if this were the case, how could individual Comanches have ini-

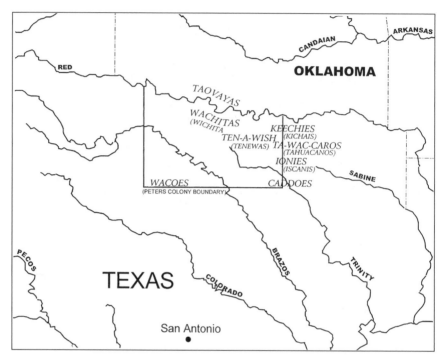

Map 4. Indians Living within the Boundaries of the Peters' Colony

tially acquired the influence to accumulate the resources upon which they based their authority?

People all over the world use kin terms and clan names to identify large numbers of relatives. But this fact alone does not explain why or how people like Comanches benefit by identifying large numbers of kinsmen. While kin terms and clan names are often associated with kinship behavior, the identification of kin is not sufficient to reduce competition and promote altruistic cooperation between relatives. Soxas's murder of Ecueracapa's son clearly demonstrates this point since both individuals presumably shared the same clan name and would have been considered kin. However, his flight to the Taovaya village after perpetrating the homicide suggests that he also had some kinship connection to these Caddoans.[69] This incident demonstrates, at once, antisocial behavior as well as altruism among various relatives.

If kinship identification alone cannot account for cooperation among kinsmen, how can we explain widespread cooperation among Comanches? In other words, what was the basis of cooperation between Ecueracapa and his adjutant, Cabeza Rapada; between the principal chiefs of the Cuchanecs, Jupes, and Yamparicas attending the council of November, 1785, at La Casa de Palo; and between

the reported thousand-man-strong Comanche and Taovaya armed force assembled for a summer campaign against the Lipan, Mescalero, and Lipiyana Apaches in 1791? All of the social behavior in these three examples involved some sort of ordering or ranking system. Various studies of Plains Indians have noticed that those societies tended to emphasize an individual's social position or rank. The explanation accepted by most students for this behavior has primarily focused on the influence of material goods in determining a persons' stature within the society.[70] However, this approach to understanding rank fails to account for the point that young men, who were probably the best hunters and warriors and most likely to be the members of Comanche society to have the greatest access to material goods, were usually far less prestigious than elders.[71]

Rank, like social behavior, probably developed originally among humans as a result of the fundamental parent-offspring relationship. For millennia, mothers and fathers have exerted parental influence upon their children who, in turn, have accepted and respected their influence. Consequently, children everywhere are considered as subordinates to their parents.[72] This relationship is the most fundamental level of rank and status among humans, and it is necessarily based on age.

Beyond the basic hierarchical status of parents and children, siblings are ranked in relation to one another by their birth order. Ecueracapa's sons demonstrated this ranking classification when they and nineteen other young warriors arrived in Santa Fe on July 15, 1786, to volunteer for military duty against the Apaches. Anza identified Oxamaquea as the leader of the Comanche force and as the *hixo* [*sic*] *mayor* ("first son") of the tribe's captain general. His younger brothers, Tomanaguene and Tahuichimpia, were listed in successive order and identified as *hijo segundo* and *hijo tercero* ("second" and "third son") respectively. This arrangement implies that younger siblings accepted the authority of the older ones and that older siblings cared for the welfare of younger ones.[73]

All kinship relationships are ranked similar to those between parents and offspring and between siblings. Every kin term suggests an extension of these fundamental relationships and facilitates rank. For example, Oxamaquea would have used terms such as *kuhnu* for his paternal grandfather, *pia* in reference to his maternal aunt, and *tua* when speaking of a nephew. Terms like these, when used literally, specified distinct birth links and implied these people's social position, or rank, in relation to Oxamaquea. *Pia,* incidentally, is not only the Comanche word for "maternal aunt" but also the word for "mother." Likewise, *tua,* the word for "nephew," also means "son." Oxamaquea's metaphorical extension of these kin terms to more distant relatives would have communicated his willingness to accept his aunt's motherlike authority and a readiness to care for his nephew as he would a son. The observation that a Comanche could call every other Comanche by a kin term of some sort suggests that individuals would have recognized their rank and responsibility in relation to another no matter how distantly related.[74]

Kinship and its social behavior serve as the basis of ranked relationships or hierarchies. In other words, a hierarchy is a social relationship based on the acceptance of parentlike authority and sacrifice. In 1786 Governors Anza of New Mexico and Cabello of Texas both alluded to the existence of this form of hierarchical leadership among Comanches. Anza explicitly notes that the chiefs attending the ratification ceremonies of that year's monumental peace treaty in Pecos "seated themselves according to order." Cabello similarly identifies the ranking order of the eastern Cuchanec leadership in a report to the commandant general of the Provincias Internas. The Comanches' concern with order, and particularly their seating order at the Pecos peace ritual, graphically communicated each participant's receptiveness to the parentlike influence of those seated ahead of them.[75]

Rank and hierarchies are fundamental to kinship cooperation because they help reduce competition, enhancing the possibility of concordance among relatives and their ability to successfully compete with outsiders. Rituals, very much like the one observed by Anza at Pecos, serve to reinforce the hierarchical social structure and help create cooperation among individuals. Comanche men participated in such rituals on a daily basis. According to José Francisco Ruíz, a council was held when the chief of an encampment, "who is *always an old man*," would send out a notice for all the warriors to "come to the pipe" (emphasis added). The chief took "the principal seat" and waited for the others to come to his tent. Upon arrival, the men, one by one, "say, 'here am I, what seat shall I occupy?' The answer is given by the Chief [*sic*], on the right or left, as the case may be and he enters and seats himself accordingly." Ruiz continued:

> each one as he enters [the tent] divest[s] himself of the ornaments and clothing he wears and deposits them in [an] enclosure in the back part of the tent — all the men having entered & seated themselves in this manner (no woman is allowed to attend) a profound silence reigns in the meeting — while the preparation is making for commencing the ceremony — the Chief then fills his pipe . . . everyone holding his nose to prevent inhaling the smoke before the ceremony commences — the Chief then lights the pipe and draws a mouthful of smoke which ascends to the top of the tent — this is intended as an offering to the sun he again fills his mouth and turning his face towards the earth blows the smoke downward and then blows smoke first to the right then to the left — After this he draws from the pipe four times and swallows the smoke — then passes the pipe to the next person sitting . . . the pipe is passed all around and smoked by everyone in the same manner as by the chief — each one after smoking rubbing himself all over — This is continued until three pipes of tobacco are consumed, the Chief carefully preserving the ashes — Consultation then commences.[76]

Everything Ruíz describes about the Comanche smoke-lodge council served to foster unanimity and reduce contention among the participants. His account of the protocol involved in seating arrangement underscores the great concern Comanches had for a hierarchical social structure and promoting social harmony. The requirement that all participants in the council remove their ornamentation and clothing also served at reducing demonstrative competition in favor of fellowship. The stereotyped cooperative behavior associated with the pipe-smoking ceremony likewise served to strengthen the individuals' social relationships with one another beyond the ritual setting.[77]

Comanches performed the religious smoke ritual at any time and for various occasions. Each morning at dawn, the men "render[ed] him [the sun] homage, bowing low before him and censing him with the first smoke of their pipes." Warriors seeking to avenge a fallen comrade also practiced this ritual prior to conducting a raid. Berlandier further remarked, "every meeting they hold, no matter what its purpose, opens with an act of homage [the smoke ritual] and respect toward him [the sun]." Like the Sun Dance among other plains peoples, this ritual venerated ancient ancestors and traditions, ultimately encouraging sacrifice and solidarity among kinsmen.[78]

Making a smoke sacrifice to the sun communicated the participants' acknowledgment of their original ancestors' authority and their responsibility to one another as siblings or co-descendants. As with all tribal religions, ancestor worship characterized Comanche religion. The image of the sun served as a symbol or metaphor for the common ancestor of all Comanches. Ruíz observed that "all their religious rites center around the worship of the sun." Closely following this, Jean Louis Berlandier noted that Comanches and other Texas Indians "look on the sun as the universal father of all that exists in nature and consequently consider themselves his children." Chief Senaco explained to Marcy in 1849 that "the Comanches' God was so far distant in the sky that they could not hear him speak, and when they wished to communicate with him they were obliged to do it through the medium of the sun, which they could see and hold converse with." Burnet's observation of Comanche religion, however, most explicitly shows that Comanches ritually honored their common ancestor, asserting that the Indians "claim supremacy to the one Great Being, whom they represent as a Big Man, that can never die, and who is the peculiar original parent of the Comanchee race."[79]

The great potential for discord at various Comanche councils and meetings compelled the encouragement of solidarity between the participants by means of religious ritual. The "consultation" that took place after the performance of the smoke ritual featured discussion over a wide range of issues, from matters of camp movements, politics, and warfare to gossip about women and personal relationships. All concerns, whether serious or trivial, had the potential to breed significant contention between individuals. Berlandier states that "it is in these reunions [councils] that they communicate the greatest secrets; often it is there that the unfortunate adulteress, unfaithful to her husband, is discovered." Bonnell mentions that disharmony among participants in Comanche councils "sometimes [produced] permanent enmities."[80]

The disagreements, indiscretions, and jealousies revealed in the context of a council probably emerged from fundamental issues concerning individuals' rank and place in the social hierarchy. Discussing the formalities of entering a Comanche lodge, Neighbors writes: "the owner . . . designates the route [a visitor] shall pass, and the seat he shall occupy. Any infringement of this rule is liable to give offence." In 1787 Jacobo Ugarte y Loyola, *comandante general* of the Provincias Internas, worried that Governor Anza's recognition of Ecueracapa as the authority of all Comanches would upset high-ranking Jupes and Yamparicas, who might refuse to subordinate themselves to a Cuchanec chief. Ugarte y Loyola based his concern over these Indians' insubordination upon an observation that Comanches were often contemptuous of individuals appointed to positions of authority that they considered equal or lesser to them in rank.[81]

Soxas's murder of Ecueracapa's son and El Sordo's disavowal of his Comanche wives demonstrated extreme contempt toward rivals. Obviously, Soxas had some sort of contention with his victim. The identity of the deceased as the son of a former prominent chief suggests that a conflict over rank and authority may have lain at the root of their differences. However, the details surrounding this dispute remain unknown. Spanish authorities explained El Sordo's behavior as a reaction to their policies regulating commerce with American traders. But students of this incident have understood the chief's actions as a response to the economic opportunities provided by that trade.[82] These explanations, however, inadequately account for why El Sordo would have disavowed his Comanche wives if his quarrel was with the governor of Texas, or how this action would have necessarily benefited his ability to trade with Americans.

Traditionally, humans have reacted to material issues in consideration to their position in hierarchical and social relationships. Tribal hierarchies can be extremely complicated and difficult to understand because they have been based on birth order, and the practice of polygyny creates a tangle of full and half, close and distant, relationships between people of great age differences. Knowing peoples' relationship to one another would have been perplexing, especially since some could be addressed by different kin terms. Comanches could use "many lines of relationship" to trace their affiliation to one another. Two or more kin terms could even be applied to the same person.[83]

Since Comanches associated rank with birth order, the type of kin term persons used had the potential to be a volatile issue when individuals challenged each other's primacy in the social hierarchy. The use of kin terms such as *pávi* ("older brother") and *tami* ("younger brother") showed that people understood one's age in relation to another.[84] By simply addressing another individual with such a kin term, people communicated an acceptance of their position or rank in the "family" hierarchy. Comanches' practice of polygyny complicated the problem of determining how one was ranked in relation to others. For example, an eldest son of a second wife may have been older than the youngest son of a first wife, but their relative rank might be disputed. The elder son could have argued that he outranked the younger one on the basis of his more advanced age. But the younger son could have alleged that he outranked his half-sibling on the basis that his mother was his father's first, and thus higher-ranking, wife. Conceivably, a younger person could have addressed a brother of greater age as *tami*. Disagreements over a person's stature within clan hierarchies provoked conflicts that sometimes forced individuals to dissociate themselves from their rival co-descendants. Even though Comanches did not know their exact age, they knew people's relative age and position within the tribal hierarchy. Ugarte y Loyola's observation of the jealousy involved in Comanche politics hinted that the issue of rank could inflame passions. Indeed, Soxas's and El Sordo's actions imply that Comanches took such disputes seriously.

The actions associated with social behavior, kin recognition, family identification, camp residency, the demise and division of individual genealogical lineages, and issues of rank between Comanches of the late eighteenth and early nineteenth centuries reveal the kinship sacrifice and altruism that constituted the rudiments of Comanche society. Social organization is an extremely complicated yet fundamental subject. Making sense of the actions of individuals such as Ecueracapa, Oxamaquea, the two Cuerno Verdes, Soxas, and El Sordo through an understanding of social and kinship behavior allows one a view of the subtle underpinnings of their society. However, social organization does not determine the actions of individuals. It is simply an effect of behaviors associated with matters pertaining to social situations. This realization allows for the development of a more complete understanding of some major behaviors associated with Comanche society prior to the 1850s, such as geographical mobility, horse pastoralism, tribal economics, and violence.

CHAPTER 2

Comanche Migration and Geographic Mobility

ON NOVEMBER 19, 1828, FRENCH NATURALIST JEAN LOUIS Berlandier, Francisco Ruíz, and about thirty Mexican dragoons accompanied a party of "fifty to eighty Comanches" led by Chiefs Quelluna (Keiuna) and El Ronco as they departed in a north-northwesterly direction from the presidio of Béxar. Berlandier had been anxious to explore the environs of "the western parts of Texas" during his expedition to the region during 1828–29, but hostilities between Comanches and Lipan Apaches had made travel in that vicinity dangerous. Lieutenant Colonel Ruíz, apparently inspired by a personal commitment to scientific discovery and confidence in his own ability to deal with any potentially hostile Indians they might come across, began to organize a hunting and exploration party to the Hill Country northwest of San Antonio. Quelluna, El Ronco, and their followers had unexpectedly appeared in Béxar just as the expedition prepared for its departure. The arrival of the Indians encouraged Ruíz to take advantage of their numbers and knowledge for the upcoming excursion. Berlandier knew of the potential difficulties associated with such an undertaking and accepted his friend's suggestion that they "go out into the wilds with [the Comanches]."[1]

The combined expedition of Tejanos — Mexican Texans — and Indians only traveled about three leagues (roughly eight or nine miles) that first day, establishing camp along Arroyo de los Olmos. Nevertheless, Berlandier immediately took notice of the distinctive nature of Comanche geographical movements as he beheld a "confusion of nomadic men" and three hundred horses "spread out over a great distance, traveling in single file or en masse, while a certain number forming an advance guard went ahead to spy out the land." One thing that especially struck him as peculiar was the imposing "silence which prevailed in the wilderness and among our travel companions." This tense quiet gave way to a more "gay and open nature" upon the entourage's arrival at the *arroyo* campsite. Berlandier remarked that while in that first night's camp, he "observe[d] a great difference in the character of the indigenes" from the suspicious, taciturn, and mysterious aura they usually emitted when visiting the towns and villages of Texas. Pleasantly surprised, and probably somewhat relieved by the friendly temperament settling over the excursion, the French scientist settled in as he prepared for an evening of curious observation.[2]

The first task at hand for the Comanches involved the erection of their "conical tents which are made of skins." After the tepees had been set up, the women spread out hides in preparation of a comfortable place for their husbands' repose and then attended to all the other necessary domestic chores. If the men did not immediately lie down to rest, they sauntered off on short outings in search for that evening's meal in the form of bison, bear, deer, or even skunk. Later, the men gathered in a lodge, established away from the camp, where they engaged in the daily pipe ritual and discussed various topics ranging from the next day's travel plans to the latest gossip pertaining to various individuals' sexual infidelities.[3]

Berlandier also found peculiar the Comanches' "imperfect" security arrangements. He could only guess that the Indians' neglected taking defensive precautions in their camps "either because of their nonchalance or because of some particular motive unknown to me." On a couple of occasions during their jaunt in the Texas hills, Berlandier witnessed episodes of alarm among the Indians. One incident occurred on November 20 at the Ojo del Agua when, with little warning, the mass of the Indians' three hundred horses and mules stampeded, "trampl[ing] everywhere through our camp, upsetting tents and people in their path, turning the fires topsy-turvy, and finally precipitating themselves in the forests to the south." In response to this chaotic turn of events, the Indians "threw themselves on their weapons," while several others "who had . . . the prudence to tether their horses in camp" went off to retrieve the scattered herd. Shortly after things had begun to calm down, some nervous individuals shouted warnings of the presence of their Lipan Apache enemy. Immediately "everything was ready for combat." Even the women armed themselves with bows, ready to defend themselves and their families. The Comanches braced themselves for an attack, but the anticipated Lipans failed to materialize. In order to reassure the campers that the warning had been a false alarm and to calm everyone's nerves, several mounted warriors armed with lances set out to patrol the surrounding darkness.[4] An uncomfortable silence eventually descended over the camp as the night advanced and sleep overcame most of the *ranchería*.

The morning routine in Comanche encampments began with "a chief, performing the role of orator, . . . g[iving] orders about what was to be done, the hour of departure, and the place where we were going to camp." All this infor-mation had been discussed and decided upon the previous night by the men at-tending the smoke-lodge gathering. At least one hour before daybreak, a chief who assumed the duties of official spokesperson, or *tlatolero*, "address[ed] the entire tribe in a loud voice . . . [g]oing from one principal point in the camp to another"; at sunrise the public crier repeated the orders in case anybody missed the information the first time around. Berlandier noted that the overall "conduct of the Indians was in accord with the recommendations of the orator," especially the orders communicating that the Indians were to have "great regard" for their visitors' well being.[5]

The retinue continued in a north-northwesterly direction on the twenty-first until they came across a small hill overlooking a "charming plain," where they pas-tured their horses. Berlandier stated that the Indians chose this particular spot be-cause it provided a vantage point to keep watch on all their horses. That night the Comanches again had to quickly mobilize their defenses due to various alarms that, like the previous night, turned out to be false. Early in the morning, the en-tourage of Tejanos and Comanches decamped and headed for the Guadalupe River. Their route passed through narrow valleys and defiles of "difficult access" teeming with black bears and deer. The caravan crossed the river around noon and proceeded to travel upstream in search of a campsite along its eastern bank. For-tunately, that evening passed without incident. The next day the camp moved to another location four leagues away near an unnamed stream, christened by the travelers "Arroyo del Lobo Blanco" after a Comanche killed a whitish-gray wolf there shortly after their arrival. On the following morning, the twenty-fourth, the Comanches abandoned Berlandier, Ruíz, and the dragoons to head for their vil-lages to the west of a deserted Spanish presidio along the San Sabá River.[6]

Berlandier and his company eventually spent a month in the wilds of north-western Texas. After departing from the company of Quelluna and El Ronco, the Mexicans ultimately circled back around to Béxar via the upper Guadalupe River, the "Cañon de don Juan Ugalde," and the Medina River. Berlandier's account of his explorations in this region not only contributed to the corpus of scientific knowledge of the world in his day, but it continues to serve scholars as a reliable source in the chronicle of the area's transformation. With regard to Comanches, Berlandier's observations should be of particular interest to students of these In-dians. The French scientist's report of this expedition includes one of the only eyewitness accounts of Comanches on the move and describes several important features of Comanche nomadic camps that probably were universal among the Indians.[7] For instance, the manner of traveling, the procedures of setting up camps, men's participation in the smoke lodge, their sensitivity toward the threat of nighttime attacks, hunting activities, the role of the *tlatolero* in the camps, and the presence of large numbers of horses all probably typified the kinds of activ-ities that occurred in Comanche campsites throughout the Comanchería. Thus,

Berlandier's description of his Comanche traveling companions has allowed students to have a firsthand view of the details associated with these Indians' nomadic and migratory behavior. What Berlandier does not tell us—it probably did not occur to him—is why these Indians behaved in such a manner? This chapter seeks to answer that question.

The geographical mobility exhibited by Comanches constituted a basic feature of their history and everyday lives. Yet this routine aspect of the Indians' past has received relatively little attention, possibly because of the general assumption that environmental and economic factors determined such movements. Indeed, the environmental and economic realities of the eighteenth-and nineteenth-century southern plains weighed heavily on individuals deciding when and where to move. Yet upon close examination, social relationships seem to have figured greatly on their decisions concerning migratory and nomadic movements. Comanche mobility in the eighteenth and nineteenth centuries was chiefly an effect of their social relations. The creation and maintenance of social relationships between family members lay at the basis of the travels of individuals. Social relations strongly influenced Comanches' mobility, including those movements that were aimed at increasing pastoral production or exploiting game reserves.

Comanches first appeared in the vicinity of New Mexico sometime around or shortly after the turn of the eighteenth century. Juan de Ulibarri's diary of his 1706 journey to "the unknown land of the plains for the ransom of the Christian Indians of the Picuríes nation" contains the first mention of Comanches in the documentary sources. His entry for July 15 mentioned the arrival of a combined force of 140 Spaniards and "friendly Indians" at Taos and noted: "After we had been welcomed by the Reverend Father Fray Francisco Ximénez, its minister, and the rest of the Indians, the inhabitants who came to see me, the Governor [Taos Pueblo chief] Don Juan Pacheco, and the rest of the chiefs then informed me that they were very certain that the infidel enemies of the Ute and Comanche tribe were about to come to make an attack upon this pueblo, which information they wished to send to the governor and captain-general." Later on the twenty-eighth while out on the plains, Ulibarri came across "an Apache Indian who had with him two women and three little boys." In response to questioning, the man "said that he was of the same tribe of the Penxayes [Apaches] and that he was going to join all the rest who live along those rivers and streams in order to defend themselves together from the Utes and Comanches, who were coming to attack them according to the information of the rest of his tribe."[8]

Ulibarri's 1706 references to Comanches not only indicate the general time period the Indians appeared in New Mexico and its outlying regions but also allude to the very beginnings of a migratory push into the vicinity of the Spanish province and eventually into the vast plains territory lying farther to the south and east. Of course, Ulibarri did not recognize the ultimate significance of the various reports of Comanches he received, but it was not too much longer before the residents of New Mexico began to fathom the implications of these Indians' presence in their neighborhood. Capt. Don Francisco Bueno y Bohorques's comment of August 19, 1719, on the increase of Comanche and Ute raiders in the Spanish colony hints that colonial officials were beginning to become aware of the migratory nature of the Indians' appearance in the region.[9]

If New Mexico governor Antonio de Valverde ever doubted reports of Comanches making a push to move into the region, his encounters with Apaches on an autumn campaign against the newcomers in 1719 surely changed his mind. Just six days into his march toward the plains northeast of New Mexico, Valverde ran across "a small adobe house where there were some . . . Apaches, who had sown and reaped their maize-fields." As the legion of over seven hundred soldiers, volunteers, and allied Indians approached, the Apaches made various demonstrations exalting the presence of such a formidable force. At once they informed the governor through interpreters that "their enemies, the Comanches, were persecuting and killing their kinsmen and others of their nation." Several hours later a "troop" of Apaches "from the *ranchería* of La Jicarilla" met up with the governor and communicated "that they were very sad and discouraged because of the repeated attacks which their enemies, the Utes and Comanches, make upon them. These had killed many of their nation and carried off their women and children captives until they now no longer knew where to go to live in safety." Valverde heard similar accounts from practically every Apache he came across. One of the recurring themes embedded in the various descriptions of the vicious attacks was about the necessity of abandoning former settlements as individuals struggled to survive the Comanche onslaught.[10] This testimony suggests that the invaders sought to either destroy or displace Apaches rather than target them as objects of transitory raids.

From the perspective of New Mexicans and Plains Apaches, havoc consumed the course of events during the 1720s. The year 1723 was an especially disastrous time for the Apache refugees, who had been amassing their defensive strength in the Jicarilla Valley since 1719. Carlana and several other Apache chiefs appeared in Santa Fe that year and reported directly to Governor Bustamante that "the Comanche nation, their enemies, had attacked them with a large number in their *rancherías* in such a manner that they could not make use of weapons for their defense. They launched themselves with such daring and resolution that they killed many men, carrying off their women and children as captives." In late January, 1724, the governor received a letter from Fray Juan Mirabal of Taos communicating a report he received concerning a Comanche attack at "La Xicarilla" that lasted five days and four nights. According to Mirabal, the Comanches finished off the settlement by either killing or seriously wounding the men and running off with all the women and children. By 1727, the surviving Apaches living in the Jicarilla vicinity had retreated to Taos and Pecos pueblos in search of safe haven.[11]

Juan Paez Hurtado's testimony at the Council of War on February 6, 1724, attests to the geographical magnitude of the Comanche migration onto the plains during the 1720s. He noted that for three years, the Indians had become arrogant because of their continuous victories over "Pananas [Pawnees], Canzeres [Kansas], Palomas, Quartelejos [also Cuartelejos], Sierras Blancas, and Escalchufines [the latter four all Apaches]." These tribal names represent a vast geographical territory. The ill-fated 1720 expedition of Pedro de Villasur encountered a large Pawnee village along the Platte River twenty miles east of the junction of its north and south branches in western Nebraska. That same year Capt. Felix Martínez and Ensign Cpl. Bartolomé Garduño each testified that the Kansas Indians lived on the eastern end of the Sierra Blanca, a mountainous spur separating the upper Arkansas and Canadian River valleys. In the fall of 1719, numerous Paloma Apaches met Gov. Antonio de Valverde y Cosio near the Arkansas River in southeastern Colorado. Their Cuartelejo cousins lived in three relatively permanent villages farther to the north. Juan de Ulibarri visited these settlements in 1706 in order to escort the runaway Picurís Indians back to New Mexico.[12] According to Garduño, the Sierra Blanca Apaches made their homes on the southern "shoulders" of the Sierra Blanca range. The Escalchufines Apaches resembled the Palomas, roaming throughout the region between the Arkansas River and the Cuartelejo settlements. Upon traversing this area during the 1719 campaign against the Utes and Comanches, Governor Valverde's Cuartelejo auxiliaries called upon their Escalchufin kinsmen to join them in their pursuit of their common enemies.[13] Thus, the area the Comanches and Utes began expanding into during the early 1720s included all the mountains, foothills, and plains from the Platte River at least as far south as the Jicarilla Valley to northeast of Taos.

By the end of the decade, Comanches had begun to penetrate deep into Apache territory toward the Spanish province of Texas. A decisive nine-day battle took place around 1723–24 somewhere between New Mexico and Texas at "El Gran Cierra de el Fierro" in which Comanches routed their Plains Apache enemies, forcing them to move toward Béxar.[14] Spanish colonists in Texas experienced limited and periodic contact with Apaches in the decades prior to 1730. After this date, the number of incidents between these Indians and Spanish Texans gradually increased. This development certainly reflected the continuation of the Comanches' push into the southerly latitudes of the Great Plains. Even though the newcomers suffered a devastating defeat sometime in the early 1740s, they continued their push south. Comanches reportedly first appeared in the vicinity of Béxar in 1743. By the fall of 1745, certain hard-pressed factions of Apaches had made several requests to the Spanish for the establishment of missions and presidios in their territory. Four years later in August, 1749, the besieged Indians came to terms with Spanish Texas. Of course, the Comanches' continued determination and bellicosity figured large in this development.[15]

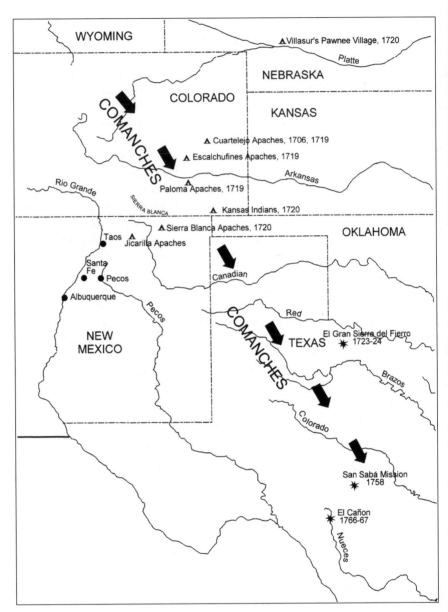

Map 5. Southern Migration of Comanches into New Mexico and Texas

The cooperative spirit engendered by the peace treaty between the Apaches and Spaniards did little to protect the Indians from the oncoming Comanches, and most likely it helped precipitate the infamous San Sabá "massacre" of 1758. Apaches continued their southward retreat during the first half of the 1750s. By 1755, a good number of the Indians had moved beyond the Rio Grande and into the province of Coahuila. Nevertheless, some individuals continued to live in the hills and plains to the north of San Antonio. Responding to the earlier requests of missionaries and Apaches alike, the viceroy in Mexico City authorized the removal of the San Xavier presidio from the San Marcos River to the upper reaches of the San Sabá River. Established in 1757, the presidio San Luis de las Amarillas and its ancillary mission became an innocent victim in the territorial conflict between Comanches and Apaches within a year's time. Around two thousand Comanches and allied Caddoan Indians descended upon the mission compound in March, 1758, stating that "they had come with the intention of killing Apaches."[16] Apparently angry with not finding any of their enemy at that location, the Indians wiled their way inside the mission's ramparts and then opened fire without warning. This treacherous episode resulted in ten deaths and the total destruction of the mission. While the attackers failed to injure any of their forsworn enemies, the destruction of the mission effectively encouraged Apaches generally to avoid the San Sabá district and to continue their retreat south. A few years later in 1762, the Spanish founded Mission San Lorenzo de la Santa Cruz at the request of Lipan Apaches along the upper Nueces River approximately eighty-eight miles to the south of San Sabá in an area known as El Cañon.[17]

Unfortunately for the Apaches, this move ultimately proved to be inadequate refuge from the persistent Comanches. The invaders made their appearance in the area shortly after the establishment of the new mission. Again, the vicinity became so harried by Comanches and Caddoans that the Lipans living there pushed southward either down the Nueces or across the Rio Grande. According to the marqués de Rubí, inspector of the interior presidios in the late 1760s, the Comanches had driven Apaches from the El Cañon region since January, 1766. Frustrated and fearful for their lives, the Lipans had completely abandoned El Cañon by the summer of 1767. That same year, Nicolás de Lafora, an engineer accompanying Rubí's inspection of New Spain's northern frontier, reported that many Lipan Apaches inhabited the mountains of Coahuila south of the Rio Grande. Texas governor Juan María, barón de Ripperdá, disclosed to Viceroy Antonio María Bucareli y Ursua in July, 1772, "that the Apaches called Lipanes, to the number of fifteen hundred or more men were on the Rivers Nuezes [sic], Frio, and Rio [sic] Grande, three or four days from this presidio [Béxar]." The following month the governor communicated to Mexico City the presence of Comanches in the vicinity of San Antonio, particularly noting that the Indians "keep us disturbed by stealing our droves of horses." By 1777, the mass of Lipans had moved farther into the region of Coahuila "under shelter of the presidios of San Juan Bautista, Monclova [Viejo], and Santa Rosa de Agua-verde." Athanase de Mézières, the Spanish ambassador to the Indians of Texas, subsequently commented to the viceroy in 1778 that Comanches "persecute[d] . . . [Apaches] with such constant war, that they have driven them from the said presidios and estates [of Texas], which the Apache also were molesting; and not being able to find them, they become angry and even suspect us of concealing them."[18]

Comanches continued to harass Apaches, Spaniards, Mexicans, and Texans well into the nineteenth century. Yet they never expanded the core of their southward migration beyond the San Antonio area. The Indians frequently visited northern Mexico from the late eighteenth century on, though these movements seem to have been motivated by revenge against enemies and opportunities for plunder as opposed to territorial expansion. Vial and Chaves mentioned in 1785 that the "Cumanches Orientales . . . extend[ed] their hostilities as far as that of Coahuila." But Comanches did not enter that region en masse until the 1830s and 1840s. The Plains Indians wrought havoc at such faraway locations as Durango, Zacatecas, San Luís Potosí, Auguascalientes, Jalisco, and Sinaloa. Some Missouri traders witnessed Comanche raids on several of "the ranches about the city [of Durango]" in 1846. According to James Josiah Webb, his men watched "from the tops of houses . . . Indians in large numbers rounding up stock . . . while another portion of the band were threatening and attacking the soldiers who remained behind their barricades on the defensive." Webb reported that the estimated loss of livestock by Comanches as a result of the raids he and his men witnessed amounted to 25,000 head.[19] Accounts like this suggest that Comanches probably could have continued their migration farther south into Mexico. Why the Indians halted to the north of San Antonio is probably related to why they began their migration in the first place at the beginning of the eighteenth century.

The Comanche migration into the southern plains has generally been explained as a response to particular environmental, economic, and technological factors present in New Mexico and on the Great Plains during the early eighteenth century. The earliest explanations of this migration, as evidenced by James Mooney's 1896 sketch of the tribe, suggest that precontact Comanches living in the region of Wyoming succumbed to hostile pressure exerted "by the Sioux and other prairie tribes."[20] Later explanations dismiss this hypothesis and focus instead on the presence of horses in Spain's northernmost frontier colonies. This argument generally claims that Indians recognized the great utility of equines in exploiting the bison resources of the Great Plains and thus were attracted to the ultimate source of the animals. Of course, the Spanish colony of New Mexico was an obvious candidate as this fount of horse technology. With regard to Comanches in particular, some have suggested that the Indians' southern migration

Map 6. Comanche Raids of Mexico

was primarily motivated by their desire for horses found in the proximity of New Mexico.[21]

Unfortunately, this approach to understanding the impetus for the Comanches' emergence onto the southern plains has not been sufficient. For instance, why did other groups susceptible to these influences not also move into the region? What explains the unwillingness of Pawnees, Crows, various other Shoshones, Cheyennes, Sioux, Mandans, Arikaras, Hidatsas, and Caddos to be drawn to the area by the same material forces that are said to have attracted Comanches there in the early 1700s? The material existence of these tribes varied in each case, but that should not have necessarily been sufficient to insulate them from the presumed allure of the technological revolution represented by horses. What, then, differentiated each of these peoples in the most fundamental sense, thus making some seemingly more responsive to these resources than others? The answer to this question has not been apparent. But the realization that tribes represented various lineages of common descent provides a clue to this answer. By following this line of reasoning, each tribe can be understood as fundamentally differentiated by the numerous lines of social relationships each one represented. The details of a tribe's social reality should be recognized as a principal consideration when determining the nature of human migrations such as that of the Comanches during the eighteenth century. This is not to say that material influences had no bearing upon the Indians' move to the southern plains. Concern for such matters certainly influenced individuals' decisions; they simply were not sufficient to have motivated the movements briefly chronicled above, nor sufficient to make them successfully.

Even though the close relationship between Comanches and Utes at the time they first appeared in New Mexico around 1706 has been clearly documented, the fundamental nature of their social relationship has remained unclear. This relationship implies that certain individual Comanches and Utes probably recognized their connection through a common ancestor. In other words, individuals of each of these lineages must have been intermarried at some point. This recognition among the Indians thus served as the basis for their social or cooperative behavior. Also (as demonstrated in the previous chapter), this cooperative behavior included individuals' residential practices. In the seventeenth century, Utes occupied the territory just to the north of New Mexico. Precontact Comanches generally lived to the north of Ute lands. Consequently, as individuals of each tribe intermarried they would, theoretically, have been free to live with either of their families. This type of behavior set the foundation for the Comanches' movement toward New Mexico and beyond.

Technically speaking, Comanches are Shoshone Indians. The lineages that made up the Comanche tribe simply were those families who became more and more geographically isolated over time from their Shoshone cousins living in the region of northwestern Colorado, Wyoming, Utah, and Idaho. The separation of Comanches from Shoshones probably came about as a result of issues similar to those contributing to the breakup of the Cuchanec clan in the early nineteenth century.

Two traditional stories reported by Wallace and Hoebel describing the split of Comanches from Shoshones hint at such issues. One story tells of a dispute between Shoshones over the distribution of a bear that had been killed. Unable to reconcile the misunderstanding, the Indians parted in opposite directions. Those going to the north continued to be called Shoshones, while those who headed south became known as Comanches. Hoebel heard the second story from one of the Comanche informants to the 1933 Oklahoma expedition of the Ethnological Field Study Group of the Santa Fe Laboratory of Anthropology. It had a similar theme:

Two bands were living together in a large camp. One band was on the east side; the other on the west. Each had its own chief.

Every night the young boys were out playing games — racing, and so forth. They were having a kicking game; they kicked each other. One boy kicked another over the stomach so hard that he died from it. That boy who was killed was from the West camp. He was the son of a chief.

When this thing happened, the West camp cried all night. In the East camp it was silent. Next day, they buried that boy.

The boy's father, the chief, had his crier go around announcing that there would be a big fight to see which camp was best so as to settle the question of his son's death. There was big excitement. Both sides had good warriors. The East camp ran to its horses. "If they really mean what they say, they will kill us," they cried.

The two sides lined up, and the chiefs met in the center. Then an old man from the East camp came up into the center. He wept and told them it wasn't right for them to fight among themselves like that. They took pity on [him]. Then other old men came out and gathered with him. "You have plenty of enemies to fight," they cried. "These were just boys playing a game. Don't take this thing so seriously. You are setting a bad example for the children. Whatever this chief wants to keep the peace, we'll do it."

That chief called it off. He said he did not realize what he was doing. So the East camp brought them horses and other things.

After that the chief had his announcer tell the people it was time to move camp. "We have had bad luck here. There has been hard feeling." While they were still there, smallpox broke out.

Then they broke up. One group went north; those are the Shoshones. The other group went west [south?].[22]

Each of these stories suggests that noncooperative or antisocial behavior contributed to the geographical separation of Comanches from Shoshones. The root of this behavior among Shoshones may possibly have been based on certain individuals' social relationship with Utes. This hypothesis is speculative at best, but El Sordo's previously mentioned association with Tahuacanos suggests that divergent tribal loyalties could foster enmity among Comanche family members. Nevertheless, we know that Comanches did set themselves apart from many of their Shoshone kinsmen and appeared in New Mexico in the accompaniment of Utes.

Once Comanches began closely associating with Utes through intermarriage, they became part of a greater New Mexican social "network," with which the latter Indians had already become a part sometime earlier during the seventeenth century. The network of social relationships that existed in the province resulted from the intermarriage of Utes, Pueblos, Apaches, Navajos, and Spaniards. Events that took place in late 1704 northwest of San Juan pueblo hints at the existence of this type of association between Utes, Navajos, and the Indians of San Juan Pueblo. *Maestre de campo* Roque Madrid reported to Lt. Gov. Juan Paez Hurtado that Utes and Navajos had recently met at Piedra Lumbre in order to establish a formal peace among them. Madrid recounted that this *amistad* was being brokered by "Christian Indians of the Pueblo of San Juan, and particularly by Joseph Tomnu of the Tano [Tewa?] nation." Upon interrogating Tomnu, Hurtado asked the Indian what motivated him to assist in establishing peace between the Navajos and Utes. He answered that some Utes who told him that they wished to be friends with the Navajos so they could go about their land and hunt without apprehension or fear had approached Bentura, the chief of San Juan pueblo. Thus, Bentura persuaded Tomnu to accompany the chief's *sobrino* to the meeting.[23]

Even though these details do not explicitly state the existence of any familial relationships between the Indians involved in this episode (except, of course, for Bentura and his nephew), the Utes did request the assistance of the San Juan Indians to serve as intermediaries for the peace talks. The Indians of San Juan pueblo probably had some familial ties with individual Utes and Navajos. Thus, as the Utes understood, the Indians of San Juan were literally natural candidates to serve as arbiters between themselves and the unrelated Navajo.

The interrelated familial ties that extended throughout New Mexico and deep into adjacent regions surrounding the province resulted from formal marriages, illicit relationships, and captivity. Indeed, the ancient human behavior of taking enemy women and children captive probably is responsible for initiating kin relationships between peoples who do not recognize a close kinship between themselves. Originally, those Indians who became Navajos mostly associated with other Athabascan, or Apache, family members. As they expanded into the Southwest, raiding the various settlements of the region, they eventually captured a number of Pueblo women and children. Close ties between Apaches and the inhabitants of those villages became cemented, as offspring of the Apaches and their Pueblo captive wives actively traced their ancestry to both peoples. By the eighteenth century, Navajos and various lineages of Pueblo Indians actively cooperated on the basis of their interrelatedness. These unique family attachments, combined with a certain amount of geographic isolation, are what have distinguished Navajos from other Apaches and presumably helps explain why they had pottery, matrilineal ancestral names, were more settled, and tended sheep.

Various Pueblo Indians interacted closely with Navajos during the seventeenth century and even lived among the Athabascan-speakers during extended times of trouble. Apparently, some Tewa Indians of San Ildefonso pueblo had become interrelated to individual Navajos. Fearful of the growing tension between the Spanish colonists and Pueblo Indians in the mid-1690s, provincial and ecclesiastical officials paid particular attention to the Indians' speech and movements. For several nights of December, 1695, Fray Francisco Corbera disguised himself in a bison pelt and secretly stood outside the *estufa,* or kiva, at San Ildefonso. On the night of the nineteenth, he overheard the Indian elders planning to abandon the pueblo. Instead of taking refuge among the mesas in the pueblo's vicinity, the Tewas stated that they would retreat to "the mesas of the Navajo." When open rebellion did finally grip the province in June, 1696, the Navajos combined with the Tewa forces at San Ildefonso. The close cooperation between Tewas and Navajos evident during 1695–96 certainly encourages the belief that these Indians were related to a certain degree. Since individual Tewa Indians of San Juan pueblo would have been able to identify close relatives among those living at San Ildefonso, they could have also probably traced some kinship link to some Navajos. But some individuals living at San Juan probably could have themselves traced a direct link to an individual among the Athabascan speakers. Bentura's nephew and Joseph Tomnu possibly were two such individuals.[24]

A similar process also must have been occurring between the Utes and Pueblo Indians during the seventeenth century. Utes began harrying the various pueblos of northern New Mexico sometime prior to the Pueblo revolt of 1680. They attacked those Indians in earnest during the years the Spanish had been exiled from the upper Rio Grande valley. Of course, the attacks resulted in the taking of captives. At least one Jémez Indian suffered captivity at the hands of the Utes prior to 1680, but it is impossible to know how many more were taken from their homes during the Spanish absence. Utes continued to raid the pueblos after the reestablishment of Spanish hegemony in 1694. Gov. Diego de Vargas stationed thirty soldiers in Taos in January, 1696, for fear of Ute attacks there. The Indians were also active in the San Juan area, running off with some of the pueblo's livestock in the first few months of 1696. Even if Ute activity around San Juan may have helped initiate some interfamilial ties between themselves and the Tewas, the incorporation of Ute captives into the pueblo probably did more to assure the development of kin connections between the Indians. At some point during the summer of 1696, some Plains Apaches entered San Juan with a large number of captive Ute women and children to sell. Thus, San Juan and the surrounding pueblos and settlements instantly became infused with a relatively large population of Utes. Some students of colonial New Mexico have noted a positive correlation between the acquisition of captive Indians and the birth of "illegitimate" children in the province. This observation essentially implies that New Mexicans (Natives and Europeans) and captive Indians produced offspring that could have come to recognize their distinctive ancestral lineages. As a result of these births, kinship connections between New Mexicans and *indios bárbaros* became established throughout the province, serving as the basis of social behavior between these peoples from Taos to Socorro. This social reality suggests why the Utes had the confidence to approach Bentura at San Juan and request his assistance to help them establish amicable relations with the Navajo.[25]

Comanches, through their interrelated association with Utes, benefited from these preexisting social connections extending across northern New Mexico. Kinship associations between Utes and New Mexicans also existed to various degrees in other northern outposts besides San Juan, in places such as Taos, Picurís, and Ojo Caliente. Taos especially became noted in New Mexico as a center for the captive trade, and this activity may explain why the first mention of Comanches in that province were associated with that pueblo. Nevertheless, kinship and the social behavior it fostered ultimately motivated Comanche-Shoshones to migrate toward New Mexico. Robert S. Neighbors recounted a similar explanation of the Comanche migration in his 1852 report on the Indians to Henry Rowe Schoolcraft. Concerning this movement, Neighbors stated: "when they [Comanches] traveled from the west . . . , [they] met with what they term the 'Mountain Spaniards' in the mountains of New Mexico. They lived with them many years, and intermarried with each other."[26] As a special U.S. agent to the Indians of Texas during the 1850s, Neighbors had intimate contact with the various Comanche lineages, and his account for the Indians' origins apparently came from them. Thus, it seems that Comanches themselves recognized the fundamental role kinship and social relationships played in their migration to the New Mexico region.

The social realities of the region spurred Comanches' movement deep into the southern plains. Once Comanches began to interact closely with Utes and New Mexicans, they also began to compete for the local pastoral and game resources. Their century-long conflict with Apaches originally emerged out of this material competition. Naturally, the struggle with Apaches in New Mexico and Texas brought about the capture of a relatively large population of women and children by both sides. For example, Jicarilla Apaches reported to Governor Valverde in September, 1719, that attacking Comanches had recently descended upon one of their *rancherías,* "causing sixty deaths, [and] carrying off sixty-four women and children."[27] The governor heard similar stories of attacks and abductions from the many Apaches he came across on his plains campaign that fall. Most of this type of activity during the eighteenth century seems to have been fundamentally antisocial in nature, but it probably also had some social consequences.

Comandante de Armas Juan Ugalde incidentally mentioned to Viceroy Manuel Antonio Flórez in 1787 that peaceful relations existed between the Comanches and Lipans at that time. Sources dating after the turn of the nineteenth century more clearly demonstrate that social relationships did indeed develop between the seemingly perpetual adversaries. Comanches and Lipans formally established a cooperative relationship in March, 1807, during a ceremonious council held at San Antonio. The Indians agreed to "suspend warring among themselves and to treat one another in a friendly manner, both in the wilderness and as well as within our [Spanish] establishments." Unfortunately, the exact social relationships encouraging this remarkable agreement have not been uncovered to date. Nevertheless, the bonds of cooperation must have been fragile because the mutual relationship between the two peoples broke down only two years later as individuals renewed their competition over the acquisition of horses.[28]

Seven years later the Indians reestablished their social ties. Intermarriage played a large, if not decisive, role in this development. Berlandier commented that the period between 1816 and 1822 composed an era of peaceful relations between the two peoples. Apparently, the Frenchman learned of this development from José Francisco Ruíz, who had lived among the Comanches and other Texas Indians from 1813 to 1821. During this period Comanches and Lipans combined forces to attack Spanish presidios in Texas and points farther south. Texas governor Antonio María Martínez reported in late June, 1818, that the post of San Marcos had suffered so much from "frequent and daily raids by large bodies of *Comanches, Tahuacanos,* and *Lipanes*" that supplies dwindled and desertions became rampant. Berlandier also noted that during the period of the Mexican struggle for independence from Spain, Lipans oftentimes "served as guides to the Comanche, since they knew the roads, the villages, and the farms, to the great detriment of all the populations along the Rio Bravo del Norte."[29]

A lack of cooperation and an event of outright hostility "dat[ing] back to the coronation of [the Mexican emperor] Iturbide [in 1822]" eventually undermined the close social relations between the two peoples. In that year Mexican authorities appointed Ruíz as an agent to the Comanches and authorized him to invite some individuals to meet with the nascent government in Mexico City. Once word of this invitation circulated throughout the Comanchería and among the Lipans, the Indians "agreed that . . . [they] would negotiate jointly as allies. It was just a matter of waiting for several other Comanche chiefs [to arrive from their country]."[30] The Lipans became impatient and sent their Chiefs Castro, Pocaropa, and others on ahead to *la Capital*. While traveling through the interior of Mexico, the Comanche delegation met up with the Lipan contingent that had already formalized their relationship with Iturbide's government and was en route to their homelands.

Berlandier remarked that while "this shabby and thoughtless trick was the original cause of disunity [among the Indians,] it was further embittered by an act of malicious mischief on the part of the Lipans." It seems that sometime after the above incident, some Lipans "without any provocation . . . stole all the horses from a Comanche encampment." Despite the Lipans' efforts to disguise their trail in order to conceal their identity, the victims of the theft finally caught up with them high along the Medina River. Upon approaching the Lipan *ranchería*, the Comanches "were greeted with a heavy fusillade." During the fighting a "gravely wounded" Comanche who had been living among the Lipans escaped and "report[ed] that the Comanche men who had married Lipan wives and stayed with their families under the protection of the laws of hospitality, all had their throats cut, despite the fact that these Comanche, for personal reasons, had sworn loyalty to the Lipans."[31] According to Berlandier, "this treacherous and inhospitable conduct" instigated the widespread bitterness and warfare that characterized the Indians' relations during the 1820s and 1830s.

This violent incident attests to the significance of intermarriage in the establishment and destruction of social relationships between Comanches and other peoples. Perhaps the most striking aspect of the periods of social intercourse established between Comanches and Lipans during the first quarter of the nineteenth century is the mere existence of such cooperative relationships, considering the deep-seated rancor that characterized relations between the Indians during most of the preceding century. Despite evidence of burgeoning social ties and instances of cooperation during the early 1800s, social relations between these Indians probably did not greatly influence the continuous southerly migration of Comanches in the 1700s. The recurrent violent competition for material resources probably hindered the successful establishment of these types of relationships during that period. Social relationships with other peoples did influence and support the Comanches move into the southern plains.

Affairs between Comanches and Caddoan-speaking Indians influenced the majority of the former peoples movement into Kansas, Oklahoma, and Texas. As Comanches pushed out of the Rocky Mountains and onto the Great Plains, they confronted various Caddoans such as Panwees, Wichitas, Taovayaces, Iscanis, Tahuacanos (Tawakonis), and Huecos (Wacos). Later in Texas they met others such as the Tejas, Bidais, Yuganis, Hainai, Navadachos, and Nacodochitos. Hostility characterized the early state of relations between Comanches and the Caddoans until 1747, when peaceful terms were established with the "Panipiquet" and shortly thereafter with the "Pananas" (Pawnees) in 1750.[32] Unfortunately, hardly any of the details of the conflict or armistice between Comanches and Caddoans have survived. We do know that these Caddoan speakers frequently engaged in hostilities against Plains Apaches during the same period that Comanches began moving into the region. While campaigning on the plains against Utes and Comanches in October, 1719, Gov. Antonio de Valverde came upon a Paloma Apache chief who "had a wound which appeared to be from a gun shot."

After examining the abdominal lesion, the governor asked the Indian how he received the injury and from whom. He answered, "the French, united with the Pawnees and Jumanos [Panipiquetes], attacked from ambush while they were planting corn." He further stated that the Caddoans had "seized their lands, and taken possession of them and held them from that time on."[33] Thus, it would seem plausible that since Comanches, Pawnees, and Panipiquetes all competed for the same territory held by Apaches, the first contact between these Indians occurred under unfriendly conditions.

As fighting between these peoples became protracted over the first decades of the eighteenth century, each side accumulated captives, some of whom they traded and others with whom they intermarried. In July, 1737, Salvador, a Pawnee servant of Taos resident Luis de Archuleta, found himself recaptured by a Comanche who had been looking for his horse. This particular individual lived among his captors until he escaped from them and returned to the pueblo eight months later.[34] Even though Salvador did not permanently associate himself socially with the Comanches, his ordeal illustrates that captive Caddoans indeed lived among the Shoshoneans of the southern plains. Almost certainly, Salvador and other Caddoans represent a very small percentage of those Indians among the Comanches prior to 1747.

There is some telling evidence suggesting that individual Comanches and Caddoan-speaking Indians had intermarried sometime during the 1700s. First of all, the violent attack upon the isolated Spanish mission on the San Sabá River in 1758 showed great levels of cooperation among various Caddoan "Nations of the North" and Comanches. An amazing number of Indians descended upon this hapless outpost. Fr. Fray Miguel de Molina, the only one of three missionaries to survive the assault upon the mission, estimated that "the attackers numbered about 2,000, equipped with at least 1,000 firearms." Another survivor, Joseph Gutiérrez, a twenty-two-year-old servant to the mission fathers, reported that "he did recognize them [the attackers] as belonging to the Texas [Tejas], Comanche, Tanague, Vidae, Yujuan, and many other nations. He said that he knew from their dress, arms, behavior, and speech that they belonged to the said tribes, and that, moreover, he heard them say so themselves."[35]

Though all of these tribes shared a great deal of enmity for Apaches, this feeling surely would not necessarily have been enough to forge an alliance between them. Indeed, the hostility Comanches showed toward Caddoans a little over a decade earlier belies the thought that common enemies could automatically forge such relations. Athanase de Mézières's report to Viceroy Bernardo de Gálvez on the Osage threat to the Los Arkansas region north of Natchitoches, dated September 14, 1777, contained an acute observation on the behavior of Caddoans and Comanches, supporting the idea that these Indians had intermarried to some degree. Speaking of the alliance between the Cadodachos, Nadacog, Nasones, Nabedakioux, Quitseys, Tancagues, Tuacanas, Xaranamas,

Taouaizes, Panis-Mahas, and Comanches in particular, de Mézières wrote: "For, as these nations, whenever they go to the aid of any warlike tribe are given the name *Techan,* similar in meaning to *comilito* [*sic*] of the Romans, and comrade [*compañero?*] in our language, and there results at once among those who use it a sort of *kinship,* a very firm union of interests, a complete sharing of common injuries, and a deep-seated opinion that the violator of so sacred a pact will receive the punishment which the supreme being has ready for liars" (emphasis added).[36] His description of the behavior associated with the word *techan* suggests that this term signified something more like "kindred" rather than the more benign, modern meaning "friend." Thus, *techan* functioned as a kin term implying a genealogical relationship through one or more (probably distant) birth links to a common ancestor between those individuals using the word.

Another compelling allusion to the likelihood of intermarriage between these Indians comes from Pedro Vial and Francisco Xavier Chaves's 1785 diary of their diplomatic mission to the Comanches. The envoys met the Indians on August 31 at "a large *ranchería* that was located on the Río del Mermellón, in a very open plain." After several days of deliberations over the terms of peace, Chiefs Ecueracapa and Cabeza Rapada invited Vial and Chaves "to tell them the reason for our coming so that all of those gathered might hear it." Vial then took it upon himself "to tell it, which I did standing up, and saying it in the Tavoayaz [a Caddoan] language, *which all the Comanches understand and speak perfectly well*" (emphasis added). Vial's ability to address the assembly of Comanches in the Taovaya language strongly suggests the existence of very close social relations between these Indians. The Comanche language is a Uto-Aztecan dialect and is not mutually intelligible with the Caddoan idiom of the Taovayas. A particular vernacular is something that is highly traditional and generally acquired by children from their parents. Although not impossible, it is much more difficult for adults to acquire a second language due simply to the changes that occur in the biological structure of the brain as one matures. Thus, it is less likely that the majority of Comanches attending Vial's speech acquired the Taovaya language simply through contact in activities such as trade. More likely, Comanches acquired this language from either mothers or fathers who were speakers of that particular Caddoan dialect.[37]

In light of the interaction outlined above between Comanches and various Caddoan-speaking peoples, Indian agent Robert S. Neighbors's report to Henry R. Schoolcraft on the Comanches clearly establishes the relationship between intermarriage and the Comanches' migration south into Texas. After speaking of this type of association between Comanches and New Mexicans, Neighbors stated that "from thence [New Mexico] they visited the prairies for the purposes of hunting, and intermarried with the other tribes inhabiting those regions. These were the Wacos, Tah-wac-car-ros [Tahuacanos], Toriuash [Taovayas], and branches of the Pawnee tribe." Comanches had first encountered these Indians along the Arkansas River in Kansas. Pressure from Comanches and Osages encouraged them to migrate south, nearer to their Caddoan relatives living in East Texas. By the late 1730s, the Tahuacanos abandoned the Arkansas and relocated to the river valleys of northern and eastern Texas. Sometime during the middle to late 1750s, all Caddoans living in the Arkansas valley had withdrawn from the region and joined their kinsmen living to the south.[38] The Comanche migration mirrored that of the Caddoans. This was not a coincidence; the two movements were intimately intertwined because of the social relationships that had been established between the two peoples. The initial appearance of Comanches in the vicinity of Béxar in 1743 probably appertained to their relationship with Caddoans as much as it did to their enmity toward Apaches.

Underscoring the interrelationship of Comanches with Caddoans and New Mexicans, Neighbors further stated that "there are at the present time [early 1850s] very few pure-blooded Comanches, having intermarried as previously stated."[39] Indeed, there would have been very few "pure-blooded" Comanches by the 1850s considering the great degree of intermarriage that occurred from the very beginning of their migration to New Mexico and the plains. Individual Comanches living in the 1850s would probably have been able to identify kin among various peoples such as Shoshones, Utes, Apaches (possibly including Navajos), Native and Spanish New Mexicans, Caddoans living in Texas and on the Missouri River, Kiowas, Cheyennes, Arapahos, Tejanos, "Anglo-Texans" (Quanah Parker, for example), former missionized Indian tribes of Texas, the "Civilized Indians" of Indian Territory, and Indian and Spanish Mexicans. Of course, all of these peoples lived across a vast territory within and surrounding the southern plains, and this intricate kinship network is what determined the boundaries of the Comanchería.

In 1886 Capt. W. P. Clark of the U.S. 2d Cavalry explained the Indian sign language symbol for Shoshone, or "Snake," Indians. He instructed: "Hold the right hand, back to right, in front of right shoulder at about height of waist and near it, first and second fingers extended, touching, and pointing to front, others and thumb closed; move the hand several inches to the front, and, by wrist action, give a wavy, sinuous [snakelike] motion to extended fingers." The sign for Comanches was exactly the same, but in reverse: "Snakes going backwards."[40] Even the Indians' sign language reflected the social realities of their kinship connections. The sign of a snake going in reverse visually explained that Comanches and Shoshones were essentially the same people, yet it denoted autonomy. As Indians probably understood, this autonomy enjoyed by the Comanches resulted not only from their geographical "distance" from the Shoshones but also from their widespread kin relationships with other peoples. Comanches were not "Snakes going backwards" simply because they migrated in a certain direction; they were called this because they initiated and maintained close social relationships with peoples other than Shoshones.

In a 1770 description of the Comanches, Athanase de Mézières explained that "the wandering life of the Comanché [*sic*] is important for their sustenance, because, not finding it in the northern region on the arrival of winter, whose frosts drive away the wild herds, they are obliged to follow them into the more temperate country of the south, whence the extreme heat of the summer again drives them along with the herds towards the cold regions."[41] De Mézières's statement expressed a common assumption about the nature of Comanche nomadism. In many ways this type of assumption continues to hold sway over persons interested in Plains Indians. This perspective unduly simplifies the complex character of the Comanches' nomadic movements. To be sure, material resources influenced when and where people moved to at any given time, but there also existed an important social component to this activity. The larger migration of Comanches into the southern plains was not a continuous push into the region; rather, it consisted of many smaller migrations associated with nomadism within local areas. By the end of the eighteenth century, these movements had culminated in a widespread geographical expansion extending throughout the southern plains as enemies became displaced and new social relations established.

Pedro Rivera, a royal inspector visiting New Mexico in 1726, commented to the viceroy on the nomadic nature of Comanches: "[They conserve] such solidarity that both on the marches which they continually make, wandering like the Israelites, as well as in the camps which they establish where they settle, they are formidable in their defense." Elsewhere he noted that the Indians were "always roaming around in battle formation because they waged war with every nation." These observations clearly suggest that Comanches were nomadic and that they frequently engaged in violent competition against numerous other peoples. Rivera did not outline the material sources of that competition, but then he did not have to. By 1726, everyone in New Mexico, New Spain, and Spain knew fully well that Indians such as the Comanches and Utes oftentimes entered the province with the intention of harrying the horse herds found there. Less apparent to Spanish observers was the affect other resources had in spurring on this conflict. The availability of game (especially bison), horses, pasturage, wood, and water influenced the movements of Comanches throughout their existence on the plains. The extent to which each of these resources affected any individual's movement is always questionable, but it is clear that these things inspired a great deal of contention among different peoples at various times. Most likely, resources influenced the movement of people more so when the need for a particular resource among individuals became especially acute. For instance, the severe drought that struck the plains area adjacent to New Mexico between 1787 and 1790 probably helped give rise to competition over local resources, thus prompting outbreaks of violent conflict and greater geographical mobility. Indeed, violence did occur between Utes and Comanches in the summer of 1789. In June and July young Utes perpetrated "various insults" upon Jupe and Yamparica Comanche horse herds despite several remonstrations from New Mexico governor Fernando de la Concha. Irritated with the governor's failure to admonish the raiders, the Comanches attacked "the *ranchería* of the Ute general named Muquisachi . . . with as much furor as one hundred and twelve [warriors could] manage . . . kill[ing] eighty persons including the said general."[42]

The bison, though, were the most conspicuous resource Plains Indians utilized and for which they competed. Interestingly, we lack documentary evidence linking violent competition over this animal with the Indians' migrations. One approach to dealing with this problem has focused on the reconstruction of historical environments in an attempt to discern the regional population of bison herds at any given time. The reasoning behind this theory suggests that beneficial environmental conditions positively affected the number of bison within particular regions of the plains. Furthermore, an assured availability of bison herds would have created a desired commodity among the Indians who exploited these animal resources. Depending upon a population's needs at given times, available game could thus spark competition (oftentimes violent) and influence migratory movements. Berlandier essentially made this same assumption in the 1830s, noting "that the peoples who still wander in the deserts of the New World are continually at war with each other. The origin of these disputes dates back to time immemorial and *little is known of their causes*. We can *assume*, however, that possession of the lands they inhabit or the exploitation of the herds [of bison] that graze there determine, or at least quite often occasion these wars" (emphasis added).[43]

Indeed, there can be no doubt that large numbers of bison wandered the plains during the early period of the eighteenth century when Comanches initially made their push into that region. Antonio de Valverde witnessed a multitude of those animals during his autumn campaign against Utes and Comanches in 1719. On October 7 the expedition descended into a canyon, "and upon entering therein they met some herds of buffalo, so that the whole camp was provided with meat." Moving on down the canyon, the body of Spanish and Apache soldiers came across a pond formed by a spring. Here, the Apache chief Carlana examined some tracks and discovered "that their enemies, the Utes and Comanches, had ranched [camped?] on that spot." Upon closer investigation, "he recognized that they had set up more than sixty tents, and following the trail along the road by which they set out, he found at a little distance the track of the tent poles which they were dragging along." The party also discovered a herd of about two hundred bison along the shoulder of nearby hill.[44] Even though Valverde and his men found evidence of a relatively large Comanche camp located in an area where the bison grazed, this observation does not necessarily associate the Indians' migration to the plains with their pursuit of the game animals.

Nevertheless, the availability of bison weighed upon the decisions of Comanches when it came time to move. Several sources mentioned the significance of bison to their nomadic behavior. French trader Pierre Sartre divulged to Gov. Vélez Cachupín that once, when he and two companions joined up with some Comanches, it took them "a month in reaching Taos from the place where this nation was living." Furthermore, he stated that this "delay was caused by the Cumanches [*sic*] having entertained them with hunting buffaloes and other animals." One of Sartre's counterparts, Louis Febre, commented that the journey to New Mexico took a month "because of having come little by little," presumably because of hunting. Likewise, Athanase de Mézières mentioned the great affect bison had upon the wanderings of Comanches in various reports in 1770, 1772, and 1778. Vial and Chaves reported in 1785 that one reason Comanches did not have "fixed *rancherías*" was because "they . . . need[ed] a place where there are many buffalo and deer for their sustenance and clothing." A year later Texas governor Cabello communicated to the *comandante general* of the Provincias Internas that "it is not possible to ascertain the number of people that constitute each of the [Comanche] *rancherías* because they are in the habit of subdividing according to their orientation to the land in which they exist, and also in relation to their hunting of bison upon which everyone's subsistence is based." David G. Burnet later explained in 1824 that "as the Comanchees [*sic*] do not cultivate the ground, but derive their subsistence from the spontaneous productions of nature, and chiefly from the animal kingdom, they are necessarily migratory, and obliged to change their encampment every ten or fifteen days." He listed "the scarcity of game, which is soon taught to avoid their dangerous neighborhood," as one of the reasons the Indians had to continuously move to a new location.[45]

Horses also greatly influenced the migratory behavior of Comanches throughout the southern plains. Unlike their association with bison, the Indians actively herded equines and thus needed to be highly mobile, not simply to access the animals but to ensure their healthy maintenance with sufficient pasturage and water. Parties of Comanche horse raiders continuously moved about the Comanchería seeking out the livestock to be found on the pastures and ranches of New Mexico, Texas, Mexico, and the various Indian tribes. During the early half of the eighteenth century, Comanches focused most of this activity toward New Mexico and the Plains Indian region to the northeast of that province. Later, especially after 1786, most Comanche horse raids targeted Texas, and as the nineteenth century progressed, they concentrated more on the interior regions of Mexico.

While the acquisition of mounts inspired much mobility among individual Comanches, the daily maintenance of the animals probably encouraged the majority of their ambulations. Pierre Sartre made the earliest and one of the most perceptive observations of this influence. Interrogated in March, 1750, by Spanish authorities for a second time within the year, Sartre explained that while living among the Indians, "he saw various rancherias [*sic*], which altogether would contain about 2,000 men; but they were dispersed, with their large droves of horses, for which reason they could not live together, having to seek sufficient pasturage and water for their horses. They change their location according to the necessities of the time." Athanase de Mézières made a somewhat similar remark in 1770, noting that the Comanches "possessed such a territory that, finding it in abundance of pasturage for their horses and an incredible number of cattle [bison] which furnish them raiment, food, and shelter, they only just fall short of possessing all the conveniences of the earth." Vial and Chaves, two of the most knowledgeable informants of the Comanches and Taovayas in the 1780s, also recognized the relationship between horses' physical needs and human movements. They reported to Texas governor Cabello that "the Cumanche [sic] nation does not have fixed rancherías because they have many horses, for which it is necessary to find pasture." American trader Anthony Glass witnessed first hand in the fall of 1808 what Vial and Chaves, de Mézières, and Sartre had all reported to their respective authorities during the eighteenth century. Traveling with a conglomeration of Taovayas, Wichitas, and Comanches "containing . . . men, women, and children near one thousand souls and three times that number of Horses & Mules," he noted that "it was impossible to remain at the same place but a short time on account of the Grass being soon Eaten up [sic]." This type of behavior explains why in 1719, Governor Valverde and his Apache allies discovered a Ute and Comanche campsite placed along a creek with an abundance of marsh grass. It also helps explain one reason why Comanches frequented Taos as much as they did during the eighteenth century. In 1776 Fray Francisco Atanasio Domínguez described "a very extensive swamp quite near the pueblo on the west . . . , [where] the Comanches . . . bring a thousand or more animals who feed there two days at most." Apparently, Comanches' periodic peaceful visits to the pueblo benefited their horses as much as it did them.[46]

Water and wood also affected Indian movements. Practically every informant's encounter with a Comanche camp occurred along river or creek bottoms, which, of course, provided the Indians with ample water and firewood. Natchitoches trader J. Gaignard encountered the "whole [Comanche] nation" at the "village of the Tavoyache [Taovayas]" on the Red River in July, 1777. In 1785 Vial and Chaves first "caught sight of a large ranchería which was located on the Río de Mermellón, in a very open plain." Visiting the plains in late June of 1790 in an attempt to drum up support among Comanches to accompany a Spanish-led attack upon the Pawnees, Sgt. Juan de Dios Peña found Chief Pujavara's ranchería consisting of seventy-two lodges along the "Rio Salado," a small tributary to the upper Canadian River. Later on July 9, Peña met up with a large gathering of Comanches consisting of 340 tepees along Trinchera Creek in southeastern Colorado. In April, 1808, an overland expedition from San Antonio to Santa Fe led by Francisco Amangual received a messenger sent by Chief Cordero "to report that . . . [the chief] had moved his village to a place where there was good grass and plenty of water." Anthony Glass spent the month of November that year trading and conversing among "ten Chiefs and near six hundred men with a large proportion of women and children" along the Colorado River in Texas. Years later in 1834, Col. Henry Dodge's regiment of U.S. dragoons encamped along southwest Oklahoma's Cache Creek across from a Comanche camp that "contains more than 200 skin lodges." In 1839 a Comanche chief "of small stature and agreeable countenance, verging on the age of fifty," informed Josiah Gregg that he came from a gathering of a great number of Comanches along a nearby creek "*en junta* to go and fight the Pawnees."[47]

In his interview with New Mexico governor Vélez Cachupín on March 1, 1750, Felipe de Sandoval recounted his experiences while living among the "Panipiques" and Comanches. Regarding Comanches and their mobility, he explained that "the Cumanches came to this rancheria [where Sandoval was living] from several others which I did not see, and went from it to others. According to what I gathered, and from what they gave me to understand, there were many rancherias in different places, which, according to the seasons, are moved from time to time in search of pasturage, wood, water, and buffaloes."[48] This statement reaffirms that Comanche mobility was motivated by natural resources and hints at the social aspect of that mobility. Sandoval's observation of individuals entering and leaving the particular *ranchería* he lived in foreshadowed Vial's, Chaves's, and Burnet's later comments on the fluid nature of Comanche camp membership.

Comanche *rancherías* never operated in isolation, thanks to a traditional system of communication that developed naturally out of the great mobility of individuals between kin groups and the insatiable human appetite for information and gossip. Hence, members of each camp generally knew where the other ones were and what the conditions of the natural resources were in those and surrounding areas. According to Ruíz, after performing the rituals associated with the nightly smoke-lodge ceremony, the men in attendance initiated consultation among themselves. In these discussions the attendants "determined how long they should occupy their position—when they shall move their encampment and where they shall reencamp &c." Upon the arrival of someone "from either another town or from an expedition," during the meeting, "the crier [*tlatolero*] announces it to the Chief—who orders that he be summoned to appear." The requested individual "then presents himself without speaking to any person in the town until after he has passed through the same ceremonies of smoking—He then tells whence he comes his adventures, the news he brings &c—Which the crier communicates by shouting thro' the town."[49] Thus, the nightly ritual of the smoke lodge not only encouraged hierarchical social behavior among Comanches but it also served as a clearinghouse of information upon which individuals could make knowledgeable decisions concerning their geographical movements, among other things.

Individuals and camps did not move just anywhere at anytime in a chaotic fashion. People planned their movements only after considering the availability of resources necessary to support a given population and the overall social situation. Whether or not personal rivals or enemies moved about a particular area surely weighed heavily on such decisions too. Unless sufficient cooperation existed among a people, they would not have been able to successfully compete for limited resources such as bison, horses, pasturage, water, and wood. Juan de Dios Peña witnessed Comanches mull over such considerations as he encouraged them to join in on an attack against the Pawnees. Sometime in 1790 the Jupe chief Paruanarimuco petitioned New Mexico governor Concha to send an armed force to escort his people on a bison hunt and campaign against the Pawnees. In late June of that year Sergeant Peña, with a small force, marched into the Comanchería with the intention of accommodating the chief's request. After a brief chance meeting with Paruanarimuco on June 24, the troop came across Chief Pujavara's camp adjacent to Salado Creek on the twenty-sixth. When the sergeant told Pujavara the reason for his visit, the chief replied that he did not want to go on the campaign because he considered the Pawnees too far and that it would place his horses in too much danger. Besides these concerns, he had orders to meet Ecueracapa, Tanqueruara, Onacama, and others to discuss this very issue. Days later, on July 7, Peña accompanied Pujavara and his people to a location along Trinchera Creek where they joined up with the camps of Tanqueruara and Onacama. By the fourteenth, Chama, Achacata, Niantine, Sampampia, Naysaras, Ecueracapa, and many of their people had arrived at the creekside meeting place. Altogether, Peña counted 340 lodges representing anywhere between seventeen hundred to twenty-seven hundred people. When the men gathered to discuss the ensuing mission, the conversation centered on the direction they might go, the availability of bison *pa[ra] comer*" (to eat) along the proposed route, and concern for the horse herds that were said to have been *"mui flaca [sic]*," or "very lean." It was decided that the campaign would be delayed for several days to allow the horses to fatten up and to while away some time in order to surprise the enemy.[50]

After waiting ten days, the mass of people finally departed north up the banks of the Trinchera towards the Purgatoire River. Several days of traveling revealed little new except for the discovery of some abandoned campsites of Pawnees who had been hunting in the area. By this time, the Comanches had for some reason lost their interest in fighting their Caddoan-speaking enemies. Ecueracapa, Paruanarimuco, and Pujavara met with Peña on the twenty-sixth and dismissed the Spanish-led force, saying that their presence had been holding up the Indians from some unexplained action.[51]

Even though Peña's mission failed, he nevertheless observed some of the main concerns Comanches pondered as they planned their movements. Worries about bison and horses played a conspicuous role in those plans. Yet not as conspicuous were those apprehensions associated with the social support needed to make various movements, especially in regions where natural resources were being contested. Paruanarimuco's request for Spanish military assistance suggests that he did not feel he had the necessary cooperation from his kinsmen for he and his followers to safely hunt bison or to conduct a raid against the Pawnees. When Peña appeared on the plains ready to assist in this undertaking, some disagreements obviously existed among the Comanches he found on the Trinchera. Indeed, Pujavara had told the sergeant that he did not want to go because of the distance and the potential threat to his horses. Paruanarimuco's direct request for an armed escort from the authorities at Santa Fe may have perturbed Chief Ecueracapa and others like Pujavara, given the former chief's position of authority over all Comanches and the propensity of individuals to be offended by insubordinate behavior.[52] It would seem that the large encampment of 340 lodges could have provided enough fighting men to conduct successful raids upon the Pawnees. Indeed, Peña had even issued firearms to some of the Indians, so the fear of being overpowered probably did not concern them. Social and political issues based on peoples' personal kin relationships and their authority and rank together with the issues of available bison herds and lean horses seem to have influenced the Comanches' judgments of whether or not to carry on with this undertaking. Thus, as Peña experienced, a complex entanglement of concerns for natural resources and social (or political) relationships characterized the nomadic movements of individuals and camps throughout the Comanchería.

The influence social relationships had on Indian migrations, nomadism, and the general geographical location at which particular groups lived has not been sufficiently appreciated. The traditional explanations for these behaviors have not been convincing because they cannot explain why certain Indians moved into a particular region while others did not. If the resources of a region like the southern plains were sufficient to attract Comanches, then why did it not also attract Sioux? The general approach to this problem has been to examine the environmental differences between the northern and southern plains and their effect upon bison and horse resources and conclude that Indians fashioned their behavior based on the availability of those resources. The discussion of whether environmental or economic factors predominated individuals' actions like migration and mobility fundamentally misunderstands the role of the environment and economics as *factors* weighing upon peoples' decisions. Likewise, social relationships among individuals did not necessarily determine the Comanches' geographical movements, but they certainly also weighed heavily upon their minds.

Kinship social behavior (cooperation) strongly influences the general behavior of human beings and is a great asset to people competing for physical resources. The social relationships Comanches established and maintained with Utes, Pueblo Indians, Caddoans, Spaniards, and even Apaches were all primarily forged by kinship ties that emerged from marriage and the birth of offspring. Only active recognition of a kinship relation formed the foundation of a social relationship in which certain individuals could cooperate in the competition for local resources. Those Shoshones who became known as Comanches just happened to migrate in a southward direction because their recognized kin relationships extended to peoples in and around the general area of New Mexico and Texas. Certainly bison, horses, and other resources played a role in this movement, but the importance of these factors must be understood in the context of social relationships.[53] Thus, the Comanches' move to the southern plains was a historical accident generated by the intermarriage and reproduction of certain geographically located lineages coupled with the availability of particular resources necessary for successful living on the plains.

CHAPTER 3

Comanche Horse
Pastoralism

THE RUSTLING SOUNDS OF URGENCY STARTLED CRISTÓBAL Torres from his midnight sleep. The calm tension that had settled over New Mexico's Rio Arriba jurisdiction on the evening of August 22 epitomized all frontier settlements in New Spain and thus gave Torres no reason to expect his slumber would be interrupted. However, once the *teniente de alcalde mayor* of Santa Cruz arose from bed, a sentry escorted a breathless messenger from San Juan pueblo into the officer's quarters. Though winded, the Indian runner summoned the energy to recount that some Utes had abducted eighteen of the town's horses earlier that night. Sensing that the culprits had safely made their escape, Torres abandoned the idea of chasing after them. Instead, he reported the incident to the captain general in Santa Fe and asked for follow-up instructions.[1]

Sixteen days later, Indians identified as "*Yutas* [or] *Cumanches*" took five more animals from the area. This time Torres set off with several San Juan Indians and three Spanish settlers in search for the rustled livestock. According to the reports of local officials, the *indios bárbaros* seemed to have completely infiltrated the countryside. Martín Fernandez reported that raiders took eleven of his horses. Meanwhile, some Pueblo Indians from Santa Clara discovered four Utes in the cornfields outside of Santa Cruz de la Cañada busy cutting off ears for their own taking. When Torres arrived in San Juan with his small militia, the inhabitants of the pueblo informed him that they had located four separate trails exhibiting fresh signs of Comanches.[2]

In response to this information, the *alférez* positioned seventeen sentinels to keep a twenty-four-hour watch over the recently trampled pathways leading into the area. The following morning around four o'clock, a sentry sighted a lone Indian on a stolen mare and promptly reported this. Scrambling to save as much time as possible, Torres set out to overcome the horse thief just as dawn broke over the crest of the Sangre de Cristo Mountains to the east. He encountered a Comanche after tracking the stolen animal for just a short amount of time. Immediately, Torres requested that the Indian surrender to him peacefully. The Comanche responded to this request by launching an arrow toward the Spaniard. Unperturbed by this attack, the *teniente alcalde* continued to extend offers of peace to the assailant. The Indian again resisted the pleas for goodwill and moved to rearm his bow. Without further warning, Torres descended on the Comanche and killed him.[3]

Despite Torres's determination to find and punish Indian horse raiders, Comanches and Utes continued to harry the herds of New Mexico's northern frontier region. In October, 1716, Sebastian Martín of the Rio Arriba jurisdiction lost his entire *caballada* to Comanches on the ninth, and six Utes ran off with the majority of the horses around Taos on the eleventh. Even a successful retaliatory campaign against the Indians failed to permanently discourage them from continuing to carry away New Mexico's horses. Three years later, in 1719, residents of Santa Fe, Santa Cruz, Rio Arriba, Pojoaque, and Taos convened a council of war to discuss the problems associated with a steadily increasing Comanche and Ute presence in the province. People like Torres and Martín expressed their perpetual frustration over the ongoing pilfering of livestock by the newcomers. Juan de Archibeque of Santa Fe and Cristóbal de la Serna of Taos both pointed out that for the seven or eight years since the Indians had been granted peace, they "stole the beasts which they found." Joseph Truxillo of Santa Cruz noted that the Indians had so depleted the horse herds of the province that they were on the verge of "crippl[ing] the neighborhood in such a manner that the settlers will not be able to march out in defense."[4]

The various opinions stated at the 1719 council of war roughly outlined a steady progression of the Comanche and Ute horse-stealing activity that afflicted the province through the second decade of the eighteenth century. However, these statements more generally implied that Comanches made great efforts to acquire large numbers of these animals during those years. The acquisition of horses by Indians has been traditionally perceived as a watershed event in Plains Indian history, and much of the inquiry into this occurrence has focused on understanding the animals' affect on Indian society. Despite the various quibbles over the nature of the cultural changes wrought by the use of horses, it has generally been accepted that horses became an indispensable resource for Indians living on the plains.[5] But the question must be asked; what motivated Indians to obtain them in the first place?

The presence of horses in colonial New Mexico and the Great Plains has been understood as attracting Comanches and other Indians to these regions from their former homelands. However, Frank Roe has suggested that accounting for the appearance of Comanches in New Mexico as a response to the presence of horses is an example of mistakenly concluding that the animals' presence caused the Comanche migration to the New Mexico region simply from the fact that it preceded or accompanied the Indians' appearance there.[6] This observation implies that the horse-stealing behavior exhibited by Comanches in the early eighteenth century could probably have been influenced by factors other than the desire to accumulate a resourceful European technology. And other considerations indeed influenced these Indians to accumulate livestock at the expense of New Mexican residents.

The raids of this period, particularly, hint at the emergence of horse pastoralism among Comanche Indians during this time. Pastoralism has generally been understood to be a distinctive subsistence strategy some human groups have adopted in response to certain conditions associated with the environment and domestic animals. This concept fails to recognize that pastoralism is primarily aimed at people rather than animals. It is the needs and desires of the people engaged in the practice that are the most important motivations of their pastoralist behavior.[7] Recognizing that pastoralism motivated Comanches to carry away New Mexico's horses helps attribute the responsibility for these actions to the Indians as opposed to an external stimulus.

Pastoralism was an integral, *but not central,* feature of Comanche society. Since kinship formed the basis of these Indians' social organization, pastoralism should be understood simply as another dimension of their society. The development of pastoralist behavior among Comanches not only attests to the effect of Spanish colonization in New Mexico but also to the ability of Indians to identify and adapt successful life strategies into their societies.

Although many observers have identified numerous universal traits among pastoralist peoples, there has been very little consensus over what constitutes the fundamental elements of this behavior. Some characteristics, such as living in environmentally marginal zones, herding livestock, dependence on livestock production, nomadism, and bellicosity, have been noted as particular traits of pastoralists. However, all of these can also apply to other types of societies as well. For centuries, Hopis maintained a tradition of agriculture in the marginal climate of the North American Southwest. Southern agricultural Indians such as the Choctaws maintained horse herds alongside their cornfields. Preindustrial Renaissance England developed a great dependence on various livestock products.[8] The hunting and gathering !Kung of South Africa are well known as a nomadic people. Furthermore, the militancy of the Hellenistic civilization under Alexander III of Macedonia equaled that of the pastoralist Huns five hundred years later. If these characteristics can be identified in various types of human societies throughout history and around the world, then what exactly constitutes pastoralism?

Even though pastoralists share many similarities, they also share just as many differences. Yet there are a few characteristics that *all* pastoral people have in common. Four necessary and sufficient conditions are required in determining whether or not a society is engaged in pastoralism. Individuals must own domesticated animals. Owned animals and their offspring must be inherited by individuals of one generation to the next. The livestock must reproduce biologically. And finally, individuals must make use of some consequence of the animals' behavior. These traits are crucial for the existence of pastoralism. Individuals — not groups — ultimately benefit from owning animals. The presumption that such property primarily benefited groups begs the question of how this behavior could have come about in the first place if individuals failed to benefit from it.[9] The bequeathal of animals from an individual of one generation to another of a later generation makes pastoralism a heritable trait. Because domesticated animals are replicable and inheritable, the occurrence of pastoralist behavior among humans is influenced by the effect it has on individuals' success in leaving descendants.[10] Whether individually owned animals reproduced by natural means or through the practice of husbandry is inconsequential. The human management of breeding in an effort to promote desirable characteristics encourages animal reproduction overall, but this behavior is not necessary for their replication. The continuance of pastoralism around the world attests to its success as an adaptation that helps individual humans reproduce.[11]

Pastoralism first emerged sometime around eight to ten thousand years ago during the period of cultural development known as the Neolithic Era. The data concerning exactly when and where this lifestyle first originated are murky and continue to be contested. However most students of this behavior agree with the view that animal domestication probably accompanied the emergence of horticulture and that *nomadic* pastoralism probably developed some considerable time afterward.[12]

There is also relative consensus that agriculture emerged independently in seven different geographical areas of the world. The primary centers are identified as the Near East, southern China, northern China, central Mexico, eastern North America, the central South American Andes, and sub-Saharan Africa.[13] While animal domestication and pastoralism accompanied the development of agriculture in certain parts of the Western Hemisphere, the antecedents of Comanche pastoralism extend back to the Old World. Despite Native Americans' domestication of animals such as dogs, turkeys, ducks, cochineal, llamas, alpacas, and guinea pigs, their later association with sheep, horses, and cattle stemmed not from knowledge of local domesticates but from the diffusion of the pastoralist culture originally developed in Asia.

The earliest dates suggested for the emergence of animal domestication occur in the area of the Near East known as the Fertile Crescent. Most of the livestock species people are familiar with originally became domesticated in this region and slowly began spreading into surrounding areas. Domestic goats, sheep, and cattle all originated there. Horses appear to have been one of the last animals tamed by humans, about twenty-five hundred to five thousand years ago, probably in central Asia.[14] Animal domestication and pastoralism then spread into neighboring regions such as southeastern Europe, northern Africa, and the central Asian steppes.

The historical details of the spread of agriculture into Europe are quite sketchy and conclusions are far from certain. But it is known from agricultural archeological sites in the Balkans and along the southern Mediterranean coast that European peoples began practicing wheat and barley cultivation and livestock herding possibly as early as eight thousand years ago. The practice of agriculture on the European continent came about as a result of human land- and sea-borne migrations from the east-southeast. Several early ditch-fortified sites in southern Italy and France suggest that early farmers were immigrants and encountered, or expected to encounter, hostility from the local hunter-gatherers living in the region. Sometime between sixty-five hundred and five thousand years ago, agriculturalists began settling the more temperate areas of central and western Europe. Several of these sites also exhibit fortifications, implying hostility between the newcomers and the original forager inhabitants. The archeological sites found in these areas also indicate a greater reliance on cattle as opposed to sheep and goats.[15] This development hints at a connection with an earlier development of agricultural complexes involving cattle in central Asia.

Near Eastern agricultural practices began expanding into the adjacent region of the central Asian steppes via southeastern Europe around seven thousand years ago. This area has been typically identified as the cradle of nomadic pastoralism, but it has a longer legacy of sedentary agriculture that includes all the main plant and animal species previously domesticated in the Fertile Crescent. However, cattle breeding became a major focus for many steppe inhabitants. The wide-ranging nomadic form of livestock pastoralism most people associate with steppe dwellers did not come about until the beginning of the first millennium B.C., some four thousand years after the introduction of agriculture and three thousand years after central Asians may have domesticated horses. Early horse herding on the steppes reflected the existing practices associated with raising cattle as a food source. By 2000 B.C., domestic horses had taken on the role of draft animal and quickly diffused across much of Eurasia. The arrival of horses in Europe complemented the earlier incorporation of wheeled vehicles and plows into the extant agrarian culture and may also be closely connected to the migration of Indo-European peoples into the continent.[16]

These cultural transformations greatly altered all of Europe, including the peripheral regions of Scandinavia, the British Isles, and the Iberian Peninsula. The first Iberian agricultural sites date back as far as the sixth millennium B.C. and most likely represent a continuation of the western migration of agriculturalists along the rim of the Mediterranean. Over the course of the next several millennia, livestock herding and cereal cultivation slowly spread elsewhere on the peninsula. As in other parts of Europe, the appearance of domesticated horses in southwestern Europe between 2000 and 1000 B.C. accompanied the arrival of immigrant humans whose agricultural practices focused more on raising and trading livestock.[17]

The new livestock-rearing culture especially gained a foothold in the southern Iberian region of Andalucía and eventually displaced the beneficiaries of the much older agricultural traditions that had originally expanded from the Levant.[18] By the middle of the first millennium, a diversified society featuring agriculture, mining, metallurgy, and trade had developed among the people of the greater Guadalquivir River valley. Known to Herodotus as Tartessos, this region became an important source of trade for the Greeks, Phoenicians, Carthaginians, and Romans. Herding and cultivation agriculture on the peninsula thrived from 206 B.C. to 1031 A.D. despite the successive occupations of Romans, Germanic barbarians, and Arabs. Sheep herding, however, may have become intensified after the Muslim conquest when Berbers migrated into the region, but southern Iberian pastoralism also continued to focus on the raising of oxen, cattle, donkeys, and horses.[19]

As Christian conquistadors pushed southward into the arid plains of the central Meseta in the eleventh and twelfth centuries, limited open-range cattle ranching developed. While cattle ranching became more widespread across the Meseta, raising sheep remained the region's dominant pastoral occupation, followed closely by swine herding. The Mesetan form of cattle pastoralism that developed most resembled the Alpine stock-raising tradition that featured unmounted, or pedestrian, herding; frequent penning; the castration of yearling bulls to ensure docility; and seasonal transhumance.[20]

In Andalucía, the ancient center of southern Iberian agriculture, true open-range cattle ranching had developed by the Late Middle Ages. Terry Jordan has pointed out that the cattle ranchers near the Guadalquivir River's delta practiced a unique, less labor-intensive form of pastoralism. Herders shifted cattle seasonally between salt marshes and surrounding brushy woodlands. But once they transported the animals to the new pastures, the beasts were cut loose on open ranges and neglected for months on end. This practice, coupled with the disregard for castrating bulls, had the tendency to encourage a wild temperament among Andalusian livestock. The unruliness of the cattle forced herders to manage the animals with lances from horseback when time came to transport them to winter and summer ranges. As a result, horse pastoralism also became a major occupation among the ranchers living alongside the marshy ranges.[21]

Many of the early Spanish colonists to the New World hailed from the cattle-herding areas of the Meseta and Andalucía. Indeed, the Andalusian port cities of Cádiz, Palos, and Sevilla served as the primary launching points of Spanish discovery and colonialism in the Western Hemisphere, and Andalusians accounted for over 20 percent of the total Iberian migration to the Americas before 1540. According to Jordan, these developments had a major influence on the development of pastoralism in the New World. Spaniards introduced the complete menagerie of livestock associated with Iberian pastoralism to their initial settlements, established on the islands of the West Indies. Sheep and goat herding languished in the newfound tropical climes, while cattle, horses, and pigs thrived and reproduced at incredible rates. The successful introduction of cattle and horses to tropical America, coupled with the high numbers of Andaluz colonists, encouraged the emergence of an Andalusian system of open-range ranching in the Antilles. Various elements of West Indies ranching distinguished American cattle ranching from its progenitor on the Iberian Peninsula. One of the most striking features of early colonial ranching was the feral nature of tremendous numbers of cattle and horses. These animals roamed the remote forested hills and mountains of the various islands and gave rise to a "hunting industry." Adapting Andalusian herding techniques to hunting feral cattle, men called matadors or lanceros pursued these animals on horseback, using lances with modified crescent-shaped hocking blades.[22]

Hernán Cortés's conquest of Mexico in 1521 ushered Spanish civilization onto the North American mainland. Naturally, Iberian-Antillean cattle-ranching practices accompanied the establishment of colonial agriculture in this "New Spain." Mexico's geography, consisting of a high central plateau and coastal lowlands, generally resembled Spain's Meseta uplands and low Andalusian plains. Consequently, the methods of cattle ranching that became established in the Mexican highlands and coastal areas exhibited the distinctive characteristics common to the corresponding regions of the mother country. Even though a vanguard of cattle ranchers led the expansion of Spanish pastoralism up the Mesa del Norte during the sixteenth century, large-scale open-range ranching quickly proved unfeasible in the more arid regions of the north. Thus, the labor-intensive mixed agricultural system of highland Spanish Extremadura emerged in the northern territories. By 1600, areas of northern Mexico began teeming with populations of *ganado mayor* (cattle and horses) and even greater numbers of *ganado menor* (sheep, goats, and pigs).[23]

This mixed-pastoralist system became transplanted into New Mexico as frontier expansion leapfrogged over the Chihuahua desert and into the upper Rio Grande valley. The final inspection of Juan de Oñate's initial colonizing expedition to New Mexico in late December, 1597, and early January, 1598, demonstrated the typical mixture of livestock that characterized northern Mexican pastoralism. Oñate had assembled 2,517 sheep, 846 goats, 799 cows, 500 calves, 383

Map 7. Spread of Spanish Pastoralism in New Spain

rams, 198 oxen, 101 mares, 96 colts, 53 hogs, and 41 mules and jackasses to help ensure the success of an isolated settlement. From the very beginning, sheep composed the fundamental basis of colonial New Mexican pastoralism. Josiah Gregg later observed in the 1830s that "nothing . . . has been more systematically attended to in New Mexico than the raising of the *sheep.*" Nonetheless, horse herding also remained an important undertaking in the colony. Gregg also noted that *nuevo mexicanos* "devoted [themselves] to equestrian exercise, [to the degree] that they have been styled a race of centaurs." New Mexican horse pastoralism seems to have conformed to patterns that could be traced back to Andalusian and Antillean origins. Settlers, colonial officials, soldiers, and missionaries relied on horses primarily for the animals' transportation and martial qualities as opposed to herding domestic cattle. This observation, however, hardly suggests origins from any particular geographical region since these attributes were probably self-evident from the moment humans began riding horses on a regular basis. New Mexicans also utilized them for hunting. Enormous droves of bison wandered the plains just to the east of the province, and the colonists did not fail to take advantage of this resource. The proximity of this incredible source of beef may have figured considerably in New Mexico's failure to become a major "cattle-ranching frontier."[24] New Mexicans did not borrow Indian pedestrian bison-hunting practices nor did they invent any new methods for procuring the animal. Instead, they simply adapted the Andalusian-Antillean cattle-herding and hunting practices to the pursuit of the plains bovine.

This adaptation became instituted in New Mexico shortly after Oñate initially colonized the region. Ginés de Herrera Horta, viceregal auditor and assessor of the New Mexico undertaking, reported that when he arrived at the colony in late 1599 or early 1600, the settlers had already consumed most of the cattle they brought with them from Mexico. Also, he received reports that the colonists had resorted to slaughtering their oxen and "were plowing with the horses." Of the four hundred or so bovines left, Horta communicated that the New Mexicans had "been killing seven animals each week . . . providing a very limited supply of meat." This rapid exhaustion of the settler's beef provisions probably encouraged them to concentrate on bison as a reliable source of meat. In 1598 Oñate commissioned some of his men in an attempt to domesticate the plains bison. Despite the overwhelming failure of the experiment, the soldiers nevertheless succeeded in killing many of the beasts.[25]

The Spaniards used methods previously developed in southern Spain and the West Indies to kill the bison. The records of the expedition's final inspection reveal that Oñate and his men had equipped themselves with tools that had long been associated with Spanish open-range cattle herding: lances, hocking blades, and saddles of the *jineta* and *estradiota* type.[26] The first New Mexicans probably utilized these familiar implements when they hunted bison. Oñate's statement to the viceroy in 1602 that bison "are much faster than our [cattle], almost as fleet as deer, so much that it was hard to kill them, as they did not stop," strongly suggests that the Spaniards used the classic horse-mounted herding and hunting technique of running alongside the target bovine and wounding or killing it with lances. It is also evident that the Plains Indians did not use this technique at this time. The early New Mexicans witnessed Apaches bow-hunting bison from "brush shelters built at the watering places." Over two hundred years later, Gregg encountered a New Mexican bison hunter, or *cibolero,* along the Santa Fe Trail.

Gregg's characterization of the man as brandishing a lance and wearing leather trousers, jacket, and flat straw hat closely mirrors geographer Terry Jordan's much later description of the classic Andalusian cowboy.[27] It is no accident that the description of the Spanish *vaquero* and the New Mexican *cibolero* closely resembles the classic image of the mounted Plains Indian bison hunter. All Plains Indians ultimately inherited this behavior directly from the Spanish colonists of New Spain. Therefore, many attributes that have been identified as exemplary of Comanches were, in their very essence, Spanish. Indeed, all of the Comanches' pastoralist behavior derived from an ancient tradition that originated as part of the initial development of agriculture in southwest and central Asia.

Understanding the concept of "culture" is the key to comprehending how and why Comanches came to be inheritors of certain elements of the Old World pastoralist tradition. An early explanation of culture suggested that it was associated with an exclusive human ability to learn. Unfortunately, learning is neither limited to humans nor does it necessarily imply culture.[28] Other explanations have suggested that culture is exemplified by shared behavior, the meanings associated with symbols (that is, words), or some combination of the two. Sadly, shared behavior also does not necessarily imply culture. Furthermore, the existence of symbols along with their associated meanings is not an indispensable condition either.[29]

Even though learning does not imply culture, the inverse — that culture implies learning — seems to hold true. Examples of cultural behavior, including art, law, religion, politics, cartography, music, and architecture, allude to some kind of learning process. The universal association of learning with cultural behavior suggests that this is an elemental condition for the existence of what has become identified as culture. However, because learning is not a sufficient criterion in itself, then at least one other condition must be present for the appearance of this phenomenon. What differentiates cultural learning from the general acquisition of knowledge is that it comes from one individual and is potentially transmittable to another. In other words, cultural behavior must be copied from someone else. For that reason, any activity learned from an individual and then copied is an example of cultural behavior.[30]

The recognition of culture as learned and copied behavior by *individuals* suggests that groups are not necessary for cultural behavior. The application of the term *culture* as a synonym for social groups has been misleading. In no society does everyone exhibit the same cultural behavior. Societies and cultural behavior are independent of one another. For example, Pedro Vial and Francisco Xavier Chaves reported in 1785 that Yamparica Comanches differentiated themselves from their eastern Cuchanec relatives by the cut of their hair. The Spaniards clearly recognized the individuals of these different clans as members of the same society, stating that they "all speak the same language, and thus they consider themselves brothers and comrades."[31] Vial and Chaves's observation of cultural differences within Comanche society simply reflect the essential difference between culture and a society.

The learning and copying involved in fashioning hairstyles epitomizes human cultural behavior. By the standards of modern society, distinct haircuts are a relatively superficial aspect of culture. But among native peoples like the Comanches, the cultural behavior associated with various decorations like hairstyles is not simply superficial learning and copying. It is *traditional*. In other words, customs, whether they consist of hairstyles, religion, or language, are cultural behaviors that have been acquired from ancestors. Thus, the traditional haircut Vial and Chaves observed among Yamparicas suggests that individual members of this clan learned and copied this particular behavior from their distinctive ancestors. Along with kinship cooperation, traditions have formed the basis of all human societies.[32]

Most of the cultural behavior exhibited by humans has been passed down from ancestors to descendants through the generations. Traditions have allowed parents to benefit their offspring by transmitting what they have learned in their lifetimes, customary or not. By transmitting behavior to offspring which may help them live successful lives and reproduce, ancestors not only increase their own success in leaving descendants but also encourage the occurrence of that behavior among individuals of later generations.[33] The agricultural tradition that first emerged among humans eight to ten thousand years ago has obviously been highly successful in helping people survive and leave descendants. This success, in turn, has encouraged the replication of this behavior to the point that the tradition of agriculture has flourished among humans throughout the world.

Thus, the spread of Old World pastoralism to the New World can ultimately be attributed to this tradition's beneficial effect upon people's lives and their ability to leave descendants. Some pre-Columbian inhabitants of the Western Hemisphere understood and experienced the auspicious results of animal domestication and the agricultural tradition, yet this tradition never became widespread across the continents of North and South America. Most New World animal species evidently did not adapt to domestication, and those that did were either small in size or, in the case of llamas and alpacas, suited only to a limited environment. Several Old World species, though, did adapt to domestication, and the nature of this development was such that it greatly influenced the quality of life and the descendant-leaving ability of those livestock species and their human owners. Indians throughout Spanish America quickly grasped the various advantages associated with Old World livestock. In Mexico, Tlaxcalan Indians had incorporated sheep, goats, and pigs into their agricultural economy by 1524, three years after Cortés's conquest of the Aztec capital, Tenochtitlan. Around 1550, various Chichimeca Indian tribes of Mexico's northern frontier began raiding livestock being driven to outposts like Zacatecas, and they quickly became accustomed to herding cattle and riding horses. As the limits of New Spain stretched into New Mexico, Apaches, Navajos, Pueblos, Utes, and Comanches learned and copied distinct aspects of the Spanish Old World pastoral legacy. Once individual Indians passed on this cultural knowledge to their offspring, it became part of their own ancestral heritage. The persistence of these particular pastoralist traditions among Indians to the present era alludes to the great success of this ancient behavior that originally evolved in the Near East.[34]

So far, we cannot be precisely certain when Comanches acquired the various Old World pastoralist traits. The earliest Spanish documents that specifically referred to Comanches mentioned them in a "matter-of-fact" manner, suggesting that Spanish colonial officials had made initial contact with these Indians some time prior to 1706. During a stopover in Taos on July 15 of that year, prior to setting out for the Plains Apache settlements of Cuartelejo, Juan de Ulibarri learned from local officials that Comanches and Utes threatened to attack the pueblo. A month later New Mexico governor Francisco Cuervo y Valdez also mentioned Comanches in a report to his superiors on the lack of missionaries for the surrounding areas of the province.[35] Neither of these men indicated any surprise associated with the appearance of Comanches in the vicinity of New Mexico, and no other documents relating an initial contact between Comanches and Spaniards have been uncovered. Even if one did come to light, it probably would not provide a sufficient amount of clues relating to the Comanches' initial adoption of Spanish pastoralist practices. For most early Comanche horse pastoralists, this process likely took place far away from the borders of New Mexico in the mountains and basins of their ancestral homelands in the Colorado, Wyoming, and Utah border area.

Both Ulibarri and Cuervo y Valdez associated Comanches with Utes in the early 1700s. Not only did Ulibarri receive a report that Comanches were supposed to accompany Utes in their attack upon Taos, but he also later discovered on his expedition to the plains that these Indians combined forces to attack two Apache *rancherías*. Governor Cuervo y Valdez also connected these two nations in his description of the boundaries of "the extensive province of Navajo." Ten years later, in 1716, New Mexicans continued to identify Comanches and Utes as almost the same people. Christóbal Torres's uncertain identification of horse raiders in the Rio Arriba area as "*Yutas* [or] *Cumanches*" is another indication of the close relationship that existed between these Indians. Likewise, the numerous testimonies at the 1719 council of war condemned both Comanches and Utes together for livestock raids and murderous attacks upon New Mexicans. Even as late as 1724, New Mexicans recognized the two peoples as "almost the same nation."[36] The extent of cooperation reported in the first two decades of the 1700s suggests that members of the two tribes either still recognized kinship with one another (through language or dress) or may have intermarried, for individuals in traditional societies collaborate regularly only with kinsmen. This realization has implications for understanding how Comanches came to embrace the behavior associated with horse pastoralism.

Utes had contact with the Spanish and their livestock some time before they introduced them to Comanches. They probably started to become knowledgeable of horses and the behavior associated with the animal's upkeep as they began to deal regularly with Spaniards, Pueblos, and Apaches sometime prior to the 1640s. Anthropologist Marvin Opler has suggested that traditional Ute stories and equestrian equipment design indicate that these Indians became initially involved with horses sometime around 1640. Indeed, this date corresponds to slave raids conducted by New Mexican governor Luis de Rosas upon Utes and Apaches in 1639. The internment of Utes in Santa Fe as forced laborers may have encouraged these Indians to become familiar with raising and using horses. Furthermore, Utes may have begun regularly acquiring horses during the 1650s as they became absorbed in the system of raiding, trading, and warfare that developed in colonial New Mexico.[37]

The 1680 revolt of the Pueblo Indians has generally been considered a catalyst influencing the spread of horses among Indians throughout the West. For ten years, Indians barred Spanish colonists from the province and assumed control over large numbers of livestock. One witness to the uprising noted that by September, 1680, insurgent Pueblos possessed enough horses, mares, and cattle "to maintain for more than four months the Apache nations." Presumably, Apaches and Utes carried away large numbers of these animals and their offspring in their ongoing wars with the various rebellious villages. The reestablishment of Spanish control over New Mexico in 1692 did nothing to disrupt the patterns of Ute horse-stealing behavior as evidenced by the Indians' seizure of thirteen mounts from San Juan pueblo in the late winter of 1696.[38]

That the Utes had become accomplished horse raiders by the early 1700s implies that this behavior became part of their traditional culture sometime during the latter half of the previous century. Even if this marauding is not evidence for the existence of pastoralism among these Indians, it at least hints that owning and managing horse herds became an important aspect of their traditional lifestyle. Although no direct documentation exists, most scholars believe that Comanches acquired their interest in horses from Utes. This hypothesis is most likely correct, primarily because humans have been highly proficient in learning and copying the behavior of others, especially relatives. Besides being highly cultural, humans also have been highly traditional. The possibility that these Indians may have intermarried on some scale during the early eighteenth century suggests that Comanches could have initially acquired their knowledge of horses from Ute ancestors. For example, the son of a Comanche man and a Ute woman might have learned about horse-raiding techniques from his Ute grandfather. In this case one could consider the boy as a recipient of a Ute cultural behavior, which would have become part of Comanche cultural tradition only at the moment the boy transmitted it to his own offspring. This process may explain the close cooperation of Utes and Comanches in the early 1700s and why Spanish observers had such a difficult time distinguishing between the two peoples.

That Comanches acquired horses as they became involved in horse raiding in the first two decades of the eighteenth century, however, does not prove that they were recipients of an ancient tradition of pastoralism passed down to them via the Spanish and Utes. The acquisition of these animals merely implies that they obtained an essential component for the possible emergence of pastoralism among them. But there are other Comanche material and behavioral traits that also allude to the Spanish legacy of livestock herding among these Indians.

In the summer of 1834, artist George Catlin observed a mounted Comanche riding a "fine and spirited wild horse" as the party of U.S. dragoons Catlin accompanied encountered the Indians for the first time. He noted the Indian's horsemanship, remarking, "he drew the reins upon a heavy Spanish bit, and at every jump, plunged into the animal's sides, till they were in a gore of blood, a huge pair of spurs." The artist's observation and remarks clearly bespoke of the fundamental Iberian nature of Comanche horsemanship. Catlin had never seen and had relatively little knowledge of these Indians prior to this encounter, yet he readily noticed the Spanish character of the Indians equestrian trappings. He explained this cultural exhibition as resulting from the Indians' "border wars, which are continually waged on the Mexican frontiers." The artist had unknowingly stumbled across a demonstration that reflects a great deal more than the influence of "civilized" war booty upon a "savage" nation. Instead, the use of Spanish bits and spurs by Comanches indicate the transference of time-honored cultural behaviors that their ancestors had consciously observed, learned, and adopted at some point in the past. Not only did Comanches learn and copy the Iberian use of bits and spurs, they also emulated the Spanish in their use of saddles, lassos, corrals, lances, herding techniques, and livestock markings and decorations.[39]

The saddle regularly used by Comanches roughly conformed to a Spanish design developed either in the Caribbean or New Spain for roping livestock from horseback. These saddles featured a narrow rawhide-bound wooden frame, or tree, with a high pommel and cantle along with stirrups. In the 1830s Josiah Gregg observed New Mexican *vaqueros* attaching lassos to the pommel of their saddles after roping wild horses. He suggested that Plains Indians captured mustangs in this manner as well. Thomas James's comment of a "sudden turn" after the noose passed over the animal's head strongly hints that Comanches indeed attached riatas to their saddle horn. Catlin also witnessed Comanches using lariats to capture horses. But instead of attaching the rope to the saddle, he reported that the Indian roper would dismount and run along with the captured horse, maintaining enough tension to choke the animal down but releasing enough slack to keep from being dragged along the ground.[40]

Comanches sometimes lassoed wild horses after first corralling them in a dry arroyo or an oval-shaped stockade built of posts and brush. James recounted the Indians driving the animals into a "deep ravine" where other individuals, who were to perform the task of hog-tying the roped creatures, had concealed themselves. Gregg reported that Comanche mustangers in Texas oftentimes used "a strong pen at some passway or crossing of a river, into which [wild horses] are frightened and caught." Members of the 1853 U.S. pacific railroad survey along the course of the Canadian River came across evidence of several such "'Corral' yards" at an abandoned Comanche campsite. Even though the prehorse ancestors of these Indians may have used arroyo and corral traps in their efforts to hunt bison, this behavior involving horses probably stems from similar Spanish practices of rounding up livestock. Indeed, the post-and-brush corral construction as witnessed by Randolph Marcy on a fork of the upper Red River in 1852 mimicked the crude branch-and-brush enclosures that existed in Andalucía, Tamaulipas, and Sonora.[41]

The Comanches also adopted the lance, another instrument fundamental to Spanish horse-mounted cattle pastoralism. As noted above, the lance was an age-old fixture of the Spanish and Mexican *vaquero*. Indians must have adopted the practice of hunting bison on horseback with lances sometime during the seventeenth century after observing New Mexicans engaged in this practice. According to Gregg, Indians oftentimes imitated the *ciboleros* by chasing bison down "with a long-handled spear or lance, which, if the horse be well trained, is still a more expeditious mode of killing them than with the bow and arrow." Even though Indians may have originally adopted Spanish lances as an efficient weapon for hunting bison, the spears also served a military purpose that probably was copied from colonial presidial cavalry troopers. Apparently, they had learned to use these weapons with deadly efficiency by 1750. Late that year, New Mexico governor Francisco Marín del Valle issued an order forbidding, among other things, the sale of lances to the Indians. Obviously, this prohibition did little to stem the Indians use of this weapon, for it had by this time become ensconced in their military tradition. The thirty-or-so Comanches encountered by Col. Henry Dodge's regiment of U.S. dragoons on July 14, 1834, all brandished spears "of fourteen feet in length."[42]

Comanches became proficient in the various herding techniques introduced to New Mexico by Spanish colonists. In contrast to the system of cattle ranching that had developed in the lowlands of Spain and Mexico, the raising of horses represented a more labor-intensive process. Generally, herders rotated horses to various pastures depending on the quality and condition of the forage. In relatively populated areas like that around San Antonio numerous herding interests regularly competed for access to pasturage. Consequently, herds belonging to presidios, missions, and private individuals oftentimes had to be grazed on fresh pastures forty to sixty miles away. In lieu of stock pens, soldiers, ranchers, and settlers hobbled their mounts at night. Many times, herders abandoned this practice when the number of animals made it impractical. Undoubtedly, the failure to secure horse herds in some manner facilitated the ability of Comanches and other Indians to run off with the animals.[43]

Comanche herding closely resembled the Spanish pattern used throughout northern New Spain in terms of pasture rotation. Unlike their Spanish counterparts, however, Comanche herders were not bound to forts, missions, and settlements, and their practice took on a more nomadic aspect. Nevertheless, the grasslands surrounding Comanche camps endured excessive overgrazing by horses. Visitors to the southern plains noticed the effect Indian horses had on local pasture resources. Lt. James W. Abert immediately took note of the overgrazed condition of the pasturage upon his arrival to a Kiowa camp situated on a small tributary of the Canadian River in September, 1845, remarking that Kiowa horses had eaten the grass very short, leaving his own steeds to forage on "indifferent pasturage." When Marcy entered Comanche country seven years later, he encountered several abandoned campsites that had "been unoccupied some two or three weeks since by the Comanches; the grass where their animals have grazed is not yet grown up." John Sherburne made a similar observation of an abandoned Comanche campsite he came across in 1853. He speculated that the Indians "must have had an immense number of horses as the ground in every direction is cut up & the grass eaten close."[44]

Comanches may have also practiced transhumance, seasonally moving their herds from lower lying lands into highlands and mountains. Many early New Mexican colonists originally came from Mesetan Castile, where this practice was widespread, especially among sheepherders. As in central Iberia, New Mexicans annually transported their vast flocks of sheep between low valleys and plains and high alpine meadows. Unlike the Navajo, Comanches did not raise sheep.[45] Nevertheless, they probably recognized that frequenting the higher elevations of the Comanchería and New Mexico during the hotter and dryer months of the year benefited the health of their horses. Comanche transhumance differed from the classical practitioners described in the anthropological literature. Instead of an annual migration of all herders and animals from lower and higher elevations, Comanches exploited higher pastures on an individual basis, incorporating this movement into their regular rotation of forage locations. Describing an extensive swampy area west of Taos pueblo, Fray Francisco Atanasio Domínguez stated that Comanches regularly pastured "a thousand or more animals who feed there two days at most, and in spite of this number repeatedly during the year, there is no lack of fodder."[46]

Along with the herding customs of pasture rotation and transhumance, Comanches further emulated colonial herders in their habit of fettering horses at night. Glass witnessed this practice when he and his trading party joined up with a Comanche village "containing of men women and children near one thousand souls and three times that number of Horses & Mules." Regarding the livestock, Glass reported, "most of them were tied with Ropes made of Buffalo skins every night." Jean Louis Berlandier noticed the same thing in 1828 among a band of Comanches he accompanied through the Texas Hill Country. He observed that "at the break of day, when they no longer need fear a surprise, they turn loose the horses which were tethered during the night." As with the Spanish, herd-security issues motivated the Comanches to engage in this behavior.[47]

If horses became lost or stolen, Comanches had a means to identify their recovered stock. When a person could not recognize an animal on sight alone, they could do so upon observing the permanent ear markings and brands Indians regularly made upon their animals. Gregg reported that Comanches "have a peculiar mark for their animals: every one which has pertained to them may always be recognized by a slit in the tip of each ear; a practice apparently universal among all their tribe." An early 1789 investigation of the theft of two Comanche horses by several New Mexican colonists from a Pecos corral revealed that two of the animals exhibited Spanish-type markings. One horse, a roan, featured some *lunettes,* or crescent-shaped markings, on its haunches. The other animal, a bay, displayed a cropped tail and split ears. These practices further reflected behaviors Comanches ultimately acquired from the Spanish pastoralist tradition. Jordan has demonstrated that personal markings on livestock in the form of brands and ear markings has long been a staple feature of ranching in southern Spain and Mexico. The use of the crescent-moon image on the roan abducted from Pecos particularly reflected Comanches' adoption of this Old World pastoralist tradition. This motif of ornamentation has been traced as far back as the ancient Phoenicians of Sidon and Tyre.[48] Comanches and other Indians adopted this design only after it had spread from the Near East, through North Africa, into Iberia, and finally across the Atlantic to North America.

The adoption of various Iberian practices such as roping, herding, and marking among Comanches is compelling evidence that not only did these Indians practice pastoralism but this behavior also constituted a major aspect of their lives and culture. The identification of these traits among historical Comanches still only *suggests* that they fashioned some of their behavior associated with horses after a Spanish model of ranching and herding. The discussion so far has not included any evidence that conclusively indicates that Comanche society indeed contained any particular aspect that can be identified as pastoralist.

Individual ownership of domesticated animals is the cornerstone of pastoralism. Ownership of animals first emerged when canines became domesticated around ten to twelve thousand years ago. Like most if not all Native Americans, Comanches inherited the ancient trait of dog ownership. Pedro Rivera, an observer of New Spain's northern frontier in the late 1720s, remarked on this longstanding tradition of animal ownership among Comanches, noting that they used their large dogs primarily as beasts of burden. Thanks in part to an earlier familiarity with owning dogs, Indians readily understood the role of equines as property once they learned from the Spanish how to use them. Anthropologist John Ewers suggested that all Plains Indians owned horses on an individual basis. Comanche ethnographer E. Adamson Hoebel also identified this behavior among Comanches.[49] The most compelling evidence for the individual ownership of horses by historical Comanches comes from their practice of marking animals. The two horses that were the object of the February, 1789, robbery investigation in New Mexico each exhibited markings that allowed the Comanche owners to personally identify their mounts. Gregg's later statement of the universality of this practice among the Indians certainly suggests that the identification of personal ownership was the aim of earmarks and other types of markings.

The ultimate motive for private ownership is social, not economic. Ownership probably emerged among human ancestors as a result of their social nature, since the very existence of private property requires individuals to sacrifice their personal interests in favor of another's. U.S. Indian agent Robert Neighbors commented on the social character of property owned by Comanches, observing that "the liberality with which they dispose of their effects on all occasions of the kind . . . would induce the belief that they acquire property merely for the purpose of giving it to others." It is apparent that Neighbors witnessed the great amounts of cooperation and sacrifice involved in their ownership of personal property. In particular, what each individual *ultimately* sacrifices in behaving socially with one another is their own selfish interest. Thus, Comanches' identification of personal ownership of livestock property ultimately reflected social behavior aimed at promoting the interests of others — primarily that of their close relatives.[50]

Inheritance provides the most fundamental way in which individuals have promoted the future well being of their relatives. Like fortuitous genes or cultural traditions, property has the potential to help people live successful lives and leave descendants. Several contemporary observers described Comanches bequeathing horses to surviving kinsfolk. Francisco Ruíz noted that if a death occurred, the brothers of the departed person "cut their hair and kill[ed] the horses which had belonged to the deceased." Apparently, Comanches did not kill every single animal owned by the dead man. He further mentioned that those "horses left by the deceased are divided among his brothers. If there are none [brothers], then the next heir is the father, and then the mother." Jean Louis Berlandier stated that Comanches only killed a dead warrior's "best horses." David Burnet reported on this behavior as well, recounting that the Indians only sacrificed some of the deceased's "horses and mules as the avarice of the living will relinquish." The only scholarly analysis of Comanche inheritance practices to date mostly agrees with these contemporaneous observations. According to this, Comanches only destroyed the effects of an individual's personal usage. Relatives could have claimed all other surplus property in correspondence to their degree of relationship to the dead person. In 1849 Marcy may have encountered a recipient of such "surplus property" when he met one of the widows of "Hois" clan chief Santa Anna. He described her as "possess[ing] a large number of very valuable horses and mules." Marcy's witness to the woman's performance of "mourning ceremonies" for her deceased husband hints that these animals might have been directly inherited from the chief's estate.[51]

Despite poignant demonstrations of bereavement, sometimes involving the sacrifice of great numbers of horses, Comanches clearly passed along some of their mounts to close relatives through inheritance.[52] Apparently, bequeathing such property had a positive effect on the probability that their posterity would endure. Otherwise, if horse ownership and pastoralism did not benefit Comanches in some way, it would have scarcely appeared among them. For pastoralists, the ultimate value of livestock lies in its ability to promote social behavior and relationships among people and ultimately the leaving of descendants. Thus, the disbursement of horses through inheritance provided relatives of Comanche pastoralists with the means to succeed.

Unlike money or land, property in the form of livestock is replicable. The ownership of domesticated animals not only can help people leave descendants but also can increase in frequency thanks to its inherent ability to reproduce. *Anything* inherited and replicable can influence its own frequency in later generations. The evolution and global spread of agriculture attests to the potent influence domesticated plants and animals had on the successful proliferation of humans. Thus, in the case of pastoralism, the reproduction of domestic animals must occur for this tradition to persist over any number of generations.

Wallace and Hoebel suggest that Comanches "became real pastoralists" because they practiced husbandry. But animal husbandry is not a condition necessary for the identification of pastoralism among humans. Domesticated animals simply needed to reproduce on their own in order for this behavior to have been passed along to later human generations. Controlling the reproduction of livestock only allowed people to better manage the possibility that the pastoralist tradition would be successfully bestowed upon future generations. Thus, Étienne Veniard de Bourgmont's 1724 report that the Comanches he visited had not been successful at raising any colts does not preclude the existence of a pastoralist tradition among them at that time in history. According to Bourgmont, Comanches acquired their mounts through trade with New Mexico, where horses were bred. It is clear that Comanches had learned how to raise colts sometime prior to 1786. In May of that year, Francisco Xavier Ortiz visited a gathering of eight Comanche *rancherías* on the northeast frontier of New Mexico. He observed that the smallest encampment of thirty teepees had "nine hundred beasts of burden, with the item of five herds of branded mares, with young up to three years." Several years earlier, Athanase de Mézières had characterized Comanches and other Indians of Texas as horse breeders, stating that they were "skillful in the management of the horse, to the raising of which they devote themselves." In an 1828 report on the Indian tribes of Texas, Francisco Ruíz flatly declared that Comanches raised horses.[53]

Not only did Comanches raise horses, they clearly made use of the animals' strength and energy for defense, the transportation of people and goods, and in their general hunting activities, most notably those associated with the pursuit of bison. Speaking of the Indians' use of horses, George Catlin specifically noted that the equine "has been of great service to the Indians living on these vast plains, enabling them to take their game more easily, to carry their burthens, &c." Josiah Gregg described Indian equestrian hunting practices: "Indians as well as Mexicans, hunt the buffalo mostly with the bow and arrow. For this purpose they train their fleetest horses to run close beside him; and, when near enough . . . they pierce him with their arrows, usually behind the short ribs, ranging forward, which soon disables and brings him to the ground." Gregg specifically remarked that the dexterity required for hunting bison in this manner "is perhaps superior to any other tribe." Interestingly, there are very few detailed observations of the Comanches' use of horses in hunting and transportation. Whenever historical observers of the Indians mentioned these practices, they did so in a manner that suggests such uses for horses were patently obvious to anyone living at the time — especially to the inhabitants of Spanish provinces. For instance, Athanase de Mézières's 1770 description of the Comanches made mention of the Indians' skillful horsemanship, hunting, and nomadic activity without ever explicitly describing their behavior associated with these activities. But they had no need for this type of description. All persons familiar with the Spanish traditions associated with horses would have clearly understood how Comanches put their animals to work.[54]

The general view of pastoralism maintains that people engaged in this pursuit either consume some nutritional product of their herd animals such as meat, milk (and milk products like cheese and butter), and blood or utilize some material such as hair or wool naturally produced by herd animals. But neither of these behaviors is necessary for the existence of pastoralism. It is clear that Comanches periodically consumed horseflesh. Jose Francisco Ruíz mentioned in a deposition on the Indians drafted sometime in the 1840s that he knew them to have "frequently" consumed horses. Robert Neighbors reported in the 1850s to Henry Schoolcraft, "when pressed by hunger from scarcity of game, they subsist on their young horses and mules. The flesh of the young wildhorse is considered a delicacy."[55] Although Comanches ate horses from time to time, their interest in horse pastoralism did not stem from this. Their interest in horses came primarily from their employment of the animals in hunting, trade, travel, and defense.

Thus, Comanches exhibited all four necessary and sufficient conditions for the existence of pastoralism. Individuals owned domesticated animals in the form of horses. They bequeathed their livestock to surviving relatives. The animals reproduced. And lastly, individuals made use of some consequence of the animal's behavior. Unfortunately, exactly when these Indians began to exhibit these fundamental pastoralist traits cannot be precisely determined. It is possible that their development occurred among some individuals prior to the appearance of Comanches in New Mexico. Nevertheless, the early eighteenth century should be considered a time when more and more Comanches incorporated pastoralism into their traditional culture. At a 1719 war council held in Santa Fe, Capt. Francisco Bueno y Bohorques reported that "according to the common opinion of the Indians of the rest of the frontiers, . . . [Utes and Comanches] have appeared in greater numbers than that in which they are accustomed to go about." Indeed, the ever-increasing presence of Comanches in New Mexico during the second decade of the 1700s might have come about as a result of their realization of the social benefits of pastoralism. It is clear that Comanches sought horses in their early raids on New Mexico. The stated opinions of Juan de Archibeque and Joseph Truxillo at the same council meeting attested to this motivation for the Indians' presence in the province.[56]

Comanches undoubtedly practiced pastoralism by the early nineteenth century, but this behavior can only be assumed to have developed in the preceding century. De Mézières's comment on the expertise demonstrated by Comanches and other Indians in Texas in the raising of horses implies the existence of pastoralist behavior among the Indians in 1778. Only ten years later, in 1789, did evidence of personal ownership of horses appear in historical documents. Evidence for inheritance of these animals during this century has not been found to date, but the logic behind the concepts of culture and tradition strongly suggest that Comanches of the eighteenth century engaged in this behavior as well.

Because cultural behavior is activity that is learned from another individual and then reproduced, there appears a close similarity between several features of Comanche and Spanish culture. The examination of the Indian's material and behavioral culture associated with horses demonstrates that they obviously mimicked the Spanish in their use of such things as horse tack, lassos, corrals, lances, herding techniques, and livestock markings and decorations. This evidence leads to the conclusion that Comanche horse culture was ultimately a manifestation of an aspect of Spanish pastoralism.

This conclusion does not necessarily mean that Comanches learned horse pastoralism directly from the Europeans. These Indians may have been recipients of Iberian behavior through cultural intermediaries, as suggested by their close association with Utes at the beginning of the eighteenth century. Like Pueblos, Apaches, and Navajos, Utes successfully learned and copied from the Spanish the various behaviors associated with maintaining horses. The moment this cultural activity became acquired by successive generations of Indians, it became part of those peoples' tradition. The first Comanches to have familiarized themselves with horses were probably recipients of Spanish tradition via the

Utes. Thus, the ancestral nature of cultural traditions suggests that Comanches became inheritors of pastoralism, probably early on, when some individuals were closely associated with Utes. That Comanches and many other Indians throughout Spanish North and South America acquired aspects of the Old World pastoralist tradition ultimately attests to its positive cumulative effect on the ability of various peoples and domestic animals to successfully endure and reproduce.

Like Old World peoples, American Indians realized the positive effects brought about by the ownership of sheep, goats, pigs, cattle, and horses. Obviously, economic and environmental considerations are deeply involved in pastoralism, but they do not explain the fundamental significance of human ownership of domestic animals.[57] The social nature of livestock ownership is probably best exemplified by Comanche marriage practices involving the gift of horses as part of the "bride price" a husband presented to his wife's family. Ruíz stated that "[when a] girl is purchased from her father or brother; the price is a horse." Berlandier closely echoed Ruíz, noting that "each wife costs her husband a gun, a horse, a mule, or a quantity of meat which he gives her family." Pedro Bautista Pino of New Mexico described the Comanche marriage ceremony as "solemnized by means of the exchange of gifts. The groom gives the father of the bride either horses or true accounts of military feats, and then receives his bride."[58]

These observers generally interpreted Comanche marriages in terms of economic exchanges. This interpretation ultimately misses the point of the ritual involved in paying the bride price. The livestock as well as the other property exchanged in this "ceremony" have social rather than economic significance. Like "true accounts of military feats," horses given away to a bride's family represented the generous nature of the groom as a potential husband and father. Thus, the practice of the bride price was not an exchange of commodities (that is, horses for women) but a demonstration of one's willingness to sacrifice one's interests in favor of another. In other words, the exchange of horses associated with Comanche marriages demonstrated social, not economic, behavior. While pastoralism has an important economic effect, the basis of this practice, as suggested by the role of horses in the bride price, is founded in Comanche social and kinship behavior.

CHAPTER 4

The Nature of
Comanche Economics

IN 1776 FR. FRAY FRANCISCO ATANASIO DOMÍNGUEZ DETAILED
the commercial activity he witnessed among Comanches and New Mexicans at Taos. He noted that the Indians entered the pueblo particularly at
times when they "are on their good behavior." During these peaceful interludes,
Comanches could be as friendly with the Taoseños as they could be their implacable enemies in times of hostility. As an amicable embassy of Indians called
upon the settlement, excitement gripped the pueblo's inhabitants. Twenty-six
years earlier, Fray Andrés Varo commented on the enthusiasm exhibited by
Taoseños at the arrival of a large Comanche trading party to the villa. Dismayed,
the priest noted that Spanish and Indian Christians abandoned "all prudence" as
they eagerly anticipated the lucrative exchange. New Mexicans called these
events *ferias,* and indeed, the periodic congregations of people from pueblo and
plains oftentimes took on the atmosphere of a medieval carnival complete with
commercial ventures, various amusements, competitions, and the ever-present
threat of rampant disorder.[1]

Trade served as the primary focus of these gatherings. Multitudes of people
would mill about the trading grounds, where Comanches busily exchanged bison
hides and meat, horses, mules, captives, guns, pistols, powder, tobacco, hatchets,
and tin pots in return for knives, bridles, corn and corn meal, horses, mules,
cloaks, blankets, and numerous other trifles. Father Domínguez declared that
the trading activity he witnessed at Taos "resembl[ed] a second-hand market in
Mexico."[2] Great quantities of goods passed hands many times during the event.

Domínguez reported that people traded one bison hide for a broad iron knife known as a *belduque*. Bridles cost two hides or a tin pot, while maize and meal were exchanged directly for tasty and nutritious bison meat. Traders especially esteemed twelve- to twenty-year-old captive girls—far more than they did those of a higher age or any males. A Comanche could exchange one of his or her prized female servants for two good horses and other associated items, including cloaks and blankets used to cover and decorate mounts. In one case, a mule with an attendant scarlet cover was the price for a young girl. Mules, the barren offspring of horses and donkeys, were relatively rare and highly valued as work and pack animals by Comanches and New Mexicans alike. Accordingly, these animals fetched "either a cover or a short cloak or a good horse," while the latter animal simply elicited offers of "a poor bridle, but garnished with rags." A pistol equaled a bridle, but these items together could pay for a horse. Based on his observations of this behavior, Domínguez concluded that Comanches "are great traders, for as soon as they buy anything, they usually sell exactly what they bought."[3]

The priest observed a general friendliness among the Comanches with whom the New Mexicans engaged in trade. Years later, the American trader Josiah Gregg noticed a similar demonstration of friendly behavior among some Comanches he encountered in 1839 while traveling across the plains from Fort Smith, Arkansas, to Santa Fe. A few days after arriving at Camp Holmes, Indian Territory, in mid-May, "a party of Comanches, who having heard of our approach came to greet us a welcome, on the supposition that it was their friend [Missouri trader Auguste Pierre] Chouteau returning to the fort with fresh supplies of merchandise."[4] Interested in learning whether or not the Canadian River valley was suited for the passage of heavily laden wagons, Gregg and his men sought out the chief of the visiting Indians. They soon found themselves introduced to Tabequena, "a corpulent, squint-eyed old fellow, who certainly had nothing in his personal appearance indicative of rank or dignity." Presented with pencil and paper, Tabequena roughly drew up a document that bore "much to our astonishment, quite a map-like appearance" and informed the wayfarers "the route up the Canadian presented no obstacles according to *his* mode of traveling." On May 18 Gregg's caravan departed in the direction of Santa Fe, while the Indians headed east toward Fort Gibson, situated in eastern Indian Territory on the banks of the Neosho River just above its confluence with the Arkansas. The following day, "Tábba-quena, and another Comanche chief, with five or six warriors, and as many squaws, including Tab's wife and infant son" caught up to Gregg and his men, communicating that they had aborted their trip to Fort Gibson in order "to return home for better horses." That night, the Indians encamped alongside the company of traders. In the morning, the chief revealed his true motivation for breaking away from the others bound for the fort, "inform[ing] us that some of his party had a few 'mulas para *swap*' [*sic*]." Upon this request, "a barter for five mules was immediately concluded upon, much to our advantage, as our teams were rather in a weak condition." Once the trade for the animals had been settled, the Comanches departed for their people who, as they informed Gregg, were located on the False Washita River.

The caravan once again encountered Comanches a couple of weeks later somewhere north of the Canadian River just west of the one hundredth meridian. On June 8 some three hundred Comanches, "including women and children," appeared before the traders as they enjoyed a noontime rest in a ravine. Gregg noted the commercial nature of the visit, observing that the Indians "had brought several mules in the expectation of driving a trade with us." As the women and children milled excitedly about the merchandise-laden wagons, the chiefs suggested that Gregg and his men distract them by carrying some goods to a central area where a trade could be opened. This done, a bartering process began. Gregg explained that "in Comanche trade the main trouble consists in fixing the price of the first animal," the value of which was settled by the chiefs. Upon the establishment of a rate of exchange, "it often happens that mule after mule is led up and the price received without further cavil." Understandably, the Indians demanded a general assortment of goods in exchange for their livestock. Thus, Gregg and his men departed with a reduced surplus of blankets, mirrors, awls, flints, tobacco, vermilion, and beads.[5]

Both Domínguez and Gregg observed a general friendliness among the Comanches with whom they engaged in trade. Domínguez used his description of Comanche trading activity at Taos as evidence to show that even though the Indians oftentimes demonstrated "so execrable an extreme of evil that the Catholic arms of our beloved Sovereign alone will be able to destroy it . . . they [could] also [be] extremely good when they are in the mood." Gregg later suggested an explanation for the good disposition exhibited by the Indians Domínguez witnessed at Taos. He noted that Comanches' fondness of commercial traffic encouraged them to be friendly to those with whom they traded. Furthermore, Gregg mentioned that the Indians welcomed the presence of traders among their people and that they generally did not commit depredations upon those foreign agents of commerce. Rather, they tended to protect those with whom they associated commercially. Gregg recognized that Comanches and other Indians acknowledged a strong connection between commerce and friendly or social behavior.[6]

Friendliness did not always epitomize Comanche trade. Hostility always loomed underneath the surface of commercial interactions and relations no matter how friendly the various transactions appeared. Among his instructions to Francisco Marín del Valle in August, 1754, New Mexico governor Thomas Vélez Cachupín advised his successor to try and maintain the "perfect and faithful friendship" that he had labored to establish between the province and the Indians. He warned Marín del Valle that he should "use the greatest efforts and observe faithfully whatever conduces to pleasing their spirits without permitting, on the occasions when they come to trade at the pueblo of Taos, the settlers and

Pueblo Indians, who also attend, to do them the slightest injury." According to Vélez Cachupín, Comanches considered extortion a very serious offense and often responded to such behavior with violence. Indeed, Vélez Cachupín had in mind such an outbreak of violence that had reportedly occurred at a Taos fair sometime in the 1740s during Joachín Codallos y Rabál's tenure as governor.[7]

While Gregg experienced nothing but good behavior among the Comanches he encountered, he learned of some of the dangers inherent in these commercial interactions from some New Mexican traders, or *Comancheros,* who managed to overtake his party en route to Santa Fe. The New Mexicans reported that they had been with those same Comanches Gregg and his party had recently encountered north of the Canadian River. After hearing from the Indians that the Americans were making their way toward New Mexico, the *Comancheros* hurried to overtake them in order to enjoy the safety of a larger caravan. Gregg found out that the traders were especially desirous of their protection because the Indians "very frequently" attacked them on their return home and would take "forcible possession" of the livestock they had previously purchased. Even though Gregg somewhat contemptuously dismissed the New Mexicans' fears, he observed "that they had considered themselves in great jeopardy, there could be no doubt whatever, for, in their anxiety to overtake us, they came very near killing their animals."[8]

These descriptions of Comanche trade are for the most part indicative of the general nature of that nation's commercial activities in the eighteenth and nineteenth centuries. As Domínguez reported, Comanches frequently visited the various pueblos and towns located within the proximity of the Comanchería and engaged the local population in a relatively lucrative and diverse trade. Taos served as the predominant center of Comanche trade in eighteenth-century New Mexico, but the Indians also sold their various wares and livestock at other communities around the province. The few settlements in Texas also entertained Comanche visitors from time to time. The scale of trade with Tejanos appears to never have approached the level of that in New Mexico. Nomadic and sedentary villages of the surrounding tribes also served as major commercial outlets for Comanche goods, and the Caddoan-speaking tribes played an especially large role in this activity. Josiah Gregg's accounts reported on another important aspect of Comanche trade, namely that of the pedestrian trader who encountered Comanches in their own villages. This behavior certainly became more widespread in New Mexico and Texas beginning in the late eighteenth century, but there is evidence that traders visited nearby Comanche camps early in the 1700s.

As Vélez Cachupín noted, and as Gregg later learned from *Comancheros,* trading with Comanches could be a congenial and dangerous experience at the same time. The tenuous circumstance of violence always loomed over this activity, whether it took place at government-regulated trade fairs among the New Mexican pueblos or in the isolated camps and trading locations scattered about the Comanchería. Overall, the Comanche trade economy encompassed a wide range of material goods, geographical settings, peoples, and attitudes.

A recent study reiterates that the ownership of property among humans in the distant and not so distant past has been motivated primarily by social rather than purely selfish aspirations. This observation hints that social behavior is fundamentally associated with economic behavior in general. The basic connection between trade and social behavior is usually not recognized. Adam Smith sensed this relationship when he suggested that trade is not a zero-sum proposition with a distinct winner and a loser. Instead, commercial activity should be seen as beneficial to both of the sides that engage in it, even though each participant is motivated by a selfish ambition to profit in some fashion.[9]

Take, for example, the Comanches and Spanish subjects Father Domínguez apparently witnessed at a 1776 Taos trade fair. Each participant had to consider foremost his or her own self-interest; neither the Comanche nor the Spanish traders necessarily had the other's interests in mind. Conceivably, each one tried to gain a perceived advantage as they negotiated the rate of exchange between such things as bison hides and *bedulques*. As the priest reported, Comanches purveyed the hides, while New Mexicans supplied the large metal knives. The objects of bison hides and *bedulques* thus represented the existence of a division of labor that had arisen out of various individuals' specializations. Comanche men, women, and children procured the hides they brought to New Mexico. Spaniards, Mexicans, and allied Indians mined the iron and then manufactured, transported, and traded the knives. Thus, Comanches and Spaniards each manufactured and owned property that the other desired. Of course, New Mexicans wanted bison hides chiefly for their use as material for garments, tarpaulins, and other such items. Comanches desired metal knives for their general-purpose utility as a cutting instrument. Because of this division of labor, the selfish desires of individual Comanches and New Mexicans to profit from trading with one another could both be satisfied.[10] Domínguez reported that bison hides and *bedulques* traded at a ratio of one to one. The traders profited because each one received something they considered valuable in return for a commodity regarded as less valuable.

American traders commented on the great profit they acquired by trading with Comanches. Thomas James boasted that in 1823 he purchased a bison robe for "one plug of tobacco, a knife and a few strings of beads, in all worth but little more than a dime." He further claimed that "one of these valuable skins . . . [was] worth at least five dollars in any of the states." Gregg mentioned that each of the mules he received from Comanches cost between ten and twenty dollars worth of goods. From Gregg's point of view, this price weighed heavily to his advantage. Traders, teamsters, and emigrants gathering in Missouri especially desired mules, primarily because of their superior endurance in comparison to oxen. Because of the high demand for these animals in the Show Me State, they generally fetched anywhere between sixty and seventy-five dollars for stock traders in the late 1840s and early 1850s. The readers of the initial 1844 printing of *Commerce of the Prairies* certainly would have understood the commercial implications of Gregg's experiences in the Comanche mule trade.[11]

Comanches themselves explained why they could sell mules and horses so cheaply. An unnamed chief visiting Natchitoches, Louisiana, in October, 1807, announced to U.S. Indian agent Dr. John Sibley that he and his people desired the Americans to send traders among them. He stated that Comanches had become familiar with the goods Americans had to offer because they received various items from those Indians who lived close to Louisiana (the Caddoan-speaking tribes). Encouraging Sibley to open up a direct commerce, the chief divulged that the non-Comanche Indians involved with them in this trade had profited handsomely, receiving "a Horse or a Mule for a Narrow Strip of Scarlet Cloth, or a Small Parcel of Vermillion." The chief undoubtedly knew of Americans' great desire to acquire these animals. Since the 1790s, people such as Philip Nolan, John S. Lewis, James Elliot, Anthony Glass, and others had made a career of eluding the Spanish authorities in Texas and entering the plains in search of equines. Besides, when a party of eighty Comanches visited Natchitoches earlier in August, they suffered the loss of at least twenty-five horses to local thieves. With the Americans' desire for horses in mind, the chief attending Sibley's October council emphasized to the Indian agent that they had plenty of animals with which to satisfy the needs of the people living in Louisiana, Mississippi, and points farther east. He exclaimed, "Horses and Mules were to them like grass they had them in Such plenty." In exchange for these animal resources, the chief expressed a desire to procure firearms, something scarce among his own people and abundant among Americans.[12]

The Comanche demonstrated his understanding of the basic economics associated with the division of labor and supply and demand. He obviously knew that he and his people were able to acquire horses and mules at a relatively low cost. Horses and mules were "like grass" to Comanches and thus practically free of cost for them. But he also understood that Americans had less access to these resources and at much greater cost. During the period of Spanish domination in Texas, American traders from Louisiana and Mississippi had to expend much time and energy to keep from being arrested for trespassing by the Spanish authorities. If they succeeded in this endeavor, they then had to expend additional resources to ensure their own protection from hostile Indians and the environment. Finally, if these traders did capture some horses and mules, they then had to dedicate themselves to protecting and transporting their investment back to friendly territory.

Similar concerns weighed upon Comanches with regard to their desire for the various goods they acquired in trade. Comanches had neither the necessary access to resources nor a knowledgeable division of labor with which to manufacture things they coveted such as firearms, ammunition, horticultural produce, cloth, vermilion, tobacco, blankets, beads, knives, and metal pots. Such articles became highly valued among Comanches because of their desire for them and the requisite investment of time and energy necessary to procure, manufacture, transport, and protect the products that allowed them to access imported goods. American trader Jacob Fowler commented on this aspect of Comanche commerce in 1821, noting that the Indians had "many [w]ants" but that they did not have the "means of [s]upplying them."[13]

Fowler found that horses were all that the Indians had to exchange for his various trade goods. Unfortunately for the Comanches, Fowler and his men did not voyage up the Arkansas River in search of horses. Instead, they sought out beaver pelts that, as they discovered, were scarce in the country that Comanches inhabited.[14] Because commercial relationships like those that existed between Comanches and Euro-Americans were based on individuals' specific demands and a division of labor, the relationship between these peoples should not necessarily be viewed as exploitative or as one based on dependency. Instead, it should be understood as a mutual relationship in which each participant benefited. Comanches profited by trading abundant and cheaply produced local commodities for various goods that they greatly desired but could not manufacture. Euro-Americans and horticultural Indians from New Mexico, Texas, Louisiana, the Indian Territory, and Missouri also gained from the Comanche trade because they acquired items such as horses, mules, and bison hides in exchange for goods they manufactured and considered as having lesser value.

If the division of labor and supply and demand can explain Comanches' commercial relations with Euro-Americans and horticultural Indians, then how can their trade relations with other Plains Indians such as the Cheyennes be explained? Both peoples lived in an area where they had relatively easy access to equine and bison resources. Each tribe lived in the same type of environment and enjoyed similar lifestyles associated with horse pastoralism and bison hunting. For the most part, Comanches and Cheyennes do not represent societies with any degree of division of labor. Much of the trade between Plains Indians was of a "redundant" nature. In other words, Indians who raised, procured, or manufactured the same items traded those goods among themselves, for instance, the exchange of horses and bison robes between Comanches and Cheyennes. Explaining this commerce has become problematic because it would appear that the members of the tribes who produced similar commodities could not have had a reason to engage in trade with each other. The traditional approach to this conundrum has been to suggest that unpredictable environmental conditions such as droughts and floods encouraged people to trade for commodities temporarily diminished by poor environments.[15]

Obviously, environmental factors sometimes influenced the needs and desires of Comanches. Spanish documents reported that a drought occurring in the

late 1780s affected the availability of bison on the southern plains, thereby resulting in the starvation of many Comanches. Yet this episode demonstrates that environmental difficulties did not necessarily result in trade. Rather, it had a stifling
effect on commerce. In June, 1788, New Mexico governor Concha reported to his
superior in Chihuahua that Comanches had not appeared to trade among the various pueblos of the province since the preceding November. The reason for the
Indians' absence, Concha informed, was due to the disappearance of bison from
the Comanchería. The Indians were broke. Without bison to hunt, they could
not produce the bison robes and meat with which they bought food and durable
goods from the New Mexicans. Comanches could not possibly have been able to
compensate for their lack of food by engaging in trade with New Mexicans or
even with other Indians, who shared their subsistence patterns, due to their tem-
porary state of poverty. Concerned with the impoverishment of his people, Chief
Ecueracapa visited Santa Fe that June and petitioned the governor to send them
desperately needed aid. Concha obliged the chief by shipping several wagons
laden with over two hundred bushels of corn to the starving Indians.[16]

Even though hungry Comanches received a generous allotment of food aid
from Governor Concha, this action cannot be considered trade or commerce.
The Indians exchanged nothing in return for the maize. They acquired the food
only by the grace and generosity of the governor and the people of New Mexico.
Concha's beneficence involved a social behavior that is fundamental to acts of
commerce as well as charity. One of the primary differences between commercial
exchange and charity is that the former requires each participant to sacrifice selfish interests in favor of the other. This idea may seem contradictory in regard to
the earlier realization that the selfish ambition to profit motivates individuals to
engage in commerce, but the contradiction is merely an apparent one that does
not hold up to further investigation.

Adam Smith suggested (rightly) that people's selfish desires motivate the
commerce that exists between them, but he did not fully understand the social
mechanisms underlying this behavior. More recently, the social mechanisms of
trade have been understood as an effect of the segregation of humans into territorial groups and the division of labor that naturally accompanies their territoriality. This explanation falls short because of the inherent insufficiency of group
explanations for people's behavior.[17] Rather, Comanches' commercial behavior
should be seen as an effect of individuals' social and kinship behavior, personal
interests, and division of labor. Kinship, and the social behavior it promoted,
served as the primary facilitator of interaction between Comanches and of their
relations with others.

The trade of material goods among human ancestors is probably an ancient
behavior originating perhaps as early as 1.4 million years ago.[18] The earliest form
of "commerce" probably resulted from the specialization and cooperation that
existed between mothers, fathers, children, and siblings as they shared the fruits

of their labors with one another. Humans' use of kin terms and clan names has allowed them to identify a great number of distantly related and geographically dispersed individuals with whom they could cooperate in many ways. One way people have interacted with their relatives has been through the exchange of material goods. As Concha's donation of corn to the Comanches in 1788 suggest, gift giving and commerce are closely related. It is possible that the difference between the two behaviors might originally have had something to do with the genealogical distance between the individuals involved. A person probably would have been more apt to give an item to a child or brother than to a distantly related nephew or cousin. The realization that gift giving and trade emerged from basic human social and kinship behavior sheds a good deal of light on the patterns of Comanche trade and acquisition of goods in the eighteenth and nineteenth centuries.

The incorporation of Comanches into the complex web of kinship relationships existing throughout New Mexico in the early eighteenth century not only precipitated their movement into the region but also gave them direct access to the province's commercial system. Clearly, Comanches' close association with Utes in the beginning of the 1700s brought about their introduction to the place and peoples of New Mexico. As Juan de Ulibarri noted in 1706, Comanches and Utes did not initially enter New Mexico with the purpose of establishing a lucrative trade. Instead, they threatened places such as Taos, Ojo Caliente, and San Juan with brigandage and violence.[19] The large captive trade centered in northern New Mexico may have helped initiate much of this violence as Utes and Comanches sought retribution for Apaches' abduction and sale of their relatives to the citizens of the province.

Taoseños especially assumed a large role in the captive trade during the early 1700s. By November, 1703, the inhabitants of this village had become accustomed to traveling to Jicarilla and other Apache *rancherías,* where they would exchange two or three horses for a captive boy or girl. Alarmed by this behavior, the *cabildo* of Santa Fe officially petitioned Governor Diego de Vargas to prohibit anyone in Taos from trading with Apaches outside of the jurisdiction of New Mexico. Governor Vargas's consequent decree prohibiting this activity apparently had little effect. In the following year, Acting Governor Juan Paez Hurtado reported that individuals from Taos and Pecos continued to enter the Apache camps with the purpose of conducting trade.[20]

The early-eighteenth-century accounts make no mention of the identity of those captives traded by Apaches to New Mexicans, but it is probable that some were Utes and Comanches. Ulibarri's documentation of Ute and Comanche aggressions against Apaches in 1706 suggests that their hostile relationship had originated some time prior to this date, and it is known that both tribes of Indians often took many enemy captives in their battles. The appearance in Santa Fe of Escalchufines and Paloma Apaches with Comanche prisoners in 1726 encourages the idea that some of those captives traded to New Mexicans in the earlier part of the century may have been Utes and Comanches.[21] The details of this trade are lacking, but it stands to reason that Comanches first became intimately associated with New Mexico through this sort of exchange.

Nevertheless, it did not take too long before social ties became established between the New Mexicans and their former Ute and Comanche enemies. Gov. Juan Ygnacio Flores Mogollon's order of December, 1712, prohibiting New Mexicans from visiting the *rancherías* of the Jicarilla and Cuartelejo Apaches, Utes, and other Indians inhabiting the plains insinuates that social and commercial relationships had become established between Comanches and New Mexicans by this time. According to a statement made by Capt. Cristóbal de la Serna in 1719, New Mexican officials had previously arranged a formal peace with Utes and Comanches sometime between 1707 and 1712 during the administration of Gov. José Chacón Medina Salazar y Villaseñor, marqués de la Peñuela.[22] This fortuitous development surely would have promoted the commercial relations that Governor Flores Mogollon sought to regulate.

An incident taking place in 1735 at Ojo Caliente demonstrated how social relationships between Comanches and New Mexicans helped facilitate commerce. On the first day of April, five or six *rancherías* of Comanches arrived at the village and proceeded to the house of Lieutenant *Alcalde Mayor* Diego Torres with the hope of opening a trade fair. Torres was not home when the Indians arrived, so they waited for his return until three or four o'clock. When neither he nor the *alcalde mayor* appeared, the Comanches prepared to depart the settlement because they feared that their newfound Ute enemies were nearby. Apparently irritated by the wasted trade opportunity, the Comanches angrily huffed that the inaction proved to them that the Spaniards preferred trading with the Utes. According to Juan García de Mora, he and several others followed the agitated Comanches to their camps in order to open up an exchange in an effort to appease them. When they arrived, they discovered Torres's Comanche servant with a pile of bison robes loaded on the back of his horse. García de Mora and Torres each charged the other with trading with Comanches outside of the law and the customary regulations. After hearing the declaration of several witness presented on behalf of both defendants, Gov. Gervasio Cruzat y Gongora convicted both men of illegal trade.[23]

This episode provides some insight into how social relationships influenced commerce between Comanches and New Mexicans. That the Comanches initially appeared at Torres's residence seeking to officially open a trade fair was most likely not simply a consequence of his official position as lieutenant *alcalde mayor* of the jurisdiction. If that had been the case, the Indians would have sought out the primary *alcalde mayor* just as well. Rather, they approached Torres because they recognized his Comanche servant as a kinsman. Apparently the lieutenant *alcalde mayor* realized the social and commercial advantage his servant gave him in the Comanche trade and used him to circumvent the provincial regulations intended to make this type of enterprise fair and safe for everyone. Unfortunately for Torres, García de Mora and the other residents of Ojo Caliente also knew how this relationship could be used to give one an unfair advantage.

Most Comanche trade with the New Mexican settlements is probably not well represented in the documentary sources because of the subtleties associated with the social and kin relationships between Comanches and New Mexicans. Torres's Comanche servant essentially served as a social and economic link between these two communities. As a Comanche, he could interact with other Comanches, and he did so freely. As a servant, the Indian maintained a social relationship with Torres, who, in turn, had other cooperative relationships extending into Spanish and Pueblo Indian societies. Trade fairs such as those held in Taos and later in Pecos are conspicuous within the documentary accounts because of their official nature. Many times the governor attended and presided over these events in person to ensure fairness and to guard against various abuses perpetrated by the traders.[24] Yet the initial desire of those Comanches at Ojo Caliente in 1735 to engage in an officially authorized trade fair demonstrates that even this context of exchange ultimately derived from the social relationships existing between various Comanches and New Mexicans.

The trade conducted outside the official bounds of the trade fair has been known as the *Comanchero* trade. Generally, this activity has been thought to have emerged as a result of the peace Governor Anza and Chief Ecueracapa established between their peoples in 1786. Upon closer examination, it appears that this Comanche commerce predated the peace treaty by many years. The periodic decrees and orders issued by the various governors of the province are good evidence for the occurrence of this type of trade throughout the eighteenth century. Mogollon's 1712 order against visiting the "wild Indians" for the purposes of trade acknowledges that New Mexicans "had on many occasions gone to the *rancherías*" of the Jicarillas, Cuartelejos, Utes, and the Indians of the plains in order "to do their trade fairs." At that time, Comanches maintained a close connection with Utes and probably were involved in the activities that concerned Mogollon. Gov. Henrique Olavide y Michelena issued a similar order in 1737 making it illegal to go to Indian villages for trade. The severity of the penalties for engaging in this behavior suggests that this activity must have been fairly widespread. Michelena decreed that offenders were subject to a fine of two hundred pesos in silver and the confiscation of all goods. For those who could not afford the monetary penalty, two hundred lashes would be administered instead. Seventeen years later, Gov. Francisco Marín del Valle reissued regulations against going to the camps of Comanches in either day or night under the pretext of having the authority to open up a trade. Once again, the governor announced harsh penalties for those persons committing such crimes — either a five-hundred-peso fine or five hundred lashes in public display.[25]

The various governors of New Mexico realized that control of this unregulated trade was very hard to achieve. The difficulty of this task resulted from the geographic dispersal of Spanish settlements and Indian pueblos and the increase of personal kinship and social ties between the citizens of the province and Comanches. The number of Comanches baptized in New Mexico rose from only three in the 1720s to a total of fifty-seven in the 1780s.[26] Many of these individuals probably entered New Mexico as captives of enemy Apaches and Utes, though some may have arrived voluntarily. Nevertheless, these numbers suggest that Comanches lived among New Mexican communities during the eighteenth century and thus provided potential social and commercial links to their relatives remaining on the plains.

At the request of the missionaries, Gov. Gaspar de Mendoza established the settlements of Valencia and Cerro de Tomé in 1740 for Indians of various nations that had been taken captive by Comanches, Apaches, Navajos, and Utes. The New Mexicans called these former captives *genízaros,* a term borrowed from the Turks for an infantry troop made up of a mixture of slaves and conscripts. Besides Valencia and Tomé, *genízaros* lived throughout New Mexico. Other *genízaro* land grants were established near Abiquiu and Ojo Caliente in 1754. In 1776 Fray Francisco Atanasio Domínguez noted the presence of former captives in Santa Fe, Santa Clara, Abiquiu, and Belén.[27]

Near the turn of the nineteenth century, San Miguel del Vado, south of Pecos pueblo on the Pecos River, became a new center of *genízaro* settlement. Among the village's original residents, thirteen persons, a full 25 percent, claimed *genízaro* status.[28] San Miguel became known throughout New Mexico and the Comanchería as a hub for the Comanche trade, as Indians made commercial visits to the village and resident *Comancheros* journeyed onto the plains in search for trade. Again, this activity emerged from the various kinship and social connections existing between Comanches and San Miguel residents.

One individual living in San Miguel who had close ties to Comanches was Alejandro Martín. His relationship with Comanches came about as a result of his abduction from Tomé in 1775 and an eleven-year captivity among the Indians. A Comanche named Tosapoy presented Martín at the 1786 Pecos peace-treaty ceremony to a Spaniard with whom the Indian had a personal quarrel. Shortly after receiving his freedom, Martín began serving the provincial government as an official interpreter of the Comanche language. In 1804 Gov. Fernando de Chacón removed Martín from the service of Chief Quegüe and transferred him to San Miguel, where he helped mediate various transactions between the settlers and Comanches. Another resident of San Miguel who had close ties to the Indians was a Comanche named José Cristóbal Guerrero.[29] Martín and Guerrero probably represented a good number of San Miguel's inhabitants, who could have either boasted of an intimate social familiarity with Comanches or traced their ancestry to the Indians.

Josiah Gregg's brief biography of Manuel, a Comanche who guided Gregg across the plains toward Van Buren, Arkansas, in 1840, is a good illustration of how these social and commercial connections became forged throughout New Mexico. According to Gregg, Manuel had been born and reared on the prairies as "a full Indian." As an adult, Manuel frequently interacted with *Comancheros* from San Miguel, and one day he accompanied them back to their village. It was there, Gregg recounted, that Manuel met a "Mexican girl" with whom "he fell in love." When Manuel and the girl married, he became a resident of San Miguel and, as Gregg put it, "has lived in that place, a sober, 'civilized' citizen for the last ten or twelve years."[30]

Alejandro Martín's report to Gov. Real Alencaster on his visit to the villages of the Yamparica chief Somiquaso in late 1805 suggests that close social and commercial connections existing between New Mexicans and Comanches extended beyond San Miguel and into the upper Rio Grande valley. When Martín arrived among Somiquaso's people, he noticed that the Indians were "well supplied and . . . [exhibited] all the signs of having traded with those from this province." For this reason, Martín and his men had little success in striking up commerce with the Indians. Frustrated, he blamed this situation on "the continuous trade [the Comanches] *have always had and still have* with the residents of the Río Arriba and jurisdiction of La Cañada, who continually, in spite of the restriction, *live among them* and are the ones of worst conduct in all the province, and with some *genízaros* and *gentiles* from [San Miguel] el Bado who were baptized" (emphasis added).[31]

Americans traveling across the southern plains during the first half of the nineteenth century often came across *Comancheros*. While traveling along the upper Arkansas River with some Comanches and Kiowas in December, 1821, Jacob Fowler learned from the Indians that they were expecting "to meet the [Spaniards] on the River above this place to [trade] With them." Earlier that year Thomas James and his party of traders encountered on the plains about fifty Spaniards who "had come from Santa Fe with their Comanche allies . . . to hunt for buffalo." Gregg noted that the *Comancheros* he met in 1838 traded to Comanches "trinkets and trumperies of all kinds" and were very knowledgeable of the Indians. Lt. James W. Abert of the U.S. Army Topographical Engineers came across a band of *Comancheros* along the Canadian River in 1845. He learned that the small collection of Spaniards "had come out [to the plains] under the guidance of . . . [a Taos] Pueblo Indian." When forty-niner Robert B. Green crossed the plains along the Canadian, he found "lots of Mexicans" scattered about the prairies and mesas about 150 miles to the east of Santa Fe.[32]

Observers such as Gregg and Abert generally characterized commercial activities of *Comancheros* as crude and unprofitable. Gregg, who was hauling about $25,000 worth of goods to Santa Fe in 1838, pointed out that the entire stock of an individual *Comanchero* "very seldom exceeds the value of twenty dollars, with which he is content . . . to return home with a mule or two, as the proceeds of his traffic." Likewise, the Americans characterized the people involved in this trade as equally crude. Gregg classified them as belonging to the "indigent and rude classes of the frontier villages." Abert remarked that the traders he came across "presented a shabby and poor appearance though we learned that they were a good specimen [example] of the class to which they belong."[33] These characterizations failed to grasp the essence of this trade. What the Americans witnessed was not a crude and unprofitable trade system but rather an economic extension of complex kinship and social relationships between New Mexicans and Comanches.

Similar kinship and social ties generated Comanches' commercial relationships with the Caddoan-speaking tribes of the southern plains and also the inhabitants of Spanish Texas. There are numerous reports of the friendly relationship between Comanches and Caddoans and the extensive trade that derived from it. Sometime in the late 1740s, Felipe de Sandoval became lost as he attempted to make his way westward to New Mexico. Luckily, he "encountered a [Comanche] youth about twenty-four years of age, who was driving three horses" and accompanied the Indian back to the Panipique, or Wichita, settlement, which Sandoval had departed only a few days before. Upon their arrival to the village, Sandoval noticed that the Panipiques received the Comanche in a cordial manner and exchanged a musket and hand axe for his horses. In 1778 Athanase de Mézières observed that Comanches and the Caddoans of Texas "all visit each other and they observe mutual friendship." Furthermore, he noted that the Comanches "do not hesitate to sell [their Caddoan friends] the horses which the others lack on account of the frequent robberies which they experience from the Apaches and Osagues [Osage]." Pedro Vail and Francisco Xavier Chaves reported to Texas governor Domingo Cabello in 1785 that the "Cumanche Orientales have as friends the Tavoayaces and Guachitas [Wichita] people. . . . Thus they maintain much trade in exchange for salt, which they lack, for which reason [they] frequently come to get it, and, in return, give them whatever they have."[34]

It is not certain if the Comanches traded with Spanish and Anglo Texas on the same scale as they did with the New Mexicans or the Plains Caddoans. It is certain that the Indians did not attend any large official trade fairs in Texas like those held at Taos and Pecos. The Comanche trade in Texas reflected the pattern that existed in New Mexico in that social relationships between individuals formed the basis of this commercial enterprise. Many people with close ties to Comanches, such as Pedro Vial and Francisco Xavier Chaves, both of whom had lived several years among Comanches as captives, called San Antonio de Béxar home in the eighteenth and nineteenth centuries. Vial spent some time in San

Antonio when he was not blazing various trails between Texas and New Mexico; Chaves became a permanent resident of San Antonio. Comanches also lived in the Spanish Texas capital. One such individual named Andrés had accompanied José Mares from Santa Fe to San Antonio in the fall of 1787. Mares, Alejandro Martín, Domingo Maese, Chief Soxas, and six other Comanches set out on the return trip to Santa Fe on January 18, 1788. Andrés, one of the accompanying Indians, returned to San Antonio on the nineteenth, telling Gov. Rafael Martínez Pacheco that he had decided to remain among the Spanish. On several occasions, Andrés served Pacheco as an envoy to the Comanches, visiting them in their *rancherías* and assisting them in San Antonio. Another resident of Béxar who had lived among the Comanches for several years and commanded considerable influence among them was José Francisco Ruíz. In 1811 he joined the insurgents revolting against Spanish authority in Mexico. When royalist troops stationed in Texas defeated the insurrectionists in 1813, Ruíz sought refuge among the Comanches and lived with them for eight years. He informed Jean Louis Berlandier that "when he was [later] assigned to the Comanches, [he] never had occasion to complain of their hospitality."[35]

The presence of persons such as Vial, Chaves, Andrés, and Ruíz in San Antonio made that village the main focus of the Comanche trade in Texas. Undoubtedly, people with similar ties to the Indians lived in other villages and presidios such as Nacogdoches, Bucareli, and la Bahia del Espiritu Santo. During times of peace, Comanches entered the settlements laden with supplies of "bear grease, bison meat, and various furs." They exchanged these goods for items they desired, including "shot and powder, loaves of sugar called *pilloncillos* [*sic*], silver ornaments for themselves and their horses, and sometime weapons such as swords which they use to make their lances, or cheap cloth to make ornaments." Many Comanches visited the villages of Texas from time to time; for instance, ninety-three of them arrived at San Antonio on December 30, 1787.[36] Almost certainly, these people brought along various wares with which to exchange for the miscellaneous items that the inhabitants of San Antonio would sell them.

The commercial situation in Texas became somewhat unsettled for Comanches as Anglo-Americans from the United States immigrated into the region in the 1820s and 1830s. Unlike the Spanish, the Americans generally resisted interacting socially or intermarrying with Indians. Less social connections between Comanches and the "Texians" translated into less commercial opportunities for the Indians. Nevertheless, trade continued in the Republic of Texas, albeit under different terms. Since Texans encouraged Indians to stay away from their settlements, much of the Texas Comanche trade moved farther out into the Comanchería. Various Indians from the Indian Territory regularly served as diplomatic and commercial intermediaries between Texans and Comanches, especially Chickasaws and Delawares. In 1840 a Chickasaw Indian on a trading expedition among the Comanches bought a young boy who had been abducted in

Texas and offered his services to ransom other Texan captives held by the Indians. Delawares such as John Conner and Jim Shaw spent much time among the Comanches and had apparently established enduring social relationships with them. Texas capitalized on these relationships by commissioning Conner and Shaw as political and economic emissaries to the Comanches. In August, 1843, Conner submitted a draft upon the Texas government for $54.50 worth of tobacco, knives, glasses, hatchets, and strouding that he had recently traded to some Comanches. Superintendent of Indian Affairs Thomas G. Western summed up the intermediate role of the Delawares in Texas-Comanche political and commercial relations, stating that "the Delaware are, as it were, the connecting link between us and the Comanche and it is important at this juncture that the best understanding should exist between them."[37]

Official trading posts established along principal rivers also provided Comanches access to Texas markets. Sometimes the trading posts took advantage of preexisting social relationships to gain access to the Comanche trade. In 1850 the trading house of George Barnard and Company on the Brazos River employed Delaware Indians to enter the Comanches' *rancherías* and distribute presents in order to encourage them to hold their council at their location. Trading outposts like those of Torrey's Trading House and Barnard and Company entertained large numbers of Comanches at times. In the spring of 1845, about a thousand Comanche lodges encamped in the neighborhood of Torrey's post on the Brazos River. Typically, these posts supplied the Indians with a variety of sundries. A list of the items distributed as presents to Comanches attending a council at Torrey's in 1845 provides a good example of the variety of goods the Indians could purchase at such stations: silk handkerchiefs; cotton cloth and shawls; "pieces [of] Blue Prints"; blue and red strouding; blue drilling; brass wire; tin pans, buckets, and cups; vermilion, butcher knives, "Cocoa handles [?]" and horn combs; ivory; files; brass tacks; thread and linen; "Fire Steels"; needles; looking glasses; indigo and verdigris; hatchets; blankets; bars of lead; and gunpowder.[38]

If trade is an effect of kinship and social behavior, then how can the commerce between Comanches and unrelated Texan and American traders such as Torrey or Thomas James be explained? The social act of giving gifts seems to be the key to understanding how social relationships become established between unrelated persons. Thomas James's experience with Comanches in the summer of 1821 is a good example of this. James and his party of nine other men first encountered Comanches on their journey to Santa Fe while traveling along the Salt Fork of the Arkansas River. One morning before breaking camp, about one hundred Comanches startled James and his men as they swiftly approached the Americans' horse herd grazing some distance away from the campsite. James succeeded in distracting the Indians by waving a flag at them. Immediately, they rushed toward the encampment and "came among us in a very hostile manner, seizing whatever they could lay their hands on." An interpreter for the Indians

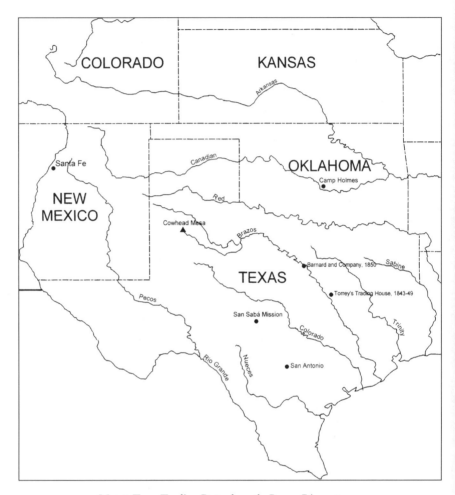

Map 8. Texas Trading Posts along the Brazos River, 1843–50

advised the Americans to appease them by giving them presents. Wanting to avoid any hostilities, James and his men then proceeded to distribute "about three thousand dollars worth of goods among them." The two chiefs among the Indians diverged in their opinions over what to do to the men. According to James, one showed friendliness to the traders, while the other only displayed hostility. Because the followers of the friendlier Comanche made up the majority of the group, the less-friendly chief and his people departed. Afterward, the remaining chief demanded that more presents be distributed to him and his men "on account of his interference in our behalf." After receiving more goods, the Indians provided James with an interpreter and guide and then departed.[39]

James and his men continued westward for New Mexico. They marched along the North Canadian (or Beaver) River to its headwaters and proceeded southward in order to meet up with the main branch of the Canadian. While encamped on this river, a large body of Comanches suddenly appeared over a nearby ridge and overwhelmed the travelers. James noticed that the friendly chief he had met earlier on the Salt Fork rode at the head of this new column of Indians. As the chief embraced James, he requested that the Americans accompany him to his village farther down the Canadian. At that moment, another Comanche snatched a brass kettle from a supply wagon and rode away. James protested to the chief and asked him if he could protect his merchandise if the traders were to go to the Comanche *ranchería*. The chief bluntly replied that he could not. James declined the invitation, but he got the chief to agree to leave a guard with them for the night.[40]

The next day, James and his men moved to the Comanche camp, which he reported as "numbering a thousand lodges, situated in the bottom near the base of a large mound." The head chief of the village, a Yamparica who James called "Big Star," coldly greeted the Americans as they arrived. Shortly after setting up their camp, about a thousand Indians gathered about the campsite and demanded presents. James proceeded to distribute "tobacco, powder, lead, vermilion, calico, and other articles, amounting to about $1,000 in value." After receiving these goods, the Comanches began breaking open bales of cloth "designed for the Spanish market" and divided it among them. Big Star intervened in the frenzy, telling everyone that they had "had enough." The next morning, more Indians arrived to the camp and demanded that they be given presents. Once again, the Indians amassed at the traders' camp and commenced breaking open and dragging about the packages of goods. The chiefs took no part in the rummage, observing the commotion while standing off to the side. James made another offering of presents to the chiefs, hoping that they would be persuaded to let him and his men continue on their journey to Santa Fe. The chiefs refused James's request and advised the traders to remain among them.[41]

The unfriendly chief whom the traders had met on the Salt Fork arrived with a hundred of his followers to the *ranchería* the following day. Apparently, the chief had become angered by the traders' presence among the Indians. Women and children scurried out of their lodges "like chickens before a hawk" as the ominously painted and heavily armed troop rode into the camp. The interpreter assigned to James quickly approached the Americans, suggesting that they hide. James claimed that he and Big Star had previously become friends as a result of presenting the chief with a particularly desirable sword. Because of this relationship, the chief took James and his men into his personal tepee, telling them that they would surely be killed if they remained outside. Big Star then asked what the other chief wanted from the Americans. He answered that he and his men must be presented with "as much cloth as his outstretched arms would once measure; and equal quantity of calico; powder, lead, vermillion, knives, beads, looking glasses, &c., and for himself the sword which he had seen on the south branch of the Salt river." James replied that he did not have the vermilion, knives, beads, or looking glasses he demanded. When he told the chief that the sword had already been given away, the chief became angry and called James a liar. Big Star then took it upon himself to give up the sword to the angry chief in an effort to save the lives of James and his men. The traders then presented the sword and five hundred yards of cloth and calico to the Indians. According to James, this action appeared to pacify the chief and his followers.[42]

Again, James asked if he and his men could be on their way, and once again the chiefs refused. They said that they were to go down the Canadian the following morning; only afterward would they permit the Americans to part from them and continue on their way to Santa Fe. The traders brought in their livestock and prepared for an early departure the next morning. Early in the morning, a hail of stones fell upon James and his men. Some boys had climbed atop a nearby mound and entertained themselves by hurling rocks on the American's camp. When the sun arose, James discovered that six of his horses had been stolen, and he ordered his men to go and find them. A friendly chief told James that it was a mistake to let his men go outside of the camp, for they would surely be murdered. At that time "about fifty of the chiefs and older Indians" followed by "a multitude of young warriors and boys," climbed to the top of the mound and sat down in a large circle. None of the chiefs friendly to the traders accompanied the other Indians. Those on the hill smoked and discussed the fate of James and his men over the course of an hour. In the meantime, the women and children disassembled their tents and headed down river, while armed men assembled before the traders.[43]

Upon the commencement of the Indians' consultation, the friendly chiefs, including Big Star, shook James's hand and bid him and his men farewell. Fearing the worst, the Americans seized whatever weapons they could find and stood silently as they faced the Comanches assembled in front of them. One Indian dressed in a bearskin emerged from the crowd, "stopped short about five paces," and began to prime his pistol. About that time a commotion broke out in the camp. Six New Mexicans, who had heard of the presence of James and his men among the Comanches, rushed into the throng of Indians and rescued the traders from their impending demise. The "Spaniards" asked the Indians why they wanted to kill the traders, and they replied "that the . . . governor at Santa Fe had commanded them not to let any Americans pass, but that [James and his men] were determined to go in spite of them. . . . [Thus in order to] keep their promise to the . . . [g]overnor, they thought they were compelled to take [the Americans'] lives."[44]

Even though James's experience with Comanches almost ended in disaster for him and his men, it showed how gifts could be used to encourage social behavior among the Indians. When Comanches first overcame the traders on the

Salt Fork, they openly threatened the Americans and communicated that peace could be achieved by distributing gifts. By doing this, James demonstrated to the Indians his willingness to sacrifice his interests in favor of the Indians. Even though the Comanches encouraged him into parting with some of his goods, they understood the social nature of the gesture, and many of them exhibited social behavior toward the Americans in return. The most influential chief of this group of Indians protected James's party from those who were not placated by the gifts and also provided the Americans with a person who could serve as an interpreter and guide to help them on their journey through the Comanchería. Thus, in certain terms, the issuance of gifts can be seen as sort of an exchange, social behavior in exchange for social behavior.

James found that he had to continuously appease each Comanche with gifts in order to protect his own life. If some Indians felt like the traders had neglected them, they became jealous of the others and expected to be provided with gifts as well. The Comanches who entered the large *ranchería* the day after the traders arrived there demanded that they be shown the same consideration their relatives had received. Similarly, the malevolent chief demanded that he and his people be recipients of the same generosity. James won the friendship of Big Star and the rancor of the antagonistic chief by giving the former the sword. Big Star returned James's social act by parting with the sword and letting him give it to the unfriendly chief in order to save the American's life. This gift had an instant pacifying effect on this chief, relieving the tension of the confrontation. The social behavior James demonstrated toward the Indians helped him win over a few friends who protected his party. For the most part, the Comanches saw the traders' actions as insufficient and thus undeserving of their social behavior. Besides, the Indians had sworn their loyalty to the Spanish governor of New Mexico with whose predecessors they had established a close relationship. So, as the Comanches figured, they had no compelling reason to allow James to pass on through their village. Were it not for the timely arrival of the New Mexicans, James and his men would have surely been killed.

James returned to the Comanches two years later. Again he had bad luck among the Indians. John McKnight, a partner of James, apparently was killed when he took off alone in search of Comanches with whom to establish a trade. When some Indians did appear, James offended them by trying to pay less than the agreed-upon price for some horses that he judged inferior. The chief in charge of the trade told James that he did not want his trade and demanded that he and his men leave the country. James bided his time among the Indians by handing out gifts to the chief and other influential Comanches until the unfriendly chief whom he had met on his previous visit appeared among them. The chief recognized James from before but this time treated James kindly. Taking him into his lodge, the chief communicated that he had previously wanted to kill the American on account that he and his men had traded with the Comanches'

Osage enemies. Shortly before the traders had appeared on the Salt Fork, the chief's brother had been killed in a battle with some Osages, and he held the traders responsible since they supplied weapons to the enemy. The chief now indicated that he was ready to bury their differences and that he was adopting James in the place of his dead brother. From then on the chief addressed James as "brother" and treated him as such, feeding him and entertaining him with mustang hunting and dance performances, among other things. The chief also assisted the Americans with their trade. Before departing, he told James that he and his people "wanted the American trade. . . . Trade with the Spaniards, [he] said, was unprofitable; they had nothing to give them for their horses except ammunition, and this they refused to sell to the Indians."[45]

Thus, Comanches responded positively to demonstrations of social behavior like that involved in gift giving. American traders, unfamiliar with the ways of Indians, quickly learned the positive effects of providing their hosts with gifts. In this way persons without any kinship or other social connections to the Comanches could begin to establish such ties through which commerce could be conducted. George Barnard of Texas obviously recognized how Comanches responded to this type of social behavior. His effort to generate traffic at his Brazos River post by distributing gifts to Comanches through Delaware intermediaries demonstrated his awareness of the Indians' typical reaction to such an act.[46]

As James's experience and the various strict trade regulations issued by New Mexico's governors have suggested, violence was something often associated with Comanche trade. The historical record documents the outbreak of hostilities in all contexts of the Comanche trade. Trade fairs, *Comanchero* enterprises, inter-Indian exchange, the American traders, and trading posts all experienced the wrath of Comanches at some point. Why would violence be associated with this commerce if trade is ultimately a product of social behavior?

People always put themselves at risk when they behave in a social manner. The essence of social behavior is that one sacrifices their interests in favor of another's. This puts anyone acting in such a manner at risk of being taken advantage of by someone who decides to favor his or her personal interests first. Unsocial or selfish behavior is threatening to others. Oftentimes, people retaliate for the antisocial behavior exhibited by others, ranging from avoidance of the antisocial person to hostile confrontation. Comanches exhibited the entire spectrum of responses when they thought they had been treated unfairly in a commercial transaction, but violence seems to have been an option most often exercised by the Indians as they sought retribution for what they felt was disrespectful behavior.

Comanche trade resulted as a result of the Indians' social relations with others within and beyond the Comanchería. Those directly involved in a particular commercial transaction did not always recognize a kinship or social connection between one another. Personal interests often stimulated commerce, and such interaction with relatives proved the easiest, least risky way to acquire goods. One could usually count on kin to behave socially and to be willing to engage in a trade. Yet a person might not have relatives who own particular desired items. In that case, one could ask their kinsman to set up a trade with another person related to that kinsman but not to oneself. The principals in the trade could thus each trace a kinship and social relation to the mediator. This type of commercial interaction may have made up the majority of the trade in which Comanches participated.

Comanches easily became offended in commercial situations when they believed they had not been respected or were offered an unfair deal. Governor Mogollon's 1712 order prohibiting New Mexicans from trading in the *rancherías* beyond the province mentioned that the residents' pernicious and offensive behavior toward the Indians often resulted in injurious circumstances. Vélez Cachupín explicitly stated to his successor that the governor and a "garrison from the presidio" of Santa Fe should attend the Taos trade fair in order to ensure peace at the event. He suggested that the soldiers should guard the Comanches' horses. This action, according to Vélez Cachupín, gave the Indians the confidence to "feel completely relieved of responsibility, a condition they appreciate in the highest degree." Furthermore, he instructed, the Comanches should be received "with every kindness and affection." Vélez Cachupín took special care to show respect to the Comanche visitors because he was well aware of the disastrous consequences that could beset the province if the Indians felt slighted in the least degree.[47]

Governor Marín del Valle took his predecessors' advice to heart and reiterated that the residents of New Mexico's villas and pueblos were not to perjure themselves with the Comanches attending the trade fairs. He noted that this behavior, along with violent robberies and other deeds of bad faith, continuously put the relationship between the Indians and the province in jeopardy. Marín del Valle attempted to restrain the crimes and violence commonly committed at trade fairs by fixing the price of bison hides, by which the value of other goods could be determined on a more agreeable basis. He suggested that most of the participants' acrimony developed in response to the process of negotiating the prices for various items. Undercutting a previously agreed price especially offended traders and led to bickering, fighting, and eventually killing. Marín del Valle claimed that by establishing a more flexible pricing system, the Comanches would then notice whether or not the Spaniards took advantage of them by asking for more than an item was worth in their eyes.[48]

Thomas James insulted a Comanche chief in 1821 by trying to purchase horses for less than the price he had agreed to pay. According to his narrative, seventeen of the horses he had bought were, to his eyes, worth the price he paid for them, but when the Indians presented him with less valuable horses, he refused to buy them. This offense enraged the chief who had arranged the trade. Later that evening, James attended a smoke-lodge council meeting in the chief's tepee, but the Indians in attendance did not offer him the pipe and only regarded him "with lowering brows." James figured this sign "portended evil and [he] feared the worst."[49]

Jacob Fowler also offended some Comanches he came across on the Arkansas River in 1821 when he and others communicated to the Indians that they had no presents for them. The Comanche chief "became in a great pas[s]ion" and told the Americans that he would kill them and take their goods. The Indians sat in council all day determining the fate of the traders until a large party of friendly Arapahos arrived and offered Fowler and the others their protection.[50]

During the winter of 1844-45, Comanches and other Indians became so agitated by the high prices of Torrey's Post No. 2 that they threatened the entire State of Texas with violence. Agents from the U.S. Bureau of Indian Affairs had to distribute goods among the Indians in an effort to make amends for the apparent insult. Because offended Comanches threatened the public order, Superintendent of Indian Affairs Thomas G. Western ordered L. H. Williams to the trading post, where he could monitor the merchants' practices. Western commanded Williams that "upon no consideration [whatever] absent yourself for a single day from your post, which is Post No. 2 at Torrey's Trading House, to which Post you are now detailed as Govt Indian Agent until further orders."[51]

Such offenses led to numerous raids and warfare throughout New Mexico and Texas as Comanches sought out retaliation for the perceived improprieties. Like commerce, the violence and hostilities that sometimes occurred within the context of trade emerged from people's interaction. Because trade required Comanches to sacrifice such a great deal of their personal interests in favor of people with whom they sometimes had no social ties, they exhibited high levels of sensitivity toward receiving appropriate reciprocal social behavior. Comanches sometimes used the threat of violence to extort others out of their goods, but this tactic could be risky and not cost effective. Comanches, like other people, generally preferred social means to acquire goods. Usually, only after being offended or insulted by their trade partner's reluctance to reciprocate did hostile posturing or violence become a possibility. When fighting did occur, Comanches became very serious about defending their interests and honor.

The realization that trade is an effect of human kinship and social behavior helps illuminate one of the most misunderstood aspects of Comanche life. Various explanations that have stressed outside influences such as the environment, geography, nutrition, and colonial market capitalism are insufficient because they characterize Comanches' economic behavior as being motivated by larger forces beyond their control. Understanding commercial exchange as an aspect of human social relationships emphasizes the point that individual Comanches determined their own economic activity. People's propensity for kinship social behavior made them more likely to interact socially and commercially with the people they considered kin. It did not necessarily determine their behavior. A particular Comanche might have chosen not to cooperate economically with a kinsman for whatever reason. Comanches were not automatically compelled to interact with their kindred in this way, but ancestral traditions strongly encouraged that they do so.[52] Assuming that Comanches behaved like most other tribal peoples, it can be surmised that they tended to favor those with whom they recognized a common ancestor. Their commercial relationships would have originally been established through kinship and kinshiplike social connections. The intermarriage of Comanches with New Mexicans, Caddoans, Kiowas, and Texans allowed the establishment of strong commercial ties between these various peoples.

Economic activity is generated by people's personal wants and desires. It is not a zero-sum game in which there must be a winner and a loser. Interpretations of Comanche economics have tended to assume a zero-sum situation in which the Indians lose through some form of dependence or exploitation by Euro-Americans. The division of labor among individuals encourages the social effect of trade because certain people own or specialize in things that others do not or cannot produce. Even though two people have personal interests in acquiring the goods the other owns, they *both* benefit by acquiring the items through social behavior as opposed to unsocial aggression. When American traders exchanged various items for Comanche mules and horses, each side considered they had gained and that it was worth their losses. From the American point of view, they received highly valued equines in exchange for cheaply produced trade goods. They saw the Comanche trade as highly profitable. On the other side, Comanches received items they valued highly in exchange for mules and horses that they could produce at little cost. From their point of view, they too saw the American trade as profitable and desirable.

The dynamics of kinship and social behavior, division of labor, and supply and demand formed the basis of all contexts of trade in which Comanches participated. Most Comanche commercial relationships were probably based on kinship social relationships. They also established these types of associations with others not recognized as kin. Comanches recognized when strangers behaved socially toward them (that is, *like* a kinsman) and often responded in kind. Unfortunately, a trader's exhibition of social behavior did not necessarily ensure that all Indians would reciprocate the generosity extended to them.

Because trade requires people to sacrifice their interests to a certain degree, the participants are vulnerable to various abuses when someone decides to take advantage of the situation. When this did happen or was thought to have happened, Comanches often responded with violence. The possibility of the Indians resorting to hostile behavior always existed when they placed themselves in vulnerable situations. Their use of violence to seize material goods demonstrated behavior different from economic exchange, even though raiding and brigandage might eventually have some economic effect. Trade is social, whereas hostile behavior is fundamentally antisocial.

Chapter 5

An Explanation of Comanche Violence

OWHEAD MESA IN SOUTHWESTERN GARZA COUNTY, TEXAS, has been described as "a typical bread-loaf-shaped western mesa, indistinguishable at a glance from dozens of others in [the] canyonlands [of the upper Double Mountain Fork of the Brazos River]." Geologically speaking, this is indeed the case. Even the fact that the mesa's walls display various petroglyphs makes it only somewhat distinct from other such surfaces across the American West. Yet there is something peculiar about this uneroded landform that distinguishes it from all other mesas in the area and even from all other rock surfaces in the world. Among the various carvings etched into the mesa's pliant walls is a pictographic account of the violent San Sabá Mission episode, apparently put there by a Comanche artist-historian sometime after the attack of March 16, 1758. The sandstone document portrays a group of figures strewn about a compound of flaming cross-crested buildings. Some of the human images are bedecked in robes, and others don three-cornered hats — obvious representations of the priests and soldiers who inhabited the ill-fated outpost. About these images are scenes of personal combat and more flames. Fire everywhere. The excessive representation of fire seems to hint at the artist's respect for the destructive force and violence that Comanches and their allies managed to inflict on that feeble Spanish post on the San Sabá River.[1]

In a striking corroboration of the Comanche record embedded into the rock of Cowhead Mesa, Spanish paper documents describing the San Sabá "massacre" also illustrate the imposing prowess the Indians wielded against people they recognized as adversaries to their way of life. Fr. Fray Miguel de Molina, the only

ries to survive the attack, testified that the Indians first
around daybreak on March 16 shortly after The Rev-
ray Alonso Giraldo de Terreros had finished celebrating
us outburst of yells and war cries" heard from outside the
he distance of a musket shot" startled Molina and rudely
oseph Santiesteban as he began reciting his personal mass.
l, some men and women of the compound rushed to Mo-
at "the Indians were upon us." People nervously scurried
about the ___ nd in search of refuge as Molina hurried to the chapel to inform Terreros of the dangerous situation. Apparently, the Indians who gathered
just beyond the mission walls sensed the defensive preparations being made inside the ramparts, for they began making "offers of peace and friendship, . . .
some in the Castilian language, and some by means of signs and gestures." Cpl.
Ascencio Cadena "recognized [the Indians] as members of the Texas [Tejas],
Tancague [Tonkawa], Vidae [Bidai], and other nations from farther inland, with
whom he had . . . experience on many previous occasions" and immediately retreated to the priests' quarters and informed them that, from his point of view,
the Indians' petitions for goodwill appeared to be genuine.

Somewhat consoled by this news, Father Terreros ventured out into the mission's courtyard to see what exactly the Indians wanted. Father Molina "filled
with amazement and fear" as he viewed a spectacle of Indians "armed with guns
and arrayed in the most horrible attire." The mass of people outside the compound gates all exhibited red and black face paint and had disguised themselves
as animals, adorned with various animal pelts, tails, horns, and feather head-
dresses. Besides muskets, the decorated warriors brandished lances, swords, and
bows and arrows. Shortly after the mission fathers appeared in the courtyard, the
Indians dismounted their horses and opened up the compound's locked gates
"by wrenching off the crossbars with their hands." Some three hundred individuals immediately crowded into the log stockade, "extending their arms to our
people . . . making gestures of civility and friendliness." When Molina witnessed
this exhibition of congeniality, he encouraged Terreros to reciprocate with bundles
of tobacco and other things highly prized by the Indians. Molina himself gave
four bundles to a mounted individual, who received the gift with but a contemptuous laugh. According to the Indians themselves, this person was a great
Comanche chief "worthy of respect."[2]

The chief's laughter unsettled Molina. It was especially chilling to the priest
because he had just finished observing other Indians ransacking the kitchen's
wares and taking the capes off the backs of several soldiers. Some of the warriors
led the horses out of the mission's corral and demanded that more of the animals
be turned over to them. In an effort to distract the Indians away from the compound, the priests communicated to them that the presidio, located just upriver,
had many more horses than they. Father Terreros quickly penned a note of in-

troduction, addressed it to the fort's commandant, and gave it to "a chieftain of the Texas nation." The Indian then grabbed Terreros's personal mount, "saying that he needed it to take the note to the Presidio." When the priest objected, the chief put the barrel of his musket to the horse's head and threatened to kill the animal. Terreros promptly rescinded his objection, whereupon the Indian departed toward the west. In the meantime, the others milled about the compound, "persist[ing] in their hostile actions, surrounding, searching, and looting the various buildings." Molina learned from conversations he had with the visitors "that they had no intention other than to fight the Apaches who had killed some of their people." They asked him whether or not there were any of their enemies at the compound. The priest denied the presence of any, even though he knew that several of them had been sheltered in Father Terreros's quarters under heavy guard.[3]

After a short time, the Texas chief returned from the presidio accompanied by "a large number of his followers, saying that he had not been allowed to enter . . . and that three of his companions had been killed and another wounded with knife cuts." To this news, Father Terreros chastised the Indian, saying that he had probably provoked the soldiers by approaching the garrison with too large of a force and by demonstrations of bad behavior. Making another effort to rid the mission of enemies, Terreros offered to accompany them back to the presidio and ordered that horses be saddled for himself and an armed escort. By the time the Spaniards had mounted their steeds, the Texas chief had disappeared "among the rabble that thronged the courtyard." While searching for the chief, Terreros rode toward the gate to see if the Indian was waiting for him outside the enclosure. As the priest made his way to the sally port, a shot rang out, "and the said Father President cried out." More shots crackled off, the mounted soldier fell to the ground, "and then began a cruel attack against all."[4]

The missionaries and soldiers scrambled, seeking asylum in the various buildings of the compound. Molina and a good number of the others made their way into Terreros's quarters, where the Apaches had been hidden. Looking through loopholes, the refugees observed the Indians setting fire to stacks of kindling they had piled up along the mission's hardwood walls. As flames consumed the complex, Indians scurried about, pillaging and plundering "the provisions stored for the Apaches." Although surrounded, the Spaniards managed to defend themselves for a time by assailing their attackers with musket fire. After midday, flames began to engulf the father president's quarters, forcing the besieged occupants to seek protection elsewhere. A house next to the church building served this need just fine, but the Indians promptly became aware of the new hiding place and proceeded to set it aflame. The church, though also ablaze, "was less badly ruined." Thus, the survivors straggled into its sanctuary, where they "remained until past midnight, when all of us escaped except Juan Antonio Gutiérrez, who could not on account of a serious wound in the thigh."[5]

Four days later, soldiers from the nearby presidio raked through the ashes of the despoiled complex. They discovered Father Terreros's body near the mission's entrance, where he had been struck down. Two other corpses found lying about the courtyard had been "burned to cinders," making recognition difficult. The lifeless figure of Juan Antonio Gutiérrez lacked a scalp as well as eyes. The investigators found the bodies of several other soldiers some distance outside of the mission walls, but they did not find the decapitated remains of Father Santiesteban until several days later. In all, eight people perished in the attack. The Indians did not even spare the lives of pets or livestock. The soldiers counted several dead cats and eighteen dead oxen among the casualties. All the buildings had been destroyed, and "the ground was strewn with smoldering debris from [their] ruins." The remnants of smashed bales of tobacco, boxes of chocolate, barrels of flour, and boxes of soap were scattered about and still burning. "Useless fragments" of church ornaments, jewels, and sacred pictures also littered the blackened ground. Even an effigy of the "Holy Saint Francis" was found overturned with its head severed from the body.[6] The scene was total destruction.

The reported level of violence perpetrated by Comanches and other Indians against the San Sabá Mission immediately sent shock waves throughout New Spain. As colonial and ecclesiastical officials questioned their policies relating to establishing missions and presidios along the Texas frontier, a military campaign set out from San Antonio the following year with the intention of punishing those who had attacked the mission. While the Spanish managed to destroy a Yojuane (a Tonkawa tribe) *ranchería* and capture 149 prisoners, they met defeat when they confronted the heavily fortified and well-armed Taovaya village on the Red River. The Spaniards' retreat from the battlefield marked the conclusion of events directly relating to the San Sabá incident. In all respects the incident and its aftermath represented a decisive victory for Comanches and their allies over their European and Apache enemies.[7]

The course of these events not only left a lasting impression upon the Spanish authorities but also has piqued the imaginations of students of Native American, colonial Texas, and the Southwest. To contemporary and later observers, the awesome display of violence and destruction the Comanches and their allies inflicted upon the mission and the people inhabiting it have suggested that there must be some particular goals or underlying motivation that can explain their hostile behavior. Yet in order to understand what provoked Comanches to act so violently at various times, one must understand what encourages humans generally to exhibit this type of behavior in the first place.

As most students of Plains Indian warfare have noted, violence occurred as an effect of competition over various resources. The resources most frequently identified as the primary focus of Comanches' competitive efforts have been territory, bison, horses, and trade goods. Access to these and other resources, such as women and children captives, water, wood, and pasturage, can have a direct influence on the ability of individuals to successfully cope with their immediate natural, political, and social challenges. Comanches certainly realized that access to these things allowed them to successfully deal with the complex environment existing on the southern plains in the eighteenth and nineteenth centuries. But as treaties and truces between Comanches and former enemies demonstrate, violence was not always necessary to access the resources they needed and wanted. The idea that "survival of the fittest" competition for these resources explains the Indians' well-documented aggressive and violent behavior is ultimately shortsighted and fails to adequately reflect the complexity of the Comanches' past reality.[8]

Kinship behavior helps explain why Comanches often exhibited violence when it came to acquiring required or desired resources. Again, kinship behavior involves social behavior toward a relation in which the degree of altruism is correlated with the genealogical distance between the individuals exhibiting this behavior. Also, because descent or clan names could be used to identify a broad range of living and dead relatives beyond immediate kin, Comanches could identify genealogically distant living co-descendants. For example, the Chiefs Pasahuoques, who visited Gov. Juan Bautista de Anza in Santa Fe on May 9, 1786, and Quahuahacante, who met with the governor later on the twenty-eighth, were both identified as Yamparicas. Because each of the men shared the Yamparica name, they could have recognized each other as kindred even though they might not have been able to address one another with a specific kin term.[9]

Comanches could also identify distant genealogical relationships by physical traits and cultural traditions. Vial and Chaves's 1785 report to Cabello described Cuchanec and Yamparica Comanches as only being differentiated by the haircut of the latter. Thus, Comanches could identify if an individual could trace their ancestry to Yamparicas simply by observing a person's hairstyle.[10]

Language, especially, is a cultural tradition that has allowed people to identify distantly related persons. Comanches realized that their common language implied their distant genealogical relationship. Vial and Chaves noted that "all [Comanches] speak the same language, and thus they consider themselves as brothers and comrades." Other traditional cultural traits associated with clothing, body painting, and artistic designs also identified individuals as Comanches. Physical traits served as the basis of discriminating against others who did not exhibit such traits and thus could be assumed to be unrelated.[11]

Kinship identification alone is not sufficient for kinship behavior to occur. The Cuchanecs' assassination of Toro Blanco in 1785 and Soxas's murder of one of Ecueracapa's sons in 1797 demonstrate that violent competition existed among people who recognized one another as kin. In traditional societies like that of the Comanches, ancestral traditions encouraged individuals to direct altruistic behavior toward genealogically distant relatives. Religious ritual played a key role in encouraging and reinforcing this among Comanches. Their worship of common ancestors served as the catalyst through which they extended kinship altruism and favoritism to their distant kinsmen. Rituals like the religious smoking ceremony that Comanches performed on various occasions promoted their respect for their common ancestor's behavioral traditions, encouraging "family-like" cooperation between distantly related individuals.[12]

When competition with outsiders over bison, horses, and trade threatened the Comanches, they could be encouraged to make extreme and sometimes life-threatening sacrifices in order to protect their close and distantly related kinsmen. The behavior promoted in the religious smoking ritual encouraged Comanches to protect and defend their "kin" over any outsiders when competition occurred. In 1828 José Francisco Ruíz mentioned that Comanches were always ready to avenge the death of one of their warriors. According to Ruíz, when someone had been killed in a battle or on a raid, the surviving male kinsmen rode into the various camps, crying many tears and urging the residents to join them in retaliation for the death of their comrade. After the announcement of their intentions, the men proceeded to the head chief's dwelling. Crying loudly, the mourners circled the tepee twice and stopped at the tent's door. After the chief invited the men to enter, he called upon his own warriors and the camp's elders to attend a council. While the collection of men sat silently, someone lit the pipe. The chief then urged the mourners to state the reason for their arrival. Once he heard the avengers' explanation for their cause, the chief was presented with the pipe. By declining the offer of the pipe, he communicated to the council that he did not deem the cause of the mourners either convincing or justified. The chief's acceptance of the pipe, however, expressed his willingness to participate in a retaliatory raid. In that case, a spokesperson wandered about the camp loudly announcing the decision. The avenging warriors then proceeded to inform the council with details of the facts surrounding who the enemies were and the time and place where their companion was killed. The visitors also presented the chief with a gift horse as a token of their gratification.[13]

Warriors who desired to avenge fallen comrades traveled across the Comanchería in search for allies to accompany them on their forays. Ruíz stated that each of the chiefs who agreed to participate in a proposed attack invited all of his relatives to go along with him. Evidence of large Comanche war parties in the eighteenth and nineteenth centuries implies the tremendous capability of the Indians' religious rituals and kinship hierarchy to promote kinship recognition among a great number of people. The size of Comanche war parties ranged from just a few people to large forces thousands of men strong.[14] Eyewitnesses of the San Sabá incident in 1758 reported that at least two thousand Indians attacked the mission. Comanches made up only a sizable portion of this force; allied Caddoan-speaking Indians made up for the rest of the brigade. The affiliation of this mixed-tribe detachment also resulted from the kinship behavior promoted by religious rituals in which both Comanches and Caddoans participated.

Caddoans such as the Hasinai also held councils in which they discussed the prospects of going off to war. In these meetings they conducted various cere-monies, including smoke rituals. Such gatherings of Comanches and Caddoans encouraged the Indians' use of the word *techan* in reference to one another. Athanase de Mézières explained that when Indians addressed one another with this term, "there arises . . . a strong tie of friendship [kinship], and the common opinion that no one can change it without fear of incurring the penalty which such perjurors [*sic*] deserve." Fray Francisco Casañas noted the use of this term among the Caddoans he lived with in the early 1690s. According to the cleric, the "name of Texias applies to all the friendly tribes although their languages may be different. And the reason why this name is so common is no other than that of their long-standing friendship [kinship]."[15] When Comanches intermarried with Plains Caddoans like the Taovayas and Tahuacanas, their children became *techan*. In other words, Comanches became genealogically distant kin of Caddoans across eastern Texas and Louisiana. As Casañas observed, this term allowed the Indians to recognize their kinship to one another even though they did not speak the same language. The combined numbers of Indians present at San Sabá in March, 1758, suggests that kinship behavior, like that indicated by the use of *techan,* could give rise to large aggregations of Comanche and Caddoan men for the purpose of defending their kin against enemies.

As the San Sabá incident demonstrates, such defense could be extremely vi-olent. There are many other reported incidents of violence perpetrated by Co-manches. Among those known are a few examples from eighteenth-century New Mexico. In January, 1724, Fray Juan de Mirabal of Taos communicated to the governor details of a particularly brutal Comanche attack on the Jicarilla Apaches, resulting in the abduction of all the women and children and the death of sixty-four men. When the Comanches descended upon the Jicarilla Valley, the Apaches sought refuge in their adobe houses. After intermittent fighting for four nights and five days, the Comanches proposed that if the Apaches gave up all the women and children, they would let the men live. The Apaches agreed to this de-mand and proceeded to transfer the women and children to their assailants. Dur-ing the process of this exchange, the Comanches opened fire on the defenseless men, exclaiming that they would kill them for meat and tan their hides.[16]

In 1777 Comanches focused their attacks on the *genízaro* settlement of Tomé. The offensive may have been instigated by the refusal of the *alcalde* to give his daughter to a Comanche chief. As a result, the Indians killed twenty-one persons in May, thirty in June, and returned in November to inflict more casualties on the village's inhabitants. The latter assault ended disastrously for the Comanche raiders, who suffered twenty dead and many wounded. Later in 1789, 112 Co-manches retaliated for various horse robberies by overrunning a Ute *ranchería* and killing eighty persons.[17]

Comanches could be extremely cruel when it came to dealing with their en-emies. Stories of shocking displays of brutality by these Indians are scattered throughout the historical record. Possibly two of the most disturbing examples involved their treatment of abducted infants. In 1836 a party of forty to fifty Comanches fell upon a wagon train of about fifteen or so refugees from Beales's failed colony in southern Texas. According to Sarah Ann Horn, the Indians first killed the eleven men and took the women and children captive. Early the next morning, shortly before sunrise, one of the infant children taken captive began to cry. When Horn requested that the Indians give it something to eat, a man approached her and seized the baby by the arms. At once the Comanche "threw it up as high as he could, and let it fall upon the ground at his feet." The Indian did this two more times until the infant was dead.[18]

A similar incident took place in Nuevo Leon in 1840, when Comanches abducted María del Carmen García along with one of her sisters and her mother from their home in Botellos. García told the Mexican authorities at Agualeguas that the Indians who abducted her also took a five-month-old infant from one of the *ranchos* they raided. When the child began crying, one of the Indians took it by the feet and threw it to the ground to silence it. The Indians wrapped the child in some cloth and gave it to García to hold. A while later the baby began crying once again. This time the Comanche took the infant, threw it up into the air, and caught it on the point of his lance. Apparently, Comanches did not tolerate crying infants when they conducted their campaigns. David G. Burnet stated that even though Comanches had been alleged of wantonly murdering women and children, "the charge is not true as to general practice, but there may be some isolated exceptions, growing out of pressing emergency or some extraordinary excitement."[19]

What explains the acts of grim and unnecessary brutality sometimes perpetrated by Comanches? Probably the best way to understand this behavior is through the perspective of their kinship behavior. By default, the Comanches' ability to recognize their kinship with a large number of people through clan names, physical traits, and the practice of religious rituals also provided them with the ability to determine who was not their kin. The recognition of a kinship connection between individual Comanches and their close and distant co-descendants encouraged altruistic, or social, behavior among them. Because the degree of altruism kinsmen extend to one another is correlated with genealogical distance, individuals extended less and less social behavior to persons more and more distantly related. When Comanches could find no genealogical link to a person, they had no reason to behave socially toward them. As far as Comanches were concerned, those persons with whom they had no relationship whatsoever did not require their benevolence. Consequently, they felt no need for self-restraint when it came to stealing livestock, abducting women and children, robbing traders, and taking the lives of anyone unrelated to them.

Comanches actively encouraged one another to exhibit this sort of hostile behavior toward unrelated persons. Ruíz described how Comanches encouraged their men to participate in raids and battles. After a chief decided to join in such an undertaking and the men made their various preparations, the party paraded past all the tents, with the chief "exhort[ing] all the Indians who have not joined to do so, explaining again the reason for the war and to induce the more recalcitrant ones." The assembly of warriors traveled from *ranchería* to *ranchería,* where the war chief consulted the leaders of each individual encampment who in turn communicated the information to their men. When everyone deciding to participate in the campaign had been mobilized, the warriors lined up in two single-file lines. Drumming commenced, and everyone began singing. The chiefs then walked down the middle of the rows followed closely by "their best warriors and children in their finest attire." As the procession filed through, the old men rode their horses on the outside, shouting out their past military exploits. They advised the young men "to die rather than commit an act of cowardice." The elders also urged the women "to marry only those who are brave and courageous in battle and to spurn the cowardly warrior." For the remainder of the day, the old men wandered about the camp continually repeating their harangue.[20]

Late in the afternoon, an elite group of warriors called the "Lobos" (wolves) arrived at the camp. This group adorned themselves with special wolf-skin belts and other ornamentations that only they were allowed to wear. Like the old men, the Lobos circulated throughout the *ranchería,* singing songs and dancing in the doorways of the tents of chiefs and warriors. According to Ruíz, the Lobos always marched separate from the other warriors. Furthermore,

> The Lobos are not allowed to retreat from the scene of the battle, not even when they are vastly outnumbered. It is their duty to die rather than surrender their ground, although the other warriors may be in full retreat. Even if their chief orders them to turn back, it is a sign of great courage to disobey such orders and to continue the fight. This kind of courage is admired greatly by the women.

> The Lobos who survive a fierce battle in which many of their number have lost their lives are forced to leave the ranchería and find a new one which has no connection with the warriors who have died. The dead Lobo's surviving kin will pursue and slay any Lobo who has escaped alive. This has happened before.

> Everyone respects the Lobos for their courage and dignity. When they ride through a ranchería their horses may trample on animal skins, meat, or other objects on the ground. They are allowed to take all the meat they desire and eat whatever else they wish without anyone hindering them.[21]

The old men's recital of their heroic war achievements, along with the Lobos, represented the epitome of sacrifice for the rank-and-file warriors to emulate. Examples and accounts of their extreme sacrificial behavior on the battlefield encouraged Comanches to demonstrate the high levels of sacrifice and cooperation necessary to defeat their enemies. Off the battlefield, the old warriors and the Lobos inspired members to demonstrate social behavior by putting the interests of others ahead of themselves. Because people recognized the profound sacrifice represented by the Lobos, they refrained from becoming angry when one behaved selfishly. The great admiration of the women for brave warriors, and the Lobos especially, also served as a powerful incentive encouraging young men to sacrifice for their kindred.

The behavior of Comanche women toward male captives also promoted social behavior among relatives and hostility toward enemies. Burnet claimed that "the largest portion of the nation's barbarity consists in the character of their women . . . [in that] [t]hey take a peculiar delight in torturing adult male prisoners, who, according to an ancient custom, are surrendered to their . . . amusements for three days succeeding their arrival in the village."[22] When a Comanche war party returned with a male captive, they delivered him up to their women, who then tied the unfortunate individual spread-eagle to stakes nailed into the ground. Burnet explained that the punishment the captive received from the women depended on whether or not the Comanches suffered heavy losses in their campaign. A prisoner taken during a successful raid only suffered "light and trivial [injuries], amounting only to a few gentle flagellations, by way of giving merriment to the dance, and cadence to the song of triumph." But if Comanches endured a grave defeat, the women severely punished the captive, which often resulted in his death.

Shortly after a prisoner had been staked to the ground, some women announced to the others to "come to the dance." Burnet stated that this invitation resulted in "the screams and yells of infuriate females, trooping impetuous[ly] to the scene of torment." The women then untied their victim and forced him to take hold of a staff adorned with scalps of his tribe. When all the women gathered into a circle, they thrust the prisoner into its center and assailed him with clubs, thongs, knives, lances, and firebrands until he collapsed. They repeated this routine for three days or until the captive succumbed to his wounds. If the enemy survived the punishment meted out by the women, the Comanches exempted him from further abuse and unconditionally considered him a member of their society. From that point on, the captive became attached to the family of the person who captured him and treated as if he were kin.[23]

Comanches extended social behavior to the few prisoners who survived the women's torture because they recognized and respected the individual's bravery and physical sacrifice. Warfare and the cruelties that Comanches sometimes inflicted on their enemies stemmed not from immoral attributes inherent to their nature but rather from the favoritism integral to kinship behavior. From the Comanches point of view, moral behavior required one to treat all persons who they recognized as kin as if they were close family members. Comanches behaved immorally if they failed to behave socially toward their relatives, no matter how distantly they were related to one another. Comanche morality did not apply to any unrelated individual, though. As a result, Apaches, Pueblos, Spaniards, Utes, Caddoans, Texans, and Mexicans all suffered the wrath of Comanches at various times since 1706. But some members of each of these groups also benefited from Comanches' social behavior because of intermarriage and the instinctive kinship behavior it fostered, especially as a result of the birth of offspring.

The issue of exactly whom Comanches considered their enemies is extremely complicated because many of their raids focused on particular individuals with whom they maintained rivalries and sought personal revenge. As the eighteenth and nineteenth centuries advanced, Comanches could trace kinship connections to an increasing number of individuals across the Comanchería and into bordering areas. The Indians did not always lash out at their enemies in an indiscriminate manner for fear of injuring a kin person or offending a co-descendant by harming one of their relatives. They probably only waged indiscriminate warfare in cases when they could be relatively certain that no kinship ties existed with their enemy. Berlandier's description of the causes of Indian warfare hint at the personal nature of Comanche campaigns. According to the French scientist, "the thirst for vengeance" drove Comanches and the other Indians of Texas to lash out at their enemies. Berlandier found that fathers cultivated this "thirst" in their children "from the tenderest of infancy . . . [and that] [t]hey are so thoroughly accustomed to the violence of this passion that they constantly invoke [it] to incite their compatriots to arms." Furthermore, he discovered that "every friend" (kinsmen) of a person killed attempted to carry out a private war against the perpetrators.[24]

There is some evidence suggesting that Comanches conducted their raids in order to avenge personal offenses exacted upon them by particular individuals. In August, 1719, some Utes and Comanches attacked the ranch of Cristóbal de la Serna at El Embudo, south of Taos, and ran off with four horses and a boy belonging to Serna. The Indians' targeting of Serna may not have been an inadvertent act. A few years earlier in 1716, Captain Serna had led a force of 112 armed soldiers, settlers, and Indians against Utes and Comanches camped at San Antonio Mountain northwest of Taos. The 1719 raid on El Embudo may have been in retribution for that offensive. A similar incident occurred, again near Taos, on August 4, 1760. On that date a large number of Comanches entered the vicinity and attacked the house of Pablo Francisco Villapando. The Spaniards fought off the assault for most of the day, but the Indians sneaked safely underneath the dwelling's parapet and set it aflame. The Comanches finished off the inhabitants as they emerged from the burning building. The attackers departed from the scene only after coupling the bodies of their male and female victims. Villapando survived; he was away when the attack took place.[25]

Josiah Gregg heard the story of this raid when he traveled to New Mexico in

1831. According to Gregg's account, Señor Villapando had gained the friendship of some Comanches and had promised one of his young daughters to a chief. When the daughter later refused to be given away, the Indians attacked the Villapando residence and killed everyone except for the betrothed girl, who they carried away in captivity. For the most part, Gregg's story seems valid. Pablo Francisco Villapando did indeed maintain a close relationship with Comanches. His testimony concerning the identity of Comanches visiting Taos in December, 1749, hints that he had traded with the Indians.[26] This activity may have served as the initial basis of his association with them. Also, the coupling together of the male and female victims at the scene of the attack may have been a sign the Indians used to communicate their indignation of Don Pablo's failure to deliver his daughter to them.

Another incident also hints that Comanches often focused their raids and wars of vengeance toward particular individuals. Representatives of the Cuchanec Comanches under the leadership of Ecueracapa met with Governor Anza to ratify their newly established peace treaty at Pecos pueblo on February 25, 1786. During the ceremony Tosacondata, the official speaker of the Indians present, arose "opposite the governor and bearing his breast made a well arranged harangue." Among other things, Tosacondata announced to the New Mexicans in attendance his people's wish to forget the past aggravations and hostilities committed by both sides. The Indian orator admitted that he felt personally ashamed by his ongoing quarrel with a particular Spaniard who sat in attendance at the council. Tosacondata announced that from that day on, he and his people would be faithful to the peace and fully comply with the orders of Anza and Ecueracapa. As a beginning to make amends with the people of New Mexico, Tosacondata approached his rival, dropped to his knees, and presented him with a gift of one of his personal captives.[27]

Comanches also retaliated indiscriminately against groups of people they considered their enemies. Their conflict with Apaches may have its roots deep in the era prior to the arrival of Europeans in the Southwest (though there has not been much research into this prospect chiefly because nomadic peoples do not leave much archeological evidence). It is known that Comanches continuously persecuted Apaches throughout the eighteenth and nineteenth centuries. In 1706 Juan de Ulibarri mentioned that Comanches and Utes had attacked the *rancherías* of the Carlana, Sierra Blanca, and Penxaye Apaches. Throughout the 1720s, Comanches overwhelmed all Apaches living to the north and east of New Mexico. The Jicarillas bore the brunt of the Comanches' hostilities until they moved close to Taos and Pecos in the late 1720s and 1730s. The Comanches' continuing harassment of Apaches culminated in their southward push into Texas and precipitated destructive events like that which occurred at the San Sabá Mission. Speaking of the conduct of Comanches toward the Apaches in Texas, Athanase de Mézières observed that the former Indians persecuted the latter to such a degree that they became angry when they had difficulties locating their enemy. Despite a couple of brief periods of peace between Comanches and Lipan Apaches in the early nineteenth century, the two peoples maintained their hostile dispositions toward each other throughout that century. U.S. Indian Agent John Rollins commented in September, 1850, on the incessant fighting between Comanches and Apaches in southern Texas. He informed Gen. George Mercer Brooke of the Eighth Military Department in San Antonio that "those Comanches who have lost relatives or friends upon the Rio Grande wished to be revenged and the Chiefs cannot govern them."[28]

It is impossible to determine exactly to what degree the violent aggression Comanches inflicted upon Apaches in the eighteenth and nineteenth centuries was aimed at particular individuals or at Apaches in general. Nonetheless, Comanches justified their indiscriminate assaults against innocent individuals because they understood these victims as relatives of enemies who had somehow injured their ancestors in the past. The hostilities between the Indians became traditional, as parents and grandparents taught their children that they should avenge their forebears. It is easy to understand how these types of traditions could become widespread among Comanches and perpetuated through the generations. For example, in February, 1808, some Osage Indians successfully attacked a Yamparica *ranchería* consisting of seventy families. The Osages enjoyed such an overwhelming victory that "not a man escaped death, not even as a captive."[29] Incidents like this surely inspired the Comanches' desire to avenge the deaths of their kin on an indiscriminate basis. Because the Osages killed such a large number of people on this particular raid, a great number of Comanches would have been offended at the loss of their close and distant relatives. Retaliatory campaigns resulting in the deaths of Osages satisfied Comanche desires for vengeance, but such actions agitated similar feelings among their enemies, creating a true vicious circle of murder and revenge.

The Spanish, though, never fully convinced Comanches that they should consider the inhabitants of New Mexico, Texas, and northern Mexico as belonging to one nation. The Indians only understood nations in terms of the original meaning of the word—belonging to lineages of one's birth—and consequently did not accept the modern metaphorical meaning of *nation* that the Spanish implied when they spoke of their provinces.[30] Comanches viewed warfare in terms of rivalries between individuals and their families. When a presidial force from San Antonio injured some of the Indians' kinsfolk, they did not seek revenge upon the residents of Santa Fe because the Indians realized that there were very few, if any, family connections between these two distant outposts. The injuries Comanches received from the residents of Texas instigated their vengeance upon those particular individuals and their kindred.

Students of Comanches and Plains Indians have correctly suggested that competition for material resources ultimately formed the basis of these people's violent rivalries, but they have generally overstated its economic function. Berlandier mentioned that, because the origin of disputes between Comanches and their enemies dated back to "time immemorial," he could only assume that they fought over bison resources. In contrast to this assumption, Robert S. Neighbors claimed that Comanches never acknowledged their exclusive rights to game and that "no dispute ever arises between tribes with regard to their hunting grounds, the whole being held in common."[31] Yet one "resource" highly valued by Comanche men could not be held in common. This so-called resource was women, and it seems to have led to a tremendous amount of violent competition between Comanches themselves and with other tribes.

The competition between men for wives is primarily a product of human sexual evolution. Among mammals, males and females represent two different reproductive strategies. Male strategy focuses on reproduction rates, while female strategy emphasizes care for offspring. One of the ways this strategy has become manifest in humans is through polygyny, or males having more than one wife at once. Comanches practiced polygyny, and several sources have commented on this behavior. Berlandier recorded that among Comanches, "polygamy is the rule, and a man marries only in order to increase the number of his servants." This explanation for the motivation of Comanche men to marry multiple women widely misses the mark in light of reproductive strategies.[32]

A great deal of competition between men for women exists in polygynous societies like the Comanches. Polygyny places a constraint on the number of women available to men because fewer men marry more wives. In such societies women are scarce or limited "commodities." The prospect of few available women for wives especially is disadvantageous to the young men, for most women marry at a young age to old men. Capt. Randolph B. Marcy, who had spent some time in the Comanchería during the late 1840s and early 1850s, took note of this practice among the Comanches, commenting "that young girls are often compelled to unite their fortunes with old men." In particular, he observed that the chief named "Ketumsee, . . . a man at least sixty years old, had four wives, the oldest of whom was not over twenty years of age." Pedro Bautista Pino of Santa Fe had made a similar observation years earlier in 1812, noticing that "men of rank [older men?] often have as many as seven wives."[33]

Neighbors reported that some of the Comanche chiefs had more than ten wives and that this hoarding of women often resulted in inconstancy. A great deal of infidelity existed as the men seduced married women and ran away with them to live in isolation. Berlandier saw many "isolated huts built by such seducers who had exiled themselves from their tribe" during his 1828 exploration of the Texas Hill Country.[34] Because jealousy caused a great deal of discord among Comanches, the transgressors had to flee from angered husbands and relatives in fear for their lives.

On May 26, 1786, a Comanche (possibly the Cuchanec Cuetaninabeni) arrived at Santa Fe with his wife "and supplicated [Governor] Anza to protect him and save his life because all the captains were conspiring to kill him as a punishment for having been discovered in adultery with one of their women." While Anza disapproved of the crime, he promised to use his authority to secure a pardon for the Indian. Two years later, the twenty-year-old brother of Chief Guaquangas, two other Comanche men, and a Comanche woman they had "stolen" appeared in San Antonio in search of refuge. Gov. Rafael Martínez Pacheco communicated to Juan de Ugalde that he thought the runaway Comanches would remain in the provincial capital for a while because the Indians "are fearful that those of their nation might kill them, as they are used and accustomed to doing to those who steal their women."[35]

The adulterers' fears of being killed or severely punished often became a reality. In December, 1808, American trader Anthony Glass witnessed the extreme response of a man who had been cuckolded by his wife. Glass recounted that when the betrayed husband found his wife in bed with another Comanche of his party on the morning of the nineteenth, he "immediately shott him dead and then deliberately loaded his gun and shott his Wife also." As far as Berlandier understood, Comanche husbands never punished men who stole their wives with death. Instead, the Indians usually demanded some form of payment and corporal punishment as recompense. Adulterers usually paid fines consisting of horses, mules, bridles, guns, or whatever else he owned. The physical punishment usually comprised several strokes across the back of the offender with a whip. Berlandier explained that if a person had to decide between a material fine and a whipping, he usually chose the latter punishment because "if he bears the vengeance of the wronged husband stoically, he earns the good opinion of his compatriots for his courage." Women adulterers, however, did not fare as well as the men. According to Berlandier, when the fugitive wife finally returned to her husband, she was often killed. Sometimes she only suffered a slash to her nose and was "put away so she will always be an object of scorn." Robert S. Neighbors's observations of the Comanches are very similar to those of Berlandier, but he claimed that husbands usually punished their unfaithful wives by cutting off their nose and only sometimes with death.[36] As Glass's observation suggests, individual Comanches reacted to each instance of infidelity differently, depending on the situation. It is also clear from Glass's experience that Comanches approached wife stealing and adultery with a deadly seriousness.

Comanches' attitudes toward stealing the women and wives of their enemies contrasted sharply with their feelings of the same activity within their own ranks. Again, because Comanches usually did not recognize kinship connections to people considered as their enemies, they felt no moral need to exercise restraint on their behalf. Also, because so much competition existed among Comanches for their own women, they encouraged their warriors to acquire wives through captivity.

The acquisition of captives, especially girls and young women, served as an additional motivation for Comanches to strike out against their enemies. Their campaign against the Apaches in the early eighteenth century clearly demonstrates this motivation for their hostilities. When New Mexico governor Antonio de Valverde began his fall campaign of 1719 against the Comanches and their Ute allies, he met with some Jicarilla Apaches from whom he learned that the Comanches had repeatedly attacked them, killing many of their nation and carrying off a large number of their women and children. A few days later, after arriving at a Jicarilla settlement, the Indians there informed the governor that their Comanche and Ute enemies had descended on a *ranchería* of their nation, killed sixty persons, and took sixty-four women and children captive. A few years later, in 1724, Comanches again stormed the Jicarillas, taking all their women and children and seriously wounded sixty-four men, who "were dying one by one."[37]

The seizure of livestock and people also encouraged the many Comanche raids into northern Mexico during the nineteenth century. As a result of these activities, Comanches took captive numerous girls and women. Berlandier claimed that Comanche raids on both sides of the Rio Grande during the 1820s netted them "so many prisoners that there are still [1830s] more than 500 captives of both sexes living among them." Comanches often acquired several captives on these forays into Mexico. A raid near Ahorcados, Coahuila, on January 21, 1841, resulted in the taking of forty-one persons, twenty-two of them women.[38]

A popular explanation of Comanche seizures of captives has focused on the Indians' need to build up their population due to the deleterious effects brought about by diseases and warfare. This explanation is insufficient, for any increase this had on their total population would have only been a result of this practice, not its cause. The motivations for this behavior can only be explained in terms of human sexuality and the intense competition between males for women in polygynous societies. The attitudes of captives toward their captivity and captors support this conclusion. One of the things Berlandier noted about those held by Comanches was their desire to stay among the Indians even when offered the means to escape. The Frenchman found that "what attaches [captives] most to these wandering hordes [Comanches] is the fact that they may win the right to marry." When Josiah Gregg traded with a group of Comanches near the Canadian River in June, 1839, he noticed a captive Mexican woman among them. He communicated with her in Spanish and learned that she had been taken from her home in Matamoros, Tamaulipas. When Gregg asked her if she wished to be released, she informed him that she "had been married to a Comanche since her captivity . . . [and] did not entertain the least desire of returning to her people."[39]

Warfare and violence played a large role in Comanches' everyday lives during the eighteenth and nineteenth centuries. Most explanations of this behavior have understood it as their reactions to the competitive dimensions of the environmental, economic, and political circumstances existing in the southern plains during those two centuries. There can be no doubt that Comanches competed against Europeans and other Indians for scarce resources, such as bison, domestic livestock, and trade goods, but this competition does not explain why Comanches often resorted to violence to attain these things. Understanding why Comanche history is filled with so many exhibitions of belligerence and violence is a complicated task primarily because these actions were ultimately motivated by the Comanches' kinship and reproductive behavior.

Comanches tended to behave altruistically to those individuals they recognized as kin. Like other people, the amount of altruism Comanches generally extended to their relatives correlated with genealogical distance, favoring their close relatives over distant ones. The religious smoke ritual Comanche men performed on an everyday basis encouraged all Comanches and their non-Comanche relatives to behave toward one another as if they were as closely related as brothers. Consequently, they encouraged each other to favor their relatives over all other nonrelated persons and to defend each against such outsiders. Sometimes Comanches' defense of their kindred could precipitate violent and gruesome episodes like that at the San Sabá Mission in 1758.

Comanches had no reason to behave socially toward persons with whom they could not trace a genealogical link. Unrelated Indians, Spaniards, Mexicans, Texans, and Americans generally suffered from the violence to which Comanches often resorted in order to compete for resources and protect their kindred. The Indians felt no restraint when it came to stealing livestock, abducting women and children, robbing traders, and taking the lives of anyone unrelated to them.

When kinsmen did commit offenses against one another, they frequently responded violently. The polygynous nature of Comanche society encouraged a high level of competition for women, which itself often encouraged adultery and the stealing of wives. Comanche men many times responded to such offences with rage and deadly violence. As Glass's observation shows, transgressors sometimes paid for their behavior with their lives. The appearance of runaway couples in Santa Fe and San Antonio in search of refuge from jealous husbands and angry kinsmen also attests to the danger such actions could bring upon fugitive couples.

While Comanches discouraged stealing one another's wives, they did encourage their men to abduct enemy women for wives. Various issues motivated Comanches to raid their enemies, and the prospect of capturing wives should be counted among them. Their battles with Apaches during the 1720s and their numerous forays against the villages and outposts of northern Mexico in the 1840s clearly demonstrate that they had a strong interest in abducting women.

Comanches could be extremely aggressive and violent at times, but this behavior did not reflect a fundamentally belligerent nature. The incentives for their aggression are found in the complexities of kinship social behavior. By demonstrating hostility toward enemies, Comanches communicated their willingness to sacrifice for their own kindred. From this perspective, Comanche belligerence toward others can be understood as an aspect of their social behavior.

Conclusion

S TUDENTS OF COMANCHE BEHAVIOR HAVE TENDED TO UNDER-
stand it as the result of an adaptation to various environmental conditions.
This type of interpretation has given rise to the perception that Comanche
society developed in response to the climatic and economic circumstances of the
Great Basin prior to 1706 and of the southern Great Plains during the eighteenth
and nineteenth centuries. According to this way of thinking, Comanches' historical behavior should be understood as a consequence of the interaction between the environment and the group.

Unfortunately, the social organization of a group does not determine people's
actions. Rather, the structure is an effect of human social and kinship behavior.
The fundamental basis of social behavior is the kinship behavior parents demonstrate in sacrificing their interests in favor of their child's. Social behavior implies
a sacrifice of one's interests in favor of the interests of another. Chief Ecueracapa
demonstrated this when he offered his three sons to the Spanish for military service against the Apaches. In this case, he literally sacrificed his and his sons' interests in favor of the welfare of Gov. Juan Bautista de Anza and Spanish New
Mexico. Anza did not misunderstand the social nature of this act. He responded
in kind by charging his soldiers to "look after and attend [the young Comanches]
with great goodwill and kindness."[1]

The social behavior involved in the parent-child relationship is ultimately
based on kinship. Comanches used kin terms and clan, or family, names to identify their ancestors and co-descendant relatives. The use of these encouraged an

extension of the sacrificial behavior normally occurring between parents and children to more distantly related co-descendants. Comanches could acknowledge their common ancestry when they called distant relatives by intimate kin terms such as *pávi* ("older brother") and *tami* ("younger brother"). Besides allowing people to recognize their common kinship, these terms also encouraged an asymmetrical form of sacrifice like that between older and younger brothers. When people's exact birth links had become obscured over the course of time, ancestral, or clan, names like Cuchanec, Jupe, and Yamparica could be used to identify distant kin with whom people could interact socially. Thus, individuals of any of these clans could associate with anyone who traced a birth link to their particular lineage. These persons need not have shared the same name because Comanches, like other peoples, recognized clan affiliations with mothers and fathers equally.

Comanches' residential units, or camps, were good examples of the tangible "organizational" consequences of kinship social relations. As contemporary observers noted, individual Comanches freely withdrew from and united with camps at their convenience. This behavior can best be explained as an effect of their ability to identify kindred and to interact with them socially. Thus, Comanches freely congregated with individuals whom they identified as co-descendant, whether they shared the same clan name or not. Individuals who identified themselves as a member of one clan — like Cuchanec — could have lived in camps associated with any other if they could trace descent from the ancestor of those camps. Besides facilitating social behavior among Comanches, their kinship behavior also served as the fundamental impetus bringing them together into residential camp groups.

Because Comanche names such as Jupe, Cuchanec, Yamparica, and Tenewa represented kinship connections between people, their existence depended on the continuation of these relationships. Comanches traced their ancestry through the male line. Therefore, the reproduction of sons was necessary and sufficient for the existence of a clan name. The history of the Jupe Comanches especially demonstrates how clans could become diminished and subject to extinction. The intermittent warfare between Comanches and New Mexicans from the 1760s to the 1780s probably initiated this ancestral group's disappearance from the province. Warfare, conflict with rival kinsmen, drought, and disease apparently had a detrimental affect on the male members of the Jupe family. A high number of deaths among them would have left fewer men to father descendants inheriting that particular clan name. Although the Jupe family ultimately endured, their history emphasizes the inherent fragility of human clans.

The appearance of new Comanche lineages throughout the eighteenth and nineteenth centuries occurred apart from the demise of former clans. The dissolution of close consanguineous ties, geographical isolation, and intermarriage with other peoples all contributed to the genesis of new Comanche clans. The eastern branch of the Cuchanec family living in Texas and Oklahoma eventually branched into some new clans due to these factors. For instance, the emergence of the Tenewa family under El Sordo in the early nineteenth century specifically characterizes how the recognition of distinct ancestral linkages could lead to the genesis of new lineages. El Sordo's geographical isolation and intermarriage with Tahuacano women encouraged Comanches to refer to him and his descendants as a related, yet distinct, clan.

The circumstances surrounding El Sordo's split from the eastern Cuchanecs and the advent of the Tenewa clan suggest that disagreements over a person's stature within family hierarchies provoked conflicts and sometimes encouraged individuals to dissociate themselves from their rival co-descendants. In tribal societies like that of the Comanches, a person's authority or power is derived from his position in the tribe's age-based hierarchy and the ability to encourage cooperation among individuals. Religious rituals such as the pipe ceremony discouraged competition between co-descendants and encouraged sacrifice, or social behavior, among the participants. By taking part in the sacred rites, Comanche men communicated their acceptance of the common ancestor's parental authority and a responsibility to associate with one another as "brothers" outside of the ceremonial setting. Their customary encouragement of ranked relationships, therefore, influenced individuals to regularly cooperate.

Understanding Comanche social organization in terms of social and kinship behavior provides a basic framework for interpreting various other behaviors these people demonstrated in the past. Geographical mobility, horse pastoralism, tribal economics, and violence can all be accounted for as stemming from this fundamental behavioral system.

Social relationships greatly influenced Comanche migrations, nomadism, and the general geographical location where they lived. Throughout the course of the eighteenth and nineteenth centuries, Comanches forged and maintained social ties with Utes, Pueblos, Caddoans, Spanish New Mexicans and Texans, and even Apaches primarily through the kinship associations that emerged from intermarriage and the birth of offspring. Kinship cooperation is advantageous to people competing for physical resources. The active recognition of ties between individual Comanches and persons of various other tribes formed the foundation of widespread social relationships through which the Indians cooperated in the competition for local resources. The Shoshones who migrated to the southern plains during the eighteenth century, becoming the Comanche Nation, depended upon particular geographically located kin relationships in order to successfully compete for bison, horses, and other necessary resources. Their migration and geographical mobility therein should ultimately be understood as historical happenstance originating from intermarriage, reproduction, and the availability of particular resources.

Comanches also exhibited all four necessary and sufficient conditions for the existence of pastoralism by the late eighteenth century: Individuals owned domesticated animals in the form of horses. They bequeathed their livestock to surviving relatives. The animals reproduced. And the Indians made use of some consequence of their horses' behavior. The pastoralism demonstrated by Comanches in the historical sources is an example of cultural behavior they ultimately acquired from Spanish colonists, who originally introduced livestock agriculture into New Mexico. Culture is any behavior that is learned from another individual and then reproduced. The material and behavioral attributes identified with horse tack, lassos, corrals, lances, herding techniques, and livestock markings and decorations suggest that Comanches learned and mimicked the associated Spanish customs too. Therefore, Comanche horse culture was ultimately a manifestation of an aspect of Spanish pastoralism.

Most likely, the first Comanche pastoralists did not learn horse pastoralism directly from the Europeans. Rather, they probably acquired Iberian pastoralist culture through related Ute intermediaries sometime prior to 1706. The close interaction between Utes and the Spanish colonists of New Mexico in the seventeenth century apparently facilitated their learning and copying of the various behaviors associated with maintaining horses. Once this cultural behavior was maintained by a successive generation of Utes, it became part of the Indians' cultural tradition. Those Comanches who first attained horses likely acquired Spanish pastoralist tradition via their intermarriage with Utes and subsequent exposure to Ute culture.

Comanches realized the positive effects brought about by the ownership of horses. Although economic and environmental considerations are deeply involved in the practice of pastoralism, neither can explain the complete significance of domestic-animal ownership. The social nature of livestock ownership is probably best exemplified by Comanche marriage practices involving the gift of horses as part of the "bride-price" a husband presented to his wife's family. The livestock and other property given away had social as well as economic significance in that it represented the generous nature of the groom as a potential husband and father. This practice was not simply an exchange of commodities (that is, horses for women), for it communicated the groom's willingness to sacrifice his interests in favor of the bride's interests and those of their children.

Comanches placed a great deal of importance in their ability to acquire various resources through commercial interaction with other peoples. The intermarriage of Comanches with New Mexicans, Texans, Caddoans, Kiowas, and other Indians not only facilitated their migration to the southern plains but also allowed for the establishment of strong commercial ties between these various peoples. Understanding commercial exchange as an effect of human kinship and social relationships emphasizes that individual Comanches determined their own economic behavior. Although people are not automatically compelled to interact socially with their kindred, ancestral traditions strongly encourage that they do so. Thus, commercial relationships probably emerged among people as a result of this heritage. The earliest form of commerce probably developed from the specialization and cooperation that existed between mothers, fathers, children, and siblings as they shared the fruits of their labors with one another.

Although people's personal interests generate economics, resultant trade is not a zero-sum game where there must be a winner and a loser. The division of labor among individuals encourages the social effect of commerce because certain people own or specialize in things that others do not or cannot produce. Although two persons have personal interests in acquiring the goods the other owns, they *both* benefit by acquiring the items through social behavior as opposed to unsocial aggression. The interrelationship between kinship and social behavior, division of labor, and supply and demand formed the basis of the various contexts of the trade in which Comanches participated. Although most of their commercial relationships were probably based on kinship social relationships, they also established these types of associations with unrelated persons. Comanches recognized when strangers behaved like a kinsmen toward them, and they responded in kind. The demonstration of social behavior, however, did not always ensure that Comanches would reciprocate the generosity extended to them. Because trade requires people to sacrifice their interests to a certain degree, traders are vulnerable to various abuses when someone decides to take advantage of a situation. Comanches often responded with violence when they thought they had been disrespected or cheated in the course of conducting a trade. Therefore, the possibility of violence always loomed over commercial encounters with these Indians.

Warfare and violence played a large role in Comanches' everyday lives during the eighteenth and nineteenth centuries. Because they tended to behave altruistically to those individuals they recognized as kin, the amount of benevolence Comanches generally extended to their relatives correlated with genealogical distance. Therefore, Comanches favored close relatives over distant ones. The religious smoking ritual performed by Comanche men encouraged all Comanches and their non-Comanche kinsmen to favor one another as if they were close relatives and to defend each other against unrelated outsiders. Comanches had no reason to behave socially toward anyone with whom they could not trace a genealogical link. Consequently, unrelated persons bore the brunt of the violent behavior the Indians often employed to compete for resources and protect their kindred. However, when kinsmen did commit offenses against one another, individual Comanches often responded violently. That Comanches exhibited extreme aggression and violence at times does not suggest that they were naturally a belligerent people. Rather, their demonstration of hostile aggression toward rivals communicated their willingness to sacrifice for the interests of their own kindred.

Viewing the Comanche past through a prism of human social and kinship behavior reveals the component behaviors that impelled the course of their history, which was generated by the actions of individuals as they coped with the natural and social environments that existed and were created everywhere Comanches lived.

Appendix 1
A Discussion of Theoretical Issues

The central thesis of this study could be wrong.[1] This acknowledgment, however, does not weaken the strength of the reasoning found herein. On the contrary, the recognition of its potential fallibility should strengthen the argument. I have attempted to state the terms of reasoning within these pages in ways that are potentially refutable and disprovable. This approach is the nature of empiricism, and it should be the character of historical scholarship as well. The strength in this method lies in its ability to allow for the establishment of reasoned or logical truth and, therefore, to the attainment of historical truth in the theoretical sense. The ongoing quibble among historians over the nature of facts and of truth is unnecessary and widely misses the mark, for past events are no longer concrete and can neither be reproduced nor tested. Only after the burning issue of the nature of historical facts is put aside can historians get down to the real business of interpreting the past in an empirical manner. Instead of worrying about the truth of facts, historians should be focused more on general methodology that embraces the tenets of empiricism, especially the criterion of disprovability. The validity of various "facts" or propositions can be established only after this type of approach is established.[2] One of the more ethereal aims of this book is to demonstrate an approach to understanding past events that embraces basic empiricism.

A problem with the study of human history is that historians have to rely on the senses of subjects and informants who are usually long dead by the time their observations are scrutinized in a scholarly fashion. Besides this concern, the issue of whether or not various subjects and informants can be considered reliable sources muddles the ability of scholars to reconstruct past reality. To know exactly how past human events came about is practically an impossible task since they involved an incomprehensibly vast amount of variables.[3] So far, it is inconceivable that anyone could account for all the variables that interacted to bring about a single historical event such as Corté's conquest of the Aztec capital of Tenochtitlan in 1521.

Historians have generally explained why historical events occurred by demonstrating how they came about. A fuller understanding of Comanche history, however, requires the comprehension of information beyond a chronological narrative of events. Narrative alone is not sufficient to answer important questions concerning the fundamental motivation behind the behavior of individual Comanches at particular moments in the past.

Although historians have outlined the general chronology of Comanche history, anthropologists have stood out in the discussion concerning the theoretical aspects of the

Comanche past since the early part of the twentieth century. Cultural determinism, or the belief that all human behavior is the result of cultural conditioning, was originally theorized by anthropologist Franz Boas and has since formed the conceptual foundation for all subsequent interpretations of the development of Indian cultural and historical behavior. The idea of cultural determinism was influenced by Immanuel Kant's postulate that human beings have the capacity to construct the character of themselves and their societies and by an intense distaste for the fashionable evolutionist anthropology at the turn of the twentieth century. Boas suggested that culture did not result from the innate qualities of human beings but that it emerged from external conditions that acted upon human attributes. He further argued that culture was in no way influenced by biology. Rather, culture represented a response of human beings to influences of the surrounding environment.[4] History and nature acted as a powerful inspiration to the development of human cultures, giving rise to distinctive group behaviors. Ultimately, this approach to understanding human behavior completely overcame any form of biological comprehension of human nature and has generally flourished within the social sciences and humanities.

Unfortunately, cultural determinism eschewed the tenets of scientific rationality, and it is inherently flawed as a means of interpreting human behavior and cultures. The rejection of the empirical approach by cultural determinists has prevented them from acknowledging cases of negative examples that refute proposed hypotheses. Instead, such contrary evidence has been viewed simply as an exception to accepted hypotheses and models. The analytical shortcomings of cultural determinism have obscured a clear understanding of Comanche culture and history.

The debate over the nature of Comanche culture and history has revealed the deficiencies of cultural deterministic reasoning. When anthropologists compared Comanches with other Plains Indians, they found that Comanches generally did not exhibit some of the typical characteristics that had become associated with the Indians living on the Great Plains in the nineteenth century. The explanations of the exceptional case of the Comanches basically followed either one of two lines of reasoning set within the general framework of cultural-deterministic thinking. Scholars generally questioned if the cultural traits exhibited by various Plains Indian cultures had originally developed as an adaptive response to the Great Plains environment or if they demonstrated the persistence of a previous adaptation to the environment of another region. These two perspectives became known as cultural adaptation and cultural persistence.[5] The general acceptance of the adaptation and persistence dichotomy forced scholars to look at Comanche culture in those terms, and the apparent anomaly Comanches represented with respect to the Plains Indian culture seemed to suggest only one of two possibilities—that they represented either adaptation or persistence. By and large, scholars believed that the one explanation necessarily eliminated the other as a possible solution to the problem, but this perspective proved to be faulty.

For years, the debate over past Comanche behavior has focused on their significance either as an example of adaptation to the Great Plains environment or as a case of the persistence of behavioral traits that developed in response to the environment of their former home in the Great Basin. Adaptation, persistence, and synthesis arguments that combine the two hypotheses cannot be substantiated primarily because of their dichotomous nature and due to cultural determinism's initial premise that culture is an identifiable unit of study.

The adaptation-persistence debate has contributed little to what we know in general of past Comanche and Plains Indian societies. The circularity of this dialogue ultimately resulted from the unverifiable nature of cultural determinism. The initial rejection of the scientific method set a powerful precedent in American anthropology, permitting hypotheses to remain untested and accepted as valid explanations of human behavior. In his examination of Margaret Mead's study of adolescent behavior in Samoa, Derek Freeman demonstrates the intellectual barrenness that exists in the antiscientific "attitude of mind" of cultural determinism.[6]

The adaptation-persistence argument is founded on the faulty reasoning associated with any false dichotomous question, that is, making an exclusive choice between two nonexclusive alternatives. The suggestion that either adaptation or persistence could explain Comanche cultural behavior implied a choice between two concepts that scholars had accepted as sufficient explanations. This thinking is faulty because neither concept necessarily excludes the other nor do they exhaust all possible solutions to the problem. Likewise, any demonstration of the coexistence of both terms, the existence of a third possibility, or a repudiation of either or both alternatives fails to sufficiently resolve the dilemma brought about by the dichotomy. These approaches fall short since they are inherently bound to the fallacious conceptualization they are trying to resolve. The most suitable resolution to a false dichotomy is to revise the inquiry on the most basic level of question framing. In other words, instead of asking whether the Comanches were an example of adaptation or persistence, one should completely dispose of that question in favor of a more open query.[7]

The first anthropologists and sociologists of the late nineteenth century accepted and established the concepts of culture and society as entities unto themselves.[8] These phenomena were seen as real entities that could be objectively studied. However, the cultural determinists of the early twentieth century suggested that culture was something that existed beyond the nature, and therefore beyond the realm, of scientific inquiry. However, the real problem with cultural determinism transcended its rejection of the scientific approach.

In his 1971 Huxley Memorial Lecture given before the Royal Anthropological Institute of Great Britain and Ireland, George Peter Murdock concluded that all concepts based on the sums of individuals (for example, culture, society, world view, social organism) are unreal conceptual abstractions inferred from the interaction of individuals with one another and their natural environments. If culture and social structure are derivative products of individuals' interaction, then human behavior can best be understood by studying individual actions rather than how a certain culture determines one's behavior. Therefore, concepts like culture and society can only be perceived as a consequence rather than a cause of individuals' behavior. According to Murdock's way of thinking, understanding human behavior as determined by culture or anything else beyond the level of the individual are inherently fallacious approaches. Murdock labeled theories like cultural determinism as simple mythology and not science. He suggested that these concepts be rejected outright since their revision or modification only perpetuates this mythology.[9]

So, the cultural deterministic notions of adaptation and persistence and the theoretical abstractions associated with terms such as *culture* and *society* should be tossed into the landfill of dead-end conceptual constructs in order to resolve the problematic false dichotomy presented by the adaptation-persistence debate and to develop a more reasonable understanding of culture and society. However, these issues can be resolved simply by discarding cultural determinism altogether in favor of a more rigorous analytical and verifiable approach.

One way to exorcize this chain-rattling specter of cultural determinism from the study of human behavior and history is to firmly establish the nature of a definition. The inability and refusal of scholars to identify the necessary and sufficient conditions giving rise to the existence of human behaviors and traits has reduced academic inquiry into these issues to the point of meaningless relativity. Definitions are logical propositions and are *not* arbitrary. As propositions, they have meaning if their referents are verifiable by observation.[10] Definitions are testable hypotheses stating the necessary and sufficient conditions for the referent of any given term. The definitions of such terms as *culture, society,* and *religion* must be verifiable and therefore potentially disprovable before they have concrete or real meaning. When definitions are constructed in this manner, they not only serve as potentially disprovable hypotheses but also establish a foundation upon which knowledge can be discovered, developed, and understood.

If cultural determinism is an ineffectual theoretical concept for approaching and explaining past human behavior, then what alternative hypothetical notion might better illuminate the enigmatic impetus of such behavior? Natural selection as conceptualized by Charles Darwin and Alfred Russell Wallace provides the insight necessary to explain the historical behavior of human beings. Natural selection, or the influence of inheritable traits on their own frequency in later generations, is not an outrageous new concept; it has been around for a good while.[11] Darwin initially proposed this idea in 1859 in his book *Origin of the Species.* Despite the ability of this theory to withstand the test of time in the discipline of biology, social scientists have generally considered it absurd to apply the idea to humans whose nature, they contend, lies outside of the biological world.

Historians have traditionally avoided ultimate questions concerning the nature of the relationship between the natural world, human behavior, and the past. But why should historians and other social scientists be concerned with natural selection? The answer to this question lies in the fact that human beings are in essence biological creatures, and as such creatures, humans are subject to the influence of natural selection just like any other living thing. The fundamental premise of cultural determinism-the denial of the biological basis of human nature in favor of the unique force of culture-has contributed very little substantive knowledge about the *ultimate* causes of human behavior. The standard social science or cultural determinist explanation of human behavior is focused primarily on *proximate* causation, or the particular sequence of events leading to a particular behavior. In other words, proximate explanations of human behavior account for how a particular behavior is influenced by something in the environment. Cultural determinism is an explanation by proximate causation, for culture is understood as the predominant environment influencing the development of human behavior. Ultimate causal analysis, however, considers *why* a behavior persists. The theory of natural selection is powerful and useful because it has the potential to explain the ultimate cause of our behavior, asking *why* do humans typically behave in particular ways as opposed to *what* stimulated the behavior. It must be stressed here that neither a proximate nor ultimate explanation is necessarily better-they are simply different. Scholars should be equally interested in explaining and understanding both causes of human behavior. However, both types of explanation can only contribute to knowledge if they can stand up to the unyielding requirements of analysis and verification. Cultural-deterministic hypotheses for human behaviors are not wrong because they are proximate explanations; they are wrong because they cannot stand up to the standard of disproof. Since proximate causes must operate within the confines of an ultimate cause, understanding the evolution of human behavior can assist historians in explaining not only *how* historical events developed but also *why* they occurred. Because the theory of natural selection is potentially disprovable, it can be used as a compelling mechanism in hypothesizing about past human behavior, ultimately advancing our substantive knowledge about our history.[12]

This book maintains that its central propositions should be testable and potentially falsifiable in some fashion. An initial way to disprove the conclusions stated above is to demonstrate that selection as proposed by Darwin and Wallace cannot be applied to our understanding of past human behavior in general. The identification of any continuous behavior detrimental to the ability of human ancestors to leave descendants in general would suggest that humans' are not affected by selection. Another means of refuting the assumptions of this book is by questioning the proposed definitions of social, kinship, cultural, and traditional behaviors and their ultimate effects on the ability of humans to leave descendants. In an evolutionary sense, social behavior refers to sacrifice, or altruism, at the expense of one's own reproduction. The identification of a social behavior that does not imply altruism or is not ultimately at the expense of one's reproduction invalidates this hypothesis. Kinship behavior is social behavior whose intensity is correlated with genealogical distance. Therefore, any identified kinship behavior not correlated with genealogical distance contradicts this conjecture. Culture is behavior that an individual learns and copies from another individual. This hypothesis would be invalidated by an example of cultural behavior that had neither been observed nor replicated from anyone else. Finally, tradition is culture that individuals acquire from their ancestors. The observation of any traditional behavior that is not acquired by ancestors, or members of previous generations, nullifies this definition. Furthermore, any of these premises can be disproved if these behaviors can be shown to have persisted despite having a negative effect on the ability of individuals to leave descendants. Because this study has argued that human social and kinship behavior is the key to comprehending eighteenth- and nineteenth-century Comanche society, the potential refutation of the hypotheses concerning these behaviors is crucial to the soundness of the thesis.

Appendix 2

A Timeline of Comanche History, 1706–1850

This timeline is based primarily on information in Elizabeth A. H. John, *Storms Brewed in Other Mens' Worlds: The Confrontation of Indians, Spanish, and French in the Southwest, 1540–1795* (1975; reprint, Lincoln: University of Nebraska Press, Bison Books, 1981); Thomas W. Kavanagh, *Comanche Political History: An Ethnohistorical Perspective, 1706–1875* (Lincoln: University of Nebraska Press, 1996); Elizabeth A. H. John, "Nurturing the Peace: Spanish and Comanche Cooperation in the Early Nineteenth Century," *New Mexico Historical Review* 59, no. 4 (1984): 345–69; John, "An Earlier Chapter of Kiowa History," *New Mexico Historical Review* 60, no. 4 (1985): 379–97.

1706: Comanches are reported in the vicinity of New Mexico in the accompaniment of Utes.

1707–12: Comanches and Utes establish peace with New Mexico during the rule of Marqués de la Peñuela.

1714: Utes harry New Mexico.
Governor Flores Mogollón arranges restitution between the Indians and restored peace to the province.

1716: Comanches and Utes raid northern New Mexico settlements under the cloak of peace.
A Spanish council of war authorizes a retaliatory force to attack a Comanche and Ute village located in the San Antonio Mountains. The autumn strike is successful in killing and capturing many Indians.

1719: Greater numbers of Comanches and Utes appear in the vicinity of New Mexico.
Comanches and Utes continue their push into the plains, launching fierce attacks against Plains Apaches and Caddoan-speaking Indians such as Wichitas and Pawnees. These raids result in the death and captivity of numerous Apaches.
Comanches and Utes raid settlements in northern New Mexico during the summer.
An August Spanish council of war decides to retaliate against Comanche and Ute

perpetrators. The September–October expedition fails to confront any Comanche or Ute enemies.

French explorers and traders make contact with the various Plains Caddo (Wichita) villages in the Arkansas River valley.

After visiting Wichitas, French explorer Claude du Tisne appears before the Comanches in September.

1720: Apaches appear in Spanish Texas for the first time and commit hostilities.

1723: Comanches and Utes unleash a ferocious offensive against Plains Apaches, resulting in the death and capture of numerous individuals.

1724: At the request of beleaguered Apaches, New Mexico governor Juan Domingo de Bustamente leads a somewhat successful campaign against the Comanches and Utes expanding into the plains northeast of New Mexico.

Comanches reportedly overwhelm Apaches in a nine-day battle somewhere in northwestern Texas at a location called El Gran Sierra del Fierro.

French trader M. Galliard presides over a springtime peace ceremony between the Comanches and Kansas.

French trader Étienne Veniard de Bourgmont establishes peace between France and the Comanches in the fall.

1726: Apaches abandon the plains northeast of New Mexico and retreat to Taos and points farther south and east toward Texas in the face of persistent Comanche and Ute attacks.

The number of Apache raids in Texas decrease substantially.

1731: Texas experiences a resumption of Apache raids.

1735: Comanches visit northern New Mexican settlements for trade.

Spanish documents suggest a dissolution of the Comanche and Ute alliance.

Apaches push beyond the Rio Grande and begin to raid the ranches and villas of Coahuila.

Tawakonis (a Plains Caddoan tribe) abandons the Arkansas River valley and flees south to the Red River sometime in the late 1730s.

1740: Apaches begin to become interested in Spanish missions in Texas under the threat of growing Comanche pressure.

Comanches launch retaliatory raids against the pueblos of Pecos and Galisteo in New Mexico.

French explorers and traders Pierre and Paul Mallet visit Comanches.

1742: New Mexicans launch two unsuccessful campaigns against the Comanches.

1743: Comanches appear in the vicinity of San Antonio de Béxar for the first time.

1746: Comanches establish peace with Plains Caddoans.
New Mexico governor Joachín Codallos y Rabal closes the Comanche trade.
Comanches launch a major attack upon Pecos in June. A Spanish force pursues the
raiders and inflict more than sixty casualties. Two weeks later Comanches attack
Galisteo.

1747: In October, Comanches and Utes attack Abiquiu.

1748: Comanches attack Pecos again in January.
French traders visit the Comanche camps.
Comanches arrive at Taos for trade.

1749: Apaches agree to a peace treaty with Spanish Texas.
By the late 1740s, the Tawakonis abandon the Red River and establish themselves
on the Sabine River to the south.
Comanches wage war against the Aa Indians.
French traders circulate among Comanches as they travel across the plains en route
to New Mexico.
Comanche raiders attack Galisteo on December 12. Several days later Comanches
arrive in Taos for trade.

1750: Comanches introduce four European traders to Taos in February.
The Wichitas mediate a peace between Comanches and Pawnees.
Some Apaches move near San Antonio in search for protection against Comanches.
Pierre Mallet has an unfriendly brush with Comanches along the Canadian River as
he travels toward Santa Fe.

1751: Allied Comanches, Wichitas, and Pawnees attack a Grand Osage village, inflicting
heavy damages.
Apaches continue to move south beyond the Nueces River and into the territory of
Coahuila.
French traders Jean Chapuis and Louis Foissy encounter Comanches in their pas-
sage to New Mexico.
During the summer, New Mexico governor Tomás Vélez Cachupín meets with Co-
manches visiting Taos and strongly encourages them to behave peacefully toward
New Mexico.
That fall, Comanches continue to raid Galisteo and Pecos.
A party of 145 Comanches is decisively defeated in November by Governor Vélez
Cachupín in retaliation for the recent raids in New Mexico.
Chief El Nimiricante Luis organizes a general meeting of Comanches to discuss
their relations with New Mexico. The Indians resolve to establish peace with the
Spanish province.

1752: Comanches forge a peaceful relationship with Vélez Cachupín and New Mexico.
Comanches establish peace with the Panismahas along the Missouri River and continue to assist their allies in the persecution of Osages, Kansas, and Apaches.

French traders continue to circulate among the Comanche villages.
Comanches maintain pressure on their Ute, Pecos, and Galisteo enemies.

1755: Natagé Apaches negotiate a peace with Coahuila settlements and ally themselves
with Julimes Indians.

1756: Viceroy of New Spain authorizes an Apache mission project in Texas.

1757: Mission Santa Cruz de San Sabá is established on the San Sabá River.
The Wichitas and Taovayas and other Plains Caddoans complete their southerly retreat from the Arkansas River to the Red River in the face of Osage attacks.

1758: Allied Tejas, Bidais, Tonkawa, and Comanche Indians destroy Mission Santa Cruz
de San Sabá.

1759: A Spanish force of 502 men led by Col. Diego Ortiz Parrilla unsuccessfully lays siege
to the Taovaya village on the Red River in a campaign designed to avenge the destruction of San Sabá Mission.

1760: Taos Indians offend visiting Comanches by performing a scalp dance with Comanche scalps.
A large Comanche force sacks Taos in August.
A Spanish retaliatory campaign is unsuccessful at finding and punishing any Comanches.

1761: Three hundred Comanches appear in Taos in December to sue for peace with New
Mexico. The New Mexicans, under the leadership of Gov. Manuel del Portillo y Ur-
risola, snub the Comanches and their request for peace by attacking the Indians,
killing two hundred men and taking the women and children captive.

1762: Tomás Vélez Cachupín is reappointed governor of New Mexico and immediately
reestablishes peaceful relations with the Comanches.
In January the Spanish establish Mission San Lorenzo de la Santa Cruz in the El
Cañon region of the upper Nueces River in Texas in an effort to serve and protect
besieged Lipan Apaches under the leadership of El Gran Cabezón.
Mission Nuestra Señora de la Candelaria is also established in El Cañon that Febru-
ary at the insistence of the Lipan chief El Turnio.
Comanches appear in the area of El Cañon in March, raiding outlying Lipan
rancherías.
Comanches and allied Indians pursue Apaches living in the vicinity of Texas
throughout the summer.
Some Apaches push south of San Antonio in a search for refuge from the hostile
Comanches and their allies.
Lipans abandon the El Cañon region in the fall. Many Apaches return the follow-
ing winter.

1763: Indians allied with the Comanches attack San Antonio in response to the protection the Spanish provide Apaches.

1764: Comanches and allied Indians continue their violent persecution of Apaches in the region west of San Antonio.

1766: Comanches maintain friendly relations with New Mexico and make regular appearances at Taos trade fairs.
Comanches and their allies attack the Spanish missions located in the El Cañon region.

1768: Large parties of Comanches and allied Indians appear in the vicinity of San Antonio and commit depredations among the outlying ranches.
Comanches raid Natagé Apaches in Nueva Vizcaya.
More than four hundred Comanches arrive in Taos in late May under a white flag of peace in order to engage in trade.
Other Comanches approaching Ojo Caliente from the north are attacked by a Spanish force of fifty soldiers stationed on San Antonio Mountain. The beleaguered Comanches flee east across the Rio Grande to Taos. Upset by the news of the attack, the Indians at Taos kill six Spanish traders and flee the pueblo.
A state of war between the Comanches and New Mexico breaks out.
New Mexico governor Pedro Fermín de Mendinueta leads an unsuccessful campaign against the Comanches.
Two-dozen Comanches raid Ojo Caliente in September.
The New Mexicans retaliate, killing twenty-one Comanches and taking two prisoners.
Fifteen Comanches raid Picurís in October.
Five hundred Comanches descend on Ojo Caliente. Cuerno Verde is killed.

1769: Comanche raiders attack the mission complex at Picurís.
Comanches raid Taos.
Comanche and Spanish forces clash again at San Antonio Mountain in August.

1770: Representatives of Taovayas, Wichitas, Iscanis, Tawakonis, and Kichais meet with Spanish envoy Athanase de Mézières at the Kadohadacho village of Chief Tinhioüen to discus the establishment of peace in Texas. Comanches oppose the establishment of peaceful relations with the Spanish in Texas and refuse to attend the conference.
Comanches become hostile toward their former Caddoan allies over the issue of peace with Spanish Texas.

1771: Comanches conclude a peace treaty with New Mexico governor Mendinueta on February 7.
Comanches and other Indians commit depredations at San Antonio and throughout Texas.

Comanches raid their former Caddoan allies.

In October, three Taovayas chiefs arrive in Natchitoches and sign a treaty of peace on behalf of their people and their allies.

1772: Comanches continue to raid New Mexican horse herds.

Comanches engage New Mexicans in trade at Taos.

Five hundred Comanche warriors attack Pecos.

Comanches launch five separate raids against Picurís.

Galisteo suffers four Comanche raids. Mendinueta overwhelms the members of the last raiding party on Galisteo, killing some of the perpetrators and recovering about sixty animals.

Comanches continue to commit depredations in Texas.

Five hundred Comanches under the leadership of Chief Povea meet Athanase de Mézières at the Wichita villages on the Brazos River.

In June Chief Povea and other representatives of the Comanches and their Caddoan allies accompany de Mézières to San Antonio to ratify and celebrate the establishment of peace between the Indians and Spanish Texas.

Comanches conduct many raids in the vicinity of San Antonio during Povea's stay there.

Apaches harass the party of Comanches and Caddoans attending the peace negotiation in San Antonio.

1773: In March and April, Comanche raiders descend upon the San Antonio region, seizing numerous Apache and Spanish horses.

Apaches retreat farther south across the Rio Grande into Coahuila and Nueva Vizcaya.

Five hundred Comanches attack Pecos in July.

That same month another five hundred Comanches attack Cochití. Governor Mendinueta pursues the raiders north to the Rio Conejos, where his force manages to kill fifteen Indians and capture their horses.

Picurís suffers five Comanche raids; Galisteo bears four raids.

Comanches trade at Taos.

That autumn, Comanches continue to commit depredations throughout Texas, diminishing Spanish confidence in the peace treaty signed the previous year.

Laredo looses 350 horses to Comanche raiders.

1774: Comanches abduct a large number of horses from San Antonio in February. A military force of 130 men unsuccessfully pursues the perpetrators.

Comanches kill two Picurís Indians on June 23.

Comanche raiders make off with the entire horse herd of Nambé pueblo on June 24.

On June 27 a large number of Comanches enter Taos to trade.

Plains Caddoans arrive in Natchitoches in late June. The Caddoans promise Athanase de Mézières that they would help avenge Comanche depredations in Texas.

A force of Tawakonis (Tahuacanos) intercepts a Comanche party returning from a raid on San Antonio and kills all fourteen of the raiders.

Tensions between Comanches and Plains Caddoans increase.

In July a large number of Comanches meet with J. Gaignard, a Spanish trader and emissary sent from Natchitoches. The Indians promise to keep the peace with the Spanish in Texas.

A large Comanche war party numbering over a thousand warriors attacks Santa Clara and San Juan pueblos as well as three settlements in the La Cañada district on July 27.

Pecos suffers from a raid on August 15. A force of 114 Spanish soldiers pursues the raiders eastward toward the plains, discovering and successfully attacking a large Comanche camp.

One hundred Comanches raid Albuquerque on August 18.

On September 19, nineteen Comanches are arrested in Taos and sent to Santa Fe under guard. All the prisoners are killed in Las Truchas as they try to escape their captors. Later in September, a Spanish force of six hundred men surprises a Comanche *ranchería*, killing and capturing over a hundred Indians.

1775: Comanches raid Pecos in early May.

Comanches attack a ranch on the outskirts of Santa Fe.

Comanche traders arrive in Taos on May 13. The Indians attack the pueblo after the *alcalde mayor* refuses to authorize a trade fair.

Comanche raiders target Nambé pueblo on May 27.

The pueblos of Sandía and La Alameda suffer Comanche raids in mid-June. A Spanish force pursues the raiders and are successful in killing some of the perpetrators and capturing a number of their horses.

Pecos once again experiences a large Comanche attack on June 25.

Comanches descend on Galisteo in August.

1776: New Mexico experiences Comanche raids in June.

Yamparica Comanches wage war against the Sabuaguanas Utes throughout the summer.

Comanches kill three hundred Apache families fleeing from a grand Spanish offensive designed to subdue the Apaches on the northern frontier of New Spain.

1777: Comanches attack Tomé in May, killing twenty-one New Mexican settlers. The Indians strike Tomé again in November, but this time the raiders endure the majority of the casualties.

1778: Comanches pester Tawakoni settlements along the Brazos River.

Comanches focus much of their raiding activities toward the ranches located near Laredo.

Comanche raiders attack a Spanish train on the road between San Antonio and the Presidio del Río Grande.

Athanase de Mézières visits the Taovayas village and charges a young Comanche to communicate the Spanish desire to establish peace with his kinsmen.

In May a Comanche peace delegation led by Chief Povea's son approaches the Spanish frontier outpost of Bucareli in an effort to meet with de Mézières. The settlers of Bucareli misinterpret the reason for the Indians' appearance and attack them. Comanches raid the New Mexico village of Tomé in early June.

The following October, Comanches make off with 240 horses from Bucareli. Kichai and Tejas Indians pursue the raiders and recover the horses near the Taovayas village. The Comanches counterattack the Caddoans and recapture the horses.

Chief Povea meets with a Tejas chief sent by de Mézières as a Spanish envoy to explain the mistake made by the settlers at Bucareli and to discuss the establishment of peace in Texas. Povea agrees to try to discourage his kinsmen from raiding the Spanish settlements.

1779: Comanches kill a Tejas Indian within view of the Tawakoni village playing host to de Mézières late that summer.

Comanche raiders steal over four hundred horses from Lipan Apaches camped in the Cañon de San Sabá.

About a dozen Comanches succumb to a Ute raid in July near Pike's Peak.

On August 31 a large Comanche *ranchería* encamped on Fountain Creek (Colorado) is surprised by a force of 762 men led by New Mexico governor Juan Bautista de Anza. A running battle ensues for about ten miles. The Spanish kill eighteen warriors and capture thirty-four women and children.

That same day, the Comanche chief Cuerno Verde (the younger) attacks Taos and is repulsed by the Taoseños, who had been forewarned of the raid by Apaches.

Upon his return to join his people on the plains, Cuerno Verde encounters Anza's force on September 3 and is killed along with his eldest son, four chiefs, a medicine man, and ten warriors.

A large number of Comanches raid the Lipan Apaches living northwest of San Antonio throughout the autumn.

Lipans continue their retreat to the south.

A couple of Comanche *rancherías* suffer ruin as a result of two wintertime attacks by American frontiersmen.

1780: Comanches attack a force from San Antonio along the Guadalupe River on New Year's Day and suffer the loss of nine warriors.

Throughout the spring, Comanches avoid the region surrounding San Antonio and make numerous overtures to establish peace with New Mexico.

In June a large Comanche war party invades Texas, seizing livestock and committing murders.

Comanches establish semipermanent camps along the ridge separating the Guadalupe and Colorado Rivers from which they launch numerous raids upon the outlying ranches and roads of Texas.

Comanche raiders steal the horses of twenty-two Mayeyes, Cocos, Bidais, and Akokisas Indians along the Brazos River.

By early autumn, signs of a Comanche presence in Texas become more evident. Comanche raiders attack the outpost of Cíbolo, killing three soldiers and stealing part of the horse herd.

1781: Comanches suffer heavy losses as a result of the 1780–81 smallpox epidemic. Comanches continue to trouble Spanish Texas.
A force of 172 men from San Antonio defeat Comanches encamped near the Medina River. The Indians suffer the loss of about one-third of their warriors, including a prominently decorated chief.

1783: Comanches appear on the outskirts of Texas. The Spanish brace for an attack, but the expected offensive never materializes.
Comanches appear in October in the vicinity of San Antonio accompanied by renegade Spaniard Miguel Jorge Menchaca, son of Capt. Luis Menchaca.
Comanches establish a large encampment of two hundred tepees at the junction of the Llano and Colorado Rivers.
The large Comanche *ranchería* moves southward. The Indians attack two settlers from Laredo on the road to San Antonio, taking ten of their horses.

1784: About forty Comanches suffer defeat by a force of Spaniards from San Antonio in July.
Comanche raiders steal the horses of Taovayas and Spanish diplomats making their way toward San Antonio from the Red River in order to discuss peace.
In December Comanche raiders enter San Antonio and steal horses from the settlement's corrals.

1785: Comanches commit depredations around San Antonio and Nacogdoches throughout the spring.
Raiders wound a soldier defending the San Antonio horse herd in March.
Two Texas settlers fall victim to Comanche raiders in two separate incidents in May.
On July 12 four hundred Comanches arrive in Taos to express their desire for peace with New Mexico.
One hundred and twenty warriors representing twenty-five Comanche *rancherías* visit Taos on July 29 to communicate their desire for peace.
That August, Eastern Cuchanec Comanches meet with the Spanish envoys Pedro Vial and Francisco Xavier Chaves to discuss making peace with the Taovayas, Wichitas, and the Spaniards of Texas.
Yamparica Comanches wage war against the Omahas and Otoes.
Hostile Jupe and Yamparica Comanches appear in New Mexico in late August intent on committing depredations. The Spanish are prepared for a defense and suffer minimal damage.
Other Jupes and Yamparicas appear in Taos on August 29 to declare their desire for peace with New Mexico.
Comanches participate in several successful trade fairs held in Taos throughout the fall.

Six hundred Comanche *rancherías* meet along the Arkansas River to discuss the issue of peace with New Mexico.

Three Cuchanec chiefs and their wives arrive in San Antonio on September 29 in the accompaniment of Vial and Chaves in order to formalize peace with Texas.

The recalcitrant Comanche chief Toro Blanco continues to raid New Mexican settlements and pueblos. Peace-minded Comanches conspire against Toro Blanco, assassinate him, and mollify his followers.

A succession of Comanches begin to make regular visits to San Antonio.

A large number of Comanches meet in November at La Casa de Palo along the Arkansas River to discuss peace with New Mexico and to choose a leader to negotiate the treaty. Chief Ecueracapa is commissioned as the Comanche leader.

In late December Comanches send a captured New Mexican Indian to Santa Fe to communicate to Governor Anza the leadership of Chief Ecueracapa and the Comanches' desire to negotiate a peace with the province.

1786: Anza responds to this news in early January by sending a diplomatic entourage to the Comanches in order to express his approval of the Indians' desires.

A band of rebel Comanches attacks Pecos and kills one Pecos Indian. Comanches apprehend the perpetrators, and Ecueracapa personally executes the leader of the mutineers.

In late January Ecueracapa dispatches a diplomatic mission to Santa Fe to apologize for the attack on Pecos and reaffirm the commitment of his people to establish peace with New Mexico.

Comanches continue to enter San Antonio on a regular basis.

On February 25 Ecueracapa arrives in Santa Fe to meet with Anza and make peace with New Mexico.

While in Santa Fe, Ecueracapa agrees to establish peace with the Utes at the urging of Anza.

A few days later, Ecueracapa and Anza perform an elaborate ceremony at Pecos pueblo, formalizing the establishment of peaceful relations between the Comanches and New Mexicans. A great trade fair is held to celebrate the new relationship.

Comanches visit Taos in April to engage in trade.

A small Comanche party suffers a Lipan attack as they approach San Antonio.

Five Comanche raiders steal two dozen horses from Santa Fe. Comanches banish the persons responsible for this act from their villages and reassert their commitment to peace with New Mexico.

Comanches participate in several campaigns alongside Spanish forces against Apaches during the spring and summer.

Numerous Comanches visit Santa Fe throughout the spring and summer.

Ecueracapa encourages Plains Caddoans to move deeper within Comanche territory in order to better defend themselves from Osage attack.

Apaches kill Cabeza Rapada, an influential chief of the Eastern Cuchanec Comanches. Ecueracapa avenges the chief's death by leading a large campaign against

Apaches along the Pecos River. Cabeza Rapada's demise leads to confusion and dissention among Eastern Comanches, who try to choose a successor.

Anza meets with a council of Comanches in the fall and ratifies the articles of peace as approved by the Spanish authorities in Mexico City.

A dozen Comanches, including Ecueracapa's son Oxamaquea, travel to Chihuahua in November to meet with Jacobo Ugarte y Loyola, lieutenant general of the Spanish Provincias Internas.

1787: Drought grips the southern plains and the Southwest. Bison become scarce.

Comanches meet with Anza again in April in a grand council to reaffirm the conditions of peace between the two peoples.

A Comanche war party searching for Apaches attacks a Spanish force escorting Mescalero Apaches on a hunt. The Comanche chief Patuarus and another chief perish as a result. The surviving Indians blame hotheaded youngsters for the incident and beg the Spanish troopers for forgiveness.

Comanches encounter Pedro Vial as he travels between Texas and New Mexico via the Taovayas village.

Jupe youths steal eighteen horses from a Spanish trading party. Ecueracapa travels to Santa Fe to apologize for the infraction.

In midsummer the Jupe Comanche chief Paruanarimuco asks Anza for assistance in building a permanent settlement on the Arkansas River.

Jupes occupy nineteen houses at San Carlos de los Jupes by September 16.

Various Comanches escort José Mares across Comanche territory via the Taovayas village as he travels from Santa Fe to San Antonio that fall.

Comanche warriors assist in two Spanish autumn campaigns against Apaches living to the west and southwest of New Mexico.

As a result of the drought conditions and the lack of bison around New Mexico, Comanches fail to attend the Taos trade fair that November. Governor Concha ships a load of corn to relieve the starving Indians.

1788: A wife of Paruanarimuco dies in early January, and following customs associated with an individual's death, Jupes abandon the settlement of San Carlos.

In January Chief Soxas and other Comanches accompany Mares as he departs San Antonio in order to search for a direct route between Texas and New Mexico, bypassing the Taovayas village on the Red River.

Comanche chief Ysampampi leads a campaign against Faraone Apaches in March. Soxas campaigns against the Mescalero Apaches.

Comanches continue to be absent from New Mexico due to the severe drought. Concha ships more corn to the hungry Indians.

Comanches escort Pedro Vial across Comanche territory as he travels from New Mexico to Natchitoches in Louisiana.

1789: In February, four Comanches guide an expedition led by Pedro Vial and Alexandre Dupont in a search for mineral ores in Taovayas and Comanche territory.

Ecueracapa journeys to Santa Fe to beg for more drought assistance. Concha and the Santa Fe community respond by shipping hundreds of bushels of corn to the Comanches.

Comanches guide Francisco Xavier Fragoso and Pedro Vial across Comanche territory from San Antonio to Santa Fe in July.

Comanches continue to beleaguer Apaches in New Mexico and Texas. Chief Zoquiné leads an expedition against the Mescalero Apaches.

Yamparica and Jupe Comanche horse herds become the target of Ute raiders. The Comanches respond to these depredations in July by attacking a Ute village and killing eighty persons.

Ecueracapa conducts a vigorous campaign throughout the fall against Apaches in New Mexico, Texas, and northern Mexico.

1790: At the request of Chief Paruanarimuco, Governor Concha provides an armed escort to accompany Comanches in a campaign against the Pawnees. The Indians abort the campaign and send the New Mexicans home to Santa Fe.

In December a Cuchanec camp on the upper reaches of the Nueces River suffers an attack by a combined force of Mescalero Apaches and their Spanish escort. The attackers kill many Comanches and take many others captive, including one of Ecueracapa's daughters.

1791: Comanches commit depredations around San Antonio and kill five men in the spring.

In April, Ecueracapa visits Concha in Santa Fe, where he accepts the governor's apology for the Mescalero attack and is reunited with his daughter and the other individuals taken captive.

1792: Once again, Comanches encounter Pedro Vial as he journeys across Comanche territory from Santa Fe toward Saint Louis in May.

In June, a large body of Comanches under the leadership of Ecueracapa, Paruanarimuco, Quenacara, and Hachaca campaign against the Lipan, Lipiyan, and Llanero Apaches.

Utes and Navajos destroy a Comanche camp, killing women and children and running off horses late in the year. Comanches retaliate for this act by wiping out a Ute camp.

Pedro Vail attempts to broker a peace treaty between Comanches and a Pawnee chief who accompanies him from Missouri to Santa Fe. The negotiations are fruitless.

1793: New Mexico governor Concha brokers a peace between Comanches and their Ute and Navajo enemies.

Ecueracapa leads a disastrous campaign against the Pawnees. Chief Hachacas is killed, and Ecueracapa suffers serious wounds from which he dies later that summer.

In early autumn, forty-five hundred Comanches meet in a council to discuss the successor to Ecueracapa. The council chooses Chief Encanaguané as the new leader.

1794: Seventy-five Comanches visit San Antonio and report that Encanaguané has been chosen as the new leader of their people.

Encanaguané requests that New Mexico governor Concha assign Pedro Vial to mediate a peace between his people and the Pawnees.

1795: The Comanche Chamanquequena visits Laredo and steals some horses upon his departure from the villa.

1797: Chief Soxas murders one of Ecueracapa's sons.

The Eastern Comanche chief Pisinampe reports to New Mexico governor Fernando de Chacón that Encanguané, the Comanche general, had died and declares that he should be recognized as the new leader of the Comanches.

Comanches hold a conference at Pecos during the summer and elect Canaguaipe as their leader.

1799: The Cuchanec Comanches suffer a smallpox epidemic.

1800: Comanches trade horses to American merchant Philip Nolan and his eighteen accomplices.

1801: Comanches visit Pecos for trade and to hold a tribal conference to elect a new leader to replace Canaguaipe, who apparently had died.

Indians migrating toward New Mexico from the north attack a Cuchanec camp on the Arkansas River in November.

Jupe Comanches force Kiowa invaders from the Arkansas River valley.

Several Comanches, including Chief Blanco's son, are killed by Spanish Texans in autumn.

Lipan Apaches surprise and kill twenty-five Comanches of Chief Yzazat's camp along the Rio Grande. Rumors that the Spanish assisted in the attack spread among the Comanches.

1802: By March, Comanches find themselves targets of Pawnee and Ute raids.

Comanches conduct an unsuccessful ninety-six-day campaign against Kiowas and Skidi Pawnees in the spring and summer. The Indians appear in Santa Fe before returning to their camps.

Also that spring, Comanches from Chief Blanco's band discover a group of hunters from San Antonio on the Blanco River and kill their leader. The surviving members of the hunting party take the life of a lone Comanche they come across on their way back to the settlements.

Renegade Comanches in favor of war with Texas threaten those who favor peaceful relations.

Chiefs Yzazat and Soxas move their camps to the Llano River to observe and control the activities of renegade Comanches.

Chief Blanco's followers kill a Spaniard in revenge for the earlier events on the Blanco River.

Comanche leaders in favor of peace with Texas gain the upper hand over their opponents by midsummer.

Yzazat leads an unsuccessful raid against Lipans. On returning from the raid in September, some warriors help themselves to Texas livestock. Yzazat recovers and returns the stolen livestock to San Antonio.

In an autumn council, Chief Chihuahua and other likeminded leaders volunteer to create a police force to control disobedient Comanches.

1803: Chief Huanacoruco visits Nemesio Salcedo, the *comandante general* of the Provincias Internas, in Chihuahua to report that the chief known as Quegüe refuses to accept the leadership of the Yamparicas and insists that one of his sons should become leader instead.

Lipans attack a Comanche family departing San Antonio in February.

Chiefs Chihuahua and Yzazat and two hundred of their followers arrive in San Antonio for a council with Gov. Juan Bautista Elguezábal and to declare their desire for peace with Texas.

Chihuahua, Yzazat, and Chief Sargento travel to Monclova, Coahuila, to establish trade relations with Gov. Antonio Cordero.

In May Huanacoruco offers his services as a guide to New Mexicans who wish to search for a rumored hill of gold located within Comanche territory.

Chief El Sordo and twenty-seven followers are arrested by Spanish soldiers for horse theft and murder and placed in a San Antonio jail. The suspects are released to Chief Chihuahua's custody.

The following August a Comanche named Cuerno Verde (also know as El Caricortado) reports to Spanish officials in Santa Fe that he had discovered the hill of gold. Huanacoruco sets out for the plains in September with Spanish gold seekers. The group fails to find the hill of gold, and Huanacoruco claims that they were hindered by the ongoing Comanche-Pawnee war.

Several Comanche chiefs visit New Mexico throughout the year.

Relations between the Comanches and Texas remain friendly throughout the year, and numerous Indians visit San Antonio.

Large Comanche war parties make their way south of Texas to raid Lipans.

1804: Huanacoruco leads another gold-seeking expedition to the plains. This time the chief blames their failure to find the hill of gold on the fact that it lies within Pawnee territory.

Great numbers of Comanches visit San Antonio throughout the year.

1805: Chiefs Chihuahua, Yzazat, Sargento, and 353 Comanches travel to San Antonio to welcome the newly appointed governor, Antonio Cordero, and to reaffirm their commitment to peace with Texas.

In March thirty-three chiefs and their two hundred followers appear and offer their services to Cordero in the event of hostilities with Americans along the Sabine River.

Comanches seize the livestock of travelers on the road from San Antonio to Laredo. One Spaniard is killed in the April attack.

Frustrated with the Comanche leaders' failure to arrest the perpetrators of the April raid, Governor Cordero forces the Texas Comanches to elect a head chief. The Indians choose Chief Sargento to fill this office. Sargento changes his name to Cordero in an act of respect for the Texas governor.

In November Yamparicas visit New Mexico governor Joachín del Real Alencaster to ratify their choice of Chief Somiquaso as the leader of the Yamparica clan. The Indians also request that the Spanish build houses for them in their territory.

1806: Yamparica Comanches and Kiowas meet at the Double Mountain Fork of the Brazos River and agree to a Spanish-brokered peace. Chief Somiquaso marries one of his daughters to the Kiowa chief El Ronco, reinforcing the alliance with the bonds of kinship.

A large number of Comanches, Lipans, and Tonkawas gather in San Antonio and talk about establishing peaceful relations between their tribes.

1807: American trader John Lewis spends a few days with Comanches during the winter. The principal leaders and large numbers of Comanches, Lipans, and Tawakonis meet in San Antonio during spring to attend a peace council mediated by Governor Cordero.

In August Comanches participate in a council in Natchitoches, Louisiana, with representatives of the United States.

A Yamparica chief and a Kiowa chief visit Santa Fe in June.

1808: Comanches assist Francisco Amangual and his party of two hundred men across Comanche territory as they make their way from San Antonio to Santa Fe.

Comanches encounter the American trader Anthony Glass along the Colorado River in Texas.

1809: In August Comanche chiefs Chimal Colorado and Pasagogo visit Gov. Josef Manrrique in Santa Fe.

In the fall a joint force of Comanches, Kiowas, and Arapahos waylay a group of Utes and Jicarilla Apaches living on the plains northeast of New Mexico.

1810: Chiefs Chihuahua and El Sordo arrive in San Antonio to complain to newly appointed Texas governor Manuel María de Salcedo about Spanish restrictions on engaging in commerce with American traders.

Chief Quegüe hosts a Spanish force tracking American trespassers in February.

Spanish soldiers arrest the American traders at Chief Pasagogo's camp later in February.

Chief Cordero leads a springtime war party against Mescalero Apaches.

During summer, a large number of Comanche warriors alongside Spanish troops from New Mexico campaign against Apaches.

Comanches and Lipans in Texas raid one another's horse herds. This activity leads to some casualties on both sides. Tensions mount between the Indians.

Comanches also steal animals from Spanish ranches along the Rio Grande; the San Sabá, Frio, and Nueces Rivers; and at Laredo, La Bahía, and San Marcos.

Chief Cordero rushes to San Antonio to discuss the situation with Governor Salcedo. The chief offers to arrest the perpetrators and return the stolen property.

Chief Cordero holds a conference of Comanche leaders at which marauders are identified and stolen property is recovered. Cordero marries his daughter to the Yamparica chief Oso Ballo.

Chief El Sordo breaks away from the Comanches and moves to live among the Tawakonis.

In October Comanche leaders travel to San Antonio to return stolen livestock and reaffirm their commitment to peace with the Lipans.

Also that month, Yamparica Comanches reportedly declare war against the Spanish.

1811: Comanches and Lipans assist royal Spanish troops in defeating Mexican insurgents fighting for their independence from Spain in Coahuila.

An August council held in San Antonio reaffirms the Comanches' pledge to live up to the peace accords of 1807.

The Yamparica chief Oso Ballo arrests followers of El Sordo and makes them return the animals they had stolen from Texas.

Oso Ballo and El Sordo each visit San Antonio that fall to warn the Texans of impending Taovayas and Tawakoni raids. Spanish authorities arrest El Sordo and four of his followers on suspicion of horse theft and incarcerate them in La Bahía. Later, the Indians find themselves shipped to a prison in Coahuila.

In December Chief Cordero sends Chief Pisinampa to San Antonio to inquire about the circumstances of El Sordo's arrest.

Oso Ballo, outraged by El Sordo's arrest, holds a council to plan an attack on Texas. Chief El Joyoso travels to Coahuila and communicates to Governor Cordero that he and other chiefs do not support Oso Ballo or El Sordo and were prepared to fight their kinsmen on behalf of the Spanish.

Comanches continue to raid Spanish outposts along the Rio Grande.

1812: Oso Ballo, Pisinampa, and Yzachá appear on the outskirts of San Antonio with a large number of warriors in April. Governor Salcedo meets with the angered Indians and encourages them to remain peaceful, thereby avoiding an attack.

1813: Some disaffected Comanches join Taovayas and Tawakonis in raiding the ranches and villas of Texas and Coahuila during April's Magee-Gutiérrez insurrection.

Two Comanches die while fighting the entrenched insurrectionists at La Bahía in November.

1814: Continuous Comanche raids on outlying Spanish haciendas around San Antonio leads to their abandonment in January.

Comanches attack Mexican supply convoys headed for San Antonio.

By August, persistent attacks by Comanches have reduced Texas almost to the point of complete destruction.

In December Chief Vicente and twenty other Comanches arrive in Santa Fe to discuss plans for establishing peace between the Indians and the province of Coahuila. Two New Mexicans later that month steal twenty of Vicente's horses. The perpetrators are arrested, tried, and found guilty of the crime.

1815:A group of 242 Comanches, including numerous chiefs, visits Santa Fe.
Comanches trade with New Mexicans who visit them in their camps.

1816: Comanches establish peace with Lipan Apaches in Texas.
Comanches trade and interact with refugee Spanish insurgents.
Chief Cordero visits the U.S. agent at Natchitoches during the summer.

1817: Northern bands of Comanches engage in commerce with a large number of American traders during the winter.
A smallpox epidemic strikes the Comanches that winter, killing about four thousand people.

1818: A Comanche camp on the Agua Negra suffers an attack by Spanish soldiers from Texas intent on recovering stolen livestock.
Chief Chihuahua visits Natchitoches.
David G. Burnet resides among the Comanches.
In late summer more than a thousand Comanches visit New Mexico for trade.
Chief Quegüe dies.

1820: A Comanche war party, smarting from an Otoe ambush, meets American soldiers at the Great Bend of the Arkansas River.

1821: Chiefs Pisinampe, Barbaquiste, and Quenoc meet a Texas peace commission led by Juan Manuel Barrera at the Tawakoni villages on the Brazos River.
Comanches kill several cows and sheep at San Miguel del Vado.
That autumn, Mexican Texas agent José Francisco Ruíz travels to Comanche territory to hold a three-day council with Pisinampe, Guonique, and Temanca.
Comanches encounter American Santa Fe trader Thomas James and his party on the Salt Fork of the Arkansas and Canadian Rivers.
Other Comanches meet American trader Jacob Fowler and his party on the Arkansas River in Colorado.

1822: Juan Manuel Barrera escorts a Comanche peace delegation to San Antonio in early 1822.
That July, Pisinampe and a group of chiefs arrive in San Antonio to negotiate a peace. Comanches sign a truce with Texas on August 11. The Comanche delegation travels to Mexico City to sign a formal peace treaty on December 13. The Indian delegation leaves the Mexican capital on January 14.

Comanches meet Thomas James again on the North Canadian, or Beaver, River and engage in trade.

1823: Comanches raid American colonies in Texas.

1824: A small number of Comanches meet with New Mexican governor Bartolomé Baca in July on the Canadian River.
Chief Ysachene, ten other chiefs, and several others make a friendly visit to San Antonio in October.
Comanches wage an unsuccessful campaign against the Osages.

1825: In January Comanche raiders harass the vicinity of El Paso and San Elizario.
Chief Joyoso visits Monclova, Coahuila, in February.
Comanche raiders strike Chihuahua in March.
Comanches raid the Mexican villas and ranches along the Rio Grande.
Chief Chimal Colorado visits Santa Fe in May and returns the captives taken from El Paso.
In June, Joyoso and 330 Comanches enter San Antonio and rob three houses, steal three horses, and kill nineteen cows.
New Mexicans from San Miguel del Vado visit Comanche camps for trade.
Chiefs Chimal Colorado, Vicente, and Genizaro visit San Miguel del Vado on September 8.
Texans later capture and arrest Joyoso for attempting to steal hoses from San Antonio.
Chimal Colorado, Vicente, and Genizaro visit San Miguel del Vado again on December 30.

1826: Comanches continue their raids into Chihuahua.
Chiefs Cordero, Ysacoruco, and Estrellas visit Santa Fe during the summer to discuss the details of renegotiating their peace with New Mexico.
Cordero and Paruaquita travel to Chihuahua in October to establish peaceful relations with that province.

1827: A Comanche war party is defeated by Mexican Texans on the Augua Fria River in July.
Comanche raiding parties beleaguer the region between Taos and Abiquiu in October.
That same month, Comanches under the leadership of Samparillena and Molote engage New Mexicans in trade in the Manzano Mountains southeast of Albuquerque.

1828: Comanches under the leadership of Quelluna and the Kiowa El Ronco escort the Mexican *Comisión de Límites* on a tour of the Texas Hill Country northwest of San Antonio.
Chief Panchoconuque makes a springtime visit to Governor Arocha of New Mexico.

Chief Paruakevitsi visits San Antonio in August.

On August 29 around six hundred Comanches meet with New Mexico governor Arocha on the Gallinas River to ratify the 1826 treaty. The Comanches attending select Toro Echicero as their leader.

Paruakevitsi returns to San Antonio in October with numerous Comanches, declaring that all of his people wish for peace with the Mexicans. The Comanches and Mexicans sign an agreement to end hostilities.

1829: Chief Paruakevitsi travels from Texas to New Mexico and meets with Governor Arocha at Bosque Redondo on July 25. Paruakevitsi agrees to Mexican vice president Bustamente's 1827 peace proclamation with frontier Indians and promises to encourage its adherence among his people.

Chief Namayajipe of the Yamparicas visits Santa Fe and requests Mexican assistance in a campaign against their enemies from the north.

Paruakevitsi visits San Antonio in the fall and reports his meeting with New Mexico governor Arocha to Texas officials.

1830: Comanches become engaged in a war against Cheyennes and Arapahos pushing into their northern territories.

Comanches visit Santa Fe throughout the year.

Sam Houston encourages Comanches and Wichitas to meet with a U.S. treaty commission at Fort Gibson, Indian Territory.

1831: Comanches serve as scouts for the Mexicans in Texas, helping track down Indian horse thieves.

In August Comanches are accused of robbing horses from San Antonio and launch a raid against Goliad, killing a Mexican and a Tonkawa chief.

Comanches meet New Mexican traders at Cuesta in the Pecos valley in early September. The Indians find themselves implicated in an attack on another party of New Mexican traders around the same time.

Toro Echicero arrives in New Mexico to reestablish amicable trade relations and attempts to acquire the release of captive Comanches held in Chihuahua.

Comanches declare war on Chihuahua in October.

Paruakevitsi returns horses stolen by Tawakonis to their owners in San Antonio. In October Yncoroy returns forty-six horses taken from Matamoros.

That same month, Tasuniqua visits the presidio of Aguaverde in Coahuila for trade. The Mexicans launch an unsuccessful campaign against the Comanches in Chihuahua.

Paruakevitsi and his son are inadvertently killed at a Tawakoni village when Mexican soldiers retaliate against Tawakoni horse raiders in November.

Yzazona returns sixteen horses stolen from Goliad, and Yncoroy and Quellune return other animals to their owners in Texas that December.

1832: Comanches visit San Antonio in January and communicate their forgiveness for Paruakevitsi's death.

The camp of Chief Yncoroy suffers an attack by Shawnees. Many Comanches are killed.

Chief Chato and twenty-six Comanches arrive in San Antonio on April 8 and declare their wish to maintain peaceful relations with Texas.

Comanches visit San Felipe, Texas, to trade furs.

Comanches visit San Fernando along the Rio Grande throughout April and early May for trade.

Comanches trade with a group of American trappers on the western edge of the Llano Estacado.

In October Comanches kill two Mexican soldiers between Leona and Buena Vista in Texas.

On October 18, Comanches kill two herders in Texas. An expedition is sent to punish the Indians, but it is unsuccessful.

Comanche raiders steal the horse herd from Villa de Rosas, Texas, on October 30. Mexican troops successfully run down the Indians and kill three of them.

That same day, two Comanche raiders are killed by Mexican troops as they attempt to make off with horses from La Bahía, Texas.

Kiowas and Comanches attack a party of American traders traveling along the Canadian River in December.

1833: Sam Houston meets with several Comanches at San Antonio in January to discuss the establishment of a treaty with the United States.

Comanches and Wichitas attack a group of Cherokee hunters.

Chief Tasuniqua makes an offer to establish peace in Texas in the summer.

1834: In May Chihuahuan Mexicans launch another campaign against the Comanches and are moderately successful.

Comanches meet a unit of U.S. dragoons escorting caravans to New Mexico along the Arkansas River in mid-June.

Chiefs Ysacoruco, Coyote Griton, Tecolote Cabezón, Zorra Alta, and Aguila del Aire sign a peace with the Mexicans on July 23 in El Paso.

1835: On February 3 a group of Comanches arrive in San Antonio with horses stolen from Chihuahua.

Chief Casimero arrives in San Antonio in April.

In May large war parties cross the Rio Grande into Mexico at Big Bend.

That same month, Comanche raiders attack several haciendas in Texas and Nuevo Leon.

Comanches trade horses stolen from Chihuahua to Texans.

By July, thousands of Comanches settle near Camp Holmes and Camp Mason on the western edge of the Cross Timbers in Indian Territory.

A large number of Comanches meet U.S. dragoons led by Col. Henry Dodge at Cache Creek in Indian Territory on July 16.

Several Comanches accompany the dragoons to Fort Gibson to participate in a peace council.

Three hundred Comanches visit San Antonio in August and then proceed to Matamoros to make a treaty with Mexican officials.

Nineteen Comanches sign a treaty with the United States on August 24 at Camp Holmes.

Comanches raid ranches near Laredo.

Comanches trade at Auguste Chouteau's new trading post near Camp Holmes.

Paul Legeste Chouteau visits Comanches on Cache Creek in the winter. The Indians communicate their dissatisfaction with the Camp Holmes treaty.

Comanche raiders strike Texan colonel Edward Burleson's camp on the Gonzalez River in December.

1836: Comanches send word to San Antonio in January of their desire to establish peace with Texas.

In the spring, Comanches attack the refugees of the La Villa de Dolores Colony in southern Texas, killing the men and taking the women and children captive.

Comanche raiders attack the Hibbens family homestead on the Guadalupe River in Texas. They kill two men and seize the women and children. The Texas Army pursues the raiders and rescues the children.

On May 19, Comanches hit Parker's Fort on the Navasota River in Texas. The Indians take five persons captive.

Comanches host Republic of Texas representative Alexander LeGrand in September to discuss the possibility of establishing a peace between the Indians and the fledgling nation.

1837: Texas Cherokee chief Bowles visits the Comanches in early summer to negotiate a treaty for the Republic of Texas. The Indians refuse to discuss the matter.

Chiefs Quinaseico and Puestia appear at Coleman's Fort in Texas to communicate their desire for peace. Noah Smithwick accompanies the Indians back to their camps and lives among them for three months.

That summer, Comanches and their Kiowa allies camped on Wolf Creek suffer a decisive defeat to the Cheyennes.

Chief Tabequena visits Chouteau's trading post near Camp Holmes in December and questions the Americans' desire for peace with the Indians.

1838: In February, 150 Comanches arrive in San Antonio asking for peace.

Fifteen Comanche chiefs host a March council with a Texas peace commission and declare their territorial limits to the Texans. The commissioners invite the Indians to make their demands to the authorities in San Antonio.

In April Chiefs Esawacany and Esamany and 150 followers visit San Antonio to discuss the issues of peace and territorial boundaries.

A Comanche trading party visits Bastrop, Texas, in April.

Chief Isacony's camp hosts a group of Texan traders led by George W. Bonnell.

Tabequena and twenty-two chiefs appear at Camp Holmes in early May. Edward Chouteau escorts Tabequena back to his village in order to encourage the Indians to refrain from retaliating against the Cheyennes.

About one hundred Comanches arrive in Houston in late May to make a peace treaty with Texas president Sam Houston. The delegates sign the "Treaty of Peace and Amity" on the twenty-ninth.

A force of Texas Rangers commanded by Col. Henry Karnes attacks a Comanche village at Arroyo Seco on August 10.

Seventy Comanches visit Bastrop on September 8 and denounce Karnes's attack. Comanches attack a group of surveyors outside of San Antonio on October 20. A party of Texans sent out to punish the attackers is defeated.

That same day, Comanches abduct six Mexicans from Texas.

A battle between Comanches and Texans at the Anadarko village on October 25 claims the life of Chief Esawacany.

Comanches release their Mexican captives at the end of November.

1839: In January a Texan-Lipan force attacks Comanches camping near the San Sabá River. Tabequena meets Josiah Gregg at Camp Holmes in May. The Indians receive about six-hundred-dollars worth of goods from the Americans.

A camp of Comanches near Wolf Creek encounters Gregg and an escort of dragoons. The Indians trade and hold council with the Americans.

1840: During the winter, Comanches ransom a number of captives taken from Texas.

On January 9, three Comanches visit San Antonio asking for peace. The Texans demand that the Indians return all captives and stolen property before peace is extended to them.

Chief Muguara along with sixty-five others arrive in San Antonio on March 19 for a trade fair at the Council House. Tempers flare as the Texans demand the release of all captives. Violence results, and thirty-five Comanches are killed in the melee. Twenty-nine Indians are taken prisoner.

Allied Comanches and Kiowas establish a truce with the Cheyennes and Arapahos in the summer.

A large Comanche war party of five hundred men attacks Victoria and the coastal town of Linnville in August. The Indians are intercepted at Plum Creek by a force of Texans.

Chief Esamany visits with other Indians to encourage the establishment of peace with Texas.

A major Comanche war party strikes Tamaulipas and Nuevo Leon in September. Another major Comanche raid strikes Tamaulipas and Nuevo Leon in October. Also that month, a force of Texans and Lipans campaign in Comanche territory and destroy a camp of sixty families on the upper Colorado River.

A third large war party campaigns in Coahuila, San Luis Potosí, and Zacatecas in December.

1841: Comanches make peace with Bent's Fort in March.

Comanches alert Mexican authorities in Santa Fe of a Texan expedition to New Mexico.

1842: Traders from Bent's Fort visit Comanches in their camps during the winter.
At the request of Comanche and Kiowa chiefs, American trader Charles Bent erects a trading post in Comanche territory on the north bank of the Canadian River during the summer.
Comanche raiders sweep along the north bank of the Rio Grande to the gulf coast.

1843: Comanches tip off Mexican authorities of the Texan Warfield-Snively expedition to attack the Santa Fe Trail.
Chief Pahayuko's village is visited by a Texas peace delegation.

1844: Chiefs Mopechucope and Potsnanquahip encounter a Texas party traveling in Comanche territory to bring an offering of peace.
Indians meet with Texas officials in May to discuss the issue of territorial boundaries.
Texas Rangers under Capt. Jack Hays attack a group of Comanches on Walker's Creek in June.
Comanche raiders suffer a serious defeat near Matamoros.
Indian Agent Robert S. Neighbors visits Comanches led by Chiefs Santa Ana and Tanacioquache on Boregas Creek. Neighbors learns that raiders are going to Laredo for horses. The Comanches communicate their desire for peace with the Texans.
Chiefs Caballero and Quilluea arrive in Santa Fe in July and report that three hundred warriors are preparing to raid Chihuahua.
Delaware scouts John Conner and Jim Shaw visit Chief Mopechucope's camp to encourage the Indians to attend that fall's peace council to be held at Torrey's Trading Post.
Potsnanquahip and Mopechucope attend the peace council at Torrey's in October. The Indians sign a peace treaty establishing a border with Texas on October 9.

1845: Three Comanches are killed on the San Marcos River by Delaware Indians in February.
In May a very large war party crosses the Rio Grande to seek revenge for the defeat of their kinsmen near Matamoros.
Comanches kill two men south of Austin, raid a ranch near Seguin, and steal horses from the German settlements in June.
Comanche raiders return from Mexico with large droves of livestock.
Chief Mopechucope entertains an expedition from Texas sent to encourage him to attend the council meeting scheduled for September.
Mopechucope and five other chiefs attend the Indian council held on Tehuacana Creek and discuss issues related to establishing peace with Texas.
A few Comanches encounter Lt. James W. Abert's expedition traveling down the Canadian River in September.
Mopechucope, Santa Anna, twelve other chiefs, and forty armed warriors meet in council with Texas representatives again in November.
Some Comanches meet with a Mexican military commander and report that they favor peace, even though their warriors were en route for Mexico.

Comanche raiders make their way to Zacatecas and spend as long as three months raiding in north-central Mexico.

Chiefs Mopechucope, Potsnanquahip, and seventeen others along with thirty-three warriors meet U.S. Commissioners Pierce M. Butler and M. G. Lewis at Comanche Peak in December to discuss peace with the United States and the newly annexed state of Texas.

Comanches establish trade relations with Osage Indians.

1846: Chiefs Pahayuko, Mopechucope, Potsnanquahip, Santa Anna, and Saviah arrive at Tehuacana Creek in early May to meet with Commissioners Butler and Lewis. On May 15 the Indians sign a treaty with the United States.

Chief Santa Anna and several other Comanches travel to Washington, D.C., in late June and meet with Pres. James K. Polk on July 1.

Seminole Indians led by Wild Cat visit the Comanches for trade.

Comanches trade with Osages, two of whom live among the Comanches. One marries a Comanche woman.

1847: Chief Ketumsee's camp is visited by German land surveyors led by John O. Meusebach to discuss a peace treaty between the Indians and German settlers pushing into Comanche territory. The German-Comanche agreement is signed on May 9.

Comanches and Kiowas engage Pawnees at Pawnee Fork. The Comanche chief Red Sleeve is killed.

Comanches request the establishment of trading houses in their territory.

U.S. Indian Agent Robert S. Neighbors visits Pahayuko, Mopechucope, and Potsnanquahip to discuss the Senate's revisions to the 1846 treaty.

Fearful of hostilities breaking out with Texas, Chiefs Mopechucope and Santa Anna move their camps to the north in July.

Throughout the summer, Comanches join in attacks on American caravans traveling along the Santa Fe Trail.

Mopechucope meets with Agent Neighbors at the Kitsai Indian village to discuss rumors of an expedition to be sent against the Comanches.

Comanches receive treaty annuities in September.

Potsnanquahip stops by Torrey's Trading Post in December on his return from a raid in Mexico.

Comanche raiders steal horses from several companies of Texas Rangers.

1848: Smallpox strikes the Comanche camps near Texas.

Mopechucope arrives at Torrey's Trading Post and returns six stolen horses belonging to the Texas Rangers.

Comanches gather in January in preparation for a springtime campaign in Mexico.

Neighbors meets with a large number of Comanches in late January to discuss various matters pertaining to Comanches' relations with Texas and the United States.

Santa Anna visits San Antonio in late May to talk with the governor and is received in a hostile manner. The Indians are told to return to the frontier. Santa Anna is offended.

Comanches attack U.S. soldiers protecting the Santa Fe Trail at Pawnee Fork on June 7.

Comanches attack another unit of U.S. soldiers camped along the Arkansas River on June 18.

On July 9 a Comanche village on the Cimarron River suffers from an attack by U.S. troops.

Comanches camp with Kiowas, Kiowa-Apaches, Cheyennes, and Arapahos at the Big Timbers on the Arkansas River below Bent's Fort during the fall.

Comanches traveling to Mexico in the fall of 1848 are attacked by Texas Rangers. The Indians steal some of the rangers' horses.

Chief Ketumsee and Agent Neighbors set out to find the stolen horses and are led to Chief Karwabebowebit. The Comanches declare that, although they maintain peace with Texas, they are at war with Mexico.

1849: Chief Pahayuko meets with a U.S. official in New Mexico.

Pahayuko relocates to the Salt Plains of the Arkansas River.

In the spring, Comanche chief Ohawakin visits the Seminole Agency in Indian Territory while accompanying Cherokee trader Jesse Chisholm.

Comanches assist Indian Agent Robert S. Neighbors and Texas Ranger John S. Ford in establishing the Butterfield Trail across Texas.

Comanches are stricken with Cholera. Chief Mopechucope and three hundred Indians die from the disease.

Comanches come in contact with numerous travelers headed for California along the Canadian River and the Santa Fe Trail.

Chief Esakeep and his followers meet an American expedition led by Capt. Randolph B. Marcy at Tucumcari.

A party of seventy-five Comanches suffers an attack by Texas Rangers at Amargosa in May.

On May 29, Texas Rangers attack another band of Comanches.

Comanches assemble at the Big Timbers with other Indians in July, awaiting the arrival of Indian Agent Thomas Fitzpatrick.

Comanches meet along the Brazos River in the fall to elect a principal chief.

Returning from New Mexico in October, Captain Marcy meets Chief Sanaco on the Clear Fork of the Brazos River.

Comanches under the leadership of Chief Mulaquetop visit Fort Lincoln, Texas.

1850: A large group of Comanches under the leadership of the female chief Tabe Peté attacks the Hacienda del Carmen in northern Chihuahua in February.

Esakeep's band encounters the Black River California Company of emigrants along the Canadian River in May.

An emigrant party known as the Knickerbocker Company meets up with a Comanche camp of eight hundred old men, women, and children.

Thirteen New Mexicans trade with Comanches.

Sometime prior to June, Comanches dispose of a package containing five separate documents relating to peace treaties in Texas. The Indians attach the package of papers to the top of a pole planted in a mound on the plains.

A large body of Comanches assembles on the Pecos River at Bosque Redondo for the purpose of making peace with the Jicarilla and Mescalero Apaches.

A Comanche raiding party appears in Santo Domingo, New Mexico, looking to recruit individuals to join them against the Navajos.

Comanches return to raid northern Chihuahua in July.

Comanches raid southern Chihuahua in August.

In September Comanche raiders visit Durango.

Chiefs Ketumsee, Saviah, Potsnanquahip, and Sanaco attend a council with U.S. Indian Agent J. H. Rollins on the Clear Fork of the Brazos River in September.

In December, eleven representatives of Comanches meet with American authorities on the San Sabá River to sign a peace treaty and boundary agreement.

Appendix 3
Glossary of Spanish Terms

alcalde mayor: the chief official of town government in colonial New Spain
alférez: second lieutenant
amistad: friendship
Andalucía: the southernmost region of Spain
Andaluz: pertaining to *Andalucía*
arroyo: a creek or small stream
auto: a judicial decree, writ, or warrant
bando: an edict or proclamation
belduque: a large broad trade knife
caballada: a drove of horses
cabildo: town council
cañon: canyon
capitán: captain
cibolero: a bison hunter
Comanchería: Comanche territory
Comancheros: New Mexicans who visited Comanche villages for trade
comandante general: commandant general
comandante inspector: commandant inspector
comer: to eat
compañero: companion, comrade, partner, or associate
en junta: conferring
estradiota: a type of saddle used by lancers
estufa: literally means stove but was used in New Mexico to refer to Pueblo Indian hogans,
   or religious meeting places
Extremadura: the westernmost region of Spain
ferias: trade fairs
flaca: lean or skinny
ganado mayor: large livestock such as cattle, horses, donkeys, and mules
ganado menor: small livestock such as sheep, goats, and pigs
genízaros: former Indian captives of Comanches, Apaches, Navajos, and Utes living in
   New Mexico
gentiles: non-Christian Indians
hijo: son

indios barbaros: "wild" or "barbarous" Indians living outside of Spanish colonial society
jineta: a Moorish-inspired combat saddle
la Capital: refers to Mexico City, the capital of New Spain
la Casa de Palo: a heavily wooded area along the Arkansas River in eastern Colorado
lanceros: lancers
lobo: wolf
luna: moon or crescent-moon shaped
lunetes: crescent-moon shaped markings
maestre de campo: chief officer
mayor: first, principal, chief, main, or major
matador: killer or slaughterer of livestock
mesa del Norte: the central Mexican highlands north of the Valley of Mexico
Meseta: the highlands of central Spain
muy: very, very much or greatly
nuevo mexicanos: New Mexicans
occidentales: westerners
ojo: literally means "eye" but was often used to refer to a spring of water
orientales: easterners
palacio gobierno: the governor's residence
para: for, to, or in
piloncillos: an unrefined loaf of sugar
presidio: garrison or fort
Provincias Internas: the office administering the internal provinces of New Spain from 1776 to 1821
ranchería: Indian camp
segundo: second
Sierra Blanca: White Mountains, northeast of New Mexico
sobrino: nephew
Tejanos: Spanish and Mexican Texans
teniente: lieutenant or assistant
tercero: third
tlatolero: an Indian public crier, announcer, or public speaker
vaquero: cowboy

Notes

Abbreviations

AGN-PI   Archivo General de la Nación, Provincias Internas, Mexico City (photographic copies, University of New Mexico, Albuquerque)

BA   Béxar Archives of Spanish and Mexican Texas, University of Texas, Austin (microfilm, Texas Tech University, Lubbock)

BATS   Béxar Archives Translation Series, University of Texas, Austin (microfilm, University of North Texas, Denton)

MANM   Mexican Archives of New Mexico, New Mexico State Records Center, Santa Fe (microfilm, University of New Mexico, Albuquerque)

SANM   Spanish Archives of New Mexico, New Mexico State Records Center, Santa Fe (microfilm, University of New Mexico, Albuquerque)

Introduction

1. See William T. Hagan, *Quanah Parker, Comanche Chief.*

2. Ibid., 6, 11.

3. Ernest Wallace, ed., "The Journal of Ranald S. Mackenzie's Messenger to the Kwahadi Comanches," *Red River Historical Review* 3, no. 2 (spring, 1978): 244.

4. Hagan, *Quanah Parker,* 25, 37.

5. Ibid., 32, 42.

6. Ibid., 103, 118–19, 120.

7. David LaVere, *Contrary Neighbors: Southern Plains and Removed Indians in Indian Territory.*

8. Christopher Hill, *The Century of Revolution, 1603–1714,* 2d ed., 1.

9. See Elizabeth A. H. John, *Storms Brewed in Other Men's Worlds: The Confrontation of Indians, Spanish, and French in the Southwest, 1540–1795;* and Thomas W. Kavanagh, *Comanche Political History: An Ethnohistorical Perspective, 1706–1875.*

Chapter 1

1. La Casa de Palo literally means "the house of wood." This term was a metaphor in reference to the wooded area along the Arkansas River in present-day southeast Colorado that was also known as the Big Timbers by English-speaking frontiersmen. See Alfred Barnaby Thomas, ed. and trans., *Forgotten Frontiers: A Study of the Spanish Indian Policy of Don Juan*

Bautista de Anza, Governor of New Mexico 1777–1787, from the Original Documents in the Archives of Spain, Mexico, and New Mexico, 73; Pedro Garrido y Duran, "An Account of Events which Have Occurred in the Provinces of New Mexico Concerning Peace Conceded to the Comanche Nation and their Reconciliation with the Utes, since November 17 of Last Year and July 15 of the Current," Chihuahua, Dec. 21, 1786, in ibid., 294–95; Kavanagh, *Comanche Political History,* 52.

2. Garrido, "Account of Events," 292; John, *Storms Brewed,* 662; Kavanagh, *Comanche Political History,* 110; "Copy of the Instruction which Don Thomas Vélez Cachupín, Governor and Captain General of New Mexico, left to his successor, Don Francisco Marín del Valle, at the order of his most excellent sir, Conde de Revilla Gigedo, viceroy of this New Spain," Santa Fe, Aug. 12, 1754, in Alfred Barnaby Thomas, ed. and trans., *The Plains Indians and New Mexico, 1751–1778: A Collection of Documents Illustrative of the History of the Eastern Frontier of New Mexico,* 133–34.

The exact date Comanches first appeared in New Mexico is unknown, but the first mention of these Indians in Spanish sources discovered so far dates to 1706. One of the earlier documents to refer to Comanches is "The Diary of Juan de Ulibarri to El Cuartelejo," 1706, published in Alfred Barnaby Thomas, ed. and trans., *After Coronado: Spanish Exploration Northeast of New Mexico, 1696–1727,* 65. Francisco Cuervo y Valdez, Spanish governor ad interim of New Mexico, 1705–1707, also commented on the Comanches in another 1706 document. In a report concerning the lack of missionaries for some of the more isolated areas of the province, and speaking particularly of the Navajo territory lying just to the northwest of New Mexico, Cuervo noted that the Comanches lived to the north of that region. What is interesting about these documents, as Kavanagh and others have pointed out, was Ulibarri's and Cuervo's casual statements about Comanches near the Spanish colonial province. While out on the plains northeast of New Mexico (possibly in the area of southeast Colorado), Ulibarri came across an Apache man with his two wives and three children fleeing to a tribal settlement along a river where their kinsmen had assembled in order to protect themselves from the attacks of Utes and Comanches. Kavanagh states that the Spanish captain's lack of surprise at the Apaches' report of the hostile Comanche presence indicates that they were probably known in the province of New Mexico by this time. Cuervo also mentioned Comanches in a similar manner in his geographical description of Navajo territorial boundaries. Francisco Cuervo y Valdez, Santa Fe, Aug. 18, 1706, in Charles Wilson Hackett, ed. and trans. *Historical Documents Relating to New Mexico, Nueva Vizcaya, and Approaches Thereto, to 1773,* 3:381. See also Kavanagh, *Comanche Political History,* 63.

Documents concerning the problems associated with trade during the eighteenth century between New Mexicans and so-called *indios barbaros* ("uncivilized Indians") such as Apaches, Navajos, Utes, and Comanches are numerous. I shall fully discuss the issue of trade and the measures taken to control the violence associated with it below in chapters dedicated to Comanche economics and violence. For an example of the types of punishment authorized for violators of official edicts regulating trade, see Henrique de Olavide y Michelena, *"Bando* in Relation to Trade with Wild Tribes," Santa Fe [?], Jan. 7, 1737, SANM, reel 7, frame 553, T-414. (The designation following the frame number is the Twitchel number, which refers to the numerical designation historian and archivist Ralph Emerson Twitchell assigned to the particular document sets contained in the SANM during the early part of the twentieth century.)

3. Council of war, Santa Fe, July 27–Dec. 10, 1716, SANM, reel 5:625–38, T-279; Isidro Armijo, ed., "Information Communicated by Juan Candelaria, Resident of this Villa de San Francisco Xavier de Alburquerque, Born 1692—Age 84," *New Mexico Historical Review* 3 (1929): 290; report of Vélez Cachupín to Conde de Revilla Gigedo, Santa Fe, Nov. 27, 1751, in Thomas,

Plains Indians and New Mexico, 68–76; Juan Bautista de Anza, "Diary of the Expedition against the Comanche Nation," Santa Fe, Sept. 10, 1779, in Thomas, *Forgotten Frontiers*, 122–39; John, *Storms Brewed*, 241–42, 321–22, 584–90; Kavanagh, *Comanche Political History*, 63–64, 74, 92.

4. Cavallero de Croix to Juan Bautista de Anza, Arispe, July 14, 1780, SANM, reel 11:77–78, T-799; John, *Storms Brewed*, 590, 668; Cavallero de Croix to Juan Bautista de Anza, Arispe, Feb. 24, 1783, SANM, reel 11:567–68, T-858; Kavanagh, *Comanche Political History*, 93, 110–11; Garrido, "Account of Events," 294, 299.

5. Garrido, "Account of Events," 295–300; John, *Storms Brewed*, 668–71, 672; Kavanagh, *Comanche Political History*, 111, 112.

6. Alfred Barnaby Thomas, "An Eighteenth Century Comanche Document," *American Anthropologist* 31, no. 2 (Apr.–June, 1929): 296, and Kavanagh, *Comanche Political History*, 113, provide Spanish and English translations of these Comanche names. The meaning of Ecueracapa is somewhat confused. As Thomas and Kavanagh note, Anza first understood Ecueracapa's name to be Contatanacapara, meaning "One without Equal in Military Achievements" (*el sin igual en hazañas militares*). This name was also thought to mean "The Orphan" (*el Huerfano*) or "Crane on the Cross" (*Grulla en Cruz*). Finally, Ecueracapa was known in Texas as Coat of Mail (*Cota de Malla*), further confusing the meaning of his name. The name "Ecueracapa" may also mean Leather Cape, from the Spanish *cuera*, meaning "leather jacket," and *capa*, meaning "cape," or "cloak." The names of the other Comanches are not quite as confusing: Tosacondata/White Crane (*Grulla Blanca*); Tosapoy/White Road (*Camino Blanco*); Hichapat/The Crafty One, or according to Kavanagh, Liar (*Ardiloso*); Paraginanchi/Ears of a Sorrel Deer, or Elk (*Orejas de Venado Alasan*); Cuetaninabeni/The Maltreated One (*El Maltratado*); Quinaneantime/He Gnaws His Master (*El Roe a su Amo*); Sonocat/Many Peppers, or possibly according to Kavanagh, Owns Many Horns (*Muchos Pimientos*); Canaguaipe/The Feeble Effeminate One, or according to Kavanagh, Poor Woman (*Amugerado flaco*); Pisimampat/The Decayed Shoe, or possibly according to Kavanagh, Smelly Shoe (*Zapato podrido*); Toyamancare/Seated on the Mountain (*Sentado en la Sierra*); and Tichinalla/Ugly Game (*Juego Feo*).

7. Garrido, "Account of Events," 303–305; John, *Storms*, 673–74; Kavanagh, *Comanche Political History*, 112. For Tosapoy's status as the official speaker, see Kavanagh, *Comanche Political History*, 38–39. He states that designated or official speakers were known as *tekwawapI* in the Comanche language. The word is basically pronounced as it looks, with the exception of the capital "I" at the end. This character represents a "voiceless vowel" that, according to Jean O. Charney, is pronounced silently with a puff of air while moving the lips in the shape of the letter. For information on the Comanche sound system as it is written and pronounced by anthropologists, see Jean O. Charney, "Notes on the Comanche Sound System," in *Comanche Political History*, xv–xvi; and Ernest Wallace and E. Adamson Hoebel, *The Comanches: Lords of the South Plains*, xvii. According to Kavanagh, *tekwawpI* were announcers and articulators of decisions and were oftentimes chiefs, as was Tosapoy.

8. Alfred Barnaby Thomas stated in "An Eighteenth Century Comanche Document" (290) that this engagement between Comanches and Apaches took place in the Sandia Mountains. He later correctly identified the Sierra Blanca Mountains in *After Coronado* (263 n. 15) as the range separating the headwaters of the Purgatoire and Canadian Rivers. On May 16, 1786, Tosapoy, his wife, and three Jupe Comanche leaders, Hisaquebera, Tuchubarua, and Encantine, visited with Anza in Santa Fe after having escorted back to the capital four Spaniards who had been sent as envoys to the Comanchería for a few weeks in April and May. Anza, anticipating the Comanche campaigns against the Apaches, suggested that they might be better off searching for their enemies in "Las Mimbres and other ranges close to the other side of the Rio

del Norte" rather than the Sierra Blanca. Apparently, the governor was not confident that the Comanche troops would find Apaches in the Sierra Blanca Mountains, hence his proposal that they should look among other ranges farther south and across the Rio Grande. Tosapoy and the Jupe captains agreed with this suggestion, and they promised to see to its pursuance. See Garrido, "Account of the Events," 312.

9. Thomas, "An Eighteenth Century Comanche Document," 294–95. The *tajara*, or tally sheet, of the campaign of May–June, 1786, against the Apaches does not clearly identify the clan affiliations of the chiefs leading the five columns employed in the operation. Clearly, Ecuera-capa and Cuetaninabeni (spelled "Quetaniaveni" on the tally sheet) were Cuchanecs, which can be verified with other documents such as Garrido, "Account of the Events," 294–321; and Juan Gasiot y Miralles, "List of Comanches Who Came to Make Peace in New Mexico, 1786," Janos, Mar. 13, 1788, in Thomas, *Forgotten Frontiers*, 325–27. This last document can also be found in Thomas, "An Eighteenth Century Comanche Document," 295–97. The clan affiliations of the others are more difficult, if not impossible, to determine. The individual identified as "Enca-jive" on the sheet may have been the Jupe chief Encantine, who visited Santa Fe on May 16, 1786, in the accompaniment of the Cuchanec chief Tosapoy. See Garrido, "Account of the Events," 312.

10. Garrido, "Account of the Events," 315; John, *Storms Brewed*, 686; Kavanagh, *Comanche Political History*, 115–16.

11. See Thomas, *Forgotten Frontiers*, 57–83; Charles L. Kenner, *A History of New Mexican–Plains Indian Relations*, 53–77; John, *Storms Brewed*, 655–96; T. R. Fehrenbach, *Comanches: The Destruction of a People*, 214–33; Thomas D. Hall, *Social Change in the Southwest, 1350–1880*, 117–18; Stanley Noyes, *Los Comanches: The Horse People, 1751–1845*, 74–81; and Kavanagh, *Comanche Political History*, 110–21.

12. One can perceive when the peace was established in New Mexico with the Comanches simply by noting the waning interest in Comanches in Spanish documentary sources. As relations became stable and routine, information on Comanche behavior became less necessary for the successful administration of the province. But incidents involving these Indians began to increase in other regions of New Spain. Texas, Nueva Vizcaya (Chihuahua), Coahuila, Nuevo Leon, and Nuevo Santander (Tamaulipas) all experienced an intensification of Comanche activity in the nineteenth century. The Indians' shift in interest can likewise be noted in the increasing volume of documents from the various parts of New Spain where they concentrated their activities. See Kenner, *History of New Mexican–Plains Indian Relations*, 53.

13. Lyle Steadman, "Kinship, the Basis of Cultural and Social Behavior" (Department of Anthropology, Arizona State University, Aug., 1996, photocopy); Lyle Steadman, "Social Behavior and Sacrifice" (paper presented at the annual meeting of the Human Behavior and Evolution Society, Ann Arbor, Mich., June 16, 1994), 1; Lyle Steadman, "Social—Not Natural, Not Sexual—Selection" (paper presented at the annual meeting of the Human Behavior and Evolution Society, Davis, Calif., July 11, 1998), 3. See also George Peter Murdock, "Anthropology's Mythology," *Proceedings of the Royal Anthropological Institute of Great Britain and Ireland for 1971* (1972): 17–23. For a discussion of George Peter Murdock's thoughts on this issue, see appendix 1.

14. Lyle Steadman, "Religion and Natural Selection: A Descendant Leaving Strategy" (Department of Anthropology, Arizona State University, Aug., 1991, photocopy), 137; Steadman, "Social Behavior and Sacrifice," 2; Garrido, "Account of the Events," 315 (quote).

15. Steadman, "Religion and Natural Selection," 15, 135; Lyle Steadman, "Kinship, Religion, and Ethnicity" (paper presented at the annual meeting of the Evolution and Human Be-

havior Society, Albuquerque, N.Mex., July 27, 1992), 1; Craig Palmer and Lyle Steadman, "Human Kinship as a Descendant-Leaving Strategy: A Solution to an Evolutionary Puzzle," *Journal of Social and Evolutionary Systems* 20, no. 1 (1997): 43. Kinship is based on birth, not on an mount of shared blood or genes. When people speak of kinship in terms of blood, the use of the word *blood* is clearly metaphorical. Likewise, many of one's kin might not share many of their genes. A grandparent who shares only a few genes with a grandchild is still considered as much family as one who shares half of their genes with that same grandchild. For approximately the past twenty years, historians of Native Americans have borrowed from anthropologists the idea that a "cultural ethos" allowed Indians to forge real kinship relationships with non–biologically related persons through adoption ceremonies and material reciprocity in the form of gift giving and trade. Those scholars adhering to this understanding of Indians' social relationships refer to this behavior as "fictive" kinship. For a couple of examples of historical works applying this concept, see Gary Clayton Anderson, *Kinsmen of Another Kind: Dakota-White Relations in the Upper-Mississippi Valley, 1650–1862*, xvi; and David LaVere, *The Caddo Chiefdoms: Caddo Economics and Politics, 700–1835*, 3. The problem with the idea of "fictive" kinship is that this behavior is actually based on metaphorical communication in an effort to promote kinshiplike social behavior among persons who do not recognize a common birth link. Neither ceremonies nor material exchanges are necessary or sufficient for humans to demonstrate this behavior. What probably has confused adherents of the idea of "fictive" kinship is that Indians and other peoples behaving in this manner explicitly denied that the use of kinship metaphors are actually metaphors. According to Lyle Steadman, the oftentimes passionate denial of a metaphor has the effect of promoting a far more intensive cooperation and altruism than that achieved by an acknowledged metaphor. See Steadman, "The Evolutionary Significance of Metaphor" (paper presented at the annual meeting of the Human Behavior and Evolution Society, Evanston, Ill., June 30, 1996), 1.

16. Steadman, "Religion and Natural Selection," 134; Steadman, "Kinship, Religion, and Ethnicity," 1–2. Because Comanches practiced polygyny, it should not be assumed that Ecueracapa's sons shared the same mother. But for the sake of argument, let us presume that the young men did have the same mother.

17. Palmer and Steadman, "Human Kinship as a Descendant-Leaving Strategy," 43; Steadman, "Kinship, Religion, and Ethnicity," 3. Thomas Gladwin's study of Comanche kin behavior centered on the identification of the relationship between kin terms and behavior patterns. He concluded that even though these titles did have some influence on behavior, it could not be said that they were the "primary factor" that determined behavior. He was confused by the difference in behavior of an individual toward two people called "brother," one a sibling, the other a cousin. "Comanche Kin Behavior," *American Anthropologist* 50 (1948): 73–94. What Gladwin failed to recognize is that calling a cousin "brother" simply acknowledges the generational equivalence of the cousins in terms of birth links. In other words, it signified that they shared ancestors two birth links up from themselves, their grandparents.

18. Comanches, like many traditional and nontraditional peoples throughout the world, practiced a traditional prohibition against mentioning the personal name of a dead person. Nobody has sufficiently explained the aim of this behavior among humans. On the one hand, Gladwin implied that this taboo had the effect of shrinking the size of Comanche kinship groups at the third ascending generation. Steadman, on the other hand, has suggested that the practice of taboos like name prohibition is a demonstration of sacrifice, which encourages the same kind of selflessness that forms the basis of social behavior. "Religion and Natural Selection," 78. Kin terms and clan names eliminate the need to mention someone's personal name in

order to trace ascending birth links and kinship. As long as a Comanche individual knew the clan name of an ancestor, they could identify those living clan members as coancestors. This capability obviously does not require one to speak the personal name of an individual. All one needs to know and speak are the kin terms for particular ancestors (identifying birth links) and the clan affiliation of the person.

19. E. Adamson Hoebel, *The Political Organization and Law-Ways of the Comanche Indians* Memoirs of the American Anthropological Association, vol. 54, 12. Here, and with Ernest Wallace in *The Comanches* (140), Hoebel claims that Comanches married within the same band. But he also mentions that they were prohibited from marrying anyone of any degree or recognized relationship. This confusion appears to stem from Hoebel's understanding of bands simply as residential groups. In *Comanche Political History* (42), Kavanagh rightly states that Hoebel incorrectly comprehended the nature of Comanche marriage, hinting that marriage occurred between bands.

20. Palmer and Steadman, "Human Kinship as a Descendant-Leaving Strategy," 44; Steadman, "Kinship, Religion, and Ethnicity," 4.

21. Gladwin, "Comanche Kin Behavior," 78; Morris W. Foster, *Being Comanche: A Social History of an American Indian Community,* 63. The representation of the Comanche term *"nuhmuhnuh"* is derived from Jean O. Charney's explanation of the Comanche sound system in Kavanagh, *Comanche Political History,* xvi.

22. Steadman, "Religion and Natural Selection," 16. Both Kavanagh and Foster agree with the assertion that Comanche divisions were not social groups, but they differ in their explanation of the significance of division names. Kavanagh claims that divisions were "political organizations composed of local residential bands linked by kinship and sodality [associative] ties and recognizing commonality of interest in *group* affairs, war, peace, and trade." *Comanche Political History,* 52 (emphasis added). Foster, though, understands divisions as "discrete gatherings focused around activities associated with larger-scale public social occasions . . . comprised of residence bands that, because of territorial proximity, tended to have more frequent ties of kinship and marriage." *Being Comanche,* 65–66. Despite their claims that divisions were not social groups, there is a group element necessary to each of these definitions. Also, they each recognize some association between the divisions and kinship, but their reluctance to acknowledge division names as clan names screened them from the fundamental connection between the names.

23. Elizabeth A. H. John, ed., and Adán Benavides Jr., trans., "Inside the Comanchería, 1785: The Diary of Pedro Vial and Francisco Xavier Chaves," *Southwestern Historical Quarterly* 98, no. 1 (July, 1994): 49; Ernest Wallace, comp., "David G. Burnet's Letters Describing the Comanche Indians," *West Texas Historical Association Year Book* 30 (1954): 124. The following are a few of many examples of this practice of naming a camp for their leader found in documentary sources: Ortiz to Anza, Santa Fe, May 20, 1786, in Thomas, *Forgotten Frontiers,* 322; "Itinerary and Diary of José Mares, Bexar to Santa Fe, Jan. 18–Apr. 27, 1788," Santa Fe, June 20, 1788, in Noel M. Loomis and Abraham P. Nasatir, *Pedro Vial and the Roads to Santa Fe,* 310; "Proceedings by the *Teniente* of the Pueblo Relative to a Small Number of Comanches Who Were Depredating in that Vicinity," Pueblo de Taos, Dec. 31, 1749, SANM, reel 8:949, T-509; and Juan de Dios Peña, "Diary and Itinerary of a Campaign in Aid of the Comanches against the Pananas [Pawnees]," Santa Fe, June12–Aug. 8, 1790, SANM, reel 12:263, T-1067. Peña often mentioned the name of a chief and added *"con su gente"* ("with his people") in reference to individual Comanche *rancherías.*

24. Garrido, "Account of the Events," 294–321; Ortiz to Anza, 322–23; Gasiot, "List of

Comanches Who Came to Make Peace," 327; John and Benavides, "Inside the Comanchería," 49; Wallace, "David G. Burnet's Letters Describing the Comanche Indians," 124, 121. Foster claims that a person "was a member of the division with which one's residence band and leader were affiliated." Foster, *Being Comanche,* 66. Burnet's "Comanchees" were Cuchanecs (also known as Kotsotekas). The "Yamparacks" were obviously the Yamparicas. Burnet's identification of the "Tenaways" is uncertain. Kavanagh argues that the Jupe name probably merged with the Yamparicas. He also suggests that the Tenewas resulted from a splinter group of Yamparicas and some Taovayas and Wichita Indians. He sees these divisional changes as peoples' political responses to the changing economic situation brought about by European colonization of Louisiana, Texas, and New Mexico. I discuss the issues surrounding the identity of the Tenewa Comanches in greater detail below.

25. Steadman, "Kinship, Religion, and Ethnicity," 4.

26. Harold W. Scheffler also observed this behavior among the inhabitants of Choiseul Island in the South Pacific. See "Choiseul Island Descent Groups," in *Melanesia: Readings on a Culture Area,* ed. L. L. Langness and John C. Weschler, 136.

27. Fernando de la Concha to Pedro de Nava, "New Mexico, Extraordinary Expenses, 1792," Santa Fe, Mar. 15, 1793, SANM, reel 13:218, T-1228; David G. Burnet, "The Comanches and Other Tribes of Texas; and the Policy to be Pursued Respecting Them," in *Historical and Statistical Information Respecting the History, Conditions, and Prospects of the Indian Tribes of the United States,* ed. Henry R. Schoolcraft, 1:231; E. E. Evans-Pritchard, *The Nuer: A Description of the Modes of Livelihood and Political Institutions of a Nilotic People,* 216. Gladwin reported that Comanches only traced three ascending generations—that is, they trace preceding birth links only up to the great-grandparent generation. With only a few descent names in existence at any time among Comanches, this number of ascending linkages may have been sufficient to connect most tribal members to one another. "Comanche Kin Behavior," 76. E. E. Evans-Pritchard notes the same phenomenon among the Neur in the 1930s. He found that the villages and cattle camps of a particular descent name contained more people identified with clan names other than the one the sites were named for.

28. Garrido, "Account of the Events," 310–11; Gasiot, "List of Comanches Who Came to Make Peace," 326; Nemesio Salcedo to Fernando Chacón, Chihuahua, Jan. 16, 1804, SANM, reel 15:177, T-1703.

29. Joaquin Real Alencaster to Nemesio Salcedo, "Report on Comanche Affairs," Santa Fe, Nov. 20, 1805, SANM, reel 15:1028, T-1925. This document is also found, translated, in in Marc Simmons, ed. and trans., *Border Comanches: Seven Spanish Colonial Documents, 1785–1819,* 33; and Kavanagh, *Comanche Political History,* 144–45. I agree with Kavanagh that Simmons mistranslated this report. In reference to Somiquaso and Quegüe, the document reads *"que les nombrar por General de un capitan nombrado Somiquaso asi como el Quegüe para los Cuchanticas respecto a que ellos querian tener una cabesa."* Simmons read *"otro"* for *"como"* and translated this statement thus, "that I should name as generals one of their captains called Somiquaso, and another from the Cuchanticas called Quegue so that they would have leaders." Kavanagh, however, correctly translates the document as stating "that I should name as generals one of their captains named Somiquaso, like Quegüe for the Kotsotekas." He is correct to make the point that the proper translation of this line is very important to our understanding of the political history of Comanches at this time. Simmons confused translation is innocent enough and probably reflects the general confusion within the Spanish documents with respect to Quegüe's clan association.

30. Alejo Garcia Cónde to Facundo Melgares, Durango, Nov. 9, 1818, SANM, reel 19:438,

T-2771; Kavanagh, *Comanche Political History,* 161. Cónde wrote that Quegüe died *"en la Marcha del Averio,"* literally "on the march of the assembly [or flock] of birds." The Spanish often applied an avian metaphor to nomadic Indians in an effort to communicate these people's apparent freedom and unpredictable movement. Kavanagh rightly translates this phrase as "on the road," meaning that Quegüe died in 1818 somewhere along the course of his people's frequent migrations within the Comanchería.

31. Tanquegüe, or Quegüe, was identified as a "Cuchantica" by New Mexico governor Joaquin Real Alencaster in 1805 and by Alejo Garcia Cónde in 1818. See Simmons, *Border Comanches,* 33; and Cónde to Melgares, Nov. 9, 1818, reel 19:438. However, he was identified as a Yamparica by the *comandante general* of Provincias Internas, Nemesio Salcedo, in 1804 and by the Spanish trailblazer Francisco Amangual in 1808. See Amangual, "Diary of Francisco Amangual from San Antonio to Santa Fe, Mar. 30–June 19, 1808," in Loomis and Nasatir, *Pedro Vial,* 489.

32. Evans-Pritchard, *The Nuer,* 204, 210. In societies that trace their descent and ancestry through the female line, each individual woman is a potential source for a new lineage or clan name.

33. Lyle Steadman, e-mail to author (subject, "Clan Names"), Apr. 6, 1998.

34. Kavanagh, *Comanche Political History,* 482, 137–38; Anza to Ugarte y Loyola, Santa Fe, Oct. 20, 1787, in Alfred Barnaby Thomas, "San Carlos: A Comanche Pueblo on the Arkansas River, 1787," *The Colorado Magazine* 6, no. 3 (May, 1929): 86–87; Ronald J. Benes, "Anza and Concha in New Mexico, 1787–1793: A Study in New Colonial Techniques," *Journal of the West* 4, no. 1 (Jan., 1965): 65–66; Max L. Moorhead, *The Apache Frontier: Jacobo Ugarte and Spanish-Indian Relations in Northern New Spain, 1769–1791,* 161–64; John, *Storms Brewed,* 732–34.

35. Council of war, Chihuahua, June 9–15, 1778, in Thomas, *Plains Indians and New Mexico,* 201 (which contains the earliest mention of the Jupes I have seen in the Spanish documentary sources); Mendinueta to Marqués de Croix, "Report of New Mexico Events from Sept. 17 to Nov. 9, 1768," extracted from Croix to Arriaga, Mexico, Jan. 30, 1769, in Thomas, *Plains Indians and New Mexico,* 167; Anza, "Diary of the Expedition against the Comanche Nation," 135; Kavanagh, *Comanche Political History,* 123, 482. For a reproduction of Bernardo Miera y Pacheco's 1778 map of the Domínguez–Velez de Escalante expedition, see either Kavanagh, *Comanche Political History,* 88–89; or Ted J. Warner, ed., and Fray Angelico Chaves, trans., *The Domínguez-Escalante Journal: Their Expedition through Colorado, Utah, Arizona, and New Mexico in 1776,* 144–45.

36. Garrido, "Account of the Events," 299. Thomas's translation states "because of his opposition to the Spaniards and the credit he enjoyed among the *Utes* and Yamparicas, [Toro Blanco] kept these two groups dissuaded from peace" (emphasis added). This mention of Toro Blanco's influence among the Utes is probably due to either a miscopied document, a mistranslation, or a simple typo; the first two seem more likely. I have not seen the original document, but the Spanish oftentimes referred to the Jupes as "Yupes" or "Yupis." A Spanish scribe in charge of making copies to be distributed to other officials throughout New Spain and the Iberian peninsula could have easily confused these terms with the word *Yuta,* which referred to the Ute Indians. But the error may be Thomas's. Having a great deal of respect for his work and translation skills, this hypothesis seems implausible to me, although it is quite possible. Kavanagh guessed that the slain leader might have been a Jupe, succeeding the younger Cuerno Verde as the leader of that band. See *Comanche Political History,* 5.

37. Thomas, *Plains Indians and New Mexico,* 34; John, *Storms Brewed,* 329–31; Kavanagh, *Comanche Political History,* 75–78.

38. Pedro de Fermín de Mendinueta to the Marqués de Croix, Santa Fe, June 18, 1768, in Thomas, *Plains Indians and New Mexico,* 159–62; Elizabeth John's questioning three hundred years later of the governor's explanation for his actions and for those of his subjects seems quite appropriate in light of the documentary sources. See *Storms Brewed,* 468; and Kavanagh, *Comanche Political History,* 78–79.

39. Mendinueta to Marqués de Croix, "Report of New Mexico Events," 165; John, *Storms Brewed,* 467–68.

40. Mendinueta to Marqués de Croix, "Report of New Mexico Events," 165–67; John, *Storms Brewed,* 469; Kavanagh, *Comanche Political History,* 79.

41. Thomas, *Plains Indians and New Mexico,* 43 (citing Bucareli to Arriaga, Mexico, Jan. 27, 1773, Archivo General de Indias, Guadalajara 513); John, *Storms Brewed,* 475–78; Armijo, "Information Communicated by Juan Canelaria," 294; Mendinueta to Bucareli, Santa Fe, Sept. 30, 1774, in Thomas, *Plains Indians and New Mexico,* 169–72; Kavanagh, *Comanche Political History,* 83–85; Mendinueta to Bucareli, Santa Fe, Oct. 20, 1774, in Thomas, *Plains Indians and New Mexico,* 174–75.

42. Mendinueta to Bucareli, Santa Fe, May 12, 1775, in Thomas, *Plains Indians and New Mexico,* 179–80; Mendinueta to Bucareli, Santa Fe, Aug. 18, 1775, in ibid., 180–83; Caballero de Croix, "Instructions to the Governor of the Province of Coahuila, Don Jacobo Ugarte y Loyola, for the Purchase and Prompt Sending of One Thousand and Five Hundred Horses Destined for New Mexico," Chihuahua, May 14, 1777, SANM, reel 10:910–25, T-700; John, *Storms Brewed,* 479–81, 481–82, 583; Kavanagh, *Comanche Political History,* 84–85; Mendinueta to Bucareli, Santa Fe, Aug. 19, 1775, in Thomas, *Plains Indians and New Mexico,* 184; Fray Francisco Atanasio Domínguez to Provincial Fray Isidro Murillo, Santa Fe, July 29, 1776, in Eleanor B. Adams and Fray Angelico Chaves, eds. and trans., *The Missions of New Mexico, 1776: A Description by Fray Francisco Atanasio Domínguez with other Contemporary Documents,* 282, 154 n. 11; Caballero de Croix to Mendinueta, Chihuahua, Jan. 8, 1778, SANM, reel 10:970, T-716; Caballero de Croix to Joseph de Gálvez, Arizpe, Oct. 30, 1781, in Alfred Barnaby Thomas, ed. and trans., *Teodoro de Croix and the Northern Frontier of New Spain, 1776–1783,* 111.

43. Thomas, *Teodoro de Croix,* 45–58; Anza, "Diary of the Expedition against the Comanche Nation," 130–35; Caballero de Croix to Gálvez, 109; Bailey H. Carroll and J. Villasana Haggard, eds. and trans., *Three New Mexican Chronicles: The* Exposición *of Don Pedro Bautista Pino, 1812; The* Ojeada *of Lic. Antonio Barreiro, 1832; and the additions by Don José Augustín de Escudero, 1849,* 129; John, *Storms Brewed,* 585–89; Kavanagh, *Comanche Political History,* 92.

44. This approximate figure concerning the number of Comanches that were either killed or captured is simply a guess based on the tallies given in the documents cited above. Of course, the Spanish officials did not record exact numbers many times, and when they did record numbers they sometimes tended to exaggerate the totals. But it is likely that the Comanches could have suffered several hundred deaths in the violent decade of the 1770s. At least three *rancherías* were destroyed as a result of this fighting. Spanish accounts record that one of these liquidated encampments consisted of eighty tents and that each dwelling possibly contained up to six persons. As many as 480 persons were possibly either captured or killed in that one instance. The loss of life on all sides of this drawn-out war was indeed staggering considering the relatively small populations of New Mexicans and Comanches. For the destruction of Comanche *rancherías,* see Mendinueta to Bucareli, Santa Fe, Oct. 20, 1774, in Thomas, *Plains Indians and New Mexico,* 174–75; and Caballero de Croix to Mendinueta, Jan. 8, 1778, reel 10:970.

45. Anza, "Diary of the Expedition against the Comanche Nation," 135–36; Cavallero de Croix to Juan Bautista de Anza, Arispe, July 14, 1780, SANM, reel 11:77–78, T-799; John, *Storms*

Brewed, 590; Cavallero de Croix to Juan Bautista de Anza, Arispe, Feb. 24, 1783, SANM, reel 11:567–68, T-858; Kavanagh, *Comanche Political History,* 93. Garrido suggests that it was Cuchanec individuals who opposed the aggressive behavior of their Jupe and Yamparica cousins and initiated the peace process with the authorities in New Mexico. "Account of the Events," 299. Cuchanecs may have been encouraged, in part, to seek peace in New Mexico after observing Athanase de Mézières' efforts to establish peace with the Indians in Texas during the 1770s. See Herbert E. Bolton, ed. and trans., *Athanase de Mézières and the Louisiana-Texas Frontier, 1768–1780.*

46. Gasiot, "List of Comanches Who Came to Make Peace," 326–27; Concha to Nava, Mar. 15, 1793, reel 13:218. Compare the documents Fernando de la Concha to Pedro de Nava, Santa Fe, Nov. 1, 1791, SANM, reel 12: 719, T-1164; and Concha to Nava, Mar. 15, 1793, reel 13:213 to verify Paruanarimuco's clan identity as a Jupe. The former document associates him with the Jupes and Yamparicas while the latter counts him with the Jupes and "Cuchanticas," or Cuchanecs. By the process of elimination, one can be certain that this person could not have had the Yamparica ancestral name. Eliminating all doubt of whether or not Paruanarimuco was a Jupe is "The Diary of Pedro Vial," Bexar to Santa Fe, Oct. 4, 1786–May 26, 1787, in Loomis and Nasatir, *Pedro Vial,* 284. In the diary entry for May 14, Vial notes that his expedition reached the villages of the "Tupis," where "the chief called Paruanarimuco brought out the Spanish flag and took us to his lodge." It seems that Vial may have heard the ancestral name "Jupes" as "Tupis," quite a reasonable mistake for someone not completely familiar with the Comanche tongue. It is also possible that scholars garbled this name in the process of the document's reproduction by scribes or its translation. Kavanagh did not make the connection between Tupis and Jupes when he claimed that Vial failed to "give a divisional identification for Paruanarimuco." Kavanagh, *Comanche Political History,* 137.

47. For an excellent introduction to biogeography and the concepts associated with minimum viable population and population viability analysis, see David Quammen, *The Song of the Dodo: Island Biogeography in an Age of Extinctions,* 512–19, 569–72.

48. Fray Francisco Atanasio Domínguez, "A Description of New Mexico," in Adams and Chaves, *Missions of New Mexico,* 213; Anza to Cavallero de Croix, Santa Fe, Nov. 1, 1779, in Thomas, *Forgotten Frontiers,* 142; José Francisco Ruíz, *Report on the Indian Tribes of Texas in 1828,* ed. John C. Ewers, trans. Georgette Dorn, 9; Wallace, "David G. Burnet's Letters Describing the Comanche Indians," 136; Burnet, "Comanches and Other Tribes of Texas," 231; Concha to Ugarte y Loyola, Santa Fe, July 6, 1789, AGN-PI, tomo 65, expediente 15, folio 2; Ugarte y Loyola to Concha, Chihuahua, Nov. 21, 1789, SANM, reel 12:225–26, T-1067; Benes, "Anza and Concha in New Mexico," 66–67; Moorhead, *The Apache Frontier,* 167–68, 738; Kavanagh, *Comanche Political History,* 177; Concha to Ugarte y Loyola, Santa Fe, June 15, 1789, AGN-PI, tomo 65, expediente 14, folio 2.

49. John and Benavides, "Inside the Comanchería," 37–38. There has been a good deal of confusion since 1786 over whether Camisa de Hierro and Ecueracapa were the same person. The source for this longstanding and ongoing uncertainty stems from the nature of Spanish colonial administration in the department of the Provincias Internas. The governors of New Mexico and Texas each sent reports about Indian affairs to Chihuahua, where they were reviewed by the *comandante general.* Because Comanches had contact with officials in both New Mexico and Texas during the 1780s, officials in Chihuahua received two separate streams of information relating to the Indians. It was almost inevitable that confusion would settle upon the office of the *comandante general* as it processed information about Comanche names and actions generated by two sources of imperfect information about what exactly was going on in

the Comanchería. Students of Comanche history have inherited this confusion as it is revealed in the documentary sources generated by the Spanish authorities. The inability of administrators to come to a conclusion over the issue of the identities of Ecueracapa, Camisa de Hierro (or Fierro), and Cota de Malla has contributed considerably to the problem scholars deal with in making a positive identity of these names today. In *Comanche Political History* (120–21), Kavanagh suggests that Camisa de Hierro and Cota de Malla were indeed the same person, but that person was not also Ecueracapa. He bases this conclusion on a conversation Comandante General Jacobo Ugarte y Loyola had through an interpreter with Ecueracapa's sons and Tosacondata about the identities of these men. The Indians were reported to say that the two were different individuals and that Camisa de Hierro had been killed in a battle with the Spanish. See Ugarte y Loyola to Marqués de Sonora, Chihuahua, Jan. 4, 1787, AGN-PI, tomo 65, expediente 2, folio 65. Kavanagh also cites the report of the Spanish officer who claimed to have killed Camisa de Hierro during the reported battle Kavanagh gleaned this report from Luis Navarro García, *Don José de Galvez y la comandancia general de las provincias internas de norte de Nueva España* (Sevilla: Consejo Superior de Investigaciones Cientificas, 1964). I have not seen this source and cannot comment on its implication for resolving this issue. Questions still persist. Elizabeth John remains convinced that the three names represented only one person. I am inclined to agree with her. She basically argues that Pedro Vial's and Francisco Xavier Chaves' notion that the three names represented one person was the most informed opinion of anybody in New Mexico and Texas since both men had lived among those Indians for some time prior to settling in San Antonio. Indeed, Vial and Chaves would have had firsthand knowledge of whether or not these men were one in the same. See John, *Storms Brewed,* 715–16. Also see Cabello to Ugarte y Loyola, San Antonio de Béxar, Sept. 24, 1786, BA, reel 17:830–32; and Cabello to Anza, San Antonio de Béxar, Oct. 3, 1786, BA, reel 17:865.

50. Garrido, "Account of the Events," 309.

51. Concha to Ugarte y Loyola, Santa Fe, June 26, 1788, in Thomas, "San Carlos," 90. For a full description of Comanche funerary traditions, see Ruíz, *Report on the Indian Tribes of Texas,* 12–13. Ruíz's account of these traditions corresponds nicely with Concha's report explaining why the Jupes abandoned San Carlos.

52. Kavanagh, *Comanche Political History,* 482; Wallace, "David G. Burnet's Letters Describing the Comanche Indians," 123; Garrido, "Account of the Events," 295, 299.

53. J. Cameron "Comanche Indians: The Country West of the Colorado," in Charles Adams Gulick Jr. and Winnie Allen, eds., *The Papers of Mirabeau Buonaparte Lamar,* 1:475; [José Francisco?] Ruis [Ruíz], San Antonio de Béxar, 1840s, "'Comanches': Customs and Characteristics," in ibid., 4:221; Benjamin Sloat [?], Council Ground, Tehuacana Creek, July 22, 1844, "Notes," in Dorman H. Winfrey and James M. Day, eds., *The Indian Papers of Texas and the Southwest, 1825–1916,* 2:82; Report from R. S. Neighbors to H. R. Schoolcraft, "The Na-ü-ni, or Comanches of Texas; Their Traits and Beliefs, and Their Divisions and Intertribal Relations," in ibid., 3:350; Carroll and Haggard, *Three New Mexican Chronicles,* 128; "Treaty with the Comanches," Chihuahua, Oct. 18, 1826, MANM, reel 5, frame 429.

54. Marín del Valle, Santa Fe, [?] 1758, "Description of the Province of New Mexico, with a map which shows its situation and towns, made under Governor Don Francisco Marín del Valle," AGN-Californias, tomo 39, expediente 1; Kavanagh, *Comanche Political History,* 76; James Mooney, *The Ghost Dance Religion and the Sioux Outbreak of 1890,* Fourteenth Annual Report of the Bureau of Ethnology, 1892–93, pt. 2, 1044–45. Out of the thirteen clan names identified by Mooney, five names had gone extinct, two were on the verge of extinction, and six others remained in existence.

55. John and Benavides, "Inside the Comanchería," 50; Garrido, "Account of the Events," 295.

56. Tomás Vélez Cachupín, *"Auto,"* Santa Fe, Mar. 5, 1750, in Charles Wilson Hackett, ed. and trans., *Pichardo's Treatise on the Limits of Texas and Louisiana,* 3:317; Donald E. Chipman, *Spanish Texas, 1519–1821,* 183; Mézières to Barón de Ripperdá, San Antonio de Béxar, July 4, 1772, in Bolton, *Athanase de Mézières,* 1:297; Jean Louis Berlandier, *The Indians of Texas in 1830,* ed. John C. Ewers, 120; Evans-Pritchard, *The Nuer,* 247; Napoleon Chagnon, *Yänomamö,* 4th ed., 145. Evans-Pritchard and, more recently, Chagnon both observed clan fragmentation within areas as small as villages. Evans-Pritchard, in particular, notes that different areas of Nuer settlements were known by the personal names of influential males. This behavior, it might be recalled, resembled the Comanche practice of naming a *ranchería* after its leader. In the case of the Nuer, lineage divisions were characterized by the association of different parts of a village with the names of brothers of an influential family. Something similar to this process occurred among the Cuchanec Comanches.

57. Elizabeth A. H. John surmises from other Spanish documents that the "Vermillion River" was the Little Wichita River. See John and Benavides, "Inside the Comanchería," 35 n. 25, 36–37.

58. Ibid., 49; Domingo Cabello to José Antonio Rengel, "Responses of the Governor of Texas to the Questions which the Comandante General of the Provincias Internas Made in his Official Letter of Jan. 27, 1786, Covering Various Circumstances of the Eastern Comanche Indians," San Antonio de Béxar, Apr. 30, 1786, BA, reel 17:419; Cabello to Anza, San Antonio de Béxar, Oct. 3, 1786, BATS 1, reel 16, vol. 142, p. 17 (also available as BA, reel 17:864–66); John, *Storms Brewed,* 695; Kavanagh, *Comanche Political History,* 109. Because some of these names have been translated into Spanish from the Comanche, while others have been recorded in their original language as they sounded to Spanish-speaking observers, it is difficult to know the true identity of some of these men. For instance, the person whose name was recorded as El Manco in this document possibly appears in another document under his Comanche name. This idiosyncracy of the Spanish sources makes it difficult to positively identify individuals. Kavanagh addressed the meaning of the names of the chiefs mentioned in this document. Of course, Cota de Malla and Camisa de Yierro were other names by which the Spanish knew Ecueracapa. These names translate to "coat of mail" and "iron shirt" respectively in English. Cabeza Rapada means "shaved head"; El Lobito, "little wolf"; Quinacaraco, "eagle sash" or "neckpiece," according to Kavanagh; Guaquangas, "trotter," also according to Kavanagh; and El Español, obviously, "the Spaniard." El Español may have been a captive from some northern province of New Spain who grew up among the Comanches. Kavanagh seems to have mistranslated the names of the remaining chiefs mentioned by Cabello. For example, Kavanagh was confused by the name El Sonnillo. This name probably was El Sorrillo, which means "skunk." Sometimes it is difficult to distinguish the difference between lower case "n"s and "r"s in the Spanish documents. The names La Boca Partida, El Surdo, and El Manco also seem to be misunderstood by Kavanagh. He claimed that La Boca Partida suggests "broken mouth." Rather, it probably translates more properly as "split mouth," suggesting that this person had the congenital physical defect known as a cleft palate. For El Surdo, Kavanagh implies that it meant "the deaf one." However, the Spanish word "sordo," not "surdo," means "deaf." "Surdo," as fans of Mexican League baseball might know, is slang for left-handed. The word is derived from the word *sur,* meaning south. "Surdo" is similar to the American slang term *southpaw* for a left-handed baseball pitcher. Of course, *sordo* and *surdo* sound very similar, and it is plausible that the recording of El Surdo may indeed have been El Sordo. Finally, Kavanagh suggests that El Manco implied "the one-armed," or "the person with one arm." Indeed, any Spanish-

English dictionary supplies this translation for *manco*. Then again, this term is also used in some parts of Mexico as slang for "someone who has a limp." A more correct translation for the word *manco* would be "defective," in the general sense of a birth defect or some injury that caused permanent damage. The individual known as El Manco may have had only one arm or hand, or he could of had a leg injury that caused him to limp.

59. "Itinerary and Diary of José Mares," 311; Concha to Nava, Mar. 15, 1793, reel 13:213, 216–17; Concha to Nava, Santa Fe, Nov. 10, 1792, SANM, reel 13:190, T-1218. The March 15 document identifies the six Comanche chiefs who arrived in Santa Fe on Apr. 7, 1792, as both Jupes and "Cuchanticas," or Cuchanecs. Hachacas, or Achacas, must have identified with either one of these clan names. The other individuals mentioned as accompanying Quenatacaro were Hachacas, Ysabupi, Ysimiacara and sixteen others who remained nameless.

60. Concha to Nava, Mar. 15, 1793, reel 13:214. The Comanche prefix "pisi," or "pisu," means "odor," or "smell." Kavanagh concurred with Anza that the name Pisimanpat translated to something like "smelly" or "decayed shoe." Apparently, Cabello only partially understood the complete meaning of this person's name, probably assuming that the sign-language motion for "smelly" suggested "skunk." Because Anza and Cabello both cite Pisimanpat and El Sorrillo as influential Cuchanecs, I am inclined to believe that these two individuals may have been the same person. Unfortunately, there is no conclusive evidence that supports this opinion. Nevertheless, the meanings of the names are close enough to suggest that these individuals were actually the same person.

61. Garrido, "Account of the Events," 295; Nava to Concha, Chihuahua, Aug. 8, 1793, in Simmons, *Border Comanches,* 29.

62. Cabello to Ugarte y Loyola, San Antonio de Béxar, July 30, 1786, BA, reel 17:607; John, *Storms Brewed,* 704–705; Kavanagh, *Comanche Political History,* 148.

63. Pedro de Nava to Manuel Muñoz, Chihuahua, Apr. 4, 1797, BA, reel 27:184. Various spellings of Soxas exist in the Spanish documents, including "Sojas," "Sosas," "Sofais," and "Chofais." Interestingly, Kavanagh did not note the murder in his treatment of the Comanche political scene in the late 1790s. The son of Ecueracapa killed in this incident could not have been Oxamaquea because he is known to have lived among the Shoshone in the early nineteenth century. D. B. Shimkin, "The Wind River Shoshone Sun Dance," *Smithsonian Bureau of Ethnology, Anthropological Papers,* Bulletin 151, no. 41 (1953): 398–484. Oxamaquea might have chosen to live with his Shoshone relatives in Wyoming because of the poisonous political climate that existed among the Cuchanecs on the southern plains.

64. Athanase de Mézières, "Report of the Expedition to the Cadodachos," Oct. 29, 1770, in Bolton, *Athanase de Mézières,* 1:212; John, *Storms Brewed,* 390; Kavanagh, *Comanche Political History,* 80; John and Benavides, "Inside the Comanchería," 50; Concha to Nava, Mar. 15, 1793, reel 13:215; report from R. S. Neighbors to H. R. Schoolcraft, "The Na-ü-ni, or Comanches of Texas," 3:348. Neighbors reported that Comanches informed him they had intermarried with the "Wacos, Tah-wac-car-ros, Toriuash, and branches of the Pawnee [Wichita] tribe" shortly after they began to migrate to the plains east of New Mexico.

65. Manuel de Salcedo, "Proceedings Concerning Oso Ballo's Conspiracy," San Fernando de Béxar, Mar. 6, 1812, BA, reel 50:633; Kavanagh, *Comanche Political History,* 149; council of war, San Fernando de Béxar [?],Oct. 1810, BA, reel 47:123, 126; "Proceedings on the Capture of El Sordo and his Followers," San Fernando de Béxar, Dec. 15, 1811, BA, reel 49:730. It is possible that El Sordo was the same person Cabello identified as El Surdo in 1786. See Cabello to Rengel, "Responses of the Governor of Texas," reel 17:419.

66. Nemesio Salcedo to Manuel de Salcedo, Chihuahua, Apr. 27, 1812, BA, reel 51:90;

Kavanagh, *Comanche Political History*, 157. For the Indian council of war and events leading to it, see the various documents associated with "Proceedings Concerning Oso Ballo's Conspiracy," San Fernando de Béxar, Mar. 6–Apr. 3, 1812, BA, reel 50:627–72.

67. "Report of G. W. Bonnell, Commissioner of Indian Affairs," Houston, Nov. 3, 1838, 3d Cong., 1st sess., in U.S. Congress, Senate Committee on Indian Affairs, *Communication from the Commissioner of Indian Affairs, and other Documents in Relation to the Indians in Texas*, 30th Cong., 1st sess., 1848, S. Rpt. 171, 42–43, 46; Robert S. Neighbors to W. Medill, U.S. Special Indian Agency [Texas], Mar. 16, 1848, in ibid., 13. Thomas Kavanagh strongly criticized Bonnell's 1838 report as a polemic "mixture of fact and folklore, more reflective of Anglo-Texan preconceptions about Comanches than objective personal observations." *Comanche Political History*, 229. Indeed, Bonnell's personal opinions about Comanches are apparent in this report, and at times he reveals his confusion over the exact relationship various Indians had to one another. But I contend that this document has value as a resource for understanding the historical behavior of individual Comanches. His observations are relatively sound when looked at in the proper context. Also, see Roger M. Keesing, "Shrines, Ancestors, and Cognatic Descent: The Kwaio and Tallensi," in *Melanesia: Readings on a Culture Area*, ed. L. L. Langness and John C. Weschler, 146. Keesing's observations on Kwaio clan segmentation parallel the splintering of the eastern Cuchanecs in the early nineteenth century. In particular, he notes that internal feuding among family members precipitates these splits.

68. According to Kavanagh, Comanches could acquire political power or authority through the control of various material resources. These derived from the exploitation of bison and horses, military campaigns and the redistribution of war booty, control of trade, and the control of "Euroamerican" political gifts. *Comanche Political History*, 57.

69. Steadman, "Kinship, Religion, and Ethnicity," 4, 6; Palmer and Steadman, "Human Kinship as a Descendant-Leaving Strategy," 43–44; Nava to Muñoz, Apr. 4, 1797, reel 27:184. Steadman, in an apparent reference to Evans-Pritchard's *Kinship and Marriage among the Nuer*, notes that ancestral or clan names among the Nuer could be used to identify thousands of co-descendants.

70. Garrido, "Account of the Events," 294; Nava to Concha, Chihuahua, July 22, 1791, SANM, reel 12:604, T-1135. Probably the most well-known study of rank among Plains Indians is Bernard Mishkin, *Rank and Warfare among the Plains Indians*. Mishkin's argument on this issue is primarily economic, focusing on warfare and raiding as the source of material goods upon which a person's stature was based. Thomas Kavanagh's treatment of Comanche status basically echoes Mishkin's materialistic interpretation. Morris Foster, though, understood this issue in terms of postmodernist thinking based on the interpersonalist tradition of Erving Goffman. According to this reasoning, the status of individual Comanches is identified with their "social 'face.'" Apparently, Foster associates "face" with social behavior, but Goffman's reasoning prevents him from making this connection explicit. See Foster, *Being Comanche*, 23–28. Unfortunately, all of these explanations of rank and status have only further complicated the issue. It appears that Mishkin sensed that a Plains Indian man's stature was founded on something other than economics. His struggle to explain the role of counting coup in determining Kiowa rank suggests as much. Unfortunately, he did not recognize the importance of one's generation in determining a man's social position vis-á-vis other individuals. *Rank and Warfare*, 61–62.

71. This situation is paralleled among the Tiwi of northern Australia. The young men of this society never have high status, even though they have the greatest access to wealth by being the best hunters and fighters. Interestingly, Tiwi women generally prefer not to marry these

young men. Instead, they choose old prominent men as husbands. Capt. Randolph B. Marcy, who had spent some time in the Comanchería in the late 1840s and early 1850s, took note of this practice among the Comanches, commenting "that young girls are often compelled to unite their fortunes with old men." In particular, he observed that the chief named "Ketumsee, . . . a man at least sixty years old, had four wives, the oldest of whom was not over twenty years of age." Pedro Bautista Pino of Santa Fe had made a similar observation years earlier in 1812, noticing that "men of rank [older men?] often have as many as seven wives." Rank and status among tribal cultures like the Tiwi and Comanches appears to have been most associated with age as opposed to material possessions. C. W. M. Hart and Arnold R. Pilling, *The Tiwi of North Australia*, fieldwork edition, 34, 82; Randolph B. Marcy, *Thirty Years of Army Life on the Border*, 49; Carroll and Haggard, *Three New Mexican Chronicles*, 130; Lyle Steadman, "Kinship Hierarchy: The Basis of Cooperation?" (paper presented at the annual meeting of the Human Behavior and Evolution Society, Tucson, Ariz., June 6, 1997), 9.

72. Steadman, "Kinship Hierarchy," 2–4.

73. Ibid., 4, 5; Garrido, "Account of the Events," 315; Juan Gasiot y Miralles, "List of Comanches Attending a Spanish, Navajo and Comanche Attack on the Apaches," July, 1786, in Thomas, *Forgotten Frontiers*, 327–28. Comanches have four terms for siblings, each specifying either older or younger brother or sister. This practice suggests that Comanches recognized rank among siblings was based on birth order. See E. Adamson Hoebel, "Comanche and H3kandika Shoshone Relationship Systems," *American Anthropologist* 41 (1939): 441.

74. Hoebel, "Comanche and H3kandika Shoshone Relationship Systems," 441; Jean O. Charney, "Notes on the Comanche Sound System," in Kavanagh, *Comanche Political History*, xv–xvi; Steadman, "Kinship Hierarchy," 5; Gladwin, "Comanche Kin Behavior," 78.

75. Steadman, "Kinship Hierarchy," 6–7; Garrido, "Account of the Events," 303; Cabello to Rengel, "Responses of the Governor of Texas," reel 17:419.

76. Steadman, "Kinship Hierarchy," 6; Hoebel, *Political Organization and Law-Ways*, 40; [Ruíz], "'Comanches': Customs and Characteristics," in Gulick and Allen, *Papers of Mirabeau Buonaparte Lamar*, vol. 4, 1:222–23; Kavanagh, *Comanche Political History*, 44–45. For a similar description of Comanche councils, see Cameron, "Comanche Indians: The Country West of the Colorado," 1:475.

77. The ritual behavior associated with the smoking ceremony is interesting. It is my contention that by first blowing a mouthful of smoke toward the sky, the chief paid homage to the Comanche's ascending ancestry. By blowing the smoke downward, the chief then honored the descendants of the ancestors and the participants. Finally, by blowing smoke to either side, the chief acknowledged the Comanches nature as co-descendents.

78. Berlandier, *Indians of Texas in 1830*, 90, 91; Ruíz, *Report on the Indian Tribes of Texas*, 10. Religion has been a problematic issue for scholars studying Comanche behavior. Most have concluded that these Indians did not concern themselves with religion as much as the Kiowa or Sioux did because they were bereft of an elaborate large gathering and religious ritual like the famous Sun Dance. The lack of such a ritual gathering of Comanches has frequently been cited as evidence for the persistence of cultural traits that developed in response to Great Basin environmental realities. The most recent treatment of this issue is Daniel Gelo, "The Comanches as Aboriginal Skeptics," *American Indian Quarterly* 17, no. 1 (winter, 1993): 69–82. In this article, Gelo rightly criticizes the idea that Comanches lacked formal religious rituals because of their skeptical nature. Yet he maintains the idea that their particular form of religious behavior could be attributed to a persistence of Shoshonean traits. I agree that Comanches inherited their religious traditions from their Shoshone ancestors, but I disagree that they were

characteristic of the Great Basin and its environment. What most students of American Indians fail to understand is that ancestor worship, something fundamental and universal among humans, is at the root of all religious behavior. Comanches did not practice the Sun Dance simply because it was not part of their ancestral tradition. But they did have the smoking ritual. While not as dramatic as the Sun Dance, this practice achieved the same aim — it encouraged cooperation among distant kin. See Lyle B. Steadman, Craig T. Palmer, and Christopher F. Tilley, "The Universality of Ancestor Worship," *Ethnology* 35, no. 1 (winter, 1996): 63–76; Steadman and Palmer, "Religion as an Identifiable Traditional Behavior Subject to Natural Selection," *Journal of Social and Evolutionary Systems* 18, no. 2 (1995): 149–64; and Steadman, "Religion and Natural Selection."

79. Ruíz, *Report on the Indian Tribes of Texas*, 15; Berlandier, *Indians of Texas in 1830*, 90; Marcy, *Thirty Years of Army Life*, 58; Wallace, "David G. Burnet's Letters Describing the Comanche Indians," 126. For the commonality of tribal ancestor worship, see Steadman, Palmer, and Tilley, "Universality of Ancestor Worship," 63–76; Steadman, "Kinship, Religion, and Ethnicity," 7; Steadman, "Evolutionary Significance of Metaphor," 3. For another observation that Comanches saw the sun as a metaphor for their original fatherly ancestor, see [Ruíz], "'Comanches': Customs and Characteristics," vol. 4, 1:221. Indeed, Berlandier may have received much of his information on Comanche behavior directly from his acquaintance with Ruíz.

80. [Ruíz], "'Comanches': Customs and Characteristics," vol. 4, 1:223; Jean Louis Berlandier, *Journey to Mexico during the Years 1826 to 1834*, trans. and ed., S. M. Ohlendorf, J. M. Bigelow, and M. M. Standifer, 344; Robert S. Neighbors to W. Medill, U.S. Special Indian Agency, Trading Post No. 2, Mar. 2, 1848, in Senate Committee on Indian Affairs, *Communication from the Commissioner of Indian Affairs*, 18; "Report of G. W. Bonnell," 42.

81. Report from R. S. Neighbors to H. R. Schoolcraft, "The Na-ü-ni, or Comanches of Texas," 3:355; Ugarte y Loyola to Anza, Chihuahua, Feb. 8, 1787, AGN-PI, tomo 65, expediente 2, folio 68.

82. Council of war, San Fernando de Béxar [?],Oct., 1810, BA, reel 47:123, 126; Kavanagh, *Comanche Political History*, 191.

83. Gladwin, "Comanche Kinship Behavior," 78–79.

84. Hoebel, "Comanche and H3kandika Shoshone Relationship Systems," 441; Gladwin, "Comanche Kinship Behavior," 74.

Chapter 2

1. Berlandier, *Journey to Mexico*, 343–44; John C. Ewers, introduction to *Indians of Texas in 1830*, by Berlandier, 12; Kavanagh, *Comanche Political History*, 223. The identity of the chief El Ronco is of some interest. El Ronco was a Kiowa Indian who married the daughter of Yamparica Comanche chief Somiquaso. In 1806 El Ronco, his wife (Somiquaso's daughter), and their small daughter accompanied carabineer Juan Lucero to Santa Fe, where they waited "an occasion for going to live with the Yamparica Comanches because of [El Ronco's] being married with a daughter of Somiquaso." See Loomis and Nasatir, *Pedro Vial*, 450. Although El Ronco was a Kiowa, his relationship to the Comanches came through his wife, a Yamparica. Thus, his "in-laws" were Yamparicas. This realization is suggestive of the clan identity of Quelluna, who probably also had close ties to the Yamparica family. But Quelluna would not necessarily have had to be identified as a Yamparica to be considered a close relative of those bearing that name.

2. Berlandier, *Journey to Mexico*, 344. Arroyo de los Olmos is now called Olmos Creek. It

lies just east of and runs parallel to westbound Interstate 10. The location of this campsite is well within the perimeter of Texas State Route Loop 1604 and the modern metropolitan limits of San Antonio.

3. Ibid., 344, 346, 348, 351; [José Francisco Ruíz], 1840s, San Antonio de Bexar, "'Comanches': Customs and Characteristics," in Gulick and Allen, *Papers of Buonaparte Lamar,* vol. 4, 1:223. Berlandier was surprised that the "Comanches . . . as well as the soldiers of the presidio [of Béxar] and almost all the inhabitants of the Interior States, consider [skunk] flesh a great delicacy." He further commented, "despite the repugnance which I then had for that food, I was very soon convinced to the contrary, and I believed myself to be eating suckling pig."

4. Berlandier, *Journey to Mexico,* 347, 346.

5. Ibid., 345. "*Tlatolero*" is a Nahuatl derived term that had been modified by the Spanish in America to refer to native public criers, or official speakers. Kavanagh explains that the word ultimately derived from the Nahuatl verb *tlatoa,* meaning "to speak." The Comanche language term for such a person was *tekwawpI,* deriving from the word *tekwa* (talk) and meaning talker. See Kavanagh, *Comanche Political History,* 38–39.

6. Berlandier, *Journey to Mexico,* 348, 349, 351. The translated text of Berlandier's account records that the party camped on the "western bank of the Guadalupe River," but this has to be a mistake. Berlandier later stated that they had crossed the river on November 22, 1828, and that their November 23 campsite was situated "not farther than four leagues at the most from the Guadalupe, situated west-northwest of the camp which we had abandoned." Thus, it seems that the caravan was traveling in a west-northwesterly direction on the northern side of the river.

7. Kavanagh, *Comanche Political History,* 223.

8. Juan de Ulibarri, "The Diary of Juan de Ulibarri to El Cuartelejo," 1706, in Thomas, *After Coronado,* 59–61, 65.

9. Opinion of Capt. Don Francisco Bueno y Boharques, council of war, Santa Fe, Aug. 19, 1719, in Thomas, *After Coronado,* 106.

10. Antonio de Valverde, "Diary of the Campaign of Governor Antonio de Valverde against the Ute and Comanche Indians," 1719, in Thomas, *After Coronado,* 112–15.

11. Juan Domingo de Bustamante, Decree for Council of War, Santa Fe, Nov. 8, 1723, in Thomas, *After Coronado,* 194; Fray Juan Mirabal to Juan Domingo de Bustamante, Taos, Jan. 29, 1724, SANM, reel 6:105–106, T-324; John, *Storms Brewed,* 254.

12. Opinion of Lt. Gen. Juan Paez Hurtado, council of war, Santa Fe, Feb. 6, 1724, SANM, reel 6:129, T-324; Pedro de Villasur, "Diary of the Reconnaissance Expedition of Colonel Don Pedro de Villasur along the Platte River," 1720, in Thomas, *After Coronado,* 136–37, 273 n. 95; declaration of Felix Martínez, Mexico City, Nov. 12, 1720, in Thomas, *After Coronado,* 171; declaration of Bartolomé Garduño, Mexico City, Nov. 15, 1720, in ibid., 174; Ulibarri, "Diary," 71. Ulibarri reported the names of the three *rancherías* of Cuartelejo: Nanahe, Adidasde, and Sanasesli. These names not only represented individual settlements, they were most likely ancestral names representing family lineages. "El Cuartelejo" means "distant outpost" in Spanish. The place name is derived from *cuartel* ("post" in the military sense) and *lejo* ("distant," or "far away"). See Ralph Emerson Twitchell, *The Spanish Archives of New Mexico,* 2:236. The Indians of these settlements practiced agriculture to a large degree. Ulibarri commented that when they arrived to Cuartelejo, they were greeted with "roasting ears of Indian corn, tamales, plums, and other things to eat" in addition to bison meat. Ulibarri in Thomas, *After Coronado,* 68. The practice of agriculture among these Indians, who chiefly identified as Apaches, most likely resulted from their close relationship with Pueblo Indians from Taos and

Picurís. Indeed, the various lineages of these Indians were probably intermarried to a great degree. Various hardships during the mid-seventeenth century in New Mexico encouraged numerous Pueblo Indians to seek refuge among the Plains Apaches. This probably belied preexisting relationships among individual Apache and Pueblo Indians based on intermarriage. Many Taos Indians lived among the Cuartelejos until the 1660s. Later, many Picurís Indians fled their pueblo to the plains in 1696 as a result of the Pueblo Indian revolt of that year. See John, *Storms Brewed,* 89–91, 145.

13. Declaration of Garduño, 174; Valverde, "Diary of the Campaign," 130.

14. Kavanagh cites *"Ynforme* of the Governor of Texas Don Domingo Cabello on the Peace with the Lipan Apaches in the Colony of Nuevo Santander," Sept. 30, 1784, AGN-PI, tomo 64, expediente 1, as the ultimate source relating to this battle. I have not seen this document, so I cannot comment on its content. However, as Kavanagh points out, there are no other contemporary sources whatsoever that allude to this supposed event. Kavanagh, *Comanche Political History,* 66. See also Bolton, *Athanase de Mézières,* 1:24–25. Bolton cites Hubert Howe Bancroft as the source for his information on this event. William Edward Dunn also cites Cabello's *Ynforme.* He suggests that the "Rio del Fierro," which Cabello reported as the place where the Apaches lived at the time of the battle, was the Wichita River in northwestern Texas. William Herbert Dunn, "Apache Relations in Texas, 1718–1750," *Texas Historical Association Quarterly* 14 (1911): 220.

15. Dunn, "Apache Relations in Texas," 225–56, 256–62; John, *Storms Brewed,* 275, 275–86; Juan Augustín Morfi, *History of Texas, 1673–1779,* trans. Carlos Eduardo Castañeda, 2:294; Kavanagh, *Comanche Political History,* 79. Dunn cites Santa Ana to the viceroy, Mar. 3, 1743, Carpeta de Correspondencia de las Provincias, 37–40

16. John, *Storms Brewed,* 287–88; deposition of Joseph Gutiérres, a servant at the Mission of San Sabá, concerning the Comanche attack, in Lesley Byrd Simpson, ed., and Paul D. Nathan, trans., *The San Saba Papers: A Documentary Account of the Founding and Destruction of San Saba Mission,* 43. Later in 1777, Texas governor Juan María, barón de Ripperdá, commented, "it is undeniable that the lamentable war which the old presidio of San Sabas as well as this province suffered, and even that with the Comanches which continues, reaching to the borders of the colony of Nuevo Santander [modern south Texas and Tamaulipas], had its origins in the fact that those nations saw that the Apaches, united with our troops, made war on them and molested them continually and found these Apaches in possession of prisoners taken from them by the latter, always under the protection of the presidio of San Sabas." Juan María, barón de Ripperdá, to Cavallero de Croix, San Antonio de Béxar, Apr. 27, 1777, in Bolton, *Athanase de Mézières,* 2:128–29.

17. John, *Storms Brewed,* 359–61.

18. "Itinerary of Señor Marqués de Rubí, Field Marshall of His Majesty's Armies, in the Inspection of the Interior Presidios that by Royal Order He Conducted in this New Spain, 1766–1768," in Jack Jackson, ed., *Imaginary Kingdom: Texas as Seen by the Rivera and Rubí Military Expeditions, 1727 and 1767,* 111; John, *Storms Brewed,* 362–69, 380, 431, 434–35; Nicolás de Lafora, *Relación del viaje que hizo a los presidios internas situados en la frontera de la América septentrional, perteneciente al rey de España,* ed. Vito Alessio Robles (Mexico City: Editorial Pedro Robredo, 1939), 182; "Report of the Journey which, by Order of the Most Excellent Viceroy, the Marqués de Cruillas, was Made by the Captain of Engineers, Don Nicolás de Lafora, in Company with the Field Marshall the Marqués de Rubí, under Commission from His Majesty to Review the Interior Presidios Situated on the Frontier of that Part of North America Belonging to the King," in Nicolás de Lafora, *The Frontiers of New Spain: Nicolas de Lafora's Description,*

1766–1768, ed. Lawrence Kinnard, 144; Juan María, barón de Ripperdá, to Antonio María Bucareli y Urasua, San Antonio de Béxar, July 6, 1772, in Bolton, *Athanase de Mézières*, 1:328; Juan María, barón de Ripperdá, to Antonio María Bucareli y Urasua, San Antonio de Béxar, Aug. 2, 1772, in ibid., 1:334; "Report of the Council at Monclova," Villa de Monclova, Dec. 11, 1777, in ibid., 2:153; Athanase de Mézières to Antonio Bucareli y Urasua, San Antonio de Béxar, Feb. 20, 1778, in ibid., 2:181. The report of the Monclova council also notes that some Apaches continued to visit the upper Nueces River in the vicinity of El Cañon. Each of the presidios mentioned in the quote were located to the southwest of San Antonio and the northwest of Laredo. Presidios Monclova Viejo and San Juan Bautista were on the western banks of the Rio Grande at the confluence of the Rio San Rodrigo and at modern-day Guerrero, Coahuila, respectively. Presidio Santa Rosa de Aguaverde was located farther to the west in the interior of Coahuila on the Rio San Diego.

19. John and Benavides, "Inside the Comanchería," 51; James Josiah Webb, *Adventures in the Santa Fé Trade, 1844–1847*, ed. Ralph P. Bieber, 240–41. For the date of Comanche mass movement into northern Mexico, see Isidro Vizcaya Canales, ed., *La invasión de los indios bárbaros al noreste de México en los años de 1840 y 1841*. For the extreme southern extent of Comanche raiding, see Ralph A. Smith, "The Comanches' Foreign War: Fighting Head Hunters in the Tropics," *Great Plains Journal* 24–25 (1985–86): 21–44.

20. Mooney, *Ghost Dance Religion*, 1043–44. A strange example of this type of explanation for the Comanche migration to the southern plains is in Ramón Gutiérrez, *When Jesus Came, the Corn Mothers Went Away: Marriage, Sexuality, and Power in New Mexico, 1500–1846*, 146–47. Speaking of this migration, Gutiérrez states, "the growing presence of French colonists in Illinois and on the eastern edges of the Great Plains pushed the *Comanche*, Pawnee, Kansas, Witchita, and Osage Indians in a southwestern direction, into Apache and Navajo hunting grounds" (emphasis added). This statement is not supported by the facts. Comanches migrated to the plains from the *west*, not the east. Also, Pawnees, Kansas, Wichitas, and Osages were never driven deeply into Apache and Navajo territory. The French presence in Illinois was never large enough to have seriously imposed on Indians living in the region of Nebraska, Kansas, and western Missouri.

21. Rupert Norval Richardson, *The Comanche Barrier to South Plains Settlement*, 19, n. 10. Other works following this reasoning are Åke Hultkrantz, "Shoshoni Indians on the Plains: An Appraisal of the Documentary Evidence," *Zeitschrift für Etnologie* 93, nos. 1–2 (1968): 63; Wallace and Hoebel, *The Comanches*, 11; Dan Flores, "Bison Ecology and Bison Diplomacy: The Southern Plains from 1800 to 1850," *Journal of American History* 78, no. 2 (Sept., 1991): 468, 471; Foster, *Being Comanche*, 38–39; Kavanagh, *Comanche Political History*, 62.

22. Wallace and Hoebel, *The Comanches*, 9–10.

23. Roque Madrid to Juan Paez Hurtado, Santa Cruz, Dec. 22, 1704, SANM, reel 3:930–31, T-104; Juan Paez Hurtado to Padre Pedro Matha, Santa Fe, Dec. 23, 1704, SANM, reel 3:934, T-104; Juan Paez Jurtado, "Interrogation of Joseph Tomnu," Dec. 24, 1704, SANM, reel 3:935–36, T-104. Madrid identified Tomnu as a member of the Tano Nation, but this association seems to have been a mistake. When Governor Hurtado questioned Tomnu about the events taking place at Piedra Lumbre, a Spanish-Tewa interpreter had to be present. This strongly suggests that Tomnu was a Tewa and not a Tano as Madrid implied.

24. John, *Storms Brewed*, 116; Fray Francisco Corbera to Fray Francisco de Vargas, San Ildefonso, Dec. 20, 1695, in J. Manuel Espinosa, ed. and trans., *The Pueblo Indian Revolt of 1696 and the Franciscan Missions in New Mexico*, 158; Jack Forbes, *Apache, Navajo, and Spaniard*, 265. The history of contact (hostile and peaceful) between Navajos and Tewa Pueblo Indians is a

long one, probably extending back to the beginnings of the Athabascan migration to the Southwest. It has been suggested that the term *Navajo* came from the Tewa term *navahu,* meaning "large area of cultivated lands." However, it has also been suggested that this term means "to take from the fields" in the Tewa language. Whatever the exact translation, that the name of the Navajo Apaches comes from Tewa speakers implies intimate contact over a long period of time. Thus, it should be of no surprise that these Indians became interrelated. See Clyde Kluckhohn and Dorothea Leighton, *The Navaho,* 24.

25. Forbes, *Apache, Navajo, and Spaniard,* 173, 263, 269–70; *auto* of Gov. Diego de Vargas, Santa Fe, Mar. 8, 1696, in Espinosa, *Pueblo Indian Revolt,* 167; *auto* of Gov. Diego de Vargas, Santa Fe, Mar. 22, 1696, in ibid., 209–10; David M. Brugge, "Navajos in the Catholic Church Records of New Mexico," *Research Reports,* No. 1, 106; Gutiérrez, *When Jesus Came, the Corn Mothers Went Away,* 199–201. E. E. Evans-Pritchard witnessed similar behavior among the Nuer. He noticed that the tribes he visited contained a large number of persons of Dinka descent. Traditionally, Dinkas had been enemies of the Nuer and the object of many raids. One consequence of these attacks was the taking of captives. As individual Dinkas lived among the Nuer, they intermarried with their captors and bore children. Most importantly for the discussion above, however, Evans-Pritchard noticed that those progeny of Dinka descent continued to recognize their Dinka lineage and maintained social connections to others recognizing that ancestral linkage. See Evans-Pritchard, *The Nuer,* 221–25.

26. Report from R. S. Neighbors to H. R. Schoolcraft, "The Na-ü-ni, or Comanches of Texas; Their Traits and Beliefs, and Their Divisions and Intertribal Relations," in Winfrey and Day, *Indian Papers of Texas and the Southwest,* 3:348.

27. Valverde, "Diary of the Campaign," 115.

28. Juan Ugalde to Manuel Antonio Flórez, Valle de Santa Rosa, Dec. 15, 1787, in Loomis and Nasatir, *Pedro Vial,* 304; Nemesio Salcedo to Manuel Antonio Cordero, Chihuahua, May 4, 1807, BATS 2, reel 23, vol. 25, p. 42; Elizabeth A. H. John, "Nurturing the Peace: Spanish and Comanche Cooperation in the Early Nineteenth Century," *New Mexico Historical Review* 59, no. 4 (1984): 356–57.

29. Ewers, introduction to *Indians of Texas in 1830,* by Berlandier, 11–12; Antonio María Martínez to Joaquín de Arredondo, Béxar, June 27, 1818, in Virginia H. Taylor, ed. and trans., *The Letters of Antonio Martinez: Last Spanish Governor of Texas, 1817–1822,* 150–51; Berlandier, *Indians of Texas in 1830,* 133. Berlandier said that when the Lipans and Comanches joined forces during this time, "the wretched troops the Spanish government could command to man the presidios were generally besieged in their homes by these two warlike nations, whom it often required as many as 500 cavalrymen to rout." *Indians of Texas in 1830,* 131. It must be remembered, however, that the second decade of the nineteenth century was a general period of rebellion throughout New Spain, including Texas. Indians like Comanches and Lipans seemed to have taken full advantage of the discord that gripped the province. Some of this activity may also have been at the encouragement of insurgents like José Francisco Ruíz who lived in exile among the Indians.

30. Berlandier, *Indians of Texas in 1830,* 133.

31. Ibid., 133–34.

32. Declaration of Luis del Fierro, Santa Fe, Apr. 13, 1749, in Hackett, *Pichardo's Treatise,* 3:303; declaration of Pierre Sartre, Santa Fe, Apr. 13, 1749, in ibid., 305; declaration of José Miguel, Santa Fe, Apr. 13, 1749, in ibid., 3:308; Thomas Vélez Cachupín to Conde de Revilla Gigedo, Santa Fe, Sept. 18, 1752, in Thomas, *Plains Indians and New Mexico,* 110. Panipiquet was the term used by the French for Wichitas, Taovayaces, Iscanis, Tahuacanos (Tawakonis), and Hue-

cos (Wacos). Broken down into its two sum parts, the word becomes *Pani* (Pawnee) and *piquet* (picket). The French probably applied this term to these Indians because they fortified their villages by surrounding them with stockades. Another possible meaning may come from an application of the Latin root term *pict,* meaning "painted," "decorated," or "tattooed." Three French traders who showed up in Taos in 1749 in the accompaniment of some Comanches mentioned that "their directions [to New Mexico] were given to them by a nation of Indians whom, in their colony, they call savages, or Panipiquetes, a nation who paints their faces." See declaration of Pierre Sartre, 3:305. The Spanish term for these Indians, *Jumano,* may also have had a meaning similar to "painted." The Spanish applied the term *Jumanos* to so many different Indians that confusion has beset scholars who have tried to identify exactly who they were talking about on any given occassion. A small industry of scholarship has been devoted to the resolution of this problem throughout the twentieth century. The latest effort to solve the various mysteries is Nancy Parrott Hickerson, *The Jumanos: Hunters and Traders of the South Plains.* I feel that this term was some indigenous word generally meaning "painted" or "decorated" and was ultimately adopted by the Spanish as a generic classification.

33. Valverde, "Diary of the Campaign," 132.

34. Declaration of Salvador [Pawnee servant of Luis de Archuleta], Santa Fe, Feb. 8, 1738, SANM, reel 7:1006–1007, T-422a; declaration of Francisco Guerrero, Taos, Mar. 20, 1738, SANM, reel 7:1008–1009, T-422a.

35. Deposition of Fr. Fray Miguel de Molina, San Luis de las Amarillas, Mar. 22, 1758, in Simpson and Nathan, *San Saba Papers,* 90; deposition of Joseph Gutiérrez, San Luis de las Amarillas, Mar., 1758, in ibid., 44.

36. Athanase de Mézières to Bernardo de Gálvez, enclosure, "Plan for a Campaign against the Osages," Natchitoches, Sept. 14, 1777, in Bolton, *Athanase de Mézières,* 2:145–46. "*Techan*" seems to be a derivative of "*techa,*" or "*teja*" as the Spanish pronounced it. This is the same term from which the State of Texas derives its name. Indeed, the official state motto is "friendship." However, this term as used by Caddoans and other Indians of Texas probably meant something more significant, like "kindred." Note that the English word "friend" comes from the Old English word "*freond,*" which means "relative" or "kin." This word is ultimately derived from the Gothic verb "*frijon,*" which means "to love." Human behaviors associated with love are ultimately derived from the sacrificial, or social, behaviors associated between close kin (i.e., mothers and offspring).

37. John and Benavides, "Inside the Comanchería," 36, 39; Stephen Pinker, *The Language Instinct: How the Mind Creates Language,* 262–96.

38. Report from Neighbors to Schoolcraft, "The Na-ü-ni," 3:348; John, *Storms Brewed,* 305, 338.

39. Report from Neighbors to Schoolcraft, "The Na-ü-ni," 3:350.

40. W. P. Clark, *The Indian Sign Language,* 336–37; Wallace and Hoebel, *The Comanches,* 5.

41. Athanase de Mézières, "Report of the Expedition to the Cadodachos," Oct. 29, 1770, in Bolton, *Athanase de Mézières,* 1:219.

42. Pedro de Rivera to Marqués de Casafuerte, Presidio del Paso del Río del Norte, Sept. 26, 1726, in Thomas, *After Coronado,* 211; Pedro de Rivera, *Diario y derrotero de la caminado, visto y observado en la visita que lo hizo a los presidios de la Nueva España septentrional,* ed. Vito Allesio Robles, 78; Kavanagh, *Comanche Politics,* 67; Concha to Ugarte y Loyola, Santa Fe, July 6, 1789, AGN-PI, tomo 65, expediente 15, folio 2; Concha to Ugarte y Loyola, Santa Fe, Nov. 18, 1789, SANM, reel 12:211, T-1064.

43. Richard White, "The Winning of the West: The Expansion of the Western Sioux in

the Eighteenth and Nineteenth Centuries," *Journal of American History* 65 (Sept. 1978): 319–43; Flores, "Bison Ecology and Bison Diplomacy," 465–85; Berlandier, *Indians of Texas in 1830*, 67.

44. Valverde, "Diary of the Campaign," 125.

45. Declaration of Pierre Sartre, Santa Fe, Apr. 13, 1749, in Hackett, *Pichardo's Treatise*, 3:306; declaration of Luis del Fierro, Santa Fe, Apr. 13, 1749, in ibid., 3:304; de Mézières, "Report of the Expedition to the Cadodachos," 1:219; Athanase de Mézières to Juan María, barón de Ripperdá, San Antonio de Béxar, July 4, 1772, in Bolton, *Athanase de Mézières*, 1:297; Athanase de Mézières to Antonio María de Bucareli y Ursúa, San Antonio de Béxar, Feb. 20, 1778, in ibid., 2:174; John and Benavides, "Inside the Comanchería," 49; Domingo Cabello to José Antonio Rengel, "Responses of the Governor of Texas to the Questions which the Comandante General of the Provincias Internas Made in his Official Letter of Jan. 27, 1786, Covering Various Circumstances of the Eastern Comanche Indians," San Antonio de Béxar, Apr. 30, 1786, BA, reel 17:418; Kavanagh, *Comanche Politics*, 108; Wallace, "David G. Burnet's Letters Describing the Comanche Indians," 124. Vélez Cachupín originally called Febre "Del Fierro." Later in 1752 the governor referred to him as "Luis Febre," which is probably more correct. See *auto* of Thomas Vélez Cachupín, Santa Fe, Aug. 8, 1752, in Thomas, *Plains Indians and New Mexico*, 103.

46. Declaration of Pedro Satran, Santa Fe, Mar. 5, 1750, in Hackett *Pichardo's Treatise*, 3:317; de Mézières, "Report of the Expedition to the Cadodachos," 1:219; John and Benavides, "Inside the Comanchería," 49; Anthony Glass, *Journal of an Indian Trader: Anthony Glass and the Texas Trading Frontier, 1790–1810*, ed. Dan L. Flores, 67–68; Valverde, "Diary of the Campaign," 126; Adams and Chaves, *Missions of New Mexico*, 111.

47. J. Gaignard, "Journal of an Expedition up the Red River," Village of the Chacto [Choctaws], Nov. 10, 1777, in Bolton, *Athanase de Mézières*, 2:93; John and Benavides, "Inside the Comanchería," 36; Juan de Dios Peña, "Diary and Itinerary of a Campaign in Aid of the Comanches against the Pananas [Pawnees]," Santa Fe, June 12–Aug. 8, 1790, SANM, reel 12:263, T-1089 (this document is out of numerical order as assigned by Twitchell and can be found on reel 12:262–65); Francisco Amangual, "Diary from San Antonio to Santa Fe, Mar. 30–June 19, 1808, in Loomis and Nasatir, *Pedro Vial*, 467; Glass, *Journal of an Indian Trader*, 71; U.S. Congress, T. B. Wheelock, *Journal of Colonel Dodge's Expedition from Fort Gibson to the Pawnee Pict Village, Fort Gibson*, 23d Cong., 2d sess., 1834–35, H. Doc. 2, 1:76; Josiah Gregg, *Commerce of the Prairies*, ed. Max L. Moorhead, 246. According to John, the "Río de Mermellón" was probably the Little Wichita River in north Texas. Artist George Catlin, who accompanied Dodge to the Comanches, commented on the dragoon's campsite, noting that the Indians "escorted us to the banks of a fine clear stream, and a good spring of fresh water, half a mile from their village." Catlin also reported that the Comanche village encamped along this creek was "composed of six or eight hundred skin-covered lodges." Wheelock's count of "more than 200 lodges" may be more accurate. See George Catlin, *North American Indians*, ed. Peter Matthiessen, 326–27; and Kavanagh, *Comanche Political History*, 237.

48. Declaration of Felipe de Sandoval, Santa Fe, Mar. 1, 1750, in Hackett, *Pichardo's Treatise*, 3:324.

49. [Ruíz], "'Comanches': Customs and Characteristics," vol. 4, 1:223.

50. Pedro de Nava to Fernando de la Concha, Chihuahua, July 26, 1791, SANM, reel 12:617, T-1137 (6); de Dios Peña, "Diary and Itinerary of a Campaign," reel 12:263; Kavanagh, *Comanche Political History*, 141. Many sources, including Spanish documents, have estimated that each tepee represented from five to eight people. The population numbers mentioned above for the 340 lodges encamped along Trinchera Creek in 1790 were computed with these

estimates in mind (5 x 340 = 1,700; 8 x 340 = 2,720). See Flores, "Bison Ecology and Bison Diplomacy," 479. In 1786 Francisco Xavier Ortiz estimated three to four "men of arms" and seven to eight women and children for each tepee. Ortiz to Juan Bautista de Anza, Santa Fe, May 20, 1786, in Thomas, *Forgotten Frontiers,* 323. These estimates may be a little high. Jean Louis Berlandier noticed that Comanches were "used to having many tents. . . . Often you may see three, five, or even ten tents clustered about the larger ones belonging to the head of the family, one the house of the warrior and his favorite wife, others for other wives, for children, and sometimes one for the slaves. Barbakista, one of the principal chiefs of the Comanche people, had 11 wives when I knew him, and consequently a number of tents." *Indians of Texas in 1830,* 43. Thus, each tent may not have necessarily represented five to eight persons.

51. De Dios Peña, "Diary and Itinerary of a Campaign," reel 12:263–64; Kavanagh, *Comanche Political History,* 141.

52. Ugarte y Loyola to Anza, Chihuahua, Feb. 8, 1787, AGN-PI, tomo 65, expediente 2, folio 68.

53. See I. M. Lewis, *A Pastoral Democracy: A Study of Pastoralism and Politics among the Northern Somali of the Horn of Africa,* 42.

Chapter 3

1. Cristóbal Torres to Juan Páez Hurtado, Santa Cruz, Aug. 22, 1716, SANM, reel 5:626, T-279.

2. Cristóbal Torres to Juan Páez Hurtado, Cañada, Sept. 7, 1716, SANM, reel 5:626–27, T-279; Diego Marquez to Juan Páez Hurtado, Cañada, Sept. 8, 1716, SANM, reel 5:627, T-279; Cristóbal Torres to Juan Páez Hurtado, Santa Cruz, Sept. 9, 1716, SANM, reel 5:628, T-279.

3. Torres to Hurtado, Sept. 9, 1716, reel 5:628–29. Marquez referred to Torres by the rank "*alférez*" ("second lieutenant") in Diego Marquez to Hurtado, Sept. 8, 1716, reel 5:627.

4. Torres to Hurtado, Sept. 9, 1716, reel 5:628–29; Cristóbal Torres to Juan García, Santa Cruz, Oct. 9, 1716, SANM, reel 5:629–30, T-279; Cristóbal Tafoya to Juan Páez Hurtado, Taos, Oct. 11, 1716, SANM, reel 5:630, T-279; council of war, Santa Fe, July 27–Dec. 10, 1716, SANM, reel 5:631–38, T-279; John, *Storms Brewed,* 241–42; Kavanagh, *Comanche Political History,* 63–64; Armijo, "Information Communicated by Juan Candelaria," 290; council of war, Santa Fe, Aug. 19, 1719, in Thomas, *After Coronado,* 99–110; council of war, opinion of Juan de Archibeque, Santa Fe, Aug. 19, 1719, in Thomas, *After Coronado,* 106–107; council of war, opinion of Cristóbal de la Serna, Santa Fe, Aug. 19, 1719, in ibid., 105–106; council of war, opinion of Capt. Joseph Truxillo, Santa Fe, Aug. 19, 1719, in Thomas, *After Coronado,* 102.

5. For a brief overview of the dialogue concerning this issue, see Alan J. Osborn, "Ecological Aspects of Equestrian Adaptations in Aboriginal North America," *American Anthropologist* 85, no. 3 (1983): 564–66; and H. Clyde Wilson, "An Inquiry into the Nature of Plains Indian Cultural Development," *American Anthropologist* 65, no. 2 (Apr., 1963): 355–57.

6. Richardson, *Comanche Barrier to South Plains Settlement,* 19 n. 10; Wallace and Hoebel, *The Comanches,* 11; John, *Storms Brewed,* 307; Frank Gilbert Roe, *The Indian and the Horse,* 213–14; Wayne A. Davis, *An Introduction to Logic,* 122–23; David Hackett Fischer, *Historians' Fallacies: Toward a Logic of Historical Thought,* 166. This is an example of the logical fallacy known as post hoc reasoning. Post hoc reasoning, or the fallacy of *post hoc, ergo propter hoc,* mistakenly concludes that A caused B simply from the fact that A preceded or accompanied B.

7. Robert E. Rhoades, "The Contemporary Ethnology of Pastoralists: A Critique of the Literature," *Papers in Anthropology* 20, no. 2 (fall, 1979):107.

8. Ibid., 101–110; Rada Dyson-Hudson and Neville Dyson-Hudson, "Nomadic Pastoralism," *Annual Review of Anthropology* 9 (1980): 17–19, 25, 44–46; James Taylor Carson, "Horses and the Economy and Culture of the Choctaw Indians," *Ethnohistory* 42, no. 3 (summer, 1995): 505–506; Terry G. Jordan, *North American Cattle-Ranching Frontiers: Origins, Diffusion, and Differentiation*, 51–52.

9. Gerald Betty, "'Skillful in the Management of the Horse': The Comanches as Southern Plains Pastoralists," 6; Charles Darwin, *The Descent of Man and Selection in Relation to Sex*, 163, 166. Darwin made a similar mistake when he attributed the natural selection of human morality to group phenomenon. Seeing this uniquely human behavior in terms of "survival of the fittest," he failed to understand how self-sacrificial behavior of individuals could help leave descendants. In *The Descent of Man*, Darwin states: "It is extremely doubtful whether the offspring of the more sympathetic and benevolent parents, or of those which were the most faithful to their comrades, would be reared in greater number than the children of selfish and treacherous parents of the same tribe. He who was ready to sacrifice his life, as many a savage has been, rather than betray his comrades, would often leave no offspring to inherit his noble nature" (163). In support of a group explanation for morality, he further notes, "it must not be forgotten that although a high standard of morality gives but a slight or no advantage to each individual man and his children over the other men of the same tribe, yet that an advancement in the standard of morality and an increase in the number of well-endowed men will certainly give an immense advantage to one tribe over another" (166). These statements pose a conundrum. If individuals of a hypothetical group could not benefit from behaving morally and therefore did not do so, then how could they behave morally as a group? In other words, what would be the foundation of that group's morality if no individual behaved morally? Darwin's mistaken reasoning exemplifies all group-selection theories and approaches to human behavior. It is important to understand that traits such as human ownership of animals benefit individuals since selection only affects individual organisms. Herein lies the importance of identifying the ownership of animals by *individuals* as a necessary condition for the existence of pastoralism among humans.

10. Lyle Steadman, "Natural Selection and the Evolutionary Status of Culture" (paper presented at the annual meeting of the Human Behavior and Evolution Society, Binghamton, N.Y., Aug. 5, 1993), 4, 14. Charles Darwin discovered that *anything* inheritable and replicable could influence its own frequency in subsequent generations. Genes are typically understood as the fundamental unit upon which natural selection acts. Steadman has pointed out that Darwin knew nothing of genes when he discovered natural selection. Therefore, natural selection does not necessarily imply genes; it only implies inheritable and replicable traits. From a human perspective, the inheritability and replication of domesticated animals and plants has promoted the increase of frequency of these traits by helping leave human descendants. Note that humans are not the only organisms that grow crops and tend herds. Several species of New World ants and African termites cultivate fungus gardens, while other ant species raise aphids. Most observers have understood this behavior in terms of mutual benefit or symbiosis. Richard Dawkins notes: "This kind of fundamental asymmetry can lead to evolutionary stable strategies of mutual cooperation. . . . Ant genes for cultivating and protecting aphids have been favored in ant gene-pools. Aphid genes for cooperating with the ants have been favored in aphid gene-pools." *The Selfish Gene*, 181. Dawkins and others, however, miss the significance of this behavior among ants, termites, fungi, aphids, humans, cattle, sheep, corn, wheat, and rice. This behavior, whether involving ants and aphids or humans and cattle, can influence its own frequency because aphids and cattle are replicable and inherit-

able. Indeed, all the organisms involved in this type of behavior benefit in some way, but that is not its ultimate evolutionary significance, nor is its effect on "gene-pools" of any ultimate significance.

11. Pastoralism should be treated as merely one of many adaptive behaviors exhibited by humans. It must be kept in mind that adaptations such as pastoralism do not necessarily imply progress over other adaptations. For example, an individual's cessation of hunting and gathering in favor of pastoralism or agriculture in no way suggests that the latter strategy is better at leaving descendants than the former one—the two are simply different means to the same end.

12. M. K. Dhavalikar, "Farming to Pastoralism, Effects of Climate Change in the Deccan," in *The Walking Larder: Patterns of Domestication, Pastoralism, and Predation,* ed. Juliet Clutton-Brock, 156; Pierre Bonte, "Non-Stratified Social Formations among Pastoral Nomads," in *The Evolution of Social Systems,* ed. J. Friedman and M. J. Rowlands, 173; S. I. Vajnshtejn, "The Problem of Origin and Formation of the Economic-Cultural Type of Pastoral Nomads in the Moderate Belt of Eurasia," in *The Nomadic Alternative: Modes and Models of Interaction in the African-Asian Deserts and Steppes,* ed. Wolfgang Weissleder, 127–28.

13. Bruce D. Smith, *The Emergence of Agriculture,* 11–13.

14. Robert Claiborne, *Climate, Man, and History,* 341–42; A. M. Khazanov, "Characteristic Features of Nomadic Communities in the Eurasian Steppes," in *The Nomadic Alternative: Modes and Models of Interaction in the African-Asian Deserts and Steppes,* ed. Wolfgang Weissleder, 119; Joel Berger, *Wild Horses of the Great Basin: Social Competition and Population Size,* 9.

15. Alasdair Whittle, "The First Farmers," in *The Oxford Illustrated Prehistory of Europe,* ed. Barry Cunliffe, 139, 150–51, 161; Smith, *Emergence of Agriculture,* 97–98, 102; Lawrence H. Keeley, *War before Civilization,* 137.

16. Khazanov, "Characteristic Features of Nomadic Communities," 119; Juliet Clutton-Brock, *Horse Power: A History of the Horse and the Donkey in Human Societies,* 55–56; Anthony Harding, "Reformation in Barbarian Europe, 1300–600 B.C.," in *The Oxford Illustrated Prehistory of Europe,* ed. Barry Cunliffe, 309.

17. Whittle, "The First Farmers," 153; Andrew Sherratt, "The Transformation of Early Agrarian Europe: The Later Neolithic and Copper Ages 4500–2500 B.C.," in *The Oxford Illustrated Prehistory of Europe,* ed. Barry Cunliffe, 184; Sherratt, "The Emergence of élites: Earlier Bronze Age Europe, 2500–1300 B.C.," in *The Oxford Illustrated Prehistory of Europe,* ed. Barry Cunliffe, 254; Clutton-Brock, *Horse Power,* 58.

18. Sherratt, "Emergence of élites," 256, 272–74. Sherratt suggests that the livestock-focused ("Bell-Beaker") culture assimilated peacefully among the preexisting cultures of southern Iberia (256). But he also notes that the arrival of the immigrants prompted an "erosion of the stability of communities like Los Millares with its small-scale horticultural base and ritual-centered polity" (273). Although Sherratt explains the disappearance of native communities as resulting from metallurgical innovations and long-term environmental degradation, he observes that some of the new settlements were located "in spectacular positions" on hilltops and surrounded by thick stonewalls (273). The obvious defensive nature of these sites implies that the settlement of southern Spain by the Bell-Beaker culture was anything but peaceful.

19. Herodotus, *The Histories,* trans. Harry Carter, 67; Barry Cunliffe, "Iron Age Societies in Western Europe and Beyond, 800–140 B.C.," in *The Oxford Illustrated Prehistory of Europe,* ed. Barry Cunliffe, 338, 341–42, 369–70; Joseph F. O'Callaghan, *A History of Medieval Spain,* 155. Rome took over the port city of Cádiz from the Carthaginians in 206 B.C.

20. O'Callaghan, *History of Medieval Spain,* 304; Jordan, *North American Cattle-Ranching Frontiers,* 35–42.

21. Jordan, *North American Cattle-Ranching Frontiers,* 20–34.

22. Ibid., 35, 70–71, 77.

23. Ibid., 93, 104, 131.

24. "Inspection Made by Juan Frías Salazar of the Expedition," in George P. Hammond and Agapito Rey, eds. and trans., *Don Juan de Oñate, Colonizer of New Mexico, 1595–1628,* 1:215–16, 220, 224; Gregg, *Commerce of the Prairies,* 133, 126. Jordan failed to see the connection between the stunted development of cattle pastoralism in New Mexico and readily accessible meat resources in the form of plains bison. New Mexicans did not need to develop a ranching industry when they could acquire ample beef supplies through trade or hunting expeditions. Jordan is right, however, to suggest that the presence of the substantial established population of Pueblo Indian irrigation farmers blocked the development of a large-scale cattle industry in the province. *North American Cattle-Ranching Frontiers,* 146–47. Another factor that probably impeded cattle raising in New Mexico was the persistent raiding of the province's livestock by Apaches, Navajos, Utes, and Comanches.

25. "Investigation of Conditions in New Mexico," 1601, in Hammond and Rey, *Don Juan de Oñate,* 2:651; Hammond and Rey, *Don Juan de Oñate,* 1:401–402; Kenner, *History of New Mexico–Plains Indian Relations,* 98–99.

26. "Inspection Made by Juan Frías Salazar of the Expedition," 1:226, 229, 231. *Jineta* saddles, according to Terry Jordan, were "Moorish-inspired" combat saddles. The *estradiota* saddle was probably more associated with the use of lances since its name is a word for a specific type of lance. *North American Cattle-Ranching Frontiers,* 93.

27. "Inquiry Concerning the Provinces in the North," 1602, in Hammond and Rey, *Don Juan de Oñate,* 2:840; Hammond and Rey, *Don Juan de Oñate,* 1:401; Gregg, *Commerce of the Prairies,* 63; Jordan, *North American Cattle-Ranching Frontiers,* 25–26. For a description of New Mexican bison hunting in the first half of the nineteenth century, see Carroll and Haggard, *Three New Mexican Chronicles,* 101–102.

28. Derek Freeman, *Margaret Mead and the Heretic: The Making and Unmaking of an Anthropological Myth,* 13–14. For example, a dog can be demonstrated to have learned the meaning of the word *ball,* but few people would describe this ability as an example of culture.

29. Steadman, "Natural Selection and the Evolutionary Status of Culture," 5, 13. Even though humans and crocodiles each share the yawning reflex it would be ridiculous to say that these creatures exhibited a common culture on the basis of this behavior. Furthermore, behavior independently learned by humans is not necessarily cultural. Two individuals on opposite sides of the globe can learn to avoid standing in ant beds after experiencing ant stings. Although the stung people would share this particular behavior, neither person would consider it as evidence of a common culture.

30. Ibid., 5, 6.

31. Ibid., 8; Lyle Steadman, "Traditions Are Not (Explained by) *r*" (paper presented at the annual meeting of the Human Behavior and Evolution Society, Santa Barbara, Calif., June 2, 1995), 2; John and Benavides, "Inside the Comanchería," 50.

32. Steadman, "Natural Selection and the Evolutionary Status of Culture," 9; Steadman, "Traditions Are Not (Explained by) *r*," 3; Steadman, "Social — Not Natural, Not Sexual — Selection."

33. Steadman, "Natural Selection and the Evolutionary Status of Culture," 9. Interestingly, like genes, culture is subject to natural selection. Essentially, this means that learned behavior copied from another individual could have an influence on its own frequency. Traditions that are successful in retaining adherents, such as religions, also tend to increase their fre-

quency, or become more popular, in later generations. Unlike genes, however, traditions can be potentially passed from ancestors to descendants at a rate of 100 percent. In contrast, only 50 percent of parent's genes can be passed to any one offspring. Because traditions are highly inheritable, they have responded rapidly to natural selection. Today the transmission of culture is becoming less traditional. Nevertheless, culture continues to be subject to natural selection. Only those traditions that influence their own frequency will continue to exist in the future.

34. Charles Gibson, *Tlaxcala en el siglo XVI,* 148–49; Philip Wayne Powell, *Soldiers, Indians, and Silver: North America's First Frontier War,* 37, 50; Forbes, *Apache, Navajo, and Spaniard,* 30; Jack D. Forbes, "The Appearance of the Mounted Indian in Northeastern Mexico and the Southwest, to 1680," *Southwestern Journal of Anthropology* 15 (1959): 190–91. For another discussion of the domestication of animals and why Old World livestock became diffused across the globe, see Jared Diamond, *Guns, Germs, and Steel: The Fates of Human Societies,* 157–75. Peter Iverson, in his study *When Indians Became Cowboys: Native Peoples and Cattle Ranching in the American West,* demonstrates the endurance of this pastoralist tradition among American Indians in the western United States. I submit that this heritage persists among Indians as well as other Westerners precisely because it is *traditional,* or passed down from ancestors to descendants.

35. Juan de Ulibarri, "The Diary of Juan de Ulibarri to El Cuartelejo," 1706, in Thomas, *After Coronado,* 61; Francisco Cuervo y Valdez, Santa Fe, Aug. 18, 1706, in Hackett, *Historical Documents,* 3:381.

36. De Ulibarri, "Diary," 76; Cuervo y Valdez, Aug. 18, 1706, 3:381; Cristóbal Torres to Juan Páez Hurtado, Cañada, Sept. 7, 1716, SANM, reel 5:626–27, T-279; council of war, Santa Fe, Aug. 19, 1719, in Thomas, *After Coronado,* 100–110; Juan Domingo de Bustamante, *Auto de Junta de Guerra,* Santa Fe, Feb. 1, 1724, SANM, reel 6:110, T-324.

37. Marvin K. Opler, "The Southern Ute of Colorado," in *Acculturation in Seven American Indian Tribes,* ed. Ralph Linton, 157; Forbes, "Appearance of the Mounted Indian," 200; Forbes, *Apache, Navajo, and Spaniard,* 133–34; John, *Storms Brewed,* 118–19. According to Opler, the Ute designs of the saddle, quirt, and other trappings are replicas of Spanish models.

38. *Auto* of Alonso García, La Isleta, Aug. 14, 1680, in Charles Wilson Hackett, ed., and Charmion Clair Shelby, trans., *Revolt of the Pueblo Indians of New Mexico and Otermín's Attempted Reconquest, 1680–1682,* 1:69; Espinosa, *Pueblo Indian Revolt,* 38; John, *Storms Brewed,* 120–21; *auto* of Governor Vargas, Mar. 8, 1696, 166–67; *auto* of Governor Vargas, Mar. 22, 1696, 209–10.

39. Catlin, *North American Indians,* 318; Fehrenbach, *Comanches,* 95. Fehrenbach also recognized the Spanish nature of Comanche horse culture and horsemanship.

40. Jordan, *North American Cattle-Ranching Frontiers,* 94; Robert Goldthwaite Carter, *On the Border with Mackenzie,* 296; Wallace and Hoebel, *The Comanches,* 96–97; Robert H. Lowie, *Indians of the Plains,* 41; Gregg, *Commerce of the Prairies,* 131, 367; Thomas James, *Three Years among the Indians and Mexicans,* 141; Catlin, *North American Indians,* 321–22. Jordan points out that scholars are uncertain of the exact origin of the American stock saddle.

41. James, *Three Years among the Indians and Mexicans,* 141; Gregg, *Commerce of the Prairies,* 367; John P. Sherburne, *Through Indian Country to California: John P. Sherburne's Diary of the Whipple Expedition, 1853–1854,* 83; Randolph B. Marcy, *Adventure on Red River: Report on the Exploration of the Headwaters of the Red River by Captain Randolph B. Marcy and Captain G. B. McClellan,* ed. Grant Foreman, 62; Jordan, *North American Cattle-Ranching Frontiers,* 25, 137, 142; George Bird Grinnell, *The Cheyenne Indians: Their History and Ways of Life,* 1:292–93.

42. Gregg, *Commerce of the Prairies,* 371; Sidney B. Brinckerhoff and Odie B. Faulk, *Lancers for the King: A Study of the Frontier Military System of Northern New Spain, with a Translation of the Royal Regulations of 1772,* 21; Max L. Moorhead, *The Presidio: Bastion of the Spanish Border-*

lands, 190; Francisco Marín del Valle, *"Bando* Prohibiting the Sale of Horses, Animals, and Arms to the Indians under Penalties Named in the Order," Santa Fe, Dec. 2, 1750, SANM, reel 8:1193, T-530; José Cortés, *Views from the Apache Frontier: Report on the Northern Provinces of New Spain,* ed. Elizabeth A. H. John and trans. John Wheat, 27; Congress, *Journal of Colonel Dodge's Expedition,* 1:75; Catlin, *North American Indians,* 318..

43. Jesús de la Teja, *San Antonio de Béxar: A Community on New Spain's Northern Frontier,* 113; Mendinueta to Bucareli, Santa Fe, May 26, 1772, in Alfred Barnaby Thomas, ed. and trans., "Governor Mendinueta's Proposals for the Defense of New Mexico, 1772–1778," *New Mexico Historical Review* 6, no. 1 (1931): 28; "Reglamento e Instruccion para los Presidios que se han de formar en la linea de Frontera de Nueva España," in Brinckerhoff and Faulk, *Lancers for the King,* 22–23.

44. James W. Abert, *Through the Country of the Comanche Indians in the Fall of 1845: The Journal of a U.S. Army Expedition led by Lieutenant James W. Abert of the Topographical Engineers,* ed. John Galvin, 39; Marcy, *Adventure on Red River,* 50; Sherburne, *Through Indian Country to California,* 90–91.

45. Jordan, *North American Cattle-Ranching Frontiers,* 146–47. Like Comanches and horse pastoralism, Navajos acquired their culture of sheep pastoralism from the Spanish colonists of New Mexico. For more information on Navajo pastoralism, see Lynn Robinson Bailey, *If You Take My Sheep— : The Evolution and Conflicts of Navajo Pastoralism, 1630–1898;* and James F. Downs, *Animal Husbandry in Navajo Society and Culture.*

46. Adams and Chaves, *Missions of New Mexico,* 111.

47. Glass, *Journal of an Indian Trader,* 67–68; Berlandier, *Journey to Mexico,* 347.

48. Gregg, *Commerce of the Prairies,* 435; Antonio Josef Ortiz, interrogation of Josef Antonio García, Santa Fe, Feb. 28, 1789, SANM, reel 12:148–49, T-1041; Jordan, *North American Cattle-Ranching Frontiers,* 26–28; LaVerne Harrell Clark, "Early Horse Trappings of the Navajo and Apache Indians," *Arizona and the West* 5 (autumn, 1963): 239–40.

49. Stuart J. Fiedel, *Prehistory of the Americas,* 83, 93; de Rivera, *Diario y derrotero de lo caminando,* 78; Kavanagh, *Comanche Political History,* 67; John C. Ewers, *The Horse in Blackfoot Indian Culture: With Comparative Material from Other Western Tribes,* 31; Hoebel, *Political Organization and Law-Ways,* 14; Wallace and Hoebel, *The Comanches,* 47, 241.

50. Matt Ridley, *The Origins of Virtue Virtue: Human Instincts and the Evolution of Cooperation,* 245; report from Neighbors to Schoolcraft, "The Na-ü-ni," 3:357. In terms of natural selection, what one ultimately sacrifices by behaving socially is their own reproduction.

51. Ruíz, *Report on the Indian Tribes of Texas,* 12, 13; Berlandier, *Indians of Texas in 1830,* 117; Wallace, "David G. Burnet's Letters Describing the Comanche Indians," 135; Burnet, "Comanches and Other Tribes of Texas," 231; Hoebel, *Political Organization and Law-Ways,* 120–22; report from Neighbors to Schoolcraft, "The Na-ü-ni," 3:350; Marcy, *Thirty Years of Army Life,* 57.

52. Wallace, "David G. Burnet's Letters Describing the Comanche Indians," 135. Burnet recounted that Comanches sacrificed "not less than 5000" horses during an 1819 smallpox epidemic that "swept off" a great number of people.

53. Wallace and Hoebel, *The Comanches,* 46; Dyson-Hudson and Dyson-Hudson, "Nomadic Pastoralism," 17–18; James Mead, "The Pawnees as I Knew Them," *Kansas Historical Collections* 10 (1907–1908): 107 n. 1; Ortiz to Anza, Santa Fe, May 20, 1786, in Thomas, *Forgotten Frontiers,* 323; Athanase de Mézières to the Viceroy [Antonio María de Bucareli y Ursúa], San Antonio de Béxar, Feb. 20, 1778, in Bolton, *Athanase de Mézières,* 2:175; Ruíz, *Report on the Indian Tribes of Texas,* 9.

54. Catlin, *North American Indians,* 323; Gregg, *Commerce of the Prairies,* 370–71; Athanase

de Mézières, "Report by de Mézières of the Expedition to Caddodachos," Fort San Juan de Baptista de Natchitoches, Oct. 29, 1770, in Bolton, *Athanase de Mézières*, 1:218–19. Interestingly, Gregg also noted that the New Mexican *ciboleros* "are scarcely if at all inferior to the Indians in this sport."

55. [José Francisco Ruíz], 1840s, San Antonio de Bexar, "'Comanches': Customs and Characteristics," in Gulick and Allen, *Papers of Buonaparte Lamar*, vol. 4, 1:221; report from Neighbors to Schoolcraft, "The Na-ü-ni," 3:356.

56. Opinion of Capt. Don Francisco Bueno y Bohorques, council of war, Santa Fe, Aug. 19, 1719, in Thomas, *After Coronado*, 106; opinion of Capt. Joseph Truxillo, council of war, Santa Fe, Aug. 19, 1719, in ibid., 102; opinion of Juan de Archibeque, council of war, Santa Fe, Aug. 19, 1719, in ibid., 107.

57. See Patricia Albers and William R. James, "Historical Materialism vs Evolutionary Ecology: A Methodological Note on Horse Distribution and American Plains Indians," *Critique of Anthropology* 6, no. 1 (Nov.–Dec., 1985): 87–100; and Osborn, "Ecological Aspects of Equestrian Adaptations." Albers and James's article is a Marxist refutation to Osborn's ecological approach.

58. Ruíz, *Report on the Indian Tribes of Texas*, 14; Berlandier, *Indians of Texas in 1830*, 118; Carroll and Haggard, *Three New Mexican Chronicles*, 130.

Chapter 4

1. Adams and Chaves, *Missions of New Mexico*, 252; "Report of the Reverend Father Provincial, Fray Pedro Serrano, to the Most Excellent Señor Viceroy, the Marquis of Cruillas, in regard to the Custodia of New Mexico, In the year 1761," in Hackett, *Historical Documents*, 3:486. The priest commented: "When the Indians trading embassy comes to these governors and their alcaldes, here all prudence forsakes them, or rather shall I say that they do not guess how completely they lose their bearings, because the fleet is in. The fleet being, in this case, some two hundred, or at the very least fifty, tents of barbarous heathen Indians, Comanches as well as other nations, of whom the multitude is so great that it is impossible to enumerate them."

2. Adams and Chaves, *Missions of New Mexico*, 252.

3. Ibid.

4. Ibid.; Gregg, *Commerce of the Prairies*, 232. Camp Holmes was located about a mile north of the Canadian River near the present town of Lexington, Oklahoma, just south of Norman. This site had previously been the location of Auguste Pierre Chouteau's "little stockade fort, where a considerable trade was subsequently carried on with the Comanches and other tribes of the southwestern prairies." See Gregg, *Commerce of the Prairies*, 231.

5. Gregg, *Commerce of the Prairies*, 232, 230, 233, 234. Gregg explained that "having learned the word *swap* of some American traders, . . . [Tabequena] very ingeniously tacked it at the tail of his little stock of Spanish." The plains expedition of U.S. dragoons under the leadership of Col. Henry Dodge had previously met Tabequena in 1834. Artist George Catlin caricatured the chief as a "huge monster, who is the largest and fattest Indian I ever saw . . . whose flesh would undoubtedly weigh three hundred pounds or more." *North American Indians*, 331–32; Gregg, Commerce of the Prairies, 249.

6. Adams and Chaves, *Missions of New Mexico*, 252; Gregg, *Commerce of the Prairies*, 251. Gregg specifically wrote: "I have always found, that savages are much less hostile to those with whom they trade, than to any other people. They are emphatically fond of traffic, and, being anxious to encourage the whites to come among them, instead of committing depredations

upon those with whom they trade, they are generally ready to defend them against every enemy."

7. "Copy of the Instruction which Don Thomas Vélez Cachupín, Governor and Captain General of New Mexico, left to his successor, Don Francisco Marín del Valle, at the order of his most excellent sir, Conde de Revilla Gigedo, viceroy of this New Spain," Santa Fe, Aug. 12, 1754, in Thomas, *Plains Indians and New Mexico*, 132–34.

8. Gregg, *Commerce of the Prairies*, 257.

9. Ridley, *Origins of Virtue*, 46, 207; Adam Smith, *An Inquiry into the Nature and Causes of the Wealth of Nations*, ed. Edwin Cannan, 14–16.

10. Ridley, *Origins of Virtue*, 199, 46.

11. James, *Three Years among the Mexicans and Indians*, 143–44; Gregg, *Commerce of the Prairies*, 250, 25; Donald Chaput, *Francois X. Aubry: Trader, Trailmaker, and Voyaguer in the Southwest, 1846–1854*, 71. Robert Luther Duffus claims that the "world-renowned Missouri mule" was introduced to the state in the 1820s as a direct result of the Santa Fe trade. "This notorious beast was a New Mexican product. He invaded Missouri from the west, filling a need which the rush of settlement into the river country was just beginning to create." Robert Luther Duffus, *The Santa Fe Trail*, 81.

12. John Sibley, *A Report from Natchitoches in 1807*, 74–75, 40–41, 45, 50–51; Loomis and Nasatir, *Pedro Vial*, 207; Glass, *Journal of an Indian Trader*.

13. Jacob Fowler, *The Journal of Jacob Fowler*, ed. Elliot Coues, 58.

14. Ibid.

15. Donald John Blakeslee, "The Plains Interband Trade System: An Ethnohistorical and Archelolgical Investigation" (Ph.D. diss., University of Wisconsin–Milwaukee, 1975), 200–204.

16. Concha to Ugarte y Loyola, Santa Fe, June 26, 1788, AGN-PI, tomo 65, expediente 5, folio 6; Moorhead, *The Apache Frontier*, 167; John, *Storms Brewed*, 738; Kavanagh, *Comanche Political History*, 177; Benes, "Anza and Concha in New Mexico," 66; Concha to Ugarte y Loyola, Santa Fe, July 6, 1789, AGN-PI, tomo 65, expediente 15, folio 2; J. Villasana Haggard, *Handbook for Translators of Spanish Historical Documents*, 76.

17. Smith, *Wealth of Nations*, 14–16; Ridley, *Origins of Virtue*, 200; Darwin, *Descent of Man*, 163, 166. As mentioned previously, Darwin made a similar mistake when he attributed the natural selection of human morality to a group phenomenon. See chapter 3, note 9, above. See also Murdock, "Anthropology's Mythology," 17–23. For a discussion of Murdock's thoughts on this issue, see appendix 1.

18. Bernard G. Campbell, ed., *Humankind Emerging*, 299. This estimate is based on the appearance in the archeological record of the primitive stone chopping tool anthropologists have labeled "the Acheulian hand axe." The name comes from the town of Saint Acheul in the Somme Valley in France, where the artifact was first discovered.

19. Juan de Ulibarri, "The Diary of Juan de Ulibarri to El Cuartelejo," 1706, in Thomas, *After Coronado*, 61.

20. Santa Fe Cabildo, "Petition to the Governor and Captain-General, [Diego de Vargas] Marqués de la Naba de Brazinas, Complaining about the Sale of Horses by Settlers to the Jicarilla Apaches," Nov. 26, 1703, SANM, reel 3:823, T-91; Santa Fe Cabildo, "Petition to the Governor and Captain-General," Santa Fe, [Nov., 1703?], SANM, reel 3:829, T-92; *auto* of Gov. Diego de Vargas, marqués de la Naba de Brazinas, Santa Fe, Nov. 27, 1703, SANM, reel 3:830–33, T-92; Juan Paez Hurtado [to Santa Fe Cabildo?], June 9, 1704, SANM, reel 3:1050–53, T-117.

21. De Ulibarri, "Diary," 65, 76; Bustamante to Casa Fuerte, Santa Fe, Apr. 30, 1727, in Thomas, *After Coronado*, 257.

22. Juan Ygnacio Flores Mogollon, *"Bando* Prohibiting the Settlers Visiting the *Rancherías* of the Wild Indians for Purposes of Barter and Trade," Santa Fe, Dec. 16, 1712, SANM, reel 4:739–40, T-185; opinion of Cristóbal de la Serna, council of war, Santa Fe, Aug. 19, 1719, in Thomas, *After Coronado,* 105, 267 nn. 48–49.

23. Antonio Truxillo, declaration, Santa Fe, Apr. 25, 1735, SANM, reel 7:377, T-402; Juan García de Mora, [testimony?], Santa Fe, Apr. 13, 1735, SANM, reel 7:365–66, T-402; Diego Torres, [testimony?], Santa Fe, [Apr. 18, 1735?], SANM, reel 7:369–70, T-402; "Declaration of an Infidel Comanche Indian Presented on Behalf of Don Juan García de Mora," Santa Fe, Apr. 14, 1735, SANM, reel 7:367, T-402; Cheryl Foote, "Spanish-Indian Trade along New Mexico's Northern Frontier in the Eighteenth Century," *Journal of the West* 24 (Apr., 1985): 24; Kavanagh, *Comanche Politics,* 67, 68; Gervasio Gongora y Cruzat, sentence of Diego Torres and Juan García de Mora, Santa Fe, May 7, 1735, SANM, reel 7:394–96, T-402.

24. Thomas Vélez Cachupín, instructions, Santa Fe, Aug. 12, 1754, in Thomas, *Plains Indians and New Mexico,* 134.

25. Kenner, *History of New Mexican–Plains Indian Relations,* 78; Juan Ygnacio Flores Mogollon, *"Bando* Prohibiting the Settlers Visiting the *Rancherías* of the Wild Indians for Purposes of Barter and Trade," Santa Fe, Dec. 16, 1712, SANM, reel 4:739, T-185; Henrique Olavide y Michelena, *"Bando* in Relation to Trade with Wild Tribes," Santa Fe [?], Jan. 7, 1737, SANM, reel 7:553, T-414; Francisco Marín del Valle, *"Bando* Prohibiting the Sale of Horses, Animals, and Arms to the Indians under Penalties Named in the Order," Santa Fe, Nov. 26, 1754, SANM, reel 8:1196, T-530.

26. Brugge, "Navajos in the Catholic Church Records," 30.

27. Frances Leon Swadesh, *Los Prímeros Pobladores: Hispanic Americans of the Ute Frontier,* 39; Adams and Chaves, *Missions of New Mexico,* 42, 119, 126, 208. According to Eleanor B. Adams and Fray Angelico Chaves, the Spanish term *"genízaro"* was derived from the Turkish words *"yeni,"* meaning "new," and *"cheri,"* meaning "troops." The English equivalent is "Janizary." *Missions of New Mexico,* 42 n. 72.

28. John Kessell, *Kiva, Cross, and Crown: The Pecos Indians and New Mexico, 1540–1840,* 416.

29. Pedro Garrido y Duran, "An Account of Events which Have Occurred in the Provinces of New Mexico Concerning Peace Conceded to the Comanche Nation and their Reconciliation with the Utes, since November 17 of Last Year and July 15 of the Current," Chihuahua, Dec. 21, 1786, in Thomas, *Forgotten Frontiers,* 304; Kavanagh, *Comanche Political History,* 112; Fernando de Chacón to Nemesio Salcedo, Santa Fe, Mar. 28, 1804, SANM, reel 15:217, T-1714; Kessell, *Kiva, Cross, and Crown,* 426. Interestingly, *guerrero* means "warrior" in Spanish.

30. Gregg, *Commerce of the Prairies,* 316 n. 1.

31. Joaquin Real Alencaster to Nemesio de Salcedo, Santa Fe, Jan. 4, 1806, SANM, reel 16:11–12, T-1942; This document is also translated in Loomis and Nasatir, *Pedro Vial,* 441–43.

32. Fowler, *Journal,* 64; James, *Three Years among the Indians and Mexicans,* 76; Gregg, *Commerce of the Prairies,* 257; Abert, *Through the Country of the Comanche Indians,* 42; Robert B. Green, *On the Arkansas Route to California in 1849: The Journal of Robert B. Green of Lewisburg Pennsylvania,* ed. J. Orin Oliphant, 45.

33. Gregg, *Commerce of the Prairies,* 257; Abert, *Through the Country of the Comanche Indians,* 42–43.

34. Declaration of Felipe de Sandoval, Santa Fe, Mar. 1, 1750, in Hackett, *Pichardo's Treatise,* 3:322–23; Athanase de Mézières to Viceroy Antonio María de Bucareli y Ursúa, San Antonio de Béxar, Feb. 20, 1778, in Bolton, *Athanase de Mézières,* 2:175; John and Benavides, "Inside the Comanchería," 50.

35. Loomis and Nasatir, *Pedro Vial*, 351; John and Benavides, "Inside the Comanchería," 27–28, 54–55; Rafael Martínez Pacheco to Jacobo Ugarte y Loyola, San Antonio de Béxar, Jan. 19, 1788, BA, reel 18:779–80 (also found in Rafael Martínez Pacheco to Jacobo Ugarte y Loyola, San Antonio de Béxar, Jan. 19, 1788, BATS 1, reel 18, vol. 151, pp. 41–43); Rafael Martínez Pacheco to Juan de Ugalde, San Antonio de Béxar, July 20, 1788, BATS 1, reel 18, vol. 155, pp. 53–54; Rafael Martínez Pacheco to Juan de Ugalde, San Antonio de Béxar, Apr. 26, 1789, BA, reel 19:754–55; Juan de Ugalde to Rafael Martínez Pacheco, Valle de Santa Rosa, May 27, 1789, BA, reel 19:834–35; Rafael Martínez Pacheco to Juan de Ugalde, San Antonio de Béxar, June 6, 1789, BA, reel 19:855–56; Rafael Martínez Pacheco to Juan de Ugalde, San Antonio de Béxar, June 22, 1789, BA, reel 19:902–903; Rafael Martínez Pacheco to Juan de Ugalde, San Antonio de Béxar, Aug. 30, 1789, BA, reel 19:996–97; Ewers, introduction to *Indians of Texas in 1830*, by Berlandier, 11; Berlandier, *Indians of Texas in 1830*, 60.

36. Berlandier, *Indians of Texas in 1830*, 120; Rafael Martínez Pacheco to Juan de Ugalde, San Antonio de Béxar, Jan. 7, 1788, BATS 1, reel 18, vol. 151, pp. 13–14.

37. A. M. M. Upshaw to Mirabeau B. Lamar, Chickasaw Agency near Fort Twoson, Ark., June 18, 1840, in Winfrey and Day, *Indian Papers of Texas and the Southwest*, 1:114; J. C. Eldredge, draft on government, Aug. 12, 1843, in ibid., 1:230; Thomas G. Western to Benjamin Sloat and L. H. Williams, Washington, D.C., Apr. 9, 1845, in ibid., 2:217. For trade between Comanches and the Indians of the Indian Territory, see Marcy, *Adventure on Red River*, 173; and Grant Foreman, *Marcy and the Gold Seekers: The Journal of Captain R. B. Marcy, with an Account of the Gold Rush over the Southern Route*, 165.

38. J. H. Rollins to G. M. Brooke, Fredericksburg, Sept. 25, 1850, in Winfrey and Day, *Indian Papers of Texas and the Southwest*, 3:125; Thomas G. Western to Robert S. Neighbors, Washington, D.C., May 11, 1845, in ibid., 2:235–36; Western to A. Coleman, Washington, D.C., May 11, 1845, in ibid., 2:236; L. H. Williams, "Report of a Council with the Comanche Indians," [Torrey's] Trading House No. 2, Nov. 23, 1845, in ibid., 2:411.

39. James, *Three Years among the Indians and Mexicans*, 67–68.

40. Ibid., 68–69.

41. Ibid., 138, 69–70. James later learned in 1823 that Big Star was a Yamparica. The true identity of this chief remains unknown. See Kavanagh, *Comanche Political History*, 210.

42. James, *Three Years among the Indians and Mexicans*, 71.

43. Ibid., 71–70.

44. Ibid., 73–75.

45. Ibid., 128–49.

46. Rollins to Brooke, Sept. 25, 1850, 3:125.

47. Flores Mogollon, *"Bando,"* Dec. 16, 1712, reel 4:739; Cachupín, instructions, 134.

48. Marín del Valle, *"Bando,"* Nov. 26, 1754, reel 8:1194–95.

49. James, *Three Years among the Indians and Mexicans*, 132.

50. Fowler, *Journal*, 56–57.

51. Thomas G. Western to L. H. Williams, Washington D.C., Apr. 29, 1845, in Winfrey and Day, *Indian Papers of Texas and the Southwest*, 2:225.

52. Steadman, "Kinship, Religion, and Ethnicity"; Steadman, "Traditions Are Not (Explained by) *r*"; Steadman, "Kinship Hierarchy"; Lyle B. Steadman and Craig T. Palmer, "Visiting Dead Ancestors: Shamans as Interpreters of Religious Traditions," *Zygon* 29, no. 2 (June, 1994): 173–89; Palmer and Steadman, "Human Kinship as a Descendant Leaving Strategy."

Chapter 5

1. Dan Flores, *Caprock Canyonlands: Journeys into the Heart of the Southern Plains,* 25–26.

2. Deposition of Fr. Fray Miguel de Molina, San Luis de las Amarillas, Mar. 22, 1758, in Simpson and Nathan, *San Saba Papers,* 84–85, 85–86.

3. Ibid., 86–87.

4. Ibid., 87–88.

5. Ibid., 88–89.

6. Joseph Antonio Flores, deposition, Presidio San Luis de las Amarillas, Mar. 21, 1758, in Simpson and Nathan, *San Saba Papers,* 56; memorandum by Colonel Parilla, in ibid., 98; Flores, deposition, 56; John, *Storms Brewed,* 297–98; Chipman, *Spanish Texas,* 161; Robert S. Weddle, *The San Sabá Mission: Spanish Pivot in Texas,* 87–88.

7. Morfí, *History of Texas,* 2:392–93; John, *Storms Brewed,* 350–51.

8. Angel de Martos y Navarrete to Toribio de Guevara, Santiago de la Monclova, Mar. 23, 1758, in Simpson and Nathan, *San Saba Papers,* 17; Domingo Valcárcel to Viceroy Agustín Ahumada y Villalón, Marqués de las Amarillas, Mexico City, Apr. 6, 1758, in ibid., 32; Morfí, *History of Texas,* 2:376; William Edward Dunn, "The Apache Mission on the San Sabá River; Its Founding and Failure," *Southwestern Historical Quarterly* 17 (1914): 414; John, *Storms Brewed,* 294–303; Lowie, *Indians of the Plains,* 109; W. W. Newcomb Jr., *The Indians of Texas,* 180; Keeley, *War before Civilization,* 41; White, "Winning of the West," 319, 319–20, 322; Mishkin, *Rank and Warfare,* 57–63. See also Frank Raymond Secoy, *Changing Military Patterns of the Great Plains (Seventeenth Century through Early Nineteenth Century),* 86–95; and Gerald Betty, "Comanche Warfare, Pastoralism, and Enforced Cooperation," *Panhandle-Plains Historical Review* 68 (1995): 1–13.

9. Steadman, "Kinship, Religion, and Ethnicity," 2–5; Pedro Garrido y Duran, "An Account of the Events Which Have Occurred in the Provinces of New Mexico Concerning Peace with the Comanche Nation and Their Reconciliation with the Utes, since November of Last Year and July 15 of the Current," Chihuahua, Dec. 21, 1786, in Thomas, *Forgotten Frontiers,* 310–11, 313–14.

10. John and Benavides, "Inside the Comanchería," 50.

11. Ibid.; Steadman, "Kinship, Religion, and Ethnicity," 5–6.

12. Pedro de Nava to Manuel Muñoz, Chihuahua, Apr. 4, 1797, BA, reel 27:184; [José Francisco Ruíz], 1840s, San Antonio de Bexar, "'Comanches': Customs and Characteristics," in Gulick and Allen, *Papers of Mirabeau Buonaparte Lamar,* vol. 4, 1:222–23; Wallace, "David G. Burnet's Letters Describing the Comanche Indians," 126; Steadman, "Kinship, Religion, and Ethnicity," 6–7. For a similar description of Comanche councils, see J. Cameron, "Comanche Indians: The Country West of the Colorado," in Gulick and Allen, *Papers of Mirabeau Buonaparte Lamar,* 1:475. See the previous chapter on Comanche social organization for a more complete description of their religious smoking ceremony.

13. Ruíz, *Report on the Indian Tribes of Texas,* 10; Steadman, "Kinship, Religion, and Ethnicity," 8.

14. Thomas Vélez Cachupín to Conde de Rivilla Gigedo, Santa Fe, Nov. 27, 1751, in Thomas, *Plains Indians and New Mexico,* 68; Pedro Fermín de Meninueta to Marqués de Croix, Santa Fe, June 18, 1768, in ibid., 160; Marqués de Croix to Julián de Arriaga, Jan. 30, 1769, in ibid., 166; Pedro Fermín de Mendinueta to Antonio María Bucareli y Ursúa, Santa Fe, Sept. 30, 1774, in ibid., 169–70, 172; Pedro Fermín de Mendinueta to Antonio María Bucareli y Ursúa, Santa Fe, Aug. 18, 1775, in ibid., 181, 183; Fernando de la Concha to Conde Revilla

Gigedo, July 20, 1792, SANM, reel 13:111, T-1200; El teniente coronel Rafael de Ugartchea a la Comandancia General e Inspección de Nuevo Leon, Los Pozos, Dec. 23, 1840, in Canales, *La invasión*, 170.

15. Herbert E. Bolton, *The Hasinais: Southern Caddoans as Seen by the Earliest Europeans*, 164–65, 170–71; Athanase de Mézières to Viceroy Antonio María de Bucareli de Ursúa, San Antonio de Béxar, Feb. 20, 1778, in Bolton, *Athanase de Mézières*, 2:181–82; Fray Francisco de Jesús María Casañas, Relación, Aug. 15, 1691, AGN, Historia, vol. 394 (cited in Bolton, *The Hasinais*, 57). Note that the English word *friend* comes from the Old English word *freond*, which means "relative" or "kin." This term is ultimately derived from the Gothic verb *frijon*, which means "to love." Human behaviors associated with love are ultimately derived from the sacrificial, or social, behaviors associated between close kin (i.e., mothers and offspring). Incidententally, the name of the State of Texas is derived from the Caddoan term *techan*, or *texias*. The modern understanding of the name has generally been assumed to mean "friend," reflecting the more recent and metaphorical understanding of that word. Rather, the name *Texas* should actually be understood to mean "kindred."

16. Fray Juan de Mirabel to Juan Domingo Bustamante, Taos, Jan. 24 [29?], 1724, SANM, reel 6:106, T-324.

17. Adams and Chaves, *Missions of New Mexico*, 154 n. 11; Joseph Rubio to Pedro Fermín de Mendinueta, Chihuahua, Jan. 8, 1778, SANM, reel 10:965, T-714; Kavanagh, *Comanche Political History*, 86; Concha to Ugarte y Loyola, Santa Fe, Nov. 18, 1789, SANM, reel 12:211, T-1064.

18. Carl Coke Rister, *Comanche Bondage*, 130.

19. El Juez Primero de Paz al Prefecto del Distrito de Cadereyta Jiménez, Agualeguas, Sept. 8, 1840, in Canales, *La invasión*, 71; Wallace, "David G. Burnet's Letters Describing the Comanche Indians," 134.

20. Ruíz, *Report on the Indian Tribes of Texas*, 10–11.

21. Ibid., 11.

22. Wallace, "David G. Burnet's Letters Describing the Comanche Indians," 129.

23. Ibid., 130.

24. Berlandier, *Indians of Texas in 1830*, 67.

25. Felix Martinez, council of war, Santa Fe, Oct. 14–Dec. 10, 1716, SANM, reel 5:637, T-279; Antonio Valverde y Cosio, Order for council of war, Santa Fe, Aug. 13, 1719, in Thomas, *After Coronado*, 99; Kavanagh, *Comanche Politics*, 64–65; Adams and Chaves, *Missions of New Mexico*, 4, 251.

26. Gregg, *Commerce of the Prairies*, 104–105; Pablo Francisco de Villapando, testimony, Taos, Dec. 31, 1749, SANM, reel 8:949, T-509.

27. Garrido, "Account of Events," 303–304. The captive Tosacondata gave his Spanish rival was Alejandro Martín, who later served the province of New Mexico as an official interpreter of the Comanche language.

28. Juan de Ulibarri, "The Diary of Juan de Ulibarri to El Cuartelejo," 1706, in Thomas, *After Coronado*, 76; Thomas, *After Coronado*, 46; Athanase de Mézières to Viceroy Antonio María de Bucareli y Ursúa, San Antonio de Béxar, Feb. 20, 1778, in Bolton, *Athanase de Mézières*, 2:181; John H. Rollins to G. M. Brooke, Fredricksburg, Sept. 25, 1850, in Winfrey and Day, *Indian Papers of Texas and the Southwest*, 3:125.

29. Manuel Antonio Cordero y Bustamante to Nemesio de Salcedo, San Antonio de Béxar, Apr. 20, 1808, BATS 2, reel 25, vol. 35, pp. 246–47.

30. The English word *nation* and the Spanish equivalent *nación* ultimately derive from the Latin *nation* and its stem, *nascī* meaning "to be born."

31. Report from R. S. Neighbors to H. R. Schoolcraft, "The Na-ü-ni, or Comanches of Texas; Their Traits and Beliefs, and Their Divisions and Intertribal Relations," in Winfrey and Day, *Indian Papers of Texas and the Southwest*, 3:354.

32. Berlandier, *Indians of Texas in 1830*, 118. For a much more detailed discussion on the evolution of human sexuality, see Donald Symons, *The Evolution of Human Sexuality*; and Matt Ridley, *The Red Queen*. For more on polygyny, see Robert Wright, *The Moral Animal*.

33. Marcy, *Thirty Years of Army Life*, 49. Carroll and Haggard, *Three New Mexican Chronicles*, 130.

34. Berlandier, *Journey to Mexico*, 344.

35. Garrido, "Account of Events," 313; Rafael Martínez Pacheco to Juan de Ugalde, San Antonio de Béxar, Mar. 3, 1788, BATS 1, reel 18, vol. 153, pp. 40–41.

36. Glass, *Journal of an Indian Trader*, 76; Berlandier, *Indians in Texas in 1830*, 118; Berlandier, *Journey to Mexico*, 344; report from Neighbors to Schoolcraft, "The Na-ü-ni," 3:355.

37. Antonio de Valverde, "Diary of the Campaign of Governor Antonio de Valverde against the Ute and Comanche Indians," 1719, in Thomas, *After Coronado*, 112–13, 115; Fray Juan de Mirabal to Juan Domingo Bustamante, Taos, Jan. 29, 1724, SANM, reel 6:105–106, T-324.

38. Berlandier, *Indians of Texas in 1830*, 119; El teniente coronel Juan J. Galán al General en Jefe del Cuerpo de Ejécito del Norte, San Fernando de Rosas, Jan. 24, 1841, Canales, *La invasión*, 198–201.

39. Berlandier, *Indians of Texas in 1830*, 119; Gregg, *Commerce of the Prairies*, 249.

Chapter 6

1. Pedro Garrido y Duran, "An Account of Events which Have Occurred in the Provinces of New Mexico Concerning Peace Conceded to the Comanche Nation and their Reconciliation with the Utes, since November 17 of Last Year and July 15 of the Current," Chihuahua, Dec. 21, 1786, in Thomas, *Forgotten Frontiers*, 316.

Appendix 1

1. This statement is inspired by Edward O. Wilson's declaration regarding the antiempiricism of ethicists: "Rarely do you see an argument that opens with the simple statement: *This is my starting point, and it could be wrong.*" See Edward O. Wilson, *Consilience: The Unity of Knowledge*, 240. Not only do you rarely see this kind of statement among ethicists, it might also be said that one seldom sees this type of statement among social scientists.

2. Alan Sokal and Jean Bricmont, *Fashionable Nonsense: Postmodern Intellectuals' Abuse of Science*, 188.

3. Ibid., 146.

4. Derek Freeman, *Margaret Mead and Samoa: The Making and Unmaking of an Anthropological Myth*, 22, 39, 30–32.

5. Thomas W. Kavanagh, "The Comanche: Paradigmatic Anomaly or Ethnographic Fiction," *Haliksa'i: UNM Contributions to Anthropology* 4 (1985): 124, 109–11; Kavanagh, "Political Power and Political Organization: Comanche Politics, 1786–1875," 3–5, 8–20.

6. Freeman, *Margaret Mead and Samoa*, 282.

7. Fischer, *Historians' Fallacies*, 9, 12, 11.

8. Murdock, "Anthropology's Mythology," 19; Freeman, *Margaret Mead and Samoa*, 46.

9. Murdock, "Anthropology's Mythology," 19; Ridley, *Origins of Virtue*, 99.

10. Albert Carl Cafagna, "A Formal Analysis of Definitions of 'Culture,'" in *Essays in the Science of Culture in Honor of Leslie A. White,* ed. Gertrude Dole and Robert L. Carneiro, 115–16.

11. Steadman, "Religion and Natural Selection," 137.

12. Wright, *The Moral Animal,* 5; Symons, *Evolution of Human Sexuality,* 7–8; Lyle Steadman, e-mail to author (subject, "Ultimate Causation"), July 9, 1997. Some historians shy away from questions relating to ultimate causation because of its seeming relationship to what David Hackett Fischer called "the fallacy of metaphysical questions." However, understanding ultimate causation through natural selection cannot be considered such a fallacy because natural selection is an empirical problem that can be resolved by empirical means. See Fischer, *Historians' Fallacies,* 14. For a clear explanation of proximate and ultimate causation, see Randy Thornhill and Craig T. Palmer, *A Natural History of Rape: Biological Bases of Sexual Coercion,* 3–5. For an overview of contemporary thinking on natural selection, see Ridley, *The Red Queen,* and *Origins of Virtue.* For a discussion on the philosophy behind the concept of natural selection, see Daniel C. Dennett, *Darwin's Dangerous Idea: Evolution and the Meanings of Life.*

Bibliography

Archival Sources and Unpublished Manuscripts

Archivo General de la Nación, Provincias Internas, Mexico City. Photographic copies, University of New Mexico, Albuquerque.

Betty, Gerald. "Comanche Pastoralism, 1700–1850." Master's thesis, Arizona State University, 1992.

Béxar Archives of Spanish and Mexican Texas. University of Texas, Austin. Microfilm edition, Texas Tech University, Lubbock.

Béxar Archives Translation Series. University of Texas, Austin. Microfilm edition, University of North Texas, Denton.

Blakeslee, Donald John. "The Plains Interband Trade System: An Ethnohistoric and Archeological Investigation." Ph.D. diss., University of Wisconsin–Milwaukee, 1975.

Canty, Carol Shannon. "New World Pastoralism: A Study of the Comanche Indians." Master's thesis, University of Texas at San Antonio, 1986.

Kavanagh, Thomas W. "Political Power and Political Organization: Comanche Politics, 1786–1875." Ph.D. diss., University of New Mexico, 1986.

Mexican Archives of New Mexico. New Mexico State Records Center, Santa Fe. Microfilm edition, University of New Mexico, Albuquerque.

Spanish Archives of New Mexico. New Mexico State Records Center, Santa Fe. Microfilm edition, University of New Mexico, Albuquerque.

Steadman, Lyle. "The Evolutionary Significance of Metaphor." Paper presented at the annual meeting of the Human Behavior and Evolution Society, Evanston, Ill., June 30, 1996.

———. "Kinship, the Basis of Cultural and Social Behavior." Department of Anthropology, Arizona State University, August, 1996. Photocopy.

———. "Kinship Hierarchy: The Basis of Cooperation?" Paper presented at the annual meeting of the Human Behavior and Evolution Society, Tucson, Ariz., June 6, 1997.

———. "Kinship, Religion, and Ethnicity." Paper presented at the annual meeting of the Evolution and Human Behavior Society, Albuquerque, N.Mex., July 27, 1992.

———. "Natural Selection and the Evolutionary Status of Culture." Paper presented at the annual meeting of the Human Behavior and Evolution Society, Binghamton, N.Y., August 5, 1993.

———. "Religion and Natural Selection: A Descendant Leaving Strategy." Department of Anthropology, Arizona State University, August, 1991. Photocopy.

———. "Social Behavior and Sacrifice." Paper presented at the annual meeting of the Human Behavior and Evolution Society, Ann Arbor, Mich., June 16, 1994.

——. "Social — Not Natural, Not Sexual — Selection." Paper presented at the annual meeting of the Human Behavior and Evolution Society, Davis, Calif., July 11, 1998.

——. "Traditions Are Not (Explained by) *r*." Paper presented at the annual meeting of the Human Behavior and Evolution Society, Santa Barbara, Calif., June 2, 1995.

Books

Abert, James W. *Through the Country of the Comanche Indians in the Fall of 1845: The Journal of a U.S. Army Expedition Led by Lieutenant James W. Abert of the Topographical Engineers.* Edited by John Galvin. San Francisco: John Howell, 1970.

Adams, Eleanor B., and Fray Angelico Chaves, eds. and trans. *The Missions of New Mexico, 1776: A Description by Fray Francisco Atanasio Domínguez with Other Contemporary Documents.* Albuquerque: University of New Mexico Press, 1956.

Anderson, Gary Clayton. *Kinsmen of Another Kind: Dakota-White Relations in the Upper Mississippi Valley, 1650–1862.* St. Paul: Minnesota Historical Society Press, 1997.

Bailey, Lynn Robinson. *If You Take My Sheep — : The Evolution and Conflicts of Navajo Pastoralism, 1630–1898.* Pasadena, Calif.: Westernlore, 1980.

Bamforth, Douglas. *Ecology and Human Organization on the Great Plains.* New York: Plenum Press, 1988.

Bannon, John Francis. *Herbert Eugene Bolton: The Historian and the Man.* Tucson: University of Arizona Press, 1978.

Berger, Joel. *Wild Horses of the Great Basin: Social Competition and Population Size.* Chicago: University of Chicago Press, 1986.

Berlandier, Jean Louis. *The Indians of Texas in 1830.* Edited by John C. Ewers. Washington, D.C.: Smithsonian Institution Press, 1969.

——. *Journey to Mexico during the Years 1826 to 1834.* Translated and edited by S. M. Ohlendorf, J. M. Bigelow, and M. M. Standifer. Austin: Texas State Historical Association, 1980.

Bolton, Herbert E. *The Hasinais: Southern Caddos as Seen by the Earliest Europeans.* Edited by Russell M. Magnaghi. Norman: University of Oklahoma Press, 1987.

——. *Texas in the Middle Eighteenth Century: Studies in Spanish Colonial History and Administration.* Berkeley and Los Angeles: University of California Press, 1915.

——, ed. and trans. *Athnanase de Mézières and the Louisiana-Texas Frontier, 1768–1780.* 2 vols. Cleveland: Arthur H. Clark, 1914.

Brinckerhoff, Sidney B., and Odie B. Faulk. *Lancers for the King: A Study of the Frontier Military System of Northern New Spain, with a Translation of the Royal Regulations of 1772.* Phoenix: Arizona Historical Foundation, 1965.

Brown, Donald E. *Human Universals.* New York: McGraw-Hill, 1991.

Campbell, Bernard G., ed. *Humankind Emerging.* Boston: Little, Brown, 1985.

Canales, Isidro Vizcaya, ed. *La invasión de los indios bárbaros al noreste de México en los años de 1840 y 1841.* Monterrey, Mex.: Instituto Technológico y de Estudios Superiores de Monterrey, 1968.

Carroll, Bailey H., and J. Villasana Haggard, eds. and trans. *Three New Mexican Chronicles: The Exposición of Don Pedro Bautista Pino, 1812; the Ojeada of Lic. Antonio Barreiro, 1832; and the additions by Don José Augustín de Escudero, 1849.* Albuquerque: Quivira Society, 1942.

Carter, Robert Goldthwaite. *On the Border with Mackenzie.* Washington, D.C.: Eynon Printing, 1935.

Catlin, George. *North American Indians.* Edited by Peter Matthiessen. New York: Penguin Books, 1989.

Chagnon, Napoleon. *Yänomamö.* 4th edition. Fort Worth: Harcourt Brace Jovanovich College Publishers, 1992.

Chaput, Donald. *Francois X. Aubry: Trader, Trailmaker, and Voyaguer in the Southwest, 1846–1854.* Glendale, Calif.: Arthur H. Clark, 1975.

Chipman, Donald E. *Spanish Texas, 1519–1821.* Austin: University of Texas Press, 1992.

Claiborne, Robert. *Climate, Man, and History.* New York: W. W. Norton, 1970.

Clark, W. P. *The Indian Sign Language.* Philadelphia: L. R. Hamersly, 1885.

Clutton-Brock, Juliet. *Horse Power: A History of the Horse and the Donkey in Human Societies.* Cambridge: Harvard University Press, 1992.

Cortés, José. *Views from the Apache Frontier: Report on the Northern Provinces of New Spain.* Edited by Elizabeth A. H. John, translated by John Wheat. Norman: University of Oklahoma Press, 1989.

Darwin, Charles. *The Descent of Man and Selection in Relation to Sex.* 1871. Reprint, Princeton, N.J.: Princeton University Press, 1981.

——. *The Origin of the Species by Means of Natural Selection or the Preservation of Favored Races in the Struggle for Life.* 1859. Reprint, London: Penguin Classics, 1985.

Davis, Wayne A. *An Introduction to Logic.* Englewood Cliffs, N.J.: Prentice-Hall, 1986.

Dawkins, Richard. *The Selfish Gene.* New edition. Oxford: Oxford University Press, 1989.

Dennett, Daniel C. *Darwin's Dangerous Idea: Evolution and the Meanings of Life.* New York: Touchstone, 1995.

Diamond, Jared. *Guns, Germs, and Steel: The Fates of Human Societies.* New York: W. W. Norton, 1997.

Dole, Gertrude, and Robert L. Carneiro, eds. *Essays in the Science of Culture in Honor of Leslie A. White.* New York: Thomas Y. Crowell, 1960.

Döring, Jürgen. *Kulturwandel bei den Nordamerikanischen Plainsindianern: Zur Rolle des Pferdes bei den Comanchen und den Cheyenne.* Berlin: Dietrich Reimer Verlag, 1984.

Downs, James F. *Animal Husbandry in Navajo Society and Culture.* University of California Publications in Anthropology, no. 1. Berkeley and Los Angeles: University of California Press, 1964.

Duffus, Robert Luther. *The Santa Fe Trail.* 1931. Reprint, St. Clair Shores, Mich.: Scholarly Press, 1971.

Espinosa, J. Manuel, ed. and trans. *The Pueblo Indian Revolt of 1698 and the Franciscan Missions in New Mexico: Letters of the Missionaries and Related Documents.* Norman: University of Oklahoma Press, 1988.

Evans-Pritchard, E. E. *The Nuer: A Description of the Modes of Livelihood and Political Institutions of a Nilotic People.* Oxford: Clarendon Press, 1940.

Ewers, John C. *The Horse in Blackfoot Indian Culture: With Comparative Material from Other Western Tribes.* Smithsonian Institution, Bureau of Ethnology, Bulletin 159. Washington, D.C.: Government Printing Office, 1955.

——. *Indian Life on the Upper Missouri.* Norman: University of Oklahoma Press, 1968.

Fehrenbach, T. R. *Comanches: The Destruction of a People.* New York: Alfred A. Knopf, 1986.

Fiedel, Stuart J. *Prehistory of the Americas.* 2d edition. New York: Cambridge University Press, 1992.

Fischer, David Hackett. *Historians' Fallacies: Toward a Logic of Historical Thought.* New York: Harper Torchbooks, 1970.

Flores, Dan. *Caprock Canyonlands: Journeys into the Heart of the Southern Plains.* Austin: University of Texas Press, 1990.

Forbes, Jack D. *Apache, Navajo, and Spaniard.* Norman: University of Oklahoma Press, 1960.

Foreman, Grant. *Marcy and the Gold Seekers: The Journal of Captain R. B. Marcy, with an Account of the Gold Rush over the Southern Route.* Norman: University of Oklahoma Press, 1939.

Foster, Morris. *Being Comanche: A Social History of an American Indian Community.* Tucson: University of Arizona Press, 1991.

Fowler, Jacob. *The Journal of Jacob Fowler.* Edited by Elliot Coues. Lincoln: University of Nebraska Press, 1970.

Fox, Robin. *Kinship and Marriage: An Anthropological Perspective.* Middlesex, Eng.: Penguin Books, 1967.

Freeman, Derek. *Margaret Mead and the Heretic: The Making and Unmaking of an Anthropological Myth.* New York: Penguin Books, 1996.

———. *Margaret Mead and Samoa: The Making and Unmaking of an Anthropological Myth.* Cambridge, Mass.: Harvard University Press, 1983.

Gibson, Charles. *Tlaxcala en el siglo XVI.* Mexico City: Fondo de Cultura Económica, 1991.

Glass, Anthony. *Journal of an Indian Trader: Anthony Glass and the Texas Trading Frontier, 1790–1810.* Edited by Dan L. Flores. College Station: Texas A&M University Press, 1985.

Green, Robert B. *On the Arkansas Route to California in 1849: The Journal of Robert B. Green of Lewisburg Pennsylvania.* Edited by J. Orin Oliphant. Lewisburg, Pa.: Bucknell University Press, 1955.

Gregg, Josiah. *Commerce of the Prairies.* Edited by Max L. Moorhead. Norman: University of Oklahoma Press, 1954.

Grinnell, George Bird. *The Cheyenne Indians: Their History and Ways of Life.* 2 vols. 1923. Reprint, Lincoln: University of Nebraska Press; Bison Books, 1972.

Gross, Paul R., and Norman Levitt. *Higher Superstition: The Academic Left and Its Quarrels with Science.* Baltimore: Johns Hopkins University Press, 1998.

Gross, Paul R.; Norman Levitt; and Martin W. Lewis, eds. *The Flight from Science and Reason.* New York: New York Academy of Sciences, 1996.

Gulick, Charles Adams, Jr.; and Winnie Allen, eds. *The Papers of Mirabeau Buonaparte Lamar.* 6 vols. Austin: Texas State Library, 1924.

Gutiérrez, Ramón. *When Jesus Came, the Corn Mothers Went Away: Marriage, Sexuality, and Power in New Mexico, 1500–1846.* Stanford, Calif.: Stanford University Press, 1991.

Hackett, Charles Wilson, ed. and trans. *Historical Documents Relating to New Mexico, Nueva Vizcaya, and Approaches Thereto, to 1773.* 3 vols. Washington, D.C.: Carnegie Institution of Washington, 1937.

———, ed. and trans. *Pichardo's Treatise on the Limits of Texas and Louisiana.* 3 vols. Austin: University of Texas Press, 1941.

Hackett, Charles Wilson, ed.; and Charmion Clair Shelby, trans. *Revolt of the Pueblo Indians of New Mexico and Otermín's Attempted Reconquest, 1680–1682.* 2 vols. Albuquerque: University of New Mexico Press, 1942.

Hagan, William T. *Quanah Parker, Comanche Chief.* Norman: University of Oklahoma Press, 1993.

Haggard, J. Villasana. *Handbook for Translators of Spanish Historical Documents.* Austin: University of Texas Press, 1941.

Hall, Thomas D. *Social Change in the Southwest, 1350–1880.* Lawrence: University Press of Kansas, 1989.

Hammond, George P., and Agapito Rey, eds. and trans. *Don Juan de Oñate, Colonizer of New Mexico, 1595–1628.* 2 vols. Albuquerque: University of New Mexico Press, 1953.

Hart, C. W. M., and Arnold R. Pilling. *The Tiwi of North Australia.* Fieldwork edition. New York: Holt, Rinehart, and Winston, 1979.

Herodotus. *The Histories.* Translated by Harry Carter. New York: Heritage Press, 1958.

Hickerson, Nancy Parrott. *The Jumanos: Hunters and Traders of the South Plains.* Austin: University of Texas Press, 1994.

Hill, Christopher. *The Century of Revolution, 1603–1714.* 2d edition. New York: W. W. Norton, 1982.

Hodge, Frederick Webb, ed. *Handbook of American Indians North of Mexico.* Smithsonian Institution, Bureau of American Ethnology, Bulletin 30. 2 vols. Washington, D.C.: Government Printing Office, 1907–1910.

Hoebel, E. Adamson. *Political Organization and Law-Ways of the Comanche Indians.* Memoirs of the American Anthropological Association, vol. 54. Menasha, Wis.: American Anthropological Association, 1940.

Iverson, Peter. *When Indians became Cowboys: Native Peoples and Cattle Ranching in the American West.* Norman: University of Oklahoma Press, 1994.

Jablow, Joseph. *The Cheyenne in Plains Indian Trade Relations, 1795–1840.* Monographs of the American Ethnological Society, no. 19. New York: J. J. Augustine, 1951.

Jackson, Jack, ed. *Imaginary Kingdom: Texas as Seen by the Rivera and Rubí Military Expeditions, 1727 and 1767.* Austin: Texas State Historical Association, 1995.

James, Thomas. *Three Years among the Indians and Mexicans.* 1846. Reprint, Lincoln: University of Nebraska Press, Bison Books, 1984.

John, Elizabeth A. H. *Storms Brewed in Other Men's Worlds: The Confrontation of Indians, Spanish, and French in the Southwest, 1540–1795.* 1975. Reprint, Lincoln: University of Nebraska Press, Bison Books, 1981.

Jordan, Terry G. *North American Cattle-Ranching Frontiers: Origins, Diffusion, and Differentiation.* Albuquerque: University of New Mexico Press, 1993.

Kavanagh, Thomas W. *Comanche Political History: An Ethnohistorical Perspective, 1706–1875.* Lincoln: University of Nebraska Press, 1996.

Keeley, Lawrence H. *War before Civilization.* New York: Oxford University Press, 1996.

Kenner, Charles L. *A History of New Mexican–Plains Indian Relations.* Norman: University of Oklahoma Press, 1969.

Kessell, John. *Kiva, Cross, and Crown: The Pecos Indians and New Mexico, 1540–1840.* 1979. Reprint, Tucson: Southwest Parks and Monuments Association, 1987.

Kluckhohn, Clyde, and Dorothea Leighton. *The Navaho.* Cambridge: Harvard University Press, 1974.

Koertge, Noretta, ed. *A House Built on Sand: Exposing Postmodernist Myths about Science.* New York: Oxford University Press, 1998.

Lafora, Nicolás de. *The Frontiers of New Spain: Nicolas de Lafora's Description, 1766–1768.* Edited by Lawrence Kinnard. Berkeley: Quivira Society, 1958.

——. *Relación del viaje que hizo a los presidios internas situados en la frontera de la América septentrional, perteneciente al rey de España.* Edited by Vito Alessio Robles. Mexico City: Editorial Pedro Robredo, 1939.

LaVere, David. *The Caddo Chiefdoms: Caddo Economics and Politics, 700–1835.* Lincoln: University of Nebraska Press, 1998.

——. *Contrary Neighbors: Southern Plains and Removed Indians in Indian Territory.* Norman: University of Oklahoma Press, 2000.

Lewis, I. M. *A Pastoral Democracy; A Study of Pastoralism and Politics among the Northern Somali of the Horn of Africa.* New York: Oxford University Press, 1961.

Loomis, Noel M., and Abraham P. Nasatir. *Pedro Vial and the Roads to Santa Fe.* Norman: University of Oklahoma Press, 1967.

Lowie, Robert H. *Indians of the Plains.* 1954. Reprint, Lincoln: University of Nebraska Press, Bison Books, 1982.

Marcy, Randolph B. *Adventure on Red River: Report on the Exploration of the Headwaters of the Red River by Captain Randolph B. Marcy and Captain G. B. McClellan.* Edited by Grant Foreman. Norman: University of Oklahoma Press, 1937.

——. *Thirty Years of Army Life on the Border.* New York: Harper and Brothers, 1866.

Meadows, William C. *Kiowa, Apache, and Comanche Military Societies.* Austin: University of Texas Press, 1999.

Mishkin, Bernard. *Rank and Warfare among the Plains Indians.* 1940. Reprint, Lincoln: University of Nebraska Press, Bison Books, 1992.

Mooney, James. *The Ghost Dance Religion and the Sioux Outbreak of 1890.* Fourteenth Annual Report of the Bureau of Ethnology, 1892–93. Pt. 2. Washington D.C.: Government Printing Office, 1896.

Moorhead, Max L. *The Apache Frontier: Jacobo Ugarte and Spanish-Indian Relations in Northern New Spain, 1769–1791.* Norman: University of Oklahoma Press, 1968.

——. *The Presidio: Bastion of the Spanish Borderlands.* Norman: University of Oklahoma Press, 1975.

Morfi, Juan Augustín. *History of Texas, 1673–1779.* Translated by Carlos Eduardo Castañeda. 2 vols. Albuquerque: Quivira Society, 1935.

Newcomb, W. W., Jr. *The Indians of Texas.* Austin: University of Texas Press, 1961.

Noyes, Stanley. *Los Comanches: The Horse People, 1751–1845.* Albuquerque: University of New Mexico Press, 1993.

O'Callaghan, Joseph F. *A History of Medieval Spain.* Ithaca, N.Y.: Cornell University Press, 1975.

Oliver, Symmes C. *Ecology and Cultural Continuity as Contributing Factors in the Social Organization of the Plains Indians.* University of California Publications in American Archeology and Ethnology, vol. 48. Berkeley and Los Angeles: University of California Press, 1962.

Pinker, Stephen. *The Language Instinct: How the Mind Creates Language.* New York: Harper-Perennial, 1995.

Powell, Philip Wayne. *Soldiers, Indians, and Silver: North America's First Frontier War.* 1952. Reprint, Tempe: Center for Latin American Studies, Arizona State University, 1975.

Quammen, David. *The Song of the Dodo: Island Biogeography in an Age of Extinctions.* New York: Touchstone, 1996.

Rathje, William, and Cullen Murphy. *Rubbish: The Archeology of Garbage.* New York: Harper-Perennial, 1992.

Richardson, Rupert Norval. *The Comanche Barrier to South Plains Settlement.* Glendale, Calif.: Arthur A. Clark, 1933.

Ridley, Matt. *The Origins of Virtue: Human Instincts and the Evolution of Cooperation.* New York: Viking Penguin, 1997.

——. *The Red Queen: Sex and the Evolution of Human Nature.* New York: Penguin Books, 1995.

Rister, Carl Coke. *Comanche Bondage.* 1955. Reprint, Lincoln: University of Nebraska Press, Bison Books, 1989.

Rivera, Pedro de. *Diario y derrotero de lo caminando, visto y observado en la visita que lo hizo a los presidios de la Nueva España septentrional.* Edited by Vito Allesio Robles. Mexico City: Secretaria de la Defensa Nacional, 1946.

Roe, Frank Gilbert. *The Indian and the Horse.* Norman: University of Oklahoma Press, 1955.

Ruíz, Jose Francisco. *Report on the Indian Tribes of Texas in 1828.* Edited by John C. Ewers, translated by Georgette Dorn. New Haven: Yale University Press, 1972.

Secoy, Frank Raymond. *Changing Military Patterns of the Great Plains Indians (Seventeenth Century through Early Nineteenth Century).* Monographs of the American Ethnological Society, vol. 21. Locust Valley, N.Y.: J. J. Augustine Publishers, 1953.

Service, Elman R. *Primitive Social Organization: An Evolutionary Perspective.* New York: Random House, 1962.

Sherburne, John P. *Through Indian Country to California: John P. Sherburne's Diary of the Whipple Expedition, 1853–1854.* Stanford, Calif.: Stanford University Press, 1988.

Sibley, John. *A Report from Natchitoches in 1807.* Indian Notes and Monographs, ed. Annie Heloise Abel. New York: Museum of the American Indian, 1922.

Simmons, Marc, ed. and trans. *Border Comanches: Seven Spanish Colonial Documents, 1785–1819.* Santa Fe: Stage Coach Press, 1967.

Simpson, Lesley Byrd, ed., and Paul D. Nathan, trans. *The San Saba Papers: A Documentary Account of the Founding and Destruction of San Saba Mission.* San Francisco: John Howell, 1959.

Smith, Adam. *An Inquiry into the Nature and Causes of the Wealth of Nations.* Edited by Edward Cannan. New York: Modern Library, 1994.

Smith, Bruce D. *The Emergence of Agriculture.* New York: Scientific American Library, 1995.

Sokal, Alan, and Jean Bricmont. *Fashionable Nonsense: Postmodern Intellectual's Abuse of Science.* New York: Picador, 1998.

Spielmann, Katherine A., ed. *Farmers, Hunters, and Colonists: Interaction between the Southwest and the Southern Plains.* Tucson: University of Arizona Press, 1991.

——. *Interdependence in the Prehistoric Southwest: An Ecological Analysis of Plains-Pueblo Interaction.* New York: Garland, 1991.

Steward, Julian. *Basin-Plateau Aboriginal Sociopolitical Groups.* Bureau of American Ethnology, Bulletin 120. Washington, D.C.: Government Printing Office, 1938.

Stoll, David. *Rigoberta Menchú and the Story of All Poor Guatemalans.* Boulder, Colo.: Westview Press, 1999.

Swadesh, Frances Leon. *Los Prímeros Pobladores: Hispanic Americans of the Ute Frontier.* Notre Dame, Ind.: University of Notre Dame Press, 1974.

Symons, Donald. *The Evolution of Human Sexuality.* New York: Oxford University Press, 1979.

Taylor, Virginia H., ed. and trans. *The Letters of Antonio Martinez: Last Spanish Governor of Texas, 1817–1822.* Austin: Texas State Library, 1957.

Teja, Jesús de la. *San Antonio de Béxar: A Community on New Spain's Northern Frontier.* Albuquerque: University of New Mexico Press, 1995.

Thomas, Alfred Barnaby, ed. and trans. *After Coronado: Spanish Exploration Northeast of New Mexico, 1696–1727.* Norman: University of Oklahoma Press, 1935.

——, ed. and trans. *Forgotten Frontiers: A Study of the Spanish Indian Policy of Don Juan Bautista de Anza, Governor of New Mexico 1777–1787, from the Original Documents in the Archives of Spain, Mexico, and New Mexico.* Norman: University of Oklahoma Press, 1932.

——, ed. and trans. *The Plains Indians and New Mexico, 1751–1778: A Collection of Documents Illustrative of the History of the Eastern Frontier of New Mexico.* Albuquerque: University of New Mexico Press, 1940.

——, ed. and trans. *Teodoro de Croix and the Northern Frontier of New Spain, 1776–1783*. Norman: University of Oklahoma Press, 1941.

Thornhill, Randy, and Craig T. Palmer. *A Natural History of Rape: Biological Bases of Sexual Coercion*. Cambridge: Massachusetts Institute of Technology Press, 2000.

Twitchell, Ralph Emerson. *The Spanish Archives of New Mexico*. 2 vols. Glendale, Calif.: Arthur H. Clark, 1914.

U.S. Congress. House. T. B. Wheelock. *Journal of Colonel Dodge's Expedition from Fort Gibson to the Pawnee Pict Village, Fort Gibson*. 23d Cong., 2d sess., 1834–35. H. Doc. 2.

——. Senate Committee on Indian Affairs. *Communication from the Commissioner of Indian Affairs, and other Documents in Relation to the Indians in Texas*. 30th Cong., 1st sess., 1848. S. Rpt. 171.

Wallace, Ernest, and E. Adamson Hoebel. *The Comanches: Lords of the South Plains*. Norman: University of Oklahoma Press, 1952.

Warner, Ted J., ed., and Fray Angelico Chaves, trans. *The Domínguez-Escalante Journal: Their Expedition through Colorado, Utah, Arizona, and New Mexico in 1776*. Salt Lake City: University of Utah Press, 1995.

Webb, James Josiah. *Adventures in the Santa Fé Trade, 1844–1847*. Edited by Ralph P. Bieber. Lincoln: University of Nebraska Press, Bison Books, 1995.

Weddle, Robert S. *The San Sabá Mission: Spanish Pivot in Texas*. Austin: University of Texas Press, 1964.

Williams, George C. *Adaptation and Natural Selection*. Princeton, N.J.: Princeton University Press, 1996.

Wilson, Edward O. *Consilience: The Unity of Knowledge*. New York: Alfred A. Knopf, 1998.

Windschuttle, Keith. *The Killing of History: How Literary Critics and Social Theorists Are Murdering Our Past*. San Francisco: Encounter Books, 1996.

Winfrey, Dorman H., and James M. Day, eds. *The Indian Papers of Texas and the Southwest, 1825–1916*. 5 vols. Austin: Texas State Historical Association, 1966.

Wissler, Clark. *The American Indian: An Introduction to the Anthropology of the New World*. New York: Douglas C. McMurtrie, 1917.

——. *The American Indian: An Introduction to the Anthropology of the New World*. 3d ed. 1938. Reprint, Gloucester, Mass.: Peter Smith, 1957.

——. *The Relation of Nature to Man in Aboriginal America*. New York: Oxford University Press, 1926.

Wright, Robert. *The Moral Animal: The New Science of Evolutionary Psychology*. New York: Vintage Books, 1994.

Articles

Albers, Patricia, and William R. James. "Historical Materialism vs. Evolutionary Ecology: A Methodological Note on Horse Distribution and American Plains Indians." *Critique of Anthropology* 6, no. 1 (November–December, 1985): 87–100.

Armijo, Isidro, ed. "Information Communicated by Juan Candelaria, Resident of this Villa de San Francisco Xavier de Alburquerque, Born 1692 — Age 84." *New Mexico Historical Review* 3 (1929): 274–97.

Benes, Ronald J. "Anza and Concha in New Mexico, 1787–1793: A Study in New Colonial Techniques." *Journal of the West* 4, no. 1 (January, 1965): 63–76.

Betty, Gerald. "Comanche Warfare, Pastoralism, and Enforced Cooperation." *Panhandle-Plains Historical Review* 68 (1995): 1–13.

——. "'Skillful in the Management of the Horse': The Comanches as Southern Plains Pastoralists." *Heritage of the Great Plains* 30, no. 1 (spring/summer, 1997): 5–13.

Bolton, Herbert E. "The Jumano Indians in Texas, 1650–1771." *Texas State Historical Association Quarterly* 15 (July, 1911): 66–84.

Bonte, Pierre. "Non-Stratified Social Formations among Pastoral Nomads." In *The Evolution of Social Systems,* edited by J. Friedman and M. J. Rowlands. London: Duckworth, 1978.

Brugge, David M. "Navajos in the Catholic Church Records of New Mexico." *Research Reports* No. 1. Window Rock, Ariz.: Research Section, Navajo Tribe, 1968.

Burnet, David G. "The Comanches and Other Tribes of Texas; and the Policy to Be Pursued Respecting Them." In *Historical and Statistical Information Respecting the History, Conditions, and Prospects of the Indian Tribes of the United States.* Edited by Henry R. Schoolcraft. 6 vols. Philadelphia: Lippincott, Grambo, 1851.

Carson, James Taylor. "Horses and the Economy and Culture of the Choctaw Indians." *Ethnohistory* 42, no. 3 (summer, 1995): 495–513.

Clark, LaVerne Harrell. "Early Horse Trappings of the Navajo and Apache Indians." *Arizona and the West* 5 (autumn, 1963): 233–48.

Cunliffe, Barry. "Iron Age Societies in Western Europe and Beyond, 800–140 B.C." In *The Oxford Illustrated Prehistory of Europe.* Edited by Barry Cunliffe. New York: Oxford University Press, 1994.

Dhavalikar, M. K. "Farming to Pastoralism, Effects of Climate Change in the Deccan." In *The Walking Larder: Patterns of Domestication, Pastoralism, and Predation.* Edited by Juliet Clutton-Brock. London: Unwin Hyman, 1989.

Dobyns, Henry F. "Trade Centers: The Concept and a Rancherian Culture Area Example." *American Indian Culture and Research Journal* 8, no. 1 (1984): 23–35.

Dunn, William Edward. "The Apache Mission on the San Sabá River; Its Founding and Failure." *Southwestern Historical Quarterly* 17 (1914): 379–414.

——. "Apache Relations in Texas, 1718–1750." *Texas Historical Association Quarterly* 14 (1911): 198–275.

Dyson-Hudson, Rada, and Neville Dyson-Hudson. "Nomadic Pastoralism." *Annual Review of Anthropology* 9 (1980): 15–61.

Eggan, Fred. "Social Anthropology: Methods and Results." In *Social Anthropology of North American Tribes.* Edited by Fred Eggan. Enlarged ed. Chicago: University of Chicago Press, 1955.

Flores, Dan. "Bison Ecology and Bison Diplomacy: The Southern Plains from 1800 to 1850." *Journal of American History* 78, no. 2 (September, 1991): 465–85.

Foote, Cheryl. "Spanish-Indian Trade along New Mexico's Northern Frontier in the Eighteenth Century." *Journal of the West* 24 (April, 1985): 22–33.

Forbes, Jack D. "The Appearance of the Mounted Indian in Northeastern Mexico and the Southwest, to 1680." *Southwestern Journal of Anthropology* 15 (1959): 189–212.

Ford, Richard I. "Barter, Gift, or Violence: An Analysis of Tewa Intertribal Exchange." In *Anthropological Papers.* No. 46. Museum of Anthropology, University of Michigan. Ann Arbor: University of Michigan, 1972.

——. "Inter-Indian Exchange in the Southwest." In *Handbook of North American Indians (Southwest).* Vol. 10. Edited by Alfonso Ortiz. Washington, D.C.: Smithsonian Institution, 1983.

Freeman, Derek. "Reflections of a Heretic." *the evolutionist* (autumn, 1996): <http://www.lse.ac.uk/depts/cpnss/evolutionist/>.

Gelo, Daniel. "The Comanches as Aboriginal Skeptics." *American Indian Quarterly* 17, no. 1 (winter, 1993): 69–82.

———. "On a New Interpretation of Comanche Social Organization." *Current Anthropology* 28, no. 4 (August–October, 1987): 551–55.

Gladwin, Thomas. "Comanche Kin Behavior." *American Anthropologist* 50 (1948): 73–94.

Hämäläinen, Pekka. "The Western Comanche Trade Center: Rethinking the Plains Indian Trade System." *Western Historical Quarterly* 29 (winter, 1998): 485–513.

Harding, Anthony. "Reformation in Barbarian Europe, 1300–600 B.C." In *The Oxford Illustrated Prehistory of Europe*. Edited by Barry Cunliffe. New York: Oxford University Press, 1994.

Hoebel, E. Adamson. "Comanche and H3kandika Shoshone Relationship Systems." *American Anthropologist* 41 (1939): 440–57.

———. "The Comanche Sun Dance and the Messianic Outbreak of 1873." *American Anthropologist* 43 (1941): 301–3.

Hultkrantz, Åke. "Shoshoni Indians on the Plains: An Appraisal of the Documentary Evidence." *Zeitschrift für Etnologie* 93, nos. 1–2 (1968): 49–72.

John, Elizabeth A. H. "Nurturing the Peace: Spanish and Comanche Cooperation in the Early Nineteenth Century." *New Mexico Historical Review* 59, no. 4 (1984): 345–69.

John, Elizabeth A. H., ed., and Adán Benavides Jr., trans. "Inside the Comanchería, 1785: The Diary of Pedro Vial and Francisco Xavier Chaves." *Southwestern Historical Quarterly* 98, no. 1 (July, 1994): 26–56.

Kavanagh, Thomas W. "The Comanche: Paradigmatic Anomaly or Ethnographic Fiction." *Haliksa'i: UNM Contributions to Anthropology* 4 (1985): 109–28.

Keesing, Roger M. "Shrines, Ancestors, and Cognatic Descent: The Kwaio and Tallensi." In *Melanesia: Readings on a Culture Area*. Edited by L. L. Langness and John C. Weschler. Scranton, Pa.: Chandler Publishing, 1971.

Khazanov, A. M. "Characteristic Features of Nomadic Communities in the Eurasian Steppes." In *The Nomadic Alternative: Modes and Models of Interaction in the African-Asian Deserts and Steppes*. Edited by Wolfgang Weissleder. The Hague: Mouton Publishers, 1978.

Krech, Shepard, III. "The State of Ethnohistory." *Annual Review of Anthropology* 20 (1991): 345–75.

Linton, Ralph. "The Comanche Sun Dance." *American Anthropologist* 37 (1935): 420–28.

Mead, James. "The Pawnees as I Knew Them," *Kansas Historical Collections* 10 (1907–1908): 106–11.

Murdock, George Peter. "Anthropology's Mythology." *Proceedings of the Royal Anthropological Institute of Great Britain and Ireland for 1971* (1972): 17–23.

Opler, Marvin K. "The Southern Ute of Colorado." In *Acculturation in Seven American Indian Tribes*. Edited by Ralph Linton. 1940. Reprint, Gloucester, Mass.: Peter Smith, 1963.

Osborn, Alan J. "Ecological Aspects of Equestrian Adaptations in Aboriginal North America." *American Anthropologist* 85, no. 3 (1983): 563–91.

Palmer, Craig, and Lyle Steadman. "Human Kinship as a Descendant-Leaving Strategy: A Solution to an Evolutionary Puzzle." *Journal of Social and Evolutionary Systems* 20, no. 1 (1997): 39–51.

Redfield, Robert. Introduction to *Social Anthropology of North American Tribes*. Edited by Fred Eggan. Expanded edition. Chicago: University of Chicago Press, 1955.

Rhodes, Robert E. "The Contemporary Ethnology of Pastoralists: A Critique of the Literature." *Papers in Anthropology* 20, no. 2 (fall, 1979): 101–16.

Rollings, Willard. "In Search of Multisided Frontiers: Recent Writing on the History of the Southern Plains." In *New Directions in American Indian History*. Edited by Collin G. Calloway. Norman: University of Oklahoma Press, 1988.

Schleffler, Harold W. "Choiseul Island Descent Groups." In *Melanesia: Readings on a Culture Area*. Edited by L. L. Langness and John C. Weschler. Scranton, Pa.: Chandler Publishing, 1971.

Sherratt, Andrew. "The Emergence of élites: Earlier Bronze Age Europe, 2500–1300 B.C." In *The Oxford Illustrated Prehistory of Europe*. Edited by Barry Cunliffe. New York: Oxford University Press, 1994.

——. "The Transformation of Early Agrarian Europe: The Later Neolithic and Copper Ages 4500–2500 B.C." In *The Oxford Illustrated Prehistory of Europe*. Edited by Barry Cunliffe. New York: Oxford University Press, 1994.

Shimkin, D. B. "The Wind River Shoshone Sun Dance." In *Smithsonian Bureau of Ethnology, Anthropological Papers*. Bulletin 151, no. 41. Smithsonian Institution. Washington D.C.: Government Printing Office, 1953.

Smith, Ralph A. "The Comanches' Foreign War: Fighting Head Hunters in the Tropics." *Great Plains Journal* 24–25 (1985–86): 54–69.

Steadman, Lyle B., and Craig T. Palmer. "Religion as an Identifiable Traditional Behavior Subject to Natural Selection." *Journal of Social and Evolutionary Systems* 18, no. 2 (1995): 149–64.

——. "Visiting Dead Ancestors: Shamans as Interpreters of Religious Traditions." *Zygon* 29, no. 2 (June, 1994): 173–89.

Steadman, Lyle B.; Craig T. Palmer; and Christopher F. Tilley. "The Universality of Ancestor Worship." *Ethnology* 35, no. 1 (winter, 1996): 63–76.

Thomas, Alfred Barnaby. "An Eighteenth Century Comanche Document." *American Anthropologist* 31, no. 2 (April–June, 1929): 289–98.

——, ed. and trans. "Governor Mendinueta's Proposals for the Defense of New Mexico, 1772–1778." *New Mexico Historical Review* 6, no. 1 (1931): 21–39.

——. "San Carlos: A Comanche Pueblo on the Arkansas River, 1787." *The Colorado Magazine* 6, no. 3 (May, 1929): 79–91.

Thurman, Melburn D. "Nelson Lee and the Green Corn Dance: Data Selection Problems with Wallace and Hoebel's Study of the Comanches." *Plains Anthropologist* 27 (August, 1982): 239–43.

——. "A New Interpretation of Comanche Social Organization." *Current Anthropology* 23, no. 5 (October, 1982): 578–79.

——. "'Reply' to Daniel J. Gelo's 'On a New Interpretation of Comanche Social Organization.'" *Current Anthropology* 28, no. 4 (August–October, 1987): 552–55.

Trivers, Robert. "Parental Investment and Sexual Selection." In *Sexual Selection and the Descent of Man*. Edited by Bernard Campbell. Chicago: Aldine de Gruyter, 1972.

Vajnshtejn, S. I. "The Problem of Origin and Formation of the Economic-Cultural Type of Pastoral Nomads in the Moderate Belt of Eurasia." In *The Nomadic Alternative: Modes and Models of Interaction in the African-Asian Deserts and Steppes*. Edited by Wolfgang Weissleder. The Hague: Mouton Publishers, 1978.

Wallace, Ernest, comp. "David G. Burnet's Letters Describing the Comanche Indians." *West Texas Historical Association Year Book* 30 (1954): 115–40.

White, Richard. "The Winning of the West: The Expansion of the Western Sioux in the Eighteenth and Nineteenth Centuries." *Journal of American History* 65 (September, 1978): 319–43.

Whittle, Alasdair. "The First Farmers." In *The Oxford Illustrated Prehistory of Europe*. Edited by Barry Cunliffe. New York: Oxford University Press, 1994.

Wilson, H. Clyde. "An Inquiry into the Nature of Plains Indian Cultural Development." *American Anthropologist* 65, no. 2 (April, 1963): 355–69.

Wissler, Clark. "The Influence of the Horse in the Development of Plains Culture." *American Anthropologist* 16 (1914): 1–25.

Index

Abert, James W., 89, 108–109
Abiquiú, N. Mex., 107
Achata (Comanche chief), 71
adaptation, environmental, 139
Adobe Walls, Tex., 4
Africa, 76, 90; and agriculture, 77; and pastoralism, 78
agriculture, 78, 84; and effect on humans, 92, and Europe, 79; global spread of, 92; origins of, 77
Agualeguas, Mexico, 128
Aguascalientes, Mexico, 54
Aguila Bolteada (Comanche chief), 27
Ahorcados, Mexico, 136
Albuquerque, N. Mex., 26
Alencaster, Joaquin del Real, 23, 108
Alexander III of Macedonia, 76
altruism, 18, 40, 45, 125, 126, 128, 143, 137
Amangual, Francisco, 23, 69
Americans, 3, 5; as bison hunters, 4; as cattlemen, 4; and conflict with Comanches 8; as forty-niners, 8, 108; and relations with Comanches, 137; in Texas, 110; as traders, 8, 36, 44, 54, 69, 97, 101, 108, 109, 111–16, 119, 135; as traders with Comanches, 99, 111, 119
ancestors, 19, 21–22, 38, 56, 64, 95, 119, 125, 126, 139, 141; Comanche, 87, 133; Comanche and Caddoan, 39; definition of, 18; human, 91; and traditions, 84; Ute, 86; worship of, 43
ancestral names: demise of, 27; disappearance of, 32; existence of, 32; and reproduction, 23
Andalucía, Spain (Andalusian): cattle herding, 82; corrals, 88; horses, 82; pastoralism, 79; ranching, 80; *vaqueros,* 83
Andes Mountains, 77
Andrés (Comanche Indian), 110
animal husbandry, 92

anthropology: early evolutionist, 146; and scientific method, 147; and Comanches, 145–46
Antilles, Spain (Antillean): cattle herding, 82; cattle hunting, 80, 82; horses, 82; pastoralism, 82; ranching, 80
anti-social behavior, 40, 57, 60, 116, 120, 137, 143
Anza, Juan Bautista de, 6, 18, 24, 28–33, 41, 42, 44, 106, 125, 132, 135, 139; and campaigns against Comanches, 27; and Comanche defeats, 6; and Cuerno Verde defeat, 15; and Pecos peace council, 16
Apaches, 18, 34, 41, 58–59, 63, 65, 124; as attacked by Comanches, 49; and bison hunting, 82; camps of, 105; captives of, 136; and captive trade, 104, 107; as children, 136; and Comanches, 141; Comanches as enemies of, 6; and intermarriage with Comanches, 131; and New Mexico raids, 86; and pastoralism, 85; and relations with Spanish Texas, 53; and retreat from the plains, 53; at San Sabá Mission, 123; as Spanish allies, 25, 67, 69; and Spanish pastoralism, 94; and social relations with Comanches, 72; in Texas, 132–33; and warfare with Caddoans, 7; and warfare with Comanches, 7–8, 16, 35, 60, 131–33, 136–37; and warfare with New Mexico, 139; and warfare with Wichitas, 7; as women, 136. *See also* Carlana (Apache chief); Cuartelejos; Escalchufines; Gilas, Jicarillas; Lipans; Mescaleros; Palomas; Penxayes; Sierra Blancas
Apaches, Plains, 6, 50, 59; and retreat to the south, 51; and warfare with Caddoans, 62
Arabs, 79
Arapaho Indians, 31, 65, 118; and warfare with Comanches, 7
Archibeque, Juan de, 75, 94
Archuleta, Luis de, 63

Arikara Indians, 55
Arkansas River, 6, 7, 8, 13, 24, 29, 30, 31, 32, 33, 36, 51, 63, 65, 97, 102, 108, 118. *See also* Rio de Napeste
Arroyo del Lobo Blanco, 46, 48
Asia: and agriculture, 83; and pastoralism, 77–78; steppes of, 78
Athabascan Indians, 58
Athens, Tex., 5
authority, 23, 32, 39, 40, 44, 72, 141; and clans, 37; and hierarchy, 38

Balkans, 78
Barnard and Company, 111
Barnard, George, 111, 116
Beale's Colony, Tex., 128
bears, 47, 48, 56
Beaver River, 113
Belén, N. Mex., 107
Bentura (San Juan Indian), 58-59; and Ute Indians, 60
Berlandier, Jean Louis, 33, 43, 46–49, 61, 67, 90, 91, 95, 110, 131, 134–36
Bidais Indians, 62, 122
Big Star (Comanche chief), 113–15
birth links, 18–19, 21, 41, 64
bison, 10, 23, 28, 33, 47, 66, 68, 70, 72, 73, 102, 103, 108, 124, 126, 141; availability of, 67, 71; and Comanches, 69; Comanche competition for, 137; horse-mounted hunting of, 54, 93; hunting of, 82, 83, 88; population of, 67; scarcity of, 29
Boas, Franz, 146
Bonnell, George W., 38
Botellos, Mexico, 128
Bourgmont, Étienne Veniard de, 92
brands (branding), 87, 91, 94, 142; Comanche, 90, 92; Mexican, 90; Spanish, 90
Brazos River, 111, 31, 34, 35, 38, 116
bride price, 95, 142
British Isles, 79
Brooke, George Mercer, 133
Bucareli, Tex., 110
Bucareli y Ursua, Antonio María, 53
Bueno y Bohorques, Francisco, 50, 94
Burnet, David G., 20, 21, 30, 31, 43, 68, 128
Burnett, Samuel Burk, 4, 5
Bustamante, Juan Domingo de, 50

Cabello, Domingo, 33–35, 42, 68, 109, 125
Cabeza Rapada (Comanche chief), 29, 34, 35, 39, 40, 64

Cache Creek, 70
Caddoan Indians, 35, 37, 38, 40, 53, 65; councils of, 126; and intermarriage with Comanches, 39, 119, 142; migration of, 7; and relations with Comanches, 6, 36, 72, 109, 141; religion of, 126; rituals of, 126; at San Sabá Mission, 126; and trade with Comanches, 99, 101, 109; and warfare with Apaches, 7, 63. *See also* Cadodachos, Caddos, Hainai, Iscanis, Jumanos, Nabedakioux, Nacodochitos, Nadacog, Nasones (Nasonis), Navadachos, Pananas, Panipiquet, Panipiquetes, Panis-Maha, Pawnees, Quitseys, Taovayas, Tahuacanos, Tejas, Vidaes (Bidais), Wacos, Wichitas, Xaranamas (Xaranames), Yuganis
Caddoans, Plains, 7, 109, 127
Caddos, 38, 55
Cadena, Ascencio, 122
Cádiz, 80
Camisa de Hierro (Comanche chief), 29, 34
Camisa de Yerro (Comanche chief), 34
Campbell, Thomas M., 5
Camp Holmes, 97
camps, 70; Apache, 104; and clan identification, 20, 21; Comanche, 26, 69, 72, 88, 99, 106, 113, 126, 140; 20; Plains Indian, 105; residents of, 20, 21
Canadian River, 4, 7, 8, 33, 51, 69, 88, 89, 98, 99, 108, 113, 114, 136
Canaguaipe (Comanche chief), 16, 20
Cañon de Don Juan Ugalde, 48
capitalism, 118
captives, 16, 50, 58, 59, 63, 97,104, 110, 111, 124; Apache, 107; Comanche, 26, 105, 107, 109, 132, 137; Navajo, 107; and New Mexico, 26; and trade, 60; Ute, 105, 107; women, 135, 137
Carlana (Apache chief), 50, 67
Carlana Indians, 132
Casañas, Fray Francisco, 127
Castro (Lipan Apache chief), 61
Catlin, George, 87, 93
cattle: in Antilles, 82; domestication of, 77, 78; in Iberia, 79
Chacón, Fernando de, 23, 107
Chama (Comanche chief), 71
charity, 103, 104
Chaves, Francisco Xavier, 20, 21, 29, 30, 33, 34, 36, 54, 64, 68–70, 83, 84, 109, 110, 125
Cherokee Indians, 8
Cheyenne Indians, 31, 55, 65, 102; and warfare with Comanches, 7
Chichimeca Indians, 84

Chickasaw Indians, 8, 110

Chihuahua, Mexico, 8, 9, 23, 80, 103

children: as captives, 50, 58–60, 124, 128, 137; Apache, 127; Comanche, 69, 70, 83, 97, 98, 113, 114; and language acquisition, 64; and warfare, 131

China, 77

Choctaw Indians, 8, 76

Chouteau, Auguste Pierre, 97

ciboleros, 82

Civilized Tribes, 65, 110, and relations with Comanches, 8

clans, 19, 21–23, 26, 29, 31–34, 44, 66, 67, 71, 92, 113, 125, 132, 133, 140, 141; and authority, 23, 35, 37, 38; demise of, 27, 28, 30; existence of, 23, 24, 32; hierarchy in, 35, 37; and names, 10, 19–24, 40, 104, 125, 128, 139, 140; and rank, 23; and residence, 20; and rivalry, 35–39; and segmentation, 32, 33, 35–39, 45; survival of, 28, 30

Clark, W. P., 65

Clear Fork Reservation, 9

Coahuila, Mexico, 8, 53, 54, 136

Cochití, 26

Codallos y Rabál, Joachín, 99

co-descendants, 19–21, 32, 33, 35, 37, 38, 43, 45, 125, 128, 131, 139, 140, 141; Comanche and Caddoan, 39; definition of, 18

Colorado, 6, 15, 24, 27, 33, 51, 56, 69, 85

Colorado River, 70

Comanche and Kiowa Reservation, 3, 4

Comanchería, 15, 30, 32, 48, 49, 61, 65, 68, 72, 71, 89, 99, 100, 107, 115, 116, 119, 126, 131, 134; and bison, 103

Comancheros, 106, 107, 108, 109, 116; and Josiah Gregg, 99

Comanches: and age, 44, 45; as allied with Caddoans, 35, 36, 63; as allied with Taovayas, 41; as allied with Utes, 50, 51; and altruism, 126, 128, 137, 143; and Americans, 7, 8; ancestors of, 22, 84, 87, 119, 125, 133, 139, 141; and antisocial behavior, 137; and Apaches, 51, 141; and authority, 35, 37, 38, 40, 72, 141; baptism of, 107; and bison, 67, 68; and bride price, 95, 142; and Caddoans, 35, 36, 65, 127, 141, 142; camps of, 20, 21, 34, 47, 48, 69–72, 88, 89, 99, 105, 106, 113, 114, 126, 129, 140; captives of, 8, 26, 50, 60, 63, 97, 104, 105, 107, 110, 111, 127, 128, 130–32, 135, 136; ceremonies of, 95; and charity from New Mexico, 104; as chiefs, 70, 98, 101, 112–15, 117, 118, 122, 126, 129; as children, 89, 97, 98, 100, 113, 114, 131, 142;

and Civilized Tribes, 8; clans of, 10, 13, 15, 19, 20–40, 54, 56, 66, 67, 71, 83, 84, 92, 108, 109, 113, 125, 128, 132, 133, 139, 140, 141; and segmentation, 35, 38, 140; co-descendants of, 128, 131, 139, 140, 141; and *Comancheros,* 99; and common ancestor, 43; and community, 10; and competition with Caddoans, 63; and competition for resources, 124, 125, 137, 141, 143; and competition for women, 134, 135; and conflict, 57; and cooperation, 34, 72, 84, 91, 126, 130, 141; and cooperation with Caddoans, 64, 126; and cooperation with Spanish, 16–18, 71; and cooperation with Utes, 87; and councils, 13, 15, 38, 40, 42–44, 114, 118, 126; and culture, 83, 84, 86, 87, 90, 94, 95, 125, 142, 146; and defense, 47, 48; and disease, 25, 32; divisions among, 43, 44; and dogs, 90, 91; and economics, 11, 101, 103, 118, 119, 142, 143; and environmental adaptation, 139; as fathers, 131, 140; as first mentioned by Spanish, 49; and food relief from New Mexico, 103; geographical separation of, 33, 37, 141; and gifts, 36, 95, 132, 142; and hierarchy, 10, 35, 37, 42–44, 70, 126, 141; and horses, 11, 29, 33, 47, 61, 62, 66–69, 74–76, 85–87, 90–95, 97, 101, 117, 142; and horsemanship, 87–89, 93; and hostilities, 11, 25, 26, 36, 50, 62, 63, 75, 76, 85, 98, 99, 104, 111, 113–16, 118, 121, 124, 128, 130–33, 135, 136, 140; and hunting, 23, 41, 47, 48, 93, 134; as husbands, 22; and influence, 40; and inheritance, 91–93, 95, 142; and intermarriage, 6, 36, 37, 39, 62, 64, 65, 73, 85, 86, 119, 131, 132, 140–42; and jealousies, 43–45, 115, 134, 137; and kinship, 21, 37, 65, 72, 73, 84, 91, 95, 103, 116, 117, 119, 125–28, 130, 131, 137, 138, 140, 143; and kinsmen, 126; and kin terms, 41, 44, 64, 108, 125, 139, 140; and Kiowas, 8, 142; language of, 64, 83, 125; and Lipans, 62, 133; and marriage, 19, 44, 45, 95, 134, 136, 142; and Mexico, 8; migration of, 7, 10, 31, 33, 49, 67–69, 71–73, 76, 89, 114, 141, 142; and migration to New Mexico, 10, 50, 56, 60, 85, 104; and migration to the plains, 51, 54, 55, 62, 66; and migration to Texas, 10, 30, 51, 53, 54, 64, 65, 132; morality of, 130, 131, 135; as mothers, 140; and mules, 47, 90, 92, 93, 97, 98, 100, 101; and New Mexico, 7, 11, 24, 25, 28, 85, 94, 96, 104–108, 132, 141, 142; and nomadism, 10, 30, 33, 46, 48, 49, 66, 68–72, 89, 93, 141; as old men, 41, 42; origins of, 56, 57, 60; and ownership, 90–93, 142; and pastoralism, 11, 49, 83, 85,

Comanches (*continued*)
86–90, 92–95, 142; and patrilineage, 19, 20,
140; and peace councils, 16, 61; and peace
with Apaches, 61, 133; and peace with New
Mexico, 6, 13, 15, 16, 17, 24, 25, 28, 132; and
Pecos peace conference, 42; and Plains Indians, 146; and politics, 39, 72; and polygyny,
44, 45, 134, 137; and poverty, 103; and prestige, 41; and property, 90, 92; and Pueblo Indians, 141; and raiding, 6, 8, 9, 26, 36, 43, 50,
54, 66–68, 74–76, 85, 87, 89, 94, 118, 126–29,
131, 132, 136, 137; and religion, 43, 125, 128,
141, 143; and rank, 10, 42, 44, 45, 72, 141; and
reproduction, 137, 140, 141; and residence,
10, 22, 33; and resources, 39, 40, 67; and retaliation, 131–33; rituals of, 16, 42–44, 47, 70,
95, 114, 125, 126, 128, 129, 130, 141, 143; rivalry
among, 27, 28, 35–38, 43–45, 131, 134; at San
Antonio, 110; at San Sabá Mission, 124, 126;
and segmentation, 36, 37; and sexual infidelity, 134, 135, 137; as Shoshones, 6; and
smoke lodge, 42, 43, 47, 48, 70, 118, 125, 127,
137, 141, 143; social behavior of, 91, 95, 103,
115, 116, 119, 128, 129, 130, 131, 137–39, 141, 143,
148; social organization of, 141; and social relationships, 72, 73; and split with Shoshones,
56–58; starvation of, 29, 32, 93, 103; at Taos,
25, 96–99, 132; as *techan*, 127; and Texas, 7–9,
11, 141, 142; and *tlatoleros*, 48, 126; and trade,
6, 7, 11, 25, 36, 70, 94–101, 103, 104, 108, 110,
111, 116–19, 132, 142, 143; and trade fairs, 96,
99, 105, 117; and trade with Americans, 8,
97–102, 111–14, 116; and trade with Caddoans,
99, 101, 109; and trade with Cheyennes, 102;
and trade goods, 96–98, 101; and trade with
Indians, 99, 101; and trade with New Mexico, 11, 16, 25, 96, 97, 98, 99, 105, 106, 108,
109, 116, 117; and trade with Texas, 11, 110,
111; and trading posts, 111; traditions of, 30,
57, 84–88, 90, 92, 95, 119, 125, 133; and transhumance, 89; and transportation, 93; and
United States, 9; and Utes, 6, 56, 60, 85–87,
94, 95, 105, 131, 132, 136, 141, 142; and
vengeance, 131–33, 135; and violence, 11, 12, 25,
50, 62, 75, 99, 104, 116, 121, 124, 125, 127, 128,
131, 133–38, 143; and war councils, 36; and
warfare, 6, 12, 32, 49–51, 66, 67, 118, 121, 124,
126, 129, 130, 131, 134, 136, 143; and warfare
with Apaches, 7, 8, 17, 34, 35, 41, 46, 50, 53,
54, 60–62, 127, 132, 133, 137; and warfare with
Arapahos, 7, 8; and warfare with Caddoans,
63; and warfare with Cheyennes, 7, 8; and
warfare with Kiowas, 7; and warfare with New
Mexico, 15, 16, 24–29, 140; and warfare with
Osages, 116; and warfare with Pawnees, 35, 71;
and warfare with Utes, 58, 66, 67, 104; as warriors, 41; and warrior societies, 129, 130; as
wives, 11, 134, 137, 142; as women, 11, 12, 46,
92, 89, 97, 98, 100, 113, 114, 129, 130, 134, 135,
137, 142; as young men, 41. *See also* Cuchanecs;
Jupes; Pibians; Tenewas; Yamparicas
Commerce of the Prairies, 101
community, 10
competition, 40–43, 61, 66, 72, 126, 133, 141,
143; Comanche and Lipan, 62; over bison,
67; for resources, 71, 124, 137; for women,
134–36
Concha, Fernando de la, 29, 36, 67, 71, 103
Conner, John (Delaware Indian), 111
conquest of Mexico, 80, 84
conquistadors, 79
cooperation, 39, 40, 42, 43, 45, 56, 61, 72, 104,
126, 141, 143; Apache and Spanish, 53; among
Comanches, 34, 71, 91, 130; Comanche and
Caddoan, 63; Comanche and Lipan, 62; Comanche and Spanish, 16–18, 71, 106; Comanche and Ute, 87; and economics, 103,
119; among kin, 84; Pueblo Indian and
Navajo, 58, 59
Corbera, Fray Francisco, 59
Cordero (Comanche chief), 69
corrals: Andalusian, 88; Comanche, 88; and
herding, 87; in Sonora, 88; in Tamaulipas, 88
Cortés, Hernan, 80, 145
Cota de Malla (Comanche chief), 34
Council House Fight, 8
councils, 38, 42–44, 61, 114, 118; Comanche, 126
Cowhead Mesa, Tex., 121
Creek Indians, 8
creeks, 69, 70
Crow Indians, 55
Cruzat y Gongora, Gervasio, 105
Cuartelejos, 51, 85, 106
Cuchanecs (Comanche clan), 13, 19–24, 27–29,
39, 40, 44, 56, 132, 140; and assassination of
Toro Blanco, 15; and authority, 34; character-
istics of, 83; cooperation among, 34; and
factionalism, 35; and hierarchy, 34; and *orien-*
tales, 32, 34–36, 54, 83, 109, 141; and *occi-*
dentales, 32, 33, 34, 35; and relations with
Caddoans, 36; and rivalry, 35, 36, and seg-
mentation, 32; traditions of, 125
Cuchanticas (Comanche clan), 13
Cuerno Verde (elder), 24–27, 39, 45

Cuerno Verde (younger), 24, 26, 28, 29, 39, 45; and defeat by Anza, 15
Cuervo y Valdez, Francisco, 85
Cuetaninabeni (Comanche chief), 15, 16, 134, 135
cultural adaptation, 146, 147, 148
cultural determinism, 10, 148, 149; and hypotheses, 146; as mythology, 147; and rejection of scientific approach, 147; and scientific rationality, 146; unverifiable nature of, 147
cultural persistence, 146, 147, 148
culture, 94, 125, 142, 149; as beyond nature, 147; and biology, 146; definition of, 11, 83; and environment, 146; and history, 146; as an objective entity, 147; as a product of individual actions, 147; as a unit of study, 147

Dallas, Tex., 5
Darwin, Charles, 148, 149
deer, 47, 48, 68
Delaware Indians, 110, 111, 116
de Mézières, Athanase, 33, 36, 54, 64, 63, 66, 68, 69, 92–94, 109, 127, 132
descendants, 56, 92; definition of, 18; and tradition, 84
disease, 23, 28, 30, 32, 136, 140; among horses, 30; smallpox, 25, 29
division of labor, 11, 100–104, 119, 143
Dodge, Henry, 70, 88
domestic animals, 76–79, 84, 90; domestication of, 77; and Europe, 79; and husbandry, 77; inheritance of, 77; and management, 77; and ownership, 77, 95; products of, 77; reproduction of, 77, 92, 95, 142
Domínguez, Francisco Atanasio, 29, 69, 89, 96, 97–100, 107
Domínguez-Velez de Escalante expedition, 24
Double Mountain Fork (Brazos River), 121
drought, 28, 66, 102, 140; in New Mexico, 29
Durango, Mexico, 8, 54

economics, 11, 45, 49, 54, 72, 101, 119, 137, 141; Comanche, 103, 118; Comanche and New Mexico, 6, 7; effect of pastoralism on, 95; and environment, 139; and kinship, 109; and marriage, 95; and plains, 67; and production, 143; and social behavior, 100, 109; and specialization, 103; and territoriality, 103; and war, 134
Ecueracapa (Comanche chief), 6, 16–18, 20–22, 24, 28–30, 34, 35, 39, 40, 44, 45, 64, 71, 72, 103, 106, 132, 139; as elected leader of Comanches, 15

El Cañon, Tex., 53
El Chama (Comanche chief), 28
El Cuartelejo, 85
El Embudo, N. Mex., 131
El Español (Comanche chief), 34
El Guaquangas (Comanche chief), 34
El Lobito (Comanche chief), 34
El Manco (Comanche chief), 34
El Paso, Tex., 16
El Ronco (Kiowa chief), 46, 48
El Sordo (Comanche chief), 36–39, 44, 45, 57, 141
El Sordo affair, 36, 37
El Sorrillo (Comanche chief), 34
El Surdo (Comanche chief), 34
Elliot, James, 101
empiricism, 145, 146, 149
Encantime (Comanche chief), 28
England, 76
environment, 49, 54, 72, 76, 102, 103, 118, 125, 136, 137; and adaptation, 139; and the Americas, 84
Escalchufines, 51, 104
Ethnological Field Study Group of the Santa Fe Laboratory of Anthropology, 57
Ewers, John C., 91
exchange rates, 96, 100, 101
exploitation, 119
extortion, 118
Extremadura, 80

false dichotomy, 147, 148
Fathers, 19, 64; and clans, 23, 140; and war, 131
Febre, Louis, 68
Fernandez, Martín, 74
Fertile Crescent, 78
Flores Mogollon, Juan Ygnacio, 105, 106, 117
Flórez, Manuel Antonio, 61
Fort Gibson, 97
Fort Sill, 4, 5
Fort Smith, 97
Fort Worth Stock Show, 5
forty-niners, 8, 108
Fowler, Jacob, 102, 108, 118
France, 78
Freeman, Derek, 147
French, 29, 33, 68, 69
Frio River, 53

Gaignard, J., 69
Galisteo, N. Mex., 26

Gálvez, Bernando de, 63
game animals, 66, 67, 134
ganado mayor, 80
ganado menor, 80
García de Mora, Juan, 105, 106
García, María de Carmen, 128
Garduño, Bartolomé, 51
Garza County, Tex., 121
genízaros, 107, 127
geography, 37, 140, 141; and trade, 118
gifts, 11, 104, 122, 126, 132, 142; and horses, 95;
    and trade, 111–14, 116, 118
Gila Apaches, 16
Glass, Anthony, 69, 89, 90, 101, 135, 137
Goodnight, Charles, 4
Great Basin, 6, 139, 146
Great Plains, 6, 51, 54, 75, 139, 146
Green, Robert B., 108
Gregg, Josiah, 70, 83, 87, 88, 90, 91, 93, 100,
    101, 108, 109, 131, 132, 136; and *Comancheros,*
    99; and trade with Comanches, 97, 98
Groom, B. B., 4
groups, 17, 20, 21, 77, 103, 139, 146; and culture,
    83
Guadalupe River, 48, 79
Guaquangas (Comanche chief), 135
Guerrero, José Cristóbal (Comanche Indian),
    107
Gutiérrez, Joseph, 63
Gutiérrez, Juan Antonio, 123, 124

Hachacas (Comanche chief), 34
Hainai Indians, 62
Harrold and Ikard, 4
Hellenistic civilization, 76
herding, 76, 78, 94, 142; cattle, 79, 80; Co-
    manche, 89; goats, 80; horses, 79; in Iberia,
    79; in New Mexico, 89; and pasturage, 88;
    pigs, 80; sheep, 80; in Spain, 89; swine, 79
Herodotus, 79
Hichapat (Comanche chief), 16
Hidatsa Indians, 55
hierarchy, 35, 39, 41–45, 70, 126; and clans, 37,
    141
Hill, Christopher, 9
Hill Country (Texas), 46, 47, 90, 134
Hoebel, E. Adamson, 56, 91, 92
Hois (Comanche clan), 32, 92
Ho'is. *See* Hois (Comanche clan)
Hoish. *See* Hois (Comanche clan)
Hopi Indians, 76
Horn, Sara Ann, 128

horsemanship: Comanche, 87, 88, 93; New
    Mexican, 87; Spanish, 87
horses, 10, 11, 16, 25, 33, 46–48, 53–56, 61–63,
    66–68, 71–76, 94, 102, 105, 109–11, 114–17,
    119, 123, 124, 126, 127, 131, 135, 141, 142; and
    Andalucía, 82; and bride price, 95; Co-
    manche, 69, 85–89, 91–94; and defense, 29;
    and disease, 29; domestication of, 77, 78; and
    Europe, 78; as gifts, 95; herding, 89; and
    hunting, 29, 82, 93; and Iberia, 79; and inher-
    itance, 92, 94; and Mexico, 88; and New
    Mexico, 26, 27, 81, 82, 90; and pastoralism,
    85; and pasturage, 89; and Pueblo Indians, 6;
    and Spain, 88; from Pecos, 101; and tack, 86;
    and trade, 93, 97, 101; and transportation, 29,
    82, 93; uses of, 93; Ute, 86
Horta, Ginés de Herrera, 82
hostilities, 11, 35, 50, 53, 76, 120–24, 133, 135, 136;
    Caddoans and Apaches, 62; and Comanches,
    28, 62, 85, 128, 132, 138; Comanches and
    Apaches, 61–63, 104, 132; Comanche and
    Caddoans, 63; Comanches and New Mexico,
    24–26; Comanches and Texas, 36; in Europe,
    78; and trade, 98, 99, 104, 111–18
Huanacoruco (Comanche chief), 22, 23
Huns, 76
hunting, 47, 48, 64, 71, 80, 102; of bison, 23,
    68, 82, 88, 93, 108; mounted, 82, 88, 93; and
    war, 134
Hurtado, Juan Paez, 51, 58, 104

Iberia, 79
Idaho, 56
Indian Territory (Oklahoma), 3, 4, 8, 65, 97,
    102, 110
indios bárbaros, 60, 74
inheritance, 95; and clan names, 19, 21; and Co-
    manches, 91–94; of domestic animals, 77; of
    horses, 91–93; of mules, 92; of property, 91;
    and women, 92
intermarriage, 56, 58–61, 63, 72, 73, 119, 141, 142;
    and segmentation, 140; between Comanches
    and Apaches, 62, 131; between Comanches
    and Caddoans, 64, 65, 127; between Coman-
    ches and Mexicans, 131; between Comanches and New
    Mexicans, 132; between Comanches and
    Pueblo Indians, 131; between Comanches
    and Spanish, 131; between Comanches and
    Texans, 131; between Comanches and Utes,
    85, 86, 131; and trade, 110
Ionies Indians, 38
Iscanis Indians, 62

Italy, 78
Iturbide, Augstín de, 61

Jalisco, Mexico, 54
James, Thomas, 87, 88, 100, 108, 111–15, 117, 118
Jémez, N. Mex., 59
Jicarilla Apaches, 15, 50, 104, 127; and captives, 136; children, 136; and trade with New Mexico, 106; and warfare with Comanches, 60, 132, 136; women, 136
Jicarilla Valley, N. Mex., 50, 51
John, Elizabeth A. H., 10
Jordan, Terry, 79, 83, 90
Joyoso (Comanche chief), 36, 37
Júez (Comanche clan), 32
Jumanos, 33, 63
Jupes (Comanche clan), 13, 19–21, 24, 28, 31, 35, 40, 44, 66, 71, 140; births, 32; and decline of lineage, 25, 27, 30; migration of, 30, 32; and warfare with New Mexico, 26

Kansas, 33, 65
Kansas Indians, 51
Kant, Immanuel, 146
Kavanagh, Thomas, 10
Keechies Indians, 38
Keiuna (Comanche chief), 46. See also Quelluna
Ketumsee (Comanche chief), 134
kinship, 5, 6, 10–12, 37–43, 45, 56, 58–60, 64, 65, 70, 72, 73, 76, 84, 91, 95, 104, 106, 107, 109, 111, 116, 118, 126, 128, 138–41, 144, 149; and ancestors, 18, 19; and birth-links, 18; and co-descendants, 18, 19; Comanche, 5, 137; Comanche and Caddoan, 127; Comanche and Ute, 85; and descendants, 18; and economics, 103; and language, 125; metaphorical, 5, 130; and physical traits, 125; and Quanah Parker, 5; and residence, 21; and trade, 105, 117, 119, 143
kinsmen, 126; and antisocial behavior, 40; and cooperation, 40
kin terms, 10, 19, 40, 41, 44, 45, 64, 104, 125, 139; Comanche, 140
Kiowa Indians, 31, 65, 108; camps of, 89; and intermarriage with Comanches, 119, 142; and overgrazing, 89; and peace with Comanches, 7; and warfare with Comanches, 7
!Kung, 76
Kwahadas (Comanche clan), 4

La Alameda, N. Mex., 26
La Bahía del Espíritu Santo, Tex., 110

La Boca Partida (Comanche chief), 34
La Casa de Palo, 40; and Comanche councils, 6, 13, 15
La Ciénega, N. Mex., 26
La Xicarilla, 50. See also Jicarillas
Lafora, Nicolás, 53
lances, 47, 79, 80–83, 88, 94, 142; used in Spanish pastoralism, 82
language, 64, 83, 127
lassos, 94, 142
Levant, 79
Lewis, John S., 101
Lipan Apaches, 41, 46, 47, 53, 54; and relations with Comanches, 61; and warfare with Comanches, 35, 62
Lipiyanas Apaches, 41
livestock, 54, 59, 80, 81, 88, 124, 128, 142; branding of, 94; cattle, 80, 86; and Comanches, 137; and Comanche raids, 136; and Comanche trade, 99, herding of, 79, 94; horses, 74, 76, 79–81, 86, 90; and Mexico, 136; mules, 81, 90; and New Mexico, 26; and production, 76; and reproduction, 92, 94
Llano Estacado, 31
Lobos, 129; rituals of, 129; and sacrifice, 129; and warfare, 129
Los Arkansas, 63
Louisiana, 101, 102, 127

Mackenzie, Ranald, 4
Madrid, Roque, 58
Maese, Domingo, 110
Mandan Indians, 55
Manuel (Comanche Indian), 108
manufactured goods, 102, 104
Marcy, Randolph B., 43, 88, 89, 92, 134
Mares, José, 34, 110
Marín del Valle, Francisco, 98, 106, 117
marriage, 19, 37, 58, 72, 136; and bride price, 95; and ceremony, 95; and Comanches, 95, 134, 142; between Comanches and Caddoans, 39; between Comanches and Lipans, 62; between Comanches and Tahuacanos, 38; between Comanches and Wichitas, 36; and economics, 95; and polygyny, 134; and rituals, 95; and trade, 108
Martín, Alejandro, 107, 108, 110
Martín, Sebastian, 75
Martínez, Antonio María, 61
Martínez, Felix, 51
Martínez Pacheco, Rafael, 110, 135
Matamoros, Mexico, 136

material resources, 10, 11, 56, 60, 66, 67, 69–73, 124, 125, 133, 137, 142, 143; competition for, 62
matrilineage, 19, 59
McKnight, John, 115
Mead, Margaret, 147
Medina River, 48, 62
Mendinueta, Fermín de, 25, 26
Mendoza, Gaspar de, 107
Mesa del Norte, Mexico, 80
Mescalero Apaches, 35, 41
Meseta, Spain (Mesetan), 79; herding, 80
Mexican War for Independence, 7, 61, 110
Mexico, 8, 65, 82, 84, 90, 133; and agriculture, 77; and Comanche raids, 8, 54, 136, 137; geography of, 80; and intermarriage with Comanches, 131; and ranching, 8, 88; and relations with Comanches, 137; and *vaqueros,* 88; and warfare with Comanches, 131
Mexico City, 53, 61
Miera y Pacheco, Bernardo, 24
migration, 49–51, 56, 68, 72; and Comanches, 76, 141; Comanche and Caddoan, 65; of Comanches to New Mexico, 60; of Comanches to southern plains, 62, 66; of Comanches to Texas, 54, 64; European, 78; and transhumance, 89
minimum viable populations, 28
Mirabal, Fray Juan de, 50, 127
missions: San Lorenzo de la Santa Cruz, 53; San Sabá, 53, 63, 121–24
Mississippi, 101
Missouri Indians, 102
Missouri River, 65
Molina, Fray Miguel de, 63, 121, 122
Mooney, James, 32, 54
morality, 130, 131
mothers, 18, 19, 20, 38, 64; and clans, 23, 140
mules, 16, 47, 81, 98, 102, 109, 119, 135; and Comanches, 69, 90, 93; and Missouri, 100; and trade, 97, 100, 101
Murdock, George Peter, 147
Musquisachi (Ute chief), 67

Nabedakioux Indians, 63
Nacodochitos Indians, 62
Nacogdoches, Tex., 110
Nadacog Indians, 63
Nambé, N. Mex., 26
Nasones Indians, 63
Natchitoches, La., 33, 63, 101
nation, 133

Nations of the North, 63
natural selection, 148; and disprovability, 149; and hypotheses, 149
Navadachos Indians, 62
Navajos, 16, 59, 65; and captives, 107; and pastoralism, 85, 94, and tradition, 94, and Utes, 58
Naysaras (Comanche chief), 71
Near East, 90; and agriculture, 77; and domestication of animals, 78; and pastoralism, 85
Nebraska, 51
Neighbors, Robert S., 38, 60, 64, 91, 93, 134, 135
Neolithic Era, 77
Neosho River, 97
New Mexicans, 114, 115
New Mexico, 8, 11, 30–33, 39, 50, 51, 55, 59, 64, 65, 67, 70, 71, 73–76, 90, 91, 110, 112, 133; births in, 60; and bison hunting, 82; and captive trade, 104, 105; and *ciboleros,* 83, 88; and Comanches, 6, 34, 66, 94, 108, 141; Comanches migrate to, 49, 54, 56; Comanches residents of, 107; and *Comancheros,* 99; and cooperation with Comanches, 16, 118, 139, herding, 88; and horses, 54, 81, 82, 92; and intermarriage, 60, 119, 142; and livestock, 142; missions in, 29; and pastoralism, 80–82, 85; and peace with Comanches, 6, 15–17, 24, 28; Pueblo Indians of, 102, 103, 107; and Pueblo Revolt, 86; and raiding, 6, 15, 86, 118, 127; and relations with Comanches, 109; and social relationships, 58; and Spanish colonialism, 80; and trade with Comanches, 6, 7, 25, 96, 97, 99, 100, 103, 106, 107, 109; and trade regulations, 106, 116, 117; and Utes, 60, 86, 94; and *vaqueros,* 87; and warfare, 15, 118; and warfare with Apaches, 139; and warfare with Comanches, 6, 15, 24–26, 28, 29, 127, 131, 136, 140
New Spain, 74, 83; geography of, 80; and pastoralism, 85
New World, 84
Niantine (Comanche chief), 71
Nolan, Philip, 101
nomadism, 48, 49, 68, 76; Comanche, 66, 93, 141; and geographic dispersal, 33; and pastoralism, 77
North America, 90
North Canadian River, 113
northern plains, 72
Nueces River, 53
Nuevo Leon, Mexico, 128
nutrition, 118

offspring, 18
Ojo Caliente, N. Mex., 6, 25, 26, 60, 104, 107; and Comanche trade, 105, 106
Ojo Caliente River, 26
Ojo del Agua, Tex., 47
Oklahoma, 33, 70, 141
Olavide y Michelena Henrique, 106
Old World, 77, 83–85
Onacama (Comanche chief), 71
Oñate, Juan de, 80, 82
Opler, Marvin, 86
Origin of the Species, 148
Ortiz, Francisco Xavier, 92
Osage Indians, 65; and warfare with Caddoans, 109; and warfare with Comanches, 7, 116, 133
Oso Ballo (Comanche chief), 36
ownership, 92, 100, 119; and Comanches, 90, 93; of domestic animals, 77, 95, 142; of horses, 86, 91, 93; by individuals, 90, 91; and property, 91; and social behavior, 91
Oxamaquea (Comanche Indian), 17, 18, 20, 41, 45

Pacheco, Juan, 49
Paloma Apaches, 51, 62, 104
Palos, Spain, 80
Panana Indians, 62
Panipiques, 70, 109
Panipiquet, 62
Panipiquetes, 63
Panis-Maha Indians, 64
Paraginanchi (Comanche chief), 15, 16
parents: relationship with children, 41, 139, 140; and influence, 41
Parker family, 4, 5
Parker, Cynthia Ann, 5; marriage to Peta Nocona, 4
Parker, Isaac, 4
Parker, Quanah (Comanche chief), 3, 4, 65; celebrity status of, 5; and kinship, 5, 6; as Kwahada chief, 4; as metaphor for Comanche society, 6
Parker, Topsannah, 4
Paruanarimuco (Comanche chief), 24, 28, 30, 71, 72
Pasahuoques (Comanche chief), 22, 125
pastoralism, 45, 86, 102, 141; as an adaptation, 77; and Africa, 78; in the Americas, 80; and Andalucía, 80; and Apaches, 85; and Asia, 78; and cattle, 79; characteristics of, 76; classic view of, 93; and Comanches, 85, 94, 142; and economics, 95, 142; and environment, 95,

142; and Europe, 78; as a heritable trait, 77; and horses, 11, 81; and Iberia, 79; and Mexico, 80; and Navajos, 85; and the Near East, 85; necessary and sufficient conditions for, 77; and New Mexico, 80–82, 85; and New Spain, 85; and the Old World, 85; and production, 49; and Pueblo Indians, 85; and social behavior, 92; and Spanish, 80, 87, 85, 142; and tradition, 85; and Utes, 85, 87
pasturage, 10, 66, 68–71, 124; and herding, 88; and Old World tradition, 83; rotation of, 89
patrilineage, 20, 23; and Comanches, 19, 140
Pawnee Indians, 51, 55, 62, 64, 69–71; and warfare with Apaches, 63; and warfare with Comanches, 7, 35
peace: and Comanches, 13, 15; between Comanches, Cheyennes and Arapahos, 8; between Comanches and Lipans, 61, 133; between Comanches and New Mexico, 13, 15–17, 28, 36, 105, 106, 132; between Comanches and Texas, 36, 110; and councils, 13, 15, 16, 28, 61, 132; and gifts, 115; and rituals, 16; treaties, 125; between Utes and Navajos, 58
Pecos, N. Mex., 29, 50; and Apaches, 132; and Comanche raids, 26, 28; and drought, 29; peace ceremony and treaty at, 22, 34, 42, 107; and theft of Comanche horses, 90, 91; and trade fairs, 13, 104, 106, 109
Pecos River, 31, 35, 107
Peña, Juan de Dios, 69, 71, 72
Penxaye Apaches, 49, 132
Peta Nocona (Comanche chief), 4
Peters' Colony, 38
Pibians (Comanche clan), 32
Picurís, N. Mex., 25, 49, 51, 60; and Comanche raids, 26
Piedra Lumbre, N. Mex., 58
Pike's Peak, 27
Pino, Pedro Bautista, 95, 134
Pisimampat (Comanche chief), 16, 34
Pisimampi (Comanche chief), 34
Plains Indians, 41, 43, 66, 67, 102, 133, 146; and bison hunting, 82, 83; history of, 75; and ownership of horses, 91; typical characteristics of, 146; and warfare, 124
Platte River, 51
Poca Ropa (Lipan chief), 61
Pojaque, N. Mex., 75
polygyny, 44, 45, 136, 137
population viability analysis, 28
poverty, 103

presidios: Monclova, 54; San Juan Bautista, 54; San Luis de las Amarillas, 53; San Xavier, 53; Santa Rosa de Aguaverde, 54
profit, 199; motivation for, 100; in Comanche trade, 100
property, 91, 92, 100; and ownership of domestic animals, 91
Provincias Internas, 23, 34, 42, 44, 68
proximate causation, 148, 149
Pueblo Indians, 49, 51, 58, 65, 74, 99, 106–108; and Comanches, 141; and horses, 6; and intermarriage with Comanches, 131; and Navajos, 59; and Spanish pastoralism, 94; and trade, 94; and Utes, 86; and warfare with Comanches, 131
Pueblo Revolt, 59, 86
Pujavara (Comanche chief), 69, 71, 72
Pujibuipuja (Comanche chief), 34
Purgatoire River, 71

Quahuahacante (Comanche chief), 125
Quartelejo Indians, 51. See also Cuartelejos
Quegüe (Comanche chief), 22, 23, 107
Quelluna (Comanche chief), 46, 48
Quenarucaro (Comanche chief), 34
Queremilla (Comanche chief), 28
Quihuaeantime (Comanche chief), 16
Quinacaraco (Comanche chief), 34
Quitsey Indians, 63

raiding, 43, 50, 54, 58, 66, 67, 75, 120, 126, 131, 128, 136; and Apaches, 86; and Comanches, 76, 85, 94, 127, 132, 137; and horses, 61, 68, 85–87; and rituals, 129; and Utes, 85, 86, 94
ranching, 79, 80
rank, 23, 42, 45, 72, 141; and age, 41, 44; and birth order, 41, 44, and material goods, 41
retaliation, 132, 131, 133
Red River, 31, 32, 35–38, 69, 88, 124
relatives, 37
religion, 125, 128, 141, 143; and ancestor worship, 43; and rituals, 43; tribal, 43
reproduction, 77; and Comanches, 137, 141; detriments to, 23; and domestic animals, 77; and effects on clans, 23, 24; female and male strategies for, 134; and mammals, 134; and pastoralist tradition, 95; and polygyny, 134; and sons, 23, 24, 140; and tradition, 84
Republic of Texas, 8, 110
residence, 45, 56; and Comanche settlement patterns, 21; and communities, 21, 22; and groups, 21

Rio Arriba, N. Mex., 74, 75, 108
Rio Bravo del Norte, 61. See also Rio Grande
Rio Conejos, 26
Rio del Norte, 30. See also Rio Grande
Rio de Mermellón, 34, 64, 69
Rio de Napeste, 24. See also Arkansas River
Rio Grande, 8, 16, 25, 53, 80, 108, 133, 136. See also Rio Bravo del Norte; Rio del Norte
Rio Salado, 69
Ripperdá, Juan María, barón de, 33, 53
rituals, 43, 44, 47, 70, 125, 127, 128, 137, 141, 143; and Comanche marriage, 95; and raids, 129; and smoke lodge, 42, 114, 126
rivalries, 39, 45, 134; and clans, 38; at Comanche councils, 43, 44; and Cuchanecs, 35, 36, 37; and warfare, 131
Rivera, Pedro, 66, 90
rivers, 69, 70
Rocky Mountains, 6, 27
Roe, Frank, 76
Rollins, John, 133
Rosas, Luis de, 86
Rubí, marques de, 53
Ruíz, José Francisco, 42, 43, 46, 48, 61, 70, 91, 93, 95, 110, 126

saddles, 82
Salado Creek, 71
Salazar y Villaseñor, José Chacón Medina, marques de la Peñuela, 105
Salcedo, Manuel María de, 36
Salcedo, Nemesio, 23
Salt Fork (Arkansas River), 111–16
Salvador (Pawnee Indian), 63
Samoa, 147
Sampampia (Comanche chief), 71
San Antonio de Béxar, 23, 32, 34, 35, 46, 48, 51, 53, 54, 61, 65, 109, 124, 133, 135, 137; and Comanche residents, 110; and Comanche trade, 110
San Antonio Mountain, 8, 15, 25, 131
San Carlos de los Jupes, 24, 30
San Juan, N. Mex., 59, 104; and Comanche raids 26; and Utes, 60; and Ute raids, 86
San Juan Indians, 58, 74
San Luis Potosí, Mexico, 54
San Marcos River, 53
San Marcos, Tex., 61
San Miguel del Vado, N. Mex., 107, 108
San Sabá massacre, 53, 121, 123, 124, 126, 127, 132, 137
San Sabá Mission, 63, 121–24

San Sabá River, 48, 53, 63, 121
Sandía, N. Mex., 26
Sandoval, Felipe de, 70, 109
Sangre de Cristo Mountains, 75
Santa Anna (Comanche chief), 92
Santa Clara, N. Mex., 107
Santa Clara Indians, 74
Santa Cruz de la Cañada, N. Mex., 26, 74, 75, 108
Santa Fe, N. Mex., 23, 33, 35, 75, 94, 97, 104, 107, 108, 110, 111, 114, 117, 133, 135, 137; and Apaches, 50; and Comanches, 15, 34, 36; and Comanche raids, 26; and Utes, 86
Santa Fe Trail, 82
Santiesteban, Fray Joseph, 122, 124
Sariarioco (Comanche chief), 36. *See also* El Sordo
Sartre, Pierre, 68, 69
Satren, Pierre, 33
Scandinavia, 79
Schoolcraft, Henry Rowe, 60, 64, 93
scientific rationality, 146
Seminole Indians, 8
Senaco (Comanche chief), 43
Serna, Cristóbal de la, 75, 105, 131
Sevilla, Spain, 80
sexual behavior, 136; evolution of, 134; and infidelity, 134, 135, 137
Shaw, Jim, 111
sheep, 59, 89
Sherburne, John, 89
Shoshone Indians, 6, 55, 57, 65, 73, 141; and Comanches, 56
Sibley, John, 101
siblings, 19
Sierra Blanca Apaches, 51
Sierra Blanca Mountains, 16, 26, 51, 132
sign language, 65
Sinaloa, Mexico, 8, 54
Sioux Indians, 54, 55, 72
skunks, 47
smallpox, 25, 29
Smith, Adam, 100, 103
smoke lodge and ritual, 47, 70, 118, 127, 137, 141, 143
Snake Indians, 65
social behavior, 10–12, 17, 41–43, 45, 48, 56, 60, 70, 92, 95, 103, 107, 109, 111, 114–18, 125, 128, 131, 137, 139–41, 144, 149; and Comanche Lobo warriors, 130; Comanches and New Mexico, 6, 7; and kinship, 91; and mothers, 18; and ownership, 91; and private property,

91; towards kin, 5, and trade, 97–100, 110, 119, 120, 143
social organization, 45, 76, 139, 141
social relationships, 11, 49, 56, 58, 60–62, 64, 65, 72, 73, 92, 105, 106, 111, 113, 116; Comanches and Caddoans, 109; Comanches and New Mexico, 109; Comanches and Texas, 109
social sciences, 146, 148
sociology, 147
Socorro, N. Mex., 60
Somiquaso (Comanche chief), 23, 108
Sonocat (Comanche chief), 16
Sonora, Mexico, 88
South America, 77
southern plains, 6, 10, 31, 49, 54–56, 62, 63, 66, 68, 72, 73, 89, 103, 108, 109, 125, 137, 141, 142
Soxas (Comanche chief), 35–37, 39, 40, 44, 45, 110, 125
Spanish: American colonies of, 79, 80, 84; and American immigrants, 7; and American traders in Texas, 36; and Apaches, 51, 53, 139; and Bourbon reforms, 27; cavalry of, 88; colonial administration of, 35; and Comanches, 6, 16, 17, 24, 25, 28, 133, 137; and conquest of Mexico, 145; and cooperation with Comanches, 16–18, 71, 139; and culture, 94, 142; and defense, 27; and frontier pacification policy, 24; and herding, 82, 88–90; and horses, 93; and intermarriage with Comanches, 131; military campaigns of, 15, 16, 18, 25, 26, 49, 60, 67, 71, 124, 136, 139; missions of, 7, 29, 51, 53, 63, 85, 88, 121–24; and New Mexico, 6, 13, 15–17, 27–29, 58, 59, 75, 76, 80, 82, 85, 86, 88, 142; and pastoralism, 80, 85, 87, 88, 90, 94, 142; and peace, 17, 27, 28; presidios of, 48, 51, 53, 54, 61, 88, 122–24, 133; and ranching, 80, 88, 90; saddles of, 82; as settlers, 7, 26, 80; and social relationships with Comanches, 72; and Texas, 7, 36, 51, 53, 54, 101, 124, 133; traditions of, 87, 90, 93, 94, 95; and Utes, 6; as *vaqueros*, 83, 88; and war with Apaches, 61; and war with Comanches, 6, 25–29, 54, 60, 61, 131, 136
Staked Plains, 31
starvation, 32, 103; and Cuchanecs, 29; and Jupes, 30
subsistence, 68, 76, 103
Sun Dance, 43
supply and demand, 101, 102, 119, 143

Tabequena (Comanche chief), 97
tack, 82, 87, 94, 142; Spanish, 86; Ute, 86

Taguayases Indians, 33, 35
Tahuacano Indians, 37, 57, 61, 62, 64, 65, 127;
and intermarriage with Comanches, 36, 38,
141
Tahuichimpia (Comanche Indian), 17, 18, 20, 41
Tah-wac-caro Indians, 38
Tamaulipas, Mexico, 8, 88, 136
Tanague Indians, 63
Tanquegüe (Comanche chief), 22
Tanqueruara (Comanche chief), 71
Taos Indians, 25, 49, 99, 108
Taos, N. Mex, 6, 15, 25, 50, 51, 59, 63, 68, 75, 85,
127; and Apaches, 132; and captive trade, 60,
104; and Comanche trade, 96, 98, 99, 117,
132; and pastuarge, 69, 89; and trade fairs, 13,
96, 99, 100, 106, 109, 117; and warfare with
Comanches, 13, 131, 132
Taovaizes Indians, 64
Taovayas Indians, 35, 36, 40, 62, 64, 109, 124,
127; and Comanches, 41, 69
techan, 64, 127
Tejanos, 46, 48, 65, 99
Tejas Indians, 62, 63, 122, 123
Ten-a-wish Indians, 38
Tenewas (Comanche clan), 31, 38, 140, 141; and
intermarriage with Caddoans, 39
Terreros, Fray Alonso Giraldo de, 122–24
Tewa Indians, 58
Texas Rangers, 5
Texas State Fair, 5
Texas, 3, 31–36, 46, 47, 54, 60, 61, 65, 69, 70, 73,
88, 127, 141; and Anglo-Americans, 30; cattle-
men from, 3, 4; and Comanches, 7, 9, 109,
137, 141; Comanche migration to, 6; and Comanche trade, 99, 110, 111, 116; and horses,
68; Indians of, 92–94, 102, 131; and intermarriage with Comanches, 119, 131, 142; and
raiding, 68, 118; and Rangers, 4; and Spanish, 7, 101, 109, 124; and trade fairs, 109; and
warfare with Comanches, 8, 118, 131; and warfare between Comanches and Apaches, 133
Tichinalla (Comanche chief), 16
tlatoleros, 16, 48, 70, 126
Tlaxcala Indians, 84
Tomanaguene (Comanche Indian), 17, 18, 20,
41
Tomé, 107, 127; and Comanche raids, 26
Tomnu, Joseph (San Juan Indian), 58, 59
Tonkawa Indians, 122
Toro Blanco (Comanche chief), 17, 24, 28, 125;
assassination of, 15
Torres, Cristóbal, 74, 75, 85

Torres, Diego, 105, 106
Torrey's Post No. 2, 118
Torrey's Trading House, 111
Tosacondata (Comanche chief), 16, 22, 132
Tosaporua (Comanche chief), 22
Tosapoy (Comanche chief), 16, 107
Towacana (Comanche chief), 38
Towacany (Comanche chief), 38
Toyamancare (Comanche chief), 16
trade, 6, 11, 126, 128, 142; and captives, 104; and
Comanches, 100; Comanches and Ameri-
cans, 36, 44, 70, 101, 115, 116; and Comanche
hostility, 137; Comanches and New Mexico,
13, 16, 25, 96–99, 108, 117, 132; and dependency, 102; and horses, 93; and early humans,
103; and environment, 103; and exploitation,
102; and kinship, 143; and motivation, 100;
redundant, 102; regulations and punishment
in New Mexico 13, 106, 107; regulations in
Texas, 36; and social behavior, 97, 103, 143;
and trade fairs, 13, 96, 99, 106, 116, 117; and
trading posts, 111, 116; Utes and New Mexico, 86; and violence, 143; and zero-sum
game, 100
trade goods, 96–100, 102, 103, 105, 108–14, 116,
119, 122, 124; competition for, 137
traditions, 24, 43, 64, 84, 91, 94, 95, 119, 126,
142, 143, 149; and agriculture, 92; Comanche, 88; definition of, 11; and hairstyles,
125; and language, 125; military, 88; and pastoralism, 79, 85, 87, 92; and raiding, 86; stories, 57; and warfare, 133; and weapons, 88
traits, 77
transhumance, 79, 89
transportation, 93
Trinchera Creek, 69, 71, 72
Trinity River, 35, 38
Truxillo, Joseph, 75, 94
Tuacana Indians, 63
Tuchubarua (Comanche chief), 28

Ugalde, Juan, 61, 135
Ugarte y Loyola, Jacobo, 29, 44, 45
Ulibarri, Juan de, 49, 51, 85, 104
ultimate causation, 148, 149
United States: and Comanches, 9; Comanche
surrender to, 3; and peace treaties, 9; Qua-
nah Parker surrenders to, 4
Utah, 6, 56, 85
Utes, 65, 67; as allied with New Mexico, 25; and
Apaches, 86; camps of, 105; and captives, 6,
59, 104, 107; and Comanches, 49–51, 56, 57,

66, 69, 94, 95, 105, 131, 136, 141; and cooperation with Comanches, 87; and culture, 86,
94; and horses, 74, 75, 86, 94; and intermarriage with Comanches, 6, 131, 142; and Navajos, 58, 60; and New Mexico, 6, 86; and pastoralism, 85, 94, 142; and Pueblo Indians, 59,
86; and raiding, 74, 75, 131; and San Juan, 60;
and social relations with Comanches, 72; and
trade with New Mexico, 106; and tradition,
86, 94; and warfare with Apaches, 50; and
warfare with Comanches, 127, 131; and warfare with New Mexico, 15, 49, 59, 86
Uto-Aztecan, 64

Valencia, N. Mex., 107
Valverde Cosio, Antonio de, 51
Valle, Francisco Marín del, 32, 88
Valverde, Antonio de, 50, 60, 62, 63, 67, 69, 136
Van Buren, Ark., 108
Vargas, Diego de, 59, 104
Varo, Andrés, 96
Vélez Cachupín, Thomas, 15, 25, 33, 68, 70, 98,
99, 117
vengeance, 131–33, 135
verification, 149
Vial, Pedro, 20, 21, 35, 54, 64, 68–70, 83, 84,
109, 110, 125
Vidae Indians, 63
Villapando, Pablo Francisco, 131, 132
Villasur, Pedro de, 51
violence, 11, 12, 23, 24, 25, 29, 30, 33–36, 45, 50,
66, 116–119, 120, 121, 123–25, 127, 128, 131,
134–37, 141, 143; Comanches and Apaches,
133; Comanches and Lipans, 62; Comanches
and New Mexico, 13, 25, 26; Comanches and
Spanish, 27; Comanches and Taos, 25

Waco Indians, 62, 64
Waggoner, Daniel, 4
Wallace, Alfred Russell, 148, 149
Wallace, Earnest, 56, 92
warfare, 11, 12, 32, 49, 50, 66, 121, 123, 126, 127,
129, 136, 143; between Comanches and Apa-
ches, 34, 35, 53, 62, 63; between Comanches
and Caddoans, 63; between Comanches and
Lipans, 62; between Comanches and New
Mexico, 16, 24–26, 28, 140; between Co-

manches and Pawnees, 35; between Co-
manches and Spanish, 24, 28, 63; between
Comanches and Utes, 67; between Utes and
New Mexico, 86; effect on Jupes, 30; and
Lobo warrior society, 129; over resources, 67;
and Plains Indians, 124; and women, 134
Washington, D. C., 3, 5
Washita River, 98
water resources, 10, 66, 69–71, 124
Webb, James Josiah, 54
western hemisphere, 77
Western, Thomas C., 111, 118
West Indies, 82. See also Antilles
Wichitas, 32, 33, 35, 37, 38, 62, 109; and Comanches, 6, 69; and intermarriage with Comanches, 36; migration of, 7; and warfare
with Apaches, 7
Williams, L. H., 118
wives, 19, 142
Wolf Creek, 8
wolves, 48
women, 9, 11, 12, 47, 92, 124; Apache, 127, 136;
as captives, 50, 58–60, 128, 136, 137; Comanche, 69, 70, 97, 98, 100, 113, 114, 129, 135, 137,
142; Jicarilla, 136; and Lobo warrior society,
130; and marriage, 134; Mexican, 136; and
polygyny, 134; and rituals, 130; treatment of
captives by, 130
wood resources, 10, 66, 69–71, 124
Wyoming, 6, 54, 56, 85

Xaranama Indians, 63
Ximenez, Fray Francisco, 49

Yamparicas (Comanche clan), 13, 19, 20, 21, 24,
27, 28, 31, 32, 35, 36, 40, 44, 66, 67, 108, 113,
125, 133, 140; characteristics of, 83; and dis-
putes over leadership, 23; hairstyle of, 125;
and tradition, 84, 125
Yoguanes Indians, 124
Ysaquebera (Comanche chief), 28
Ysarumachi (Comanche chief), 21, 28
Yuganis Indians, 62
Yujuan Indians, 63

Zacatecas, Mexico, 8, 54, 84
zero-sum game, 119, 143

ISBN 1-58544-190-2

90000